Confronting Right-wing Extremism and Terrorism in the USA

Is there a right-wing extremist threat in America? Are domestic terrorists gaining strength? How does America respond to the challenge of the extreme right?

Right-wing extremism in the United States has received considerable attention in recent years, yet few studies have simultaneously examined the response of government and non-governmental organizations to the threat these groups embody. The unique constitutional tradition of civil liberties in America means that the government is unable to disband a group simply because it has unpopular ideas; as a result private non-governmental organizations (NGOs) have stepped in to heavily influence this area of US public policy.

Confronting Right-wing Extremism and Terrorism in the USA provides a detailed portrait of the contemporary extreme right in the US, and includes interviews with several of the movement's leading figures from groups such as the Ku Klux Klan, the militias, American Renaissance and White Aryan Resistance. The author persuasively explains how the activities of these racist groups have been curbed due to the campaigning efforts of anti-racist and anti-fascist watchdogs. This study draws upon declassified government documents, NGO reports and extremist literature to provide a thought-provoking account of the extreme right challenge in America. It will provide an invaluable resource to students of terrorism, political violence and right-wing extremism, as well as appealing to the general reader with an interest in contemporary American politics.

George Michael is a veteran of both the US Air Force and the Pennsylvania Air National Guard, and has worked as a civilian operations research analyst for the US Army. He received a Ph.D. in public policy from George Mason University in 2002. Currently he is an associate professor of political sciencer and administration of justice at the University of Virginia College at Wise.

Routledge studies in extremism and democracy

Editors: Roger Eatwell
University of Bath
Cas Mudde
University of Antwerp-UFSIA

This new series encompasses academic studies within the broad fields of "extremism" and "democracy". These topics have traditionally been considered largely in isolation by academics. A key focus of the series, therefore, is the (inter)*relation* between extremism and democracy. Works will seek to answer questions such as to what extent "extremist" groups pose a major threat to democratic parties, or how democracy can respond to extremism without undermining its own democratic credentials.

The books encompass two strands:

Routledge studies in Extremism and Democracy includes books with an introductory and broad focus which are aimed at students and teachers. These books will be available in hardback and paperback. Titles include:

Understanding Terrorism in America
From the Klan to Al Qaeda
Christopher Hewitt

Routledge studies in Extremism and Democracy offers a forum for innovative new research intended for a more specialist readership. These books wil be in hardback only. Titles include:

1 **Uncivil Society?**
   Contentious politics in post-communist Europe
   Edited by Petr Kopecky and Cas Mudde

2 **Political Parties and Terrorist Groups**
   Leonard Weinberg and Ami Pedahzur

3 **Western Democracies and the New Extreme Right Challenge**
   Edited by Roger Eatwell and Cas Mudde

4 **Confronting Right-wing Extremism and Terrorism in the USA**
   George Michael

Confronting Right-wing Extremism and Terrorism in the USA

George Michael

LONDON AND NEW YORK

First published 2003 by Routledge
2 Park Square, Milton Park, Abingdon, Oxon OX14 4RN

Simultaneously published in the USA and Canada
by Routledge
711 Third Avenue, New York, NY 10017
Routledge is an imprint of the Taylor & Francis Group

First issued in paperback 2012

© 2003 George Michael
Typeset in Baskerville by Taylor & Francis Books Ltd

All rights reserved. No part of this book may be reprinted or reproduced or utilized in any form or by any electronic, mechanical, or other means, now known or hereafter invented, including photocopying and recording, or in any information storage or retrieval system, without permission in writing from the publishers.

British Library Cataloguing in Publication Data
A catalogue record for this book is available from the British Library

Library of Congress Cataloging in Publication Data
Michael, George, 1961-
Right wing terrorism and exttremisim in the USA / by George Michael.
     p. cm -- (Routledge studies in extremism and democracy)
Includes bibliographical references and index.
ISBN 0–415–31500–X
1. Radicalism -- United States. 2. Right-wing extremists -- United States. 3. Terrorism -- United States. I. Title. II. Series.
HN90.R3.M42 2003
322.4```2'0973 –dc21
                           2002155138

ISBN13: 978-0-415-31500-5 (hbk)
ISBN13: 978-0-415-62844-0 (pbk)

For Anna and Wolfie

Contents

List of tables viii
Series editors' preface ix
Acknowledgements xiii

1 Introduction 1

2 Who are the watchdogs? 10

3 Overview of the contemporary American far right 39

4 The far right and terrorism 93

5 The US government's response to right-wing extremism 129

6 The watchdogs' response to the far right 171

7 Conclusion 190

Notes 207
Bibliography 259
Index 276

Tables

1.1	Regional breakdown of far-right groups in the United States for 1999	2
4.1	Terrorist fatality victims classified by type	94
6.1	Hate crime incidents in the United States (1992–9)	174
6.2	Number of hate crime victims in the United States (1996–9)	175
7.1	Financial assets and annual income of top three watchdog groups	191
7.2	Most important factors involved in the capture of terrorists	193

Series editors' preface
Roger Eatwell and Cas Mudde

I

For much of the "short twentieth century," history was characterized by the clash of great ideologies, internal violence and major wars. Although most catastrophic events took place outside the Western world, Europe and the USA were not immune from the turmoil. Two world wars and a series of lesser conflicts led to countless horrors and losses. Moreover, for long periods Western democracy – especially in its European form – seemed in danger of eclipse by a series of radical forces, most notably communist and fascist.

Yet by the turn of the 1990s, liberal democracy appeared destined to become the universal governmental norm. Dictatorial Soviet communism had collapsed, to be replaced in most successor states by multi-party electoral politics. Chinese communism remained autocratic, but in the economic sphere it was moving rapidly towards greater freedoms and marketization. The main manifestations of fascism had gone down to catastrophic defeat in war. Neo-fascist parties were damned by omnipresent images of brutality and genocide, and exerted little appeal outside a fringe of ageing nostalgics and alienated youth.

In the Western world, political violence had disappeared, or was of minimal importance in terms of system stability. Where it lingered on as a regularly murderous phenomenon, for instance in Northern Ireland or Spain, it seemed a hangover from the past – a final flicker of the embers of old nationalist passions. It was easy to conclude that such tribal atavism was doomed in an increasingly interconnected "capitalist" world, characterized by growing forms of multi-level governance that were transcending the antagonism and parochialism of old borders.

However, as we move into the new millennium there are growing signs that extremism, even in the West, is far from dead – that we celebrated prematurely the universal victory of democracy. Perhaps the turn of the twenty-first century was an interregnum, rather than a turning point? In Western Europe there has been the rise of "extreme right" and "populist" parties such as Jean-Marie Le Pen's Front National, which pose a radical challenge to existing elites – even to the liberal political system. In the USA, the 1995 Oklahoma mass-bombing has not been followed by another major extreme-right attack, but there is simmering resentment towards the allegedly over-powerful state among well armed militias and other groups. More generally across the West, new forms of green politics, often linked by a growing hostility to globalization-Americanization, are taking on more violent forms (the issue of animal rights is also growing in importance in this context).

In the former Soviet space, there are clear signs of the revival of "communist" parties (which often masquerade as "socialists" or "social democrats"), whose allegiance to democracy is (in varying degrees) debatable. In Latin America, there remain notable extremist movements on the left, though these tend not to be communist. This trend may well grow both in response to globalization-Americanization and to the (partly linked) crises of many of these countries, such as Argentina. This in turn increases the threat to democracy from the extreme right, ranging in form from paramilitary groups to agro-military conspiracies.

The rise of Islamic fundamentalism has been an even more notable feature of recent years. This is not simply a facet of Middle Eastern politics. It has had an impact within some former Soviet republics, where the old nomenklatura have used the Islamic threat to maintain autocratic rule. In countries such as Indonesia and India, Muslims and other ethnic groups have literally cut each other to pieces. More Al-Qaeda bombings of the 2002 Bali-type, threaten economic ruin to Islamic countries which attract many Western tourists.

It is also important to note that growing Islamic fundamentalism has had an impact within some Western countries. The terrorist attacks on the World Trade Center and elsewhere in the USA on 11 September 2001 are perhaps the most graphic illustration of this impact. But in democracies generally, the rise of religious and other forms of extremism poses vital questions about the limits of freedom, multiculturalism and tolerance. This is especially the case in countries which have experienced notable Islamic immigration and/or which face the greatest threat of further terrorist attack.

Democracy may have become a near-universal shibboleth, but its exact connotations are being increasingly challenged and debated. As long as the "evil empire" of communism existed, Western democracy could in an important sense define itself by the "Other" – by what it was not. It did not have overt dictatorial rule, censorship, the gulags, and so on. But with the collapse of its great external foe, the spotlight has turned inward (although Islam is in some ways replacing communism as the "Other"). Is (liberal-Western) democracy truly democratic? Can it defend itself against terrorism and new threats without undermining the very nature of democracy?

These general opening comments provide the rationale for the *Routledge series on extremism and democracy*. In particular, there are three issues which we seek to probe in this series:

- Conceptions of democracy and extremism
- Forms of the new extremism in both the West and the wider world
- How democracies are responding to the new extremism.

II

George Michael's book (the third to appear in this series) deals mainly with the second and especially the third of these issues. Like the first work in the series (Chris Hewitt's *Understanding Terrorism in America: From the Klan to Al Qaeda*, which can be read fruitfully with this one), it is not another attempt to jump on the bandwagon of current interest in terrorism. It is based on extensive original research, begun well before 11 September 2001 (9/11). A particularly notable feature of Michael's work is his emphasis on the response of NGOs to the resurgence of the right in the USA – an area which has been largely neglected in the literature on extremism and terrorism.

As Michael notes in the Introduction, it is impossible to find an accurate term which covers the multi-faceted varieties of the contemporary American right-wing fringe. Some commentators chose terms like "extreme," "far" and "radical" right as convenient shorthands (sometimes substituting them in a thesaurus-like way) – highlighting the way in which some of these groups advocate violence against opponents, even the state. Others prefer terms like "populism" – stressing the ways in which many groups have links with a more law-abiding American political tradition, for example a suspicion of big government and predilection for conspiracy theory. However, this book is not essentially concerned with typological refinement.

Rather, Michael's main task in the opening part of the book is to survey the post-1990 resurgence of the American extreme right, setting it firmly in an historical context. Unlike in parts of Europe, the recent revival of the extreme right has not been manifested in election results in the US. Whilst some of the issues raised by these groups (such as the right to carry arms and hostility to abortion) have a relatively wide resonance, the extreme right has been perceived in general as beyond the pale. At the turn of the new millennium, there appear to have been around 25,000 hard core right-wing supporters, with perhaps 150,000–175,000 sympathizers. Most of these were to be found in the militias, which began to form in the early 1990s, or various wings of the Christian Identity movement. The radical and violent groups, such as the neo-Nazi National Alliance, White Aryan Resistance and the skinheads, tended to be much smaller. However, various "lone wolves," often with only very loose affiliations to formal organizations, were responsible for the most significant acts of right-wing violence including the bombing of a government building in Oklahoma City in 1995, resulting in well over 100 dead (the greatest loss of life through a terrorist incident on US soil until 9/11).

The main part of this book concerns responses to these developments. Within hours of the Oklahoma explosion, President Clinton vowed that the country would not be intimidated by "evil cowards." Even before this incident, there had been growing US government interest in terrorism, prompted by the growth of the fringe right, fears of single-issue groups (like anti-abortionists and eco-warriors) and the 1993 bombing of the World Trade Center by international terrorists. After Oklahoma City, there was a flurry of new anti-terrorist laws and measures (although in general the focus before 9/11 remained on domestic terrorism rather than the threat from Al-Qaeda and foreign groups).

Crucial in the response to the extreme right was a set of NGOs. Among the best known of these are: the the Anti-Defamation League; the American Jewish Committee; the Center for Democratic Renewal; Political Research Associates; the Simon Wiesenthal Center; and the Southern Poverty Law Center. Among their main activities in this field have been: encouraging the government to implement new legislation on issues such as hate crime; providing intelligence about extremist groups to both government and the media; themselves inaugurating lawsuits against extremist groups, often using the civil law; seeking to limit internet access; and direct confrontation.

Michael offers several reasons why these NGOs have played a notable role in this field. One concerns the First Amendment and strong American predisposition to civil liberties, which before 9/11 made the government wary of taking too strong initiatives in this field. A second concerns the good access which these groups have to many politicians, policy makers and the media. Third, the policy demands of these groups in general appealed to politicians as popular law and order measures and (before 9/11) relatively costless. Last but not least, concerns the relative wealth of these NGOs compared to the fringe right: it has been estimated that in 2000 the top eight NGOs commanded collective assets of over $300 million and had an annual income of half this.

One particular feature that stands out in Michael's study is the extensive field research that he conducted among the various actors involved on all sides of this issue. This study contains interviews with some of the most notorious figures in the American far right, as well as prominent former government officials and representatives from NGOs that seek to counter the far right. These interviews are often exciting and provocative, as they include comments on very controversial topics such as race, civil liberties and terrorism.

However, this book also points out that the role of these NGOs prompts various concerns. For example, the BATF's handling of the siege at Waco in 1993 appears to have been influenced by spurious evidence from a cult-watching group (and the deaths of Branch Davidian sect members at Waco directly influenced Timothy McVeigh to plant the 1995 Oklahoma bomb). More generally, prior to 9/11 these groups largely monitored law-abiding members of the right, and their activities raise a host of issues about undercover activities and agents-provocateurs.

Since 9/11 the focus of American anti-terrorist concern has become international, and government has enacted swingeing new laws which increase state power to monitor, and even to try suspects in special courts. Michael briefly reviews these developments, noting that many of the NGOs which had previously focused on the right now monitor domestic Arab and Muslim activities. Again, this in many ways provides an important additional safeguard – but it also raises concerns about the future of democracy in "the land of the free."

Acknowledgements

Many people have helped in one way or another with this book, which began as my dissertation for a Ph.D. in public policy at George Mason University. I am indebted to those on my committee who reviewed my study and offered their advice and direction, including Francis Fukuyama, James Pfiffner, Chris Hewitt, Walter Laqueur and Seymour Martin Lipset. It was truly an honor to have such distinguished scholars serve on my committee.

I would like to thank several persons and Routledge for their help and guidance. Roger Eatwell and Cas Mudde provided useful feedback on my manuscript. Craig Fowlie and Zoë Boterill helped with administrative issues. Their courtesy and professionalism are much appreciated.

Many of the figures presented in this study were very helpful and offered their insights into this topic. I express my gratitude to the former deputy director of the FBI, Oliver "Buck" Revell and former US Attorney General Edwin Meese. Various representatives from the NGOs were helpful, including Chip Berlet from Political Research Associates, Chris Freeman from the Center for Democratic Renewal, Ken McVay from the Nizkor Project, Mark Potok from the Southern Poverty Law Center, Bill Wassmuth, formerly from the Northwest Coalition Against Malicious Harassment, Todd Ferguson from Anti-Racist Action, and Dr Mark Pitcavage from the Anti-Defamation League. Finally, numerous rightist activists and personalities offered me their insights, including the late Dr William Pierce, Sgt Steven Barry, Tom Metzger, Jared Taylor, Gordon Baum, Kirk Lyons, Harold Covington, Ernst Zündel, Dr Ingrid Rimland, Matthew Hale, Willis Carto, Mike Piper, Pövl Riis-Knudsen, Mark Coterill, John Trochmann, Norm Olson, Thom Robb, Milton John Kleim, Roy Armstrong, Richard Barrett, and Ron Doggett.

Laird Wilcox and the staff at the Wilcox Collection of Contemporary Political Movements in the Kenneth Spencer Research Library at the University of Kansas were most helpful in retrieving important materials used in this study. I strongly recommend that scholars interested in political extremism avail themselves of this valuable research center.

The staff at the FBI's Freedom of Information Reading Room assisted me in retrieving declassified government files pertaining to this public policy issue.

My friend Reg Orem meticulously proofread my manuscripts several times. I greatly appreciate his efforts.

Finally, I thank my wife Anna and my son Wolfie for their patience and support throughout this project. It is they to whom this book is dedicated.

1 Introduction

By most accounts, right-wing extremism appeared to make a comeback in the United States during the 1990s. Although, this did not manifest itself in electoral success due in large part to the nature of the American electoral system, the far right seemed to gain ground as a social movement. What is more, recent trends in technology, such as the internet, have enabled the far right to reach out to a potentially larger audience than it has in the past. Finally, some high profile confrontations with law enforcement authorities and horrific acts of political violence – most notably the 1995 bombing of Murrah federal building in Oklahoma City – have seared the issue of right-wing terrorism into the public's mind.

Previously, America was seen as relatively safe from a serious domestic terrorist threat. However, some high-profile terrorist incidents have done much to alter this image. And over the past few years there has been a flurry of new anti-terrorist laws and measures enacted.[1] The Clinton administration placed a high priority on counter-terrorism.

The pattern of domestic terrorism is in a state of flux. Left-wing terrorism is in retreat and Puerto Rican separatist terrorism, though still sporadic, appears to be attenuating perhaps due to the recent referendum in which Puerto Ricans decided by a large majority to reject independence and remain a part of the United States. However, the Federal Bureau of Investigation (FBI) of the US Department of Justice, has identified new actors that threaten to fill the void. First, are the so-called single-issue terrorists such as the eco-terrorists and extremist anti-abortion groups. Second, are the international terrorists who can take advantage of America's porous borders and liberal immigration laws and conduct activities inside American territory. Finally, there are domestic right-wing terrorists who have captured much attention after the bombing of the Murrah federal building in Oklahoma City. Although small in numbers, right-wing terrorists are among the most active of all terrorist categories in the United States.[2] Moreover, the American far right is widely dispersed with adherents in all major regions of the country as Table 1.1 illustrates.[3] Finally, according to a 1996 Center for Democratic Renewal estimate there are roughly 25,000 "hard core" members and another 150,000 to 175,000 active sympathizers who buy literature, make contributions, and attend periodic meetings.[4]

Compared to most of the other Western democracies, the situation as regards

Table 1.1 Regional breakdown of far-right groups in the United States for 1999

Region	KKK	Neo-Nazi	Skinhead	Christian Identity	Other	Patriot/ Militia	Total
East	16	23	6	1	30	16	92
South	69	28	6	20	54	51	228
Midwest	39	39	10	9	58	54	209
Southwest	9	9	12	2	23	36	91
West	5	31	6	14	51	60	167
Total	138	130	40	46	216	217	787

political extremism is unique in the United States. For instance, in the Federal Republic of Germany, there is an agency called the Office of the Protection of the Constitution, which can recommend to judiciary the dissolution of extremist groups that it deems a threat to Germany's constitutional democracy.[5] Likewise, the British government has invoked the 1965 Race Relations Act to justify raids on homes and offices of right-wing extremists including the National Front and the British National Party. And even in Israel, where the far right enjoys significant grassroots support, the government outlawed the late Meir Kahane's Kach movement because of its extremist platform.[6] Other democracies would appear to have much more legal latitude in responding to political extremism and violence.

By contrast, the United States has a strong civil liberties tradition. While it is axiomatic to say that terrorism is usually perpetrated by extremists, the vast majority of extremists are not terrorists. This presents somewhat of a conundrum in that because of First Amendment protections, the government does not officially have the authority to disband groups just because they espouse unpopular ideas. From a comparative legal perspective the US government appears to be more constrained in responding to political extremism. However, what is often ignored is that private non-governmental organizations (NGOs) have interjected themselves into this area of public policy and have done much to fill the void. Compared to other Western nations, the federal government's response to right-wing terrorism and extremism is unique insofar as it engenders much greater participation from NGOs. Moreover, these NGOs have persuaded the government to take a strong position *vis-à-vis* the far right. In essence, the response to right-wing extremism in America is a joint effort by both the government and private watchdog groups.

Thus the US response to right-wing terrorism and extremism is qualitatively different than the response to other variants of terrorism and political extremism insofar as it engenders much greater participation from NGOs. NGOs are much less likely to be involved in the response to other forms of political extremism and violence. Although historically some NGOs have been involved in countering other forms of political extremism, the number involved has been much fewer, and the scope of that involvement has been much more limited. To bring this issue into sharper focus, this study includes some comparative analysis between the responses to right-wing extremism and other variants of political extremism. NGOs have been instrumental in shaping the government's response to right-wing extremism in a number of ways including, *inter alia*, collaboration with law enforcement agencies and sponsoring legislation, which is primarily aimed at neutralizing the far right. Moreover, some of these NGOs often take it upon themselves to respond to the far right in more direct ways without the assistance of the state. Examples range from civil suits to physical confrontations in the streets. By and large the government responds to other variants of political extremism relatively independently, unencumbered by the influence of private interest groups. Thus the response to right-wing extremism is unique.

What is the effect of NGOs on the formation of the US government's response to right-wing terrorism and extremism? Why have private groups been able to exert so much influence on this public policy agenda? Like many other areas of American public policy, NGOs have a significant influence on public policy and this area is one more, but unexplored, example. This study explores the US government and NGOs' responses in this area by examining public policies and other measures, which take aim largely at the far right. This study is grounded in NGO and interest group theory, and to put in its proper context, examines not only the NGOs and the government agencies involved, but also the far right, including its major groups, figures, ideologies and patterns of terrorism.

Before going any further a clarification of terms is in order. Specifically, what is meant by the term "far right"? Many observers and scholars have belabored this issue and there is no general consensus. What's more, in the context of American politics the term is even more difficult to define owing to the vast geographic size, large population, and heterogeneity of the country. There are several different permutations, not only in the more respectable mainstream American right wing but within the far right as well.

One should not confuse the far right as an extrapolation of the conservative right wing. The contemporary conservative right wing for the most part espouses principles such as limited government, fiscal restraint, and support for business and free enterprise. The far right by contrast often has a quasi-socialist populist element along with a suspicion of big business and global capitalism. In general, economic issues do not loom large in the far right's agenda; cultural issues figure more prominently. Indeed, the far right is a different entity.

That said, most observers seem to be able to instinctively recognize the phenomenon of right-wing extremism. As the esteemed historian Walter Laqueur once remarked, it resembles pornography "in that it is difficult – perhaps impossible to define – in an operational, legally valid way, but those with experience know it when they see it."[7]

Examining right wing and reactionary movements in American history, Chip Berlet and Matthew N. Lyons use the term "right-wing populist" to designate those movements that have sought to mobilize against "liberation movements, social reform, or revolution." In their view, right-wing populist movements in America have historically reflected the interests of two types of social groups: (a) middle-level groups in the social hierarchy (usually White) that have a stake in the traditional arrangement of social privilege, but resent the power that upper-class elites hold over them; and (b) "outsider" factions of the elites that occasionally use forms of anti-elitism to further their own interests and bid for power. Furthermore, Berlet and Lyons coined the term "producerism" to denote a doctrine that "champions the so-called producers in society against both 'unproductive' elites and subordinate groups defined as lazy or immoral." They argue that this cognitive model leads to scapegoating, "conspiracism," and apocalypticism – elements that have traditionally figured prominently in right-wing extremism. They cite various examples of such movements, including the Jacksonian populism of the early nineteenth century, which represented an alliance between lower-class Whites and certain factions of elites and the Reconstruction Era Ku Klux Klan, which represented an alliance between Southern lower- and middle-class Whites and wealthy Southern planters who sought to regain the power and privileges they had lost as a result of the Civil War.[8] Berlet and Lyon's thesis offers interesting insights into the nature and style of populist movements, but still does not really constitute a definition of the core characteristics that compose right-wing extremism. As noted by observers, populism is primarily a style of political organizing rather than a separate political ideology. Indeed, styles of populism can be harnessed by various political ideologies all across the political spectrum.

Although somewhat vague, Roger Griffin, borrowing from the terminology of biology, succinctly captured the essence of one variant of right-wing extremism – fascism – by defining it as an ideology, which has at its core an ultra-nationalist palingenetic myth (i.e. process of death and rebirth). This definition has a great deal of merit insofar as many variants of fascism and right-wing extremism espouse the creation of a "new order" built upon the ruins of a perceived decadent and decrepit "old order."[9] Thus he sees a strong revolutionary element in right-wing extremism, which certainly would adequately describe much of the contemporary American far right. Other important characteristics that observers have cited as principal to the fascist variant of right-wing extremism are exaltations of "the people" or nation and some form of anti-elitism.[10]

Griffin's definition however, fails to adequately describe some of the other variants of the American far right, such as the Christian Patriot movement, which does not really view itself as revolutionary, but rather as preserver of the true heritage and principles of the American republic. Such a movement would more aptly be labeled "preservatist"[11] than revolutionary. Perhaps one could argue that the Christian Patriot movement should therefore not be included in the designation of the far right and should be examined separately. This has been Jeffrey Kaplan's approach, as he has focused exclusively on the racialist segment of the far right in his excellent studies of this topic. For Kaplan, the primacy of race, religiosity, and a revolutionary ethos are what characterizes the "racist radical right."[12]

However, in the history of the American far right, there has been a considerable degree of overlap, migration, cross-fertilization of ideas, and cross-membership between the Patriot and racialist segments. Moreover, the response by the government and watchdog community has usually targeted both segments contemporaneously. Measures they employ, such as anti-paramilitary training statutes and intelligence sharing, are often employed against both segments of the far right.

In surveying the twenty-six different definitions of right-wing extremism in the literature, Cas Mudde found no fewer than fifty-eight features that are mentioned at least once. Of those features, only five are mentioned in one form or another by at least half of the authors: nationalism, racism, xenophobia, anti-democracy and the strong state.[13] Mudde focused on five extreme right parties in Europe (the Republikaner Party and the Deutsche Volksunion in Germany, the Vlams Blok in Belgium, and the Centrumdemocraten and Centrumparti '86 in the Netherlands) and found evidence to suggest the existence of an extreme right "party family" with a shared core ideology. This core is built around the nucleus of nationalism, in particular internal homogenization, i.e. that the state should endeavor to create a monocultural society. Other core features include xenophobia, welfare chauvinism – the belief that the state should only serve the economic interests of its "own people," – and law and order.[14] Arguably, these characteristics would apply to many segments of the American far right as well.

However, Mudde's focus is primarily on the European far right. What is more, he focused on programmatic political parties that regularly contest elections in Europe In America by contrast, rarely do even a few far-right organizations run candidates for political office. At the present time, the American far right resembles more a loose social movement than a collection of like-minded political parties or organizations. There are, moreover, some subtle differences between the American and European variants of right-wing extremism, most notably the esteem in which the state is held; whereas the former tends to be anti-statist, the latter is more likely to view the state as an organic outgrowth of the nation. The term "nationalism" also is much more ambiguous in the American context. Whereas in Europe it often coincides with ethnicity, in America, which contains no majority ethnic group as such, it can be viewed as perhaps a more chauvinistic style of patriotism.

This therefore presents a definitional problem for researchers and scholars. With the preceding discussion, I have tried to make clear that is very difficult to rigidly define the term "far right." Thus I have endeavored to develop a list of characteristics which, although it does not rigidly define the far right, I believe adequately *describes* and captures the essence of the far right:

Particularism Unlike other political ideologies and orientations, the far right usually takes a more parochial outlook, as it is more concerned with a smaller locus of identity such as the nation, republic, race or ethnic group. It tends not to have ambitions to proselytize the whole world to its belief system. This is in contrast to other ideologies such as liberal democracy, communism, and some variants of socialism, which are seen as suitable, indeed desirable, for export, and the whole world is encouraged to adopt them as its model.

Low regard for democracy Although far-right political organizations and individuals by and large tend to play by the democratic rules of the game, they seem to be less enthusiastic for democracy than mainstream political orientations. For example, even members of the ultra-patriotic militia movement like to point out that technically the American political system was designed as a republic and not a democracy.

Anti-statism Right-wing extremism often evinces a severe disaffection with the government or at least the scope of government. Although certain segments of the racialist right – most notably those which draw inspiration from National Socialism – may in principle approve of the idea of a strong state, they regard the current US government as hopelessly under the control of outsiders who use their power in such a way that is inimical to the national community.

A conspiracy view of history Denizens of the far right have a tendency to look beneath the surface of American politics and find elite cabals at work subverting society.

A racial or ethnic component which includes usually at least one of the following:

- racism
- anti-Semitism
- xenophobia
- ethnic chauvinism

Although *all* of the preceding characteristics may not pertain to each and every far-right group and figure examined in this study, I believe that at least *enough* of these characteristics apply to each of them so that they could reasonably be classified as "far right" and "right-wing extremist." This admittedly represents some arbitrariness on my part. However, I believe that these descriptive characteristics are adequate enough to guide readers and describe the far-right subjects in this study. What's more, it allows both members of the racialist right and the Patriot movement to be examined in one study. Essentially, the final descriptive characteristic – the racial or ethnic component – is what separates the racialist right and Patriot movements. It is integral to the former and usually much less prominent in the latter.

A definition of the term "terrorism" is also in order. Scholars have long struggled with this term as well. There are many variants of political violence, which are sometimes designated under the rubric of terrorism, including guerilla warfare, sabotage, assassination, and, according to some recent observers, hate crimes. Moreover, the study of terrorism is not without its normative squabbles, as the cliché "one man's terrorist is another man's freedom fighter" demonstrates. It follows that scholars, depending on their perspective, will often classify and interpret political violence through their own national or ideological lens. For example, during their guerilla struggle against the Soviets during the 1980s, the Afghan *Mujihadeen* were looked upon as valiant freedom fighters by many observers in the West. However, their image today is that of the terrorist network *par excellence*, giving aid and comfort to the likes of Osama Bin Laden, the chief conductor of contemporary international terrorism against the West. And left-wing sympathizing scholars occasionally sympathized with left-wing terrorists and characterized them as desperate idealists who were driven by conditions such as poverty and oppression into terrorism. However, the rise of right-wing terrorism in the 1980s and 1990s has removed much of the idealistic veneer of terrorism in the academic community.[15]

The FBI – the chief government agency responsible for investigating and preventing domestic terrorism – offers one of the most succinct and practical definitions of terrorism, and it will be used for this study:

> the unlawful use of force or violence against persons or property to intimidate or coerce a government, the civilian population, or any segment thereof, in furtherance of political or social objectives.[16]

Further, the FBI defines *domestic* terrorism as

> the unlawful use, or threatened use, of force of violence by a group or individual based and operating entirely within the United States or Puerto Rico without foreign direction committed against persons or property to intimidate or coerce a government, the civilian population, or any segment thereof in furtherance of political or social objectives.[17]

One further word is in order. Much of the response to the far right is predicated on the notion that it presents a high potential for violence. Moreover, as I shall demonstrate, the government and the watchdog community respond to both the violent as well as the non-violent extreme right. I believe that the response to both segments ought to be examined in the same study. However, it is important to keep in mind that terrorists compose only a small number of right-wing extremists. During the course of my fieldwork some far rightists took some exception to being included in a study that dealt in part with terrorism. For the sake of clarity and propriety, I make efforts to distinguish between the two.

A number of studies have examined counter-terrorism. However, there is a dearth of literature on the response to domestic right-wing terrorism in the United States. Previous studies have been confined to specific terrorist incidents or groups. Moreover, the role of NGOs in this area of public policy has been given short shrift. It is hoped that this study will make several contributions:

- Provide a diachronic overview of right-wing terrorism in the United States; previous literature lacks a broad longitudinal perspective.

8 *Introduction*

- Examine the role of NGOs in this area of public policy. This is important because without addressing the role that NGOs play, one is left with an incomplete understanding of this area of domestic counter-terrorism. Furthermore, inasmuch as this study would be grounded in NGO theory, it would make a contribution to the knowledge of how interest groups interact with several other actors, including the media, law enforcement agencies, and the executive, legislative and judicial branches of government.
- Explain how the US government responds to a specific variant of terrorism and political extremism. Previous studies in counter-terrorism have tended to focus on the domestic far left or the international arena. Today many government entities are involved in domestic counter-terrorism, and their participation warrants closer examination.
- Describe the far right, including its major groups, ideologies, and patterns of terrorism. The literature on right-wing extremism could benefit greatly from an examination of the various ideologies that motivate the various individuals and groups in the movement. Inasmuch as there are several variants of terrorism and political extremism, public policy makers should be cognizant of their differences. Different brands of terrorism warrant different public policy approaches. The fiascos at Ruby Ridge and Waco illustrate the tragedies that can take place when authorities ignore the nuances of extremist groups and individuals.

The following is a preview of what lies ahead.

Chapter 2 introduces the major NGOs, which figure prominently in the area of domestic counter-terrorism policy, including the Anti-Defamation League (ADL), the American Jewish Committee, the Simon Wiesenthal Center, the Southern Poverty Law Center (SPLC), the Center for Democratic Renewal, Political Research Associates, The Northwest Coalition Against Malicious Harassment, the Center for New Community, Hatewatch, the Nizkor Project, the Militia Watchdog, and Anti-Racist Action. There has been very little research into these groups and thus the secondary literature in this area is somewhat sparse; however, the watchdogs have produced quite a bit of material from which researchers can draw to gain an understanding of who the so-called watchdogs are.

Chapter 3 provides an overview of the contemporary American far right. The major groups and individuals that populate these movements are classified and explained. I draw upon a robust secondary literature, extremist publications, and first-person interviews to give the reader a better understanding of this subterranean world.

Chapter 4 looks closely at the relationship between the far right and domestic terrorism. It endeavors to find patterns of right wing terrorism that have punctuated American history. Also, the major episodes of right-wing terrorism over the past couple of decades are reviewed. Finally, this chapter explores the considerable amount of theorizing on the strategic, tactical and normative implications of terrorism that has gone on within the far right.

Chapter 5 looks at the US government's response to right-wing terrorism and extremism. It identifies the chief government agencies which deal with the issue, and explains how they are organized to do so. There are several studies in the secondary literature on the US government's efforts to counter terrorism and political extremism. Also, there are documents from government agencies that have been involved in these efforts, including the FBI, Department of Defense, and General Accounting Office.

Chapter 6 examines the methods by which NGOs have attempted to counteract the far right. This often involves interfacing with the government. For example, NGOs have drafted and lobbied for various hate crime, anti-paramilitary training, and anti-common law court statutes. More recently, some of these NGOs have encouraged the government and internet service providers to curtail the operations of right-wing extremists on the internet. On occasion, NGOs share intelligence with law enforcement agencies, and thus help to keep surveillance on various far-right organizations. Finally, there are the less formal efforts by watchdogs to isolate their far-right adversaries from the population at large, which are worth closer examination. This chapter draws upon several sources, including material published by the various NGOs and interviews with representatives from this sector. Also, there are declassified government documents that reveal past cooperation between government agencies and NGOs.

Chapter 7 concludes with a summary along with a few final observations. First, it lists what I believe to be the reasons for the success of the NGOs in this field of public policy. Second, it addresses some of the civil liberties implications of the collaboration between the government and NGOs. Third, it provides some public policy recommendations. Fourth, a speculative threat assessment of the far right is given and its significance for the future is discussed. Finally, I explore how the events of September 11, 2001 have impinged on this public policy issue.

It is now time to take a closer look at the chief NGOs which figure prominently in the area of countering domestic right-wing terrorism and extremism.

2 Who are the watchdogs?

Introduction

This chapter introduces the reader to some of the prominent organizations that compose the watchdog community. The number of so-called watchdog groups, which monitor the activities of the extreme right, has grown considerably over the past two decades. In fact, a recent study estimates that there are now approximately 300 such groups nationwide.[1] Consistent with the disturbance theory of interest group formation, many of these organizations were created in response to some crisis or disturbance.[2] Once a threatening environment or conflict emerges, individuals are more willing to join groups. Often there is some precipitating event or condition, which serves as a catalyst for group formation.

Like its far-right opponents, the watchdog community is a variegated combination of groups. It is far from monolithic, as there is a great degree of nuance among the various organizations. There seems to be a good deal of variation in the staff compositions and orientations of the various watchdog groups. For example, the Anti-Defamation League (ADL) is concerned mostly with Jewish issues including countering anti-Semitism and building support for the state of Israel. The members of ADL's upper-management are primarily Jewish in ethnic background and their political orientations appear to be for the most part generally liberal. By contrast, groups such as the Center for Democratic Renewal and Political Research Associates are concerned with a much broader range of so-called progressive issues such as environmentalism, women's rights, affirmative action and economic rights, in addition to countering the far right. This is understandable insofar as many of the staff members of these groups had sojourned in left-wing and progressive organizations prior to their involvement in the watchdog movement. Despite these differences, however, there remains a good deal of cooperation between these groups.

Although the various organizations which compose the watchdog community may generally agree on certain issues, such as opposition to the far right, white racism, anti-Semitism and homophobia, there is a considerable difference of opinion on other issues. The most salient disagreement is on the tactics employed to counter the far right. The more established watchdog groups such as the Anti-Defamation League and the Southern Poverty Law Center (SPLC) often work closely with government agencies including those of law enforcement. Other groups, primarily those with a left-wing or progressive orientation, are much less likely to do so.

There is also considerable variation in how the general public views the different watchdog groups. For the most part, the more established groups are seen as the pillars of the community. Morris Dees, the founder of the SPLC, is often feted by admiring audiences on the lecture circuit, and has been the subject of laudatory television movies and documentaries. The ADL has a great deal of clout in politics as politicians regard it as a powerful lobby. ADL banquets in which prominent individuals are awarded honors for their contributions to civil rights and Jewish causes serve as venues to build credibility and respectability for the organization and its goals.

In stark contrast, other groups, most notably Anti-Racist Action (ARA), do not receive the near-unanimous approbation from the public as the more established watchdog groups do. Their more direct confrontational approach to the far right, including street demonstrations, at times puts off authorities and the local population in the communities in which they are active. Moreover, such groups often take a more oppositional position *vis-à-vis* the society at large, which they view as inherently racist and sexist. However, a process of moderation appears to occur in some of these organizations, which start off with a left-wing orientation. Through the course of time, several factors, including the quest for lucrative grants, public recognition and respectability, tends to moderate their radicalism to a certain degree.

The purpose of this chapter is to give the reader a better understanding of the various groups in the watchdog community. Although the list of organizations covered is far from comprehensive, they are among the most important players in the watchdog movement for a number of reasons including, *inter alia*, their resources, level of support, access to the media and opinion makers, notoriety and staff expertise. I have created a typology of watchdog groups, which includes the following categories: Jewish defense, civil litigation, progressive-oriented, regional, internet-based, and miscellaneous. There is considerable overlap among the various organizations in these various categories, but the typology is offered to give the reader a better conceptual understanding of how the various groups are organized and the differences between them. What follows is a thumbnail sketch for the rest of this chapter.

First, the American interest group structure is examined. As I explain, the "exceptional" character of American civil society has been amenable to the development of a robust interest group constellation in the United States.

Second, the major Jewish watchdog groups are examined. Inasmuch as anti-Semitism looms so large in many segments of the far right, it is not surprising that Jewish interest groups would concern themselves in countering this movement. The most prominent group in this category – and indeed the watchdog community as a whole – is the Anti-Defamation League. Other groups in this category include the American Jewish Committee and the Simon Wiesenthal Center.

Third, the Southern Poverty Law Center (SPLC) is examined. The SPLC is unique and in a category of its own. Although it began with a progressive orientation – and still concerns itself with such issues as poverty, homelessness, voting rights, etc. – it is best known as a civil litigation watchdog group. It is arguably second only to the ADL, the most influential watchdog group. It has pioneered the use of civil suits to hold far right groups responsible for the actions of their individual members. Some of these civil suits have resulted in very large judgments and in doing so, bankrupted several far-right groups. Thus the Southern Poverty Law Center is among the most feared of the watchdog groups by the far-right. The major Jewish defense groups together with the SPLC constitute, in my opinion, the first level of watchdog organizations. Those that follow are essentially second-level organizations.

Watchdog groups with a progressive orientation are reviewed next. Prominent in this category are the Center for Democratic Renewal and Political Research Associates. Inasmuch as the groups in this category are politically left-leaning, it is understandable that they would organize against the political right. Unlike the more established watchdog groups they tend to concern themselves with a broader range of social justice issues.

The next section takes a closer look at some of the more prominent regional watchdog groups. Typically, they are created in response to local right-wing extremism in their area. The Northwest Coalition Against Malicious Harassment and The Center for New Community are among the most notable in this category.

In recent years right-wing extremists have taken to the internet with great enthusiasm. Consequently, their opponents have created websites to counter their online propaganda. Some important examples in this category are the Nizkor Project, which focuses primarily on countering the claims of Holocaust revisionists; Hatewatch, which seeks to warn web surfers of the threat of online extremists; and the Militia Watchdog, which tracks the activities of those in the Christian Patriot/militia movement.

I have included a miscellaneous category to review an organization known as Anti-Racist Action, which appears to be rather anarchist in character. Although it does not command the resources and influence of its more respected counterparts in the watchdog community, it has established many chapters in North America and offers an interesting contrast in approaches to countering the far right.

Finally, I conclude this chapter by making some generalizations about the watchdog community. It is hoped that certain common characteristics of these groups will be more evident after reading this chapter.

The American interest group structure

Interest groups and non-governmental organizations (NGOs) have a long tradition in American politics and civil society, and often strongly influence public policy. There is a general consensus among observers that over the last thirty years an explosion of interest groups has occurred in America, as more Americans have sought to involve themselves in organized interest groups.[3] Essentially an interest group is "any group that is based on one or more shared attitudes and makes certain claims upon other groups or organizations in the society."[4] Interest group formation is actually nothing new in America; as the famous French observer of the early republic, Alexis de Tocqueville, noted, Americans have a proclivity for creating associations.[5]

American political culture differs markedly from other countries with similar levels of economic and political development. Several observers have commented on the nature of "American exceptionalism," including Seymour Martin Lipset. He identifies five components of what he calls the "American Creed," which in his estimation shape the ethos of the American nation: liberty, egalitarianism, individualism, populism and laissez-faire. Lipset identifies sectarian Protestantism as determinative in the development of the American creed. To put it succinctly, in the American version of Protestantism, individual believers could appeal to God directly for salvation, unmediated by ecclesiastic authorities. Furthermore, America never established a state church. Thus a sectarian religious culture enabled the "free coinage of religion." This unique denominational structure and religious freedom helped foster a civil society marked by a volunteerism. This greatly influenced the character of the American group structure, as many associations are religious in origin.[6] A comparison with eleven other countries in a 1982 study, demonstrated that Americans are more likely to be members of voluntary associations of a non-economic variety.[7] Specifically, two types that stand out are church-related and civic-political groups.[8] Furthermore, the proportion of citizens belonging to economic groups – not only labor unions but professional associations as well – is actually substantially higher in many other countries than it is in the United States.[9]

Other factors have shaped America's unique interest group structure as well. Unlike Europe, America has no feudal past. Consequently, America does not have a rigid class system as Europe formerly had. Although there are great inequalities of income, wealth and status, America has an egalitarian ethos and a class system that allows for social mobility. This encourages individual initiative and volunteerism in its interest group structure. Moreover, America has a revolutionary tradition. It was the first colony to wrest itself free from the mother country and establish independence. In that sense it was the "first new nation," and developed a political culture that was suspicious of governmental authority and an intrusive state. Consequently, America has a relatively smaller government sector *vis-à-vis* other Western democracies with similar levels of economic and social development.[10] This is in marked contrast to the more statist orientations of interest group formation found in Canada and continental Europe, namely corporatism, in which interest groups are accorded official recognition and are considered an organic part of society. In fact interest groups often have a negative connotation in American political discourse, conjuring up images of backroom deals that subvert the national interest.

Despite this image, America has not been uncongenial to organized interest groups. First, the American experiment, with its limited government coupled with a strong civil society, has encouraged private initiative on the part of self-help associations and interest groups. This fostered the creation of voluntary association, for in areas in which there is a dearth of state involvement, non-governmental organizations (NGOs) often tend to fill the void.[11] One theory posits that when the scope of government intervention is limited in an aspect of public policy, NGOs tend to be pick up the slack and take measures on their own to deal with the problem.[12] Moreover, the American interest group system is more fluid, decentralized, and entrepreneurial compared to other democracies. Finally, the American system contains many entrance points. If interests are defeated in one branch of government area such as the legislature, they can attempt to press their claims in another branch such as the executive. Taken together, these characteristics and traditions discussed above fostered an interest group system in which organizational initiative was left to private interests and state interference was discouraged. Consequently these conditions provide a "highly felicitous context for interest group politics."[13]

As mentioned in Chapter 1, the response to domestic right-wing terrorism is qualitatively different than the response to other forms of terrorism, insofar as NGOs tend to be more active and influence much of the policy agenda. However, it is not uncommon for NGOs to impinge upon public policy. For example, organizations such as the American Farm Bureau Federation, the National Farmers' Union and the National Farmers Organization have been very effective in representing the interests of farmers in the field of agriculture. In the realm of education, the National Education Association (NEA) has been effective in shaping policy not only at state and local levels, but at the national level as well. It achieved a major lobbying coup in 1979 when then President Jimmy Carter established the Department of Education as a cabinet level department. Moreover, the NEA was able to defeat President Reagan's attempts to dismantle the department. Until recently the American Medical Association was virtually an unchallenged authority in the field of health care policy. The involvement of ethnic associations in American foreign policy is yet another case where NGOs impinge greatly on public policy. Eastern European émigrés, Cuban-Americans and Greek-Americans have been very successful in this regard, even when their lobbying goals may have been against the long-term interests of America's foreign policy. The American-Israeli Public Affairs Committee's lobbying on behalf of the state of Israel is legendary in the

Congress and the State Department.[14] Thus the involvement of NGOs in the policy arena is not unique.

The Jewish defense organizations

The Anti-Defamation League

The most important watchdog group involved in countering right-wing extremism is undoubtedly the Anti-Defamation League. The ADL was founded in 1913 in Chicago, Illinois when an attorney, Sigmund Livingston, persuaded the Independent Order of B'nai B'rith to establish a defense agency for Jews in America.[15] Although mild strains of anti-Semitism had hitherto occurred throughout American history, it began to emerge for the first time in significant fashion as large numbers of Eastern European Jews arrived in America. As with virtually all newcomers, the native host population met the Jewish immigrants with some degree of hostility. Furthermore, unlike previous Jewish immigrants from the nineteenth century who were primarily German in national origin and well established in their communities, many of the new Jewish immigrants were from Eastern Europe and tended to be economically and socially marginalized in background. They brought with them their own unique dress and customs, which were viewed as peculiar and with suspicion by many Americans. Jews quickly became the butt of jokes in vaudeville routines and in the fledgling motion picture industry.[16] Thus a chief aim of the ADL was to counter negative stereotypes and caricatures of Jews in the media. These developments coincided with a period of renascent nativism in America. The Ku Klux Klan was resurrected at Stone Mountain, Georgia in 1915 and a wave of white Anglo-Saxon Protestant nationalism swept virtually all regions of the country. Finally, the Leo Frank affair of 1913–15 shocked the Jewish community and added a sense of urgency for the creation of new Jewish defense agencies.[17] In this newly charged and potentially hostile atmosphere, the ADL set out to protect Jewish interests. This pattern of organizational development fits the previously mentioned disturbance theory of interest group formation as described by Truman and Wilson. In this instance the emergence of widespread anti-Semitism for the first time in America impelled the formation of Jewish defense organizations.[18]

The ADL quickly expanded its operations and soon attained a great deal of respectability and political clout. The ADL devoted much of this influence to one of its highest priorities: exposing and countering right-wing extremists. In 1931, then ADL national director Richard Gutstadt founded the fact-finding department, which gathered intelligence on extremist organizations.[19] By the inter-war years, the ADL had gained access to various law enforcement agencies, including the US Department of Justice, with which it developed a good working relationship, and by its own admission, supplied information on native fascists and right-wing extremists.[20] The ADL sought to conceal this cooperation it had with law enforcement authorities from the press so that it would not fuel hostility from some quarters of the public.[21]

As an ADL publication once explained, the ADL has not depended on rigid formulae to pursue its interests and goals. Rather it has adapted its tactics to meet the changing threat to Jews and other minority groups.[22] However, one technique that it frequently has applied is public exposure of its extremist opponents. The purpose of this is to isolate and marginalize the extremist from the society at large.

The ADL's effectiveness in countering right-wing extremism stems in large part from its ability to control much of the information about this subject. Towards this end, the ADL moved its national headquarters from Chicago to New York in 1947 in an effort to take better advantage of the mass media of communications.[23] It publishes numerous reports on right-wing groups and their leaders, and this has greatly influenced the perception of the far right in the eyes of policy makers and academic researchers.[24]

Over the years, the ADL has gained considerable strength as it has accumulated substantial resources. In the postwar era there has been an increasing professionalization of its staff as qualified individuals perform specialized tasks.[25] Concomitant with this development has been the compartmentalization of its functions. Several departments concentrate on specific issues and areas including fact-finding, civil rights, research, international affairs, government affairs, legal affairs and education. Moreover, the ADL is very well financed; for the year 2000, the ADL recorded assets of $17,737,259 and received an annual income of $48,693,379.[26] It employs over 400 people, including an extensive legal staff.[27] Finally, it maintains thirty-three regional offices in various American cities, as well as foreign countries including Austria, Canada and Israel.

Much of the ADL's strength and continuity can be explained by the fact that many American Jews – their material and social success notwithstanding – still feel a strong sense of insecurity and believe that anti-Semitism remains a serious problem in the United States.[28] Despite the relative weakness of the contemporary American far right, many American Jews believe that under certain conditions, an anti-Semitic movement could become stronger.[29] Consequently, many Jewish-Americans are willing to make generous donations not only to the ADL and other Jewish defense organizations, but to other watchdog groups as well.

Over the years, the ADL has identified several different organizations as a serious threat not only to the American Jewish community, but to the democratic structure of America as well. Judging by the ADL's literature, the John Birch Society was regarded as the most serious threat during the 1960s. The ADL released several publications warning of the undemocratic tendencies of the Birch Society. Some of these were even published as books that were carried by major publishing houses.[30] At first it may seem odd that the ADL felt threatened by the Birch Society; there were vociferous anti-Semites active during this time, such as George Lincoln Rockwell of the American Nazi Party and Gerald L. K. Smith of the Christian National Party. However, neither commanded the resources nor the followers of the Birch Society during that era, which was estimated at its peak to have 50,000–60,000 members.[31] Thus the Birch Society demonstrated the potential of becoming a formidable mass movement. Furthermore, earlier research suggested that that the seemingly innocuous conspiracy theories propounded by the Birch Society could potentially be transformed into anti-Semitic conspiracy theories.[32]

By the 1970s, the Birch Society began to run out of steam. Moreover, to the relief of the ADL, it never transformed itself into an anti-Semitic vehicle. In fact, as mentioned earlier, it expelled those members who outspokenly expressed anti-Semitism. But the ADL identified a new threat in the Liberty Lobby. In 1964 the Lobby began publication of *The Liberty Letter*, which was a very small publication. However, in 1975 this evolved into its weekly newspaper, *The Spotlight*, which attained a circulation estimated at its peak to be approximately 315,000.[33] Moreover, the Liberty Lobby dabbled in other media such as radio, with a program called *This is the Liberty Lobby*, which was aired on radio stations around the country. Finally, Willis Carto, the Liberty Lobby's leader, was the main figure who gave Holocaust revisionism an institutional basis. For these reasons, Willis Carto and the Liberty Lobby were identified as the leading anti-Semite and leading anti-Semitic organization respectively throughout the 1970s to the 1990s.

By the late 1990s, though, the ADL identified Dr William Pierce's National Alliance as "the single most dangerous organized hate group in the United States today."[34] By far-right standards, Pierce has built an impressive multi-media propaganda apparatus with his Resistance Records, National Vanguard Books, and *American Dissident Voices* radio program. What's more, through his authorship of the *Turner Diaries* and his long experience in extremist politics, he is regarded as a well respected elder statesman in the far-right milieu. For these reasons, the ADL has expressed consternation over the increasing influence of the National Alliance. However, Dr Mark Pitcavage, the current chief fact-finder for the ADL, was vague in identifying the threat from the far right:

> Well, you know, you can measure the threat in all sorts of different ways. The movement that tends to be the most violent is the white supremacist movement. On the other hand, the movement that has given authorities the most problem is the sovereign citizen freemen movement. I really hate to sort of come up with enemy number one.[35]

(Parenthetically, it is important to keep in mind that Pitcavage had held that position for only a few days at the time of our interview and thus may have not really had a chance to formulate a more specific opinion while he settles into his new position. Prior to his arrival at the ADL, he ran the Militia Watchdog project and thus focused primarily on the Christian Patriot/militia segment of the far right.)

In recent years the ADL has taken the lead in countering the far right through various measures including, *inter alia*, the promotion of legislation (e.g. anti-paramilitary training statutes and hate crime legislation), cooperation with law enforcement agencies, training programs that alert the public to the threat of right extremism, and the promotion of software that blocks access to extremist websites. Its current national director, Abraham Foxman, is considered an important public figure with substantial political clout.[36] Despite occasional setbacks, overall, today the organization appears to be in good shape and is a formidable opponent to the far right.[37]

The American Jewish Committee

Like the ADL, the American Jewish Committee (AJC) was also founded in response to a crisis, in this case an international one. In the early part of the twentieth century pogroms convulsed Jewish populations in Russia and parts of Eastern Europe. In order to address this crisis several prominent American Jews, including the financier Jacob Schiff, the jurist Oscar Straus and the philanthropist Cyrus L. Sulzberger, met in New York City in 1906 to create an organization to aid their co-religionists overseas.[38] Hence was born the American Jewish Committee. During the early part of its history, the AJC proved to be quite adept in lobbying in the field of foreign policy. In fact it saw itself as instrumental in persuading the United States government's decision in 1911 to abrogate its 1832 commercial treaty with Russia.[39]

Up until the 1930s, the AJC focused primarily on issues facing Jews overseas. However, as World War II approached the AJC began to concern itself more with defense issues affecting Jews residing in the United States. The impetus for this repositioning was a renascent far right in America and the rise of Hitler's Nazi movement in Germany. Many far-right groups sprouted all over the country, drawing inspiration from European fascists in continental Europe. During this period, the focus of this movement's hostility shifted away from anti-Catholicism to anti-Semitism and anti-communism. This understandably was a worrisome development for the Jewish community. To meet this threat, the AJC took various measures. First, it created a Legal and Investigative Department to obtain information on its far-right opponents. Dossiers were made on them and much of this information was provided to government authorities. Inasmuch as the ADL had been ahead of the game in this area, the AJC agreed to coordinate its efforts with the former.[40] Both the ADL and the AJC worked closely with and provided information to government authorities including congressional committees, Army and Navy Intelligence, and the FBI.[41] The results of these investigations were often funneled to sympathetic journalists who wrote stories and editorials against the threat of native fascism and fifth column subversion.[42] At the close of World War II the AJC retreated from the area of investigating domestic right-wing extremism. That mission, for the most part, returned solely to the ADL. However, the AJC would occasionally issue a report on the topic.[43]

One major strategic contribution that the AJC has made to the strategy of combating right-wing extremism is the notion of "quarantine" or "dynamic silence." Dr Solomon Andhil Fineberg of the AJC is given credit for the creation of this tactic. It was first devised in the late 1940s to meet the challenge of one Gerald L. K. Smith,[44] one of the most notable anti-Semitic far-rightists of the last century. This approach was also refined to counter the antics of George Lincoln Rockwell and his American Nazi Party in the 1960s.[45] Essentially this tactical approach consists of two components. The first is the coordination among the major American Jewish community organizations to minimize public confrontations between far-right figures and their opponents, in order to deny the former a dramatic event that could generate publicity. The second component is to convince the media that absent a violent confrontation between far-rightists and their opponents, there was little newsworthy about them and thus they should be ignored.[46] A consensus among the Jewish defense groups to adhere to the dynamic silence approach has held up well over the years. An ADL publication once commented on the approach:

> At certain points, for certain agitators and groups, silence is the best course. Publicity can sometimes help a demagogue who is not well known; to ignore him is to consign him to limbo. In other situations, exposure of the agitator's background and affiliations will sharply cut his influence, depriving him of the support of decent people.[47]

Generally speaking, according to this measure, anti-Semites are to be ignored until they attain a certain level of notoriety at which time the Jewish defense organizations publicly respond. However, new developments such as the emergence of the internet and the medium of popular television talk shows, which provides a means of access for extremists to present their case directly to American public, have made the quarantine approach a bit more problematic to maintain.

In recent years the AJC has demonstrated renewed interest in combating domestic right-wing extremism, primarily by issuing reports on the topic. Its primary researcher on the topic, Kenneth Stern, published a top selling book on the militias in 1996 titled *A Force upon the Plain*.[48] More recently the AJC has supported other measures to counter the far right, such as supporting hate crime legislation. The AJC has also shown renewed interest in tracking developments in Europe as well. In 1998 it opened a permanent office in Berlin, Germany, to monitor right-wing extremism in that country.[49] Although the AJC is less involved in this area than the ADL, it enjoys considerable political influence and has formidable resources. As of 2000 the organization had assets of $70,055,959, and its annual income for that same year was reported at $39,793,811.[50] Its national headquarters is in New York and in addition it maintains thirty-two regional offices in major cities nationwide and overseas offices in Jerusalem, Berlin, Geneva and Warsaw. Harold Tanner is the AJC president and David A. Harris is executive director.

The Simon Wiesenthal Center

The Simon Wiesenthal Center (SWC), the most recent of the major Jewish defense organizations, was founded in 1977 and named after the celebrated Nazi hunter. However, the leading figure behind the Center is Rabbi Marvin Hier. The center has its headquarters in Los Angeles, California. Over the years it has expanded it operations and currently has offices in New York, Toronto, Miami, Jerusalem, Paris and Buenos Aires.

Of all the American Jewish defense organizations, the Simon Wiesenthal Center is the most internationally oriented. A perusal of its periodical, *Response*, suggests that the Center is often more focused on manifestations of right-wing extremism overseas than in the United States. Issues impinging on the security of Israel and Jews residing in other parts of the world are also given high priority. Towards this end, the SWC monitors terrorist developments in the Middle East and other regions of the world in which Jews are the primary targets. One of its chief preoccupations is exposing and lobbying for the prosecution of suspected Nazi war criminals.

In recent years the SWC has also expanded the scope of its domestic agenda. It opened its Museum of Tolerance in 1993 to foster awareness of the Holocaust and issues related to racism, bigotry and right-wing extremism. Moreover, the SWC promotes Holocaust studies and tolerance education in public schools, workplaces and other institutions. Increasingly the SWC has been involved in hate crime policy issues. In the past, it has occasionally offered monetary rewards in return for information leading to the arrest and conviction of perpetrators of such crimes.

The Center has also started monitoring right-wing extremist groups in the United States and abroad. In one instance, which received international attention, the Simon Wiesenthal Center underwrote the expenses of a former Israeli intelligence officer who infiltrated the German far-right underground.[51] This resulted in much publicity, and the Simon Wiesenthal Center presented the findings of this investigation to the US Congress, the FBI, and German authorities.[52]

One area of particular concern to the SWC is the proliferation of Holocaust revisionist material. In 1991, the Center's National Task Force Against Hate was established and soon after launched a campaign to alert the editors of college newspapers of the efforts of Holocaust revisionist historians to place ads in college newspapers on this subject. The SWC has also pressured authorities overseas to prosecute promoters of such materials in countries where such material is illegal under the rubric of hate speech. Its efforts in these areas have not gone unnoticed by right-wing extremists. For example, Buford O'Neal Furrow, the gunman who terrorized a Jewish day care center and later fatally shot an Asian American postal carrier, had in fact originally planned on attacking the Center but was dissuaded after reconnoitering the facility in Los Angeles and observing the tight security there.[53]

Like the other Jewish defense organizations reviewed earlier, the Simon Wiesenthal Center has established itself as a very influential watchdog group. It has obtained substantial funding as indicated by its assets of $72,576,026 as of 2000, and an annual income for that same year of $31,619,383.[54] Furthermore, the SWC occasionally receives lucrative government grants.[55] Moreover, the SWC is well respected in the general society and has frequently gained access to prominent politicians, celebrities and opinion makers.

The civil litigation watchdog: the Southern Poverty Law Center

The Southern Poverty Law Center is one of the most high-profile and formidable watchdog groups. It is best known for its innovative use of civil suits to combat its far-right opponents. This has brought the organization considerable attention and critical acclaim from liberal and civil rights well-wishers over the past decade and a half, which the organization has been able to parlay into a veritable fundraising juggernaut. With assets of $147,441,903 and an annual income of $32,520,416 (as of 2000), it is estimated to be the wealthiest civil rights organization in the United States.[56]

In 1971 two attorneys – Morris S. Dees Jr and Joseph J. Levin – founded the Southern Poverty Law Center in Montgomery, Alabama. At first the Center focused primarily on various progressive issues such as fighting poverty and discrimination. In its early days the Center also gave a very high priority to eradicating the death penalty from the American criminal justice system.

The SPLC owes much of its success to the efforts of one man: Morris Dees. He is arguably the most well known figure in the entire watchdog movement – praised by supporters in the civil right community and despised by those in the far right. Thus a brief examination of the man is in order. According to the exchange theory, the key element in interest group formation is the organizer or entrepreneur of the group.[57] The main figure behind the SPLC, Morris Dees, speaks volumes for this theory. An indefatigable organizer and master of self-promotion, Dees himself has acknowledged that he evinced a great talent for salesmanship for nearly as far back in his life as he can remember. Before founding the SPLC, he operated a very lucrative mail order business selling cookbooks, which made him a wealthy man. Eventually his business partner, Milliard Fuller, would sell his share to Dees, give the money he had made to charity, and go on to found the Habitat for Humanity.[58]

During the 1970s Dees became very involved in political fundraising as he worked on electoral campaigns of several very prominent Democratic Party candidates for high political office. For example, in 1972 he served as the finance director for George McGovern's 1972 presidential campaign and raised approximately 24 million dollars.[59] By some accounts, it was the first time in American politics that direct mail solicitation had played such an important role in campaign finance. Dees drew an astounding 15 per cent response from his fundraising appeal letter for the campaign, which caught the attention of well seasoned political fundraisers.[60] Four years later, Dees applied his mail fundraising skills to Jimmy Carter's successful presidential campaign.[61] Prominent members of the Democrat Party took notice and Dees established some very important political connections. More important, through his work on these campaigns, Dees was able to compile a massive mailing list of prospective donors. And through his work on civil rights issues, he forged friendships with some very prominent civil rights leaders and liberal celebrities as well.[62] As a result of these experiences, Dees has become a notable figure in the liberal establishment.

To lend credibility to his fledging SPLC, Dees asked civil rights activist and then Georgia State Senator Julian Bond to serve as the Center's president, a largely honorary position. Dees was also able to pull together several other civil rights luminaries to serve on the SPLC's Council of Civil Rights, thus further buttressing the organization's reputation.[63]

In 1979, Dees made a decision to shift the focus of the Center's activities by creating the Klanwatch Project. Part of its mission would be to serve as a clearing-house for information on the Ku Klux Klan as well as other extremist right-wing groups. In the wake of revelations of the COINTELPRO controversy in the mid-1970s, Dees saw a gap in the intelligence gathering apparatus of the FBI that he thought needed to be filled. Congressional and public calls for reform led to the creation of new guidelines, which forbade the FBI from gathering intelligence on extremist groups for which there was no evidence of a criminal predicate. Moreover, the FBI had come under sharp criticism for the way in which it handled some of its Klan informants.[64] Dees came up with the idea of gathering intelligence and sharing it with contacts that he had made over the years in law enforcement.[65] Although the ADL had been doing this for a long time, Dees saw a gap that he could fill. He would add a litigation component to these efforts by bringing civil suits against far-right groups that could be held civilly liable for their transgressions.[66] Such a novel legal maneuver would also generate valuable publicity for the SPLC.

Ingratiating his organization with law enforcement was not easy at first for Dees. In fact, much of the earlier work of the SPLC had alienated it from law enforcement authorities in the South.[67] The Center was a strong opponent of the death penalty in the American criminal justice system. Also, in an important suit initiated by the Center, the Alabama State Police was ordered to establish a very strong quota-oriented affirmative action hiring program.

Eventually, however, the SPLC compiled extensive files on right-wing extremists that authorities occasionally found helpful to utilize. In the mid-1990s, the SPLC established the "Militia Task Force" to keep tabs on the activities of the militia/Christian Patriot movement. That, along with its Klanwatch project, comprises its intelligence gathering arms. As part of this effort, the SPLC began publication of a newsletter called *The Intelligence Report* in the early 1980s. Today, as a quarterly magazine, it is widely distributed to law enforcement agencies, government officials, educators, the press, and of course, its donors. This publication got a shot in the arm in 1997 when a writer for the newspaper *USA Today*, Mark Potok, took over the reins of the publication as editor. Potock recounted for how he came to work for the SPLC:

> I've been a reporter for over twenty years. I worked for a bunch of different newspapers, the last of which was *USA Today* where I worked for about four

years – I covered Waco. I covered for *USA Today* the trial of the surviving Davidians and then started running around the country and [covering] things that seemed like obvious offshoots to that. Basically, I started writing stories about the birth of the militia movement and wound up becoming, in effect, *USA Today's* reporter on the radical right. I covered the McVeigh trial and things like the standoff in Texas – The reason I came to the Southern Poverty Law Center was because, really there was an opportunity. They had a newsletter, which had grown some over the years, but it needed some serious work. I came in very largely to kind of remake the newsletter into a real magazine [that] it has become. For me dealing with *The Intelligence Report* was really about making it into a credible, serious, effective magazine, something that would be taken seriously.[68]

In addition to *The Intelligence Report*, Dees has published books on the topic of right-wing extremism including *Gathering Storm: America's Militia Threat*, *A Season for Justice*, and *Hate on Trial*, which have helped shaped the public's perceptions of this topic.[69]

Judging by its publications and the organizations at which its civil suits are aimed, it would appear that the Southern Poverty Law Center has regarded the Ku Klux Klan as a serious threat. However, in recent years, there has been a perceptible shift away from its emphasis on the Klan to other groups in the far-right milieu. Mark Potok gave me his thoughts on this issue:

Well, I think in many ways the greatest threat comes not from the Klan or even some of the hot neo-Nazi groups out there, so much as the larger groups that present themselves as mainstream. I'm talking about groups like the Council of Conservative Citizens and the League of the South, which are vastly bigger than the other groups. The League of the South has 9,000 people. The Council of Conservative Citizens has 15,000. That's exponentially larger than the vast majority of groups we cover. And that's the reason I say they're more dangerous. Certainly the Klan groups and the Aryan Nations are dangerous in a sense that some people are going to get hurt by members or associates of these groups. That's perfectly clear. It happens consistently. But no one is going to be elected. A representative of the Aryan Nations is not going to be elected senator or even president. But, you look at a group like the Council of Conservative Citizens and what you're looking at is a racist group that plays a great deal of footsy with the Senate majority leader [Trent Lott] among others. So my point is that if a group like the Council of Conservative Citizens is allowed to get away with calling themselves mainstream or conservative, we may very well see our next senator or, god help us, president, as a member of this group. The white supremacists that don't come in pointed white hats or with shaved heads [are] as a general rule the more dangerous from a political point of view.[70]

In recent years the SPLC has taken up other issues that seek to counter right-wing extremism, such as lobbying in favor of hate crime and anti-terrorism laws. However, this gradual shift in orientation of the Center away from traditional civil rights issues to fighting right-wing extremism has alienated some on the staff of the Center. For example, in one instance in 1986, the entire legal staff, excluding Dees, resigned along with one additional employee.[71] Several of the employees thought that this emphasis on right-wing extremism was draining resources away from more important projects such as death penalty cases, homelessness, and voting rights cases.

The SPLC has won some very highly publicized civil suits against some of the most prominent groups and individuals of the far right, including the United Klans of America, Tom Metzger and his organization WAR, Dr William Pierce, the chairman of the National Alliance, and most recently, the Aryan Nations. Dees often follows these legal victories with emotive fundraising appeals to his donors.[72] The publicity from these high-profile trials has generated much goodwill among liberals and civil right supporters who have supported him with substantial donations. Ironically, this success has now brought Dees and the SPLC their most serious criticism to date as it has begun to raise eyebrows even among liberals. Commenting on Dees' fundraising efforts, Milliard Farmer, an Atlanta death penalty lawyer and former Dees ally once referred to the SPLC as a "Jim and Tammy Faye Baaker operation" and Dees as "the civil rights movement's television evangelist."[73] More seriously, the American Institute of Philanthropy – an organization that rates charitable institutions according to several criteria – gave the SPLC an "F" rating on a scale from A through F.[74] At about the same time a very critical series in the *Montgomery Advertiser* reported that the Center had amassed a huge surplus, and as of 1993 had never spent more than 31 per cent of the money it was bringing in on its various programs. By contrast, most non-profits spend about 75 per cent on programs.[75] Previously most of the criticism of the SPLC has been localized and confined to small local newspapers and right-wing critics. However, a recent *Harper's Magazine* revisited many of these charges.[76] Finally, a recent segment of 'The O'Reilly Factor' on *Fox News* questioned the fundraising and charitable propriety of the SPLC.[77] Some critics in the civil rights community are now complaining that the wealthy SPLC is siphoning off much-needed dollars that could be put to better use by other charities and civil rights organizations.[78]

This recent criticism notwithstanding, the SPLC remains a very formidable opponent of the far right. The threat of lawsuits that could bankrupt their organizations has undoubtedly had a chilling effect on its leaders and made them think twice about engaging in violent activism. Indeed, no other figure in the watchdog community is so reviled by the far right as Morris Dees. On several occasions he has been marked for assassination by right-wing terrorists seeking retribution for his activism.[79] Moreover, in one incident in 1983, the SPLC's facilities were subjected to an arson attack.[80] On another occasion in 1986, members of a right-wing group allegedly conspired to blow up the SPLC building with a military rocket.[81] These incidents demonstrate that the SPLC is considered a serious enemy in the far right. To my knowledge, no other figure in the watchdog community has received as many threats as Morris Dees. Despite the recent criticism, and whatever shortcomings the man may have, his supporters will more than likely continue to back him, thus making him and the SPLC major players in the watchdog community for some time to come.

The progressive-oriented watchdog groups

The Center for Democratic Renewal

The Center for Democratic Renewal (CDR) of Atlanta, Georgia is one of the most prominent of the progressive-oriented watchdog groups. As is so often the case, this particular organization was founded in response to a crisis. In this instance a November 3, 1979 Greensboro, North Carolina confrontation between Neo-Nazis and Klansmen on the one hand and counter-demonstrators on the other. What began as a "Death to the Klan" march ended in a bloody shootout in which five members of the Communist Workers Party were killed. The Klansmen and neo-Nazis came out of the confrontation generally unscathed.[82] This event did much to mobilize the "counter-hate" movement. Sympathizers of the slain founded the National Anti-Klan Network (NAKN) shortly thereafter.[83]

In 1985 the organization changed its name to the Center for Democratic Renewal to better reflect the increasing scope of its agenda, which has come to include a broad range of progressive issues including reproductive rights, discrimination, minority rights, ameliorating poverty, support for new immigrants, hate crimes, and of course, countering the far right. What distinguishes the progressive watchdog groups from others is that they tend to be critical of a broader segment of the right-wing spectrum, and not just the far right. Chris Freemen explains how the mission of the CDR evolved over the years:

> People got together after that incident [the Greensboro Massacre] and formed the National Anti-Klan Network. I think we went through some ideological changes over the years and our outlook and our mission changed somewhat. It went from a strictly anti-Klan organization to one that's involved in broader issues. That was one of the reasons the name was changed in 1985 to the CDR. ... We used to do a lot of community organizing-type of work, but now we focus more on research. We have a very small staff so we're not able to go out in the field as much as we'd like. So we turned into more of an educational organization. We send materials out to community-based organizations. We're not able to do the kind of activist work that we used to. But we still consider ourselves a grassroots organization in the sense that we're small and we still have a lot of local community contacts. We're not as disengaged from the community as a lot of the other [watchdog] organizations.[84]

The progressive orientation of the CDR stems from the fact that several of its staffers have sojourned in Marxist-Leninist style organizations.[85] This has brought the organization some criticism, as it is accused of applying a double standard in that it exposes right-wing extremists while tending to obscure its own left-wing background to achieve greater respectability. For his part, Chris Freemen denied any such double standard:

> I don't think that we're trying to push an agenda or ideology on anybody. I think the CDR is its own ideology as an organization as a whole. The people who work within the CDR have their own ideologies. I know I have. Personally, I consider the CDR as pretty much a mainstream liberal kind of organization. I don't really see a lot of radical-type stuff. Some of the CDR's earlier literature quite possibly was because of some of the people that were there in the beginning when it was the National Anti-Klan Network. But even then I didn't think that this was something they were trying to hide.
>
> For me personally, I would consider myself pretty much a far-left person. I have a critique of capitalism and the economic structure of the country. But at the same time, when I go to speak at an event or write something, I keep in mind that it is not the CDR's ideology. That's my ideology. That's what we try to do here. We go basically by the mission statement of the CDR, which doesn't have any ideological underpinnings.[86]

A staple of the CDR's early work consisted of counter-demonstrating against right-wing groups. Over the years, the CDR as an organization has become less involved in such activities, although individual members still occasionally participate in them.

The CDR endeavors to create broad-based coalitions of community and progressive activists in its efforts to counter the right wing. This often includes liberal Catholic, Protestant and Jewish religious organizations. Consistent with its progressive orientation, the CDR often cites economic factors such as unemployment and inequality in its analyses of right-wing extremism. It has on occasion worked closely with local human relations commissions and task forces at the state and local level to respond to tensions surrounding right-wing extremism. In sum, the CDR has favored a grassroots approach by encouraging citizens in communities to get involved in this issue. Towards this end, CDR published a book as a guide called *When Hate Groups Come to Town: A Handbook of Effective Community Response*.

The CDR does on occasion cooperate with law enforcement agencies, but not to the same degree as the major watchdog organizations such as the Southern Poverty Law Center and the ADL. One reason for this is because many of the community-based organizations, with which the CDR works, are very wary of the government. The limited size of the CDR is another reason. However, the CDR does maintain contacts in the FBI and various police agencies in the state of Georgia and other places. Usually, though, when the CDR gets involved in this type of activity it will contact the ADL in an area that has contacts with other government agencies in a region. In general, the CDR's relationship with law enforcement is less direct than that of the ADL and the SPLC. Law enforcement agencies occasionally prevail upon the CDR for information and the latter will from time to time conduct training seminars on right-wing extremism for the former.[87]

The CDR also publishes reports critical of far-right groups, and thus influences the perceptions of the media on this topic. CDR representatives are often called upon for interviews, and in doing so act as experts on this topic. Not long ago, a former CDR researcher, Leonard Zeskind, was awarded a $295,000 grant by the MacArthur Foundation to write a study on right-wing extremism.[88] The CDR has also endeavored to establish international ties with like-minded organizations in Europe such as *Searchlight*.[89] Furthermore, the CDR occasionally also cooperates with domestic watchdog groups; it works very closely with Political Research Associates and to a lesser degree with some other organizations such as the ADL, the Southern Poverty Law Center, and the Northwest Coalition Against Malicious Harassment.[90] Although it is not as well funded as the Jewish defense organizations and the SPLC, the CDR does occasionally pick up grants and has enough funding to survive albeit with a modest staff. As of 2000 the organization was reported to have had assets of $102,290 and an annual income of $543,282.[91]

Political Research Associates

Jean Hardisty, a Ph.D. in political science, founded an organization called Midwest Research in Chicago in 1981. The organization had humble origins, as it began as a library archive to assemble primary source references for people who wanted to either study the American political right wing or organize against some of its public policy positions.[92] In 1987, the organization moved to Somerville, Massachusetts and changed its name to Political Research Associates. Much like the CDR, several members of its staff have progressive and left-wing political backgrounds.[93]

Also like the CDR, PRA monitors a broad segment of the American right-wing spectrum. Unlike most of the other watchdog groups, PRA is first and foremost a research institution. One major asset in this regard is the organization's senior analyst, Chip Berlet, who has established a reputation as an authority on right-wing extremism. Although his research is not sympathetic to the right wing, he has endeavored to establish academic standards for PRA's research. This emphasis on research is what distinguishes PRA from the other watchdog groups.

One characteristic that differentiates the progressive watchdog groups from their better established counterparts is their relationship to law enforcement agencies, as they are much less likely to get involved in intelligence sharing. Berlet is quick to distinguish the PRA from the more established watchdog groups in this area. In the past, Berlet has been very critical of this collusion between law enforcement and some of the NGOs:

We have a very different way of dealing with law enforcement. We have a policy of treating law enforcement and government agencies like any other library patron. If law enforcement wants to move beyond that, we require a subpoena. Period. We have no backdoor relationship with law enforcement whatsoever. Either they come and use our library like anyone else, which happens extremely rarely, or we request that they subpoena the information or subpoena the individual. And, I've been subpoenaed more by defense counsels. ... Other than that, there is no relationship with law enforcement, which is extremely different from the Anti-Defamation League and the Southern Poverty Law Center ...

I co-wrote an op-ed in *The New York Times* that was critical of the ADL. And I've been on the record as having some differences of opinion with a number of the watchdog groups for many years. There are two separate issues. One, is the issue of whether you have a kind of cozy relationship with law enforcement and the other, as in the case of the ADL, where despite their publicity, they were clearly involved in illegally trading information with law enforcement in San Francisco. Although they admitted no wrongdoing, the evidence is quite clear that they did.[94]

Berlet has also been a strong critic of police and intelligence abuses, primarily against the political left, but he has also on occasion criticized government repression against the political right as well.[95] Berlet believes that much of this misconduct stems from what he refers to as "centrist/extremist" theory, which seeks to pathologize those ideological areas which are beyond the center of the political spectrum.[96] He blames previous social science research for this development:

I oppose the concept that dissidence is a sign of pathology, which is sort of a central core theme of Mr [Seymour Martin] Lipset's work.[97] I oppose the idea that dissidence always leads to criminality or violence, which is one of the central themes of the pluralist school. And, I think that if you make those assumptions, then you make the mistakes that the ADL has made and the FBI has made and other agencies have made by going in and assuming that the people they're studying who are angry and have a grievance are somehow motivated by some mental illness or some irrational response. I simply don't think that is true. I have a book coming out in November [2000] that I co-wrote with Matthew Lyons, which takes the position that right-wing populism is in fact internally consistent and reflects the grievances, which sometimes are expressed in the narrative form of a conspiracy theory.[98] But that does not make the people who do this either crazy or criminal – They sometimes certainly spread conspiracy theories pretty far-fetched. But that doesn't make them criminal. ...

I think that Mr Lipset's theory, which is that extremists of the left and right are a sign that there's something wrong with the society which they can't cope with, is half-right. The people who organize dissident movements on the left and right are definitely sensing that something is wrong with society. But it's not because they're crazy. In other words, the basic theme of Lipset is wrong. Dissent is a normal part of life. A society without dissent is moribund, whether it's on the left or on the right. ... What centrist-extremist theory does is idealize the center and say that the center is where things should be and that's where all democratic dialogue takes place, and that so-called pathological extremists of the left and right are marginal.[99]

PRA has proven to be quite adept in interfacing with the media. Chip Berlet frequently grants interviews and answers media inquiries on this subject.[100] PRA also puts out a periodical, *The Public Eye*, which tracks developments on the political right. One thing that sets Berlet apart from other figures in the watchdog community is his willingness to both debate and dialogue with his right-wing opponents. This is in contrast to the tacit "we don't debate extremists" policy, which prevails throughout most of the watchdog community.

The PRA tends to avoid overtly influencing public policy like the better established watchdog groups, although it does occasionally get involved in some progressive activist work. It provides resource materials, organizing advice, and speakers to community-based groups that challenge the political right. Also, PRA staffers occasionally provide expert testimony on various issues. For example, Berlet briefed Congress about right-wing extremism in the US military. He also prepared a bibliography for the Office of Policy and Planning for the Justice Department after the Oklahoma City bombing, so that the government could better understand the differences between and among the Patriot movement, the armed militia movement, and the neo-Nazi movement. Finally, Berlet has on occasion participated in law enforcement training classes in which he cautions police officers to avoid oversimplifying extremist movements, because such presumptions can lead to mistakes such as Waco. Despite these informational activities, the PRA tries to stay away from involvement in any kind of legislative or political campaign.[101]

Although its roots are left wing and progressive, PRA has established a good deal of respectability and credibility. In fact, as Berlet explains, PRA has not really done anything to hide their political orientation:

> We in fact are a progressive, left-leaning group. We're not unmindful of civil liberties issues. We're set up to study the American political right wing. If you see the world as the ideal center threatened by extremists from the left and the right, you're using a social science model that is flawed. That's my argument. The fact that we work on the left and have certain individuals, who are well known for fighting right-wing activists, what does that have to do with anything? That's guilt by association. That's one of the fallacies of logic. You're not arguing to the point. The point is when we put out a study, do we accurately represent the facts? When we put out material, are we trying to be fair, are we helping people understand the complexity of the situation? What does it matter that I used to write for *The Guardian* and that

was a Marxist newspaper? Does that make me a Marxist? Really, it doesn't. We are transparently who we are.[102]

PRA has been able to secure adequate funding from progressive groups and donors (as of 2000, the organization's assets were $737,022 and annual income was $708,556), and in doing so has established itself well in the constellation of watchdog organizations.[103] This is in large measure because it has developed a reputable research facility with a media outreach program. It has a small but capable staff of regular and affiliate researchers, besides Hardisty and Berlet, including Holly Sklar, Sara Diamond and Russ Bellant.[104]

The regional watchdog groups

The Northwest Coalition Against Malicious Harassment

The Northwest Coalition Against Malicious Harassment is perhaps the most prominent of the regional watchdog organizations. It currently has its headquarters in Seattle, Washington. Like several of the other watchdog groups, the impetus for its creation was tension between far-rightists and their neighbors in the surrounding community. During the 1980s, the Aryan Nations compound, located in Hayden Lake, Idaho, had been the epicenter of the American extreme right. During that decade a virtual "who's who" of the most radical elements of the radical right had on one occasion or another attended its annual Aryan Congresses that were regularly held in the summer. The Aryan Nations' founder and elder statesman of the American far right, Richard Butler, was a good shepherd of sorts in the far-right underground insofar as he often opened the compound's doors to ex-convicts and some criminally inclined extremists. What's more, due to the notoriety that the compound received it attracted a good deal of informants and agents-provocateurs. All of these factors proved at times to be a volatile mix, which spilled over to the surrounding community. Thus the Northwest Coalition was founded in 1986 as a community-based initiative to counter the Aryan Nations in that area. The chief figure behind its formation was a Catholic priest, Bill Wassmuth. He recalls its formation.

> In 1986, the Kootenai County Task Force on Human Relations had a human rights rally in Couer d'Alene Park at the same time that the Aryan Nations had their White supremacist rally in Hayden Lake. And in that rally we invited participation from throughout the five Northwest states because Richard Butler [leader of the Aryan Nations] had announced plans to take over those five states as a white Aryan homeland.[105] And so our human rights celebration was very successful. As a number of us were debriefing afterwards, we concluded that it would be helpful in the Northwest to have

some kind of on-going sort of coalition, because in many cases, the White supremacists would move into rural areas that were low on resources.

So we put together a steering committee of people from the five northwest states, Oregon, Washington, Idaho, Montana, Wyoming and [also] Colorado. We met in the fall of 1986 through the spring 1987 and came up with the Northwest Coalition against Malicious Harassment. It's a coalition of organizations and individuals and it's meant to provide both education and community organizing and a coordinated response to White supremacy, as well as to provide direction and leadership for respect for diversity and justice.[106]

The Northwest Coalition employs a variety of strategies to counter the far right. First, it provides assistance to communities to prevent acts of racist violence and harassment. Second, it seeks to educate communities about far-right groups and issues related to that such as bias crime. Third, it monitors far-right groups and publishes a periodical, *The Northwest Beacon*, which provides analysis on this topic. Finally, it promotes legislation such as hate crime laws.[107]

Like virtually all representatives of the watchdog community, Wassmuth refuses to debate his right-wing extremist opponents. His comments are illustrative of this sentiment:

> I've never considered that to be my duty or my role. My role is to point out injustice and there's no dialogue about that. There's no compromising about civil rights. You don't dialogue about that. Some other people have attempted to meet with Richard Butler and to essentially talk him out of his position. And they have not been successful with that.
>
> We [Butler and Wassmuth] wouldn't have anything to talk about. Nor would he do the same with me I'm sure. But it's not personal. I mean it's an ideological battle. It's a battle for the heart and soul of the region. He really wants to turn the heart and soul of the region into a White supremacist, bigoted, racist community. And I, among with a lot of other human rights people, don't think that that's the way our country is meant to be. So, it's not been my goal to meet anybody halfway because that's not what justice is about. And it hasn't been my goal to turn them around. My goal has been to stop them.[108]

The NWC was originally designed to be very inclusive so that it could attain broad-based community support.[109] Over the years it has successfully brought together a broad coalition, especially of liberal religious organizations, but also state and local politicians, and minority group and community-based organizations. It cooperates with governmental and law enforcement agencies as well. Bill Wassmuth explains:

> As a non-profit group, we promote and encourage education about hate crime legislation and bias crime legislation. But we work with law enforcement to

create community-based groups that do organizing and community education on these issues. Each of the governors from the six states we represent has a representative on our board of directors. There's a representative from law enforcement from each one of these states. There's a place for that on the board of directors. And when we advocate in terms of community organizing, we advocate the involvement of law enforcement there as well.[110]

The NWC also cooperates with other watchdog groups. For example, the ADL is a member organization of the Coalition, and the Southern Poverty Law Center works closely with the NWC.[111]

Much of the success of the NWC can be attributed to Bill Wassmuth, as he has been its chief spokesman and organizer. He served as its executive director from 1989 through 1999 and departed on what appear to be amicable terms after a considerable tour of duty. Despite the loss of Wassmuth, the NWC appears to be on a pretty solid organizational footing. Over the years the NWC has attained moderate but adequate funding (for the year 2000 its assets were reported at $507,450 and annual income $256,886) and is well respected in the Pacific Northwest region of the country.[112] As Wassmuth mentioned, each governor from the six states represented in the Coalition has a representative on its board of directors. Moreover, both local and national media have occasionally given Wassmuth and the NWC attention and good publicity. However, being a visible representative of the watchdog community has in the past put Wassmuth in harm's way, as his home was once the target of a pipe bomb attack. Those responsible – members of a small right-wing group known as the Brüder Schweigen Strike Force II – had further plans to assassinate him but the plot was foiled before it could be carried out.[113] Despite the ordeal, Wassmuth did not disengage from his activism. He has, however, since left the priesthood and now works as a consultant and lectures on the subject of hate crimes and the far right to audiences around the country.

The Center for New Community

The Center for New Community is a regional watchdog group based in Chicago, Illinois with a faith-based approach, which enlists support primarily from liberal religious organizations, but also civic, education, labor, business and government agencies. Its primary focus is on regional far-right activity such as Matt Hale's World Church of the Creator, which until recently located its headquarters in East Peoria, Illinois, and Midwestern Christian Identity groups. The *Midwest Action Report* is the organization's publication, which monitors far-right activity with special attention to that which occurs in the Midwest. It also conducts workshops and public presentations to educate the public on issues such as racism, bias crime, and right-wing extremism. On occasion it collaborates with some of the other watchdog groups. For example, it prepared a special report on the World Church of the Creator for the American Jewish

Committee.[114] Much of its staff appears to be composed of church-based activists.[115]

The organization is still young, as it was only founded in 1995, which makes it a bit too early to see if the Center for New Community will establish itself as a viable watchdog group. However, it has demonstrated on past occasions that it is capable of conducting investigative research such as its exposé of the efforts of far-rightists to infiltrate the Reform Party and Pat Buchanan's 2000 electoral campaign.[116] What is more, the Center for New Community has already established a sound financial footing on a par with the second-level watchdog groups examined earlier, as its assets as of the year 2000 were $507,450 and annual income was $256,886.[117] Finally, insofar as there are no other major regional watchdog groups in the Midwest, it is geographically well placed to fill a void in that part of the country.[118]

The internet-based watchdog groups

The Nizkor Project

The Nizkor Project[119] is a Canadian based website that was created by Ken McVay to counter the claims of the so-called Holocaust revisionist historians. McVay was so angered by the proliferation of revisionist material on the web that he decided to create an internet archive of Holocaust-related materials, which now consists of literally thousands of documents and is estimated to the largest of such archives on the World Wide Web.[120] The archiving has taken two forms: first, the archiving of Holocaust-related material (e.g. the transcripts from the Nuremberg Tribunal and the Eichmann trial) and second, the analysis of major Holocaust denial claims, coupled with well documented responses to those claims.[121] In recent years, the Nizkor Project has also expanded its scope to include articles on the contemporary far right. As McVay explained to me, he considers them to be bedfellows of the deniers and as such cannot be considered separately:

> Holocaust denial is about Hitler-cleansing coupled with overt hatred for Jews. The people who espouse this racism, without exception, associate and collaborate with the extreme right. ... The extremists are the bedfellows of the deniers. They are one and the same and cannot be considered separately. That is why I have continued to add material about extremist groups.[122]

Unlike the other watchdog organizations, the Nizkor Project seldom works with other groups in the community. However, McVay mentioned that he has shared podiums from time to time with individuals within the ADL who were presenting at the same conferences that both had attended, and that they discussed various issues informally.[123]

McVay occasionally does some consulting work for the Canadian government, with respect to providing examples of the "state of hate" on the internet and identifying the nature of the problem.[124] McVay's home country of Canada happens to be perhaps the strictest country in the Western world with regard to issues of "hate speech." However, McVay himself related to me that he "consistently and persistently campaigned against such restrictions."[125] Although the Nizkor Project is basically a one-man operation, McVay has created an impressive online resource for those interested in studying the Holocaust and related issues.

The Militia Watchdog

The Militia Watchdog began as a website in 1995 in the aftermath of the Oklahoma City bombing. Its founder, Dr Mark Pitcavage, felt that there was a great need for information on the topic of anti-governmental extremism to be made more readily available.[126] It is not surprising that Pitcavage would have an interest in this topic, after all he wrote his doctoral dissertation on the decline of state militia movements during the nineteenth century.

Despite its humble origins and the fact that it is a virtual one-man operation, Pitcavage's Militia Watchdog project has developed into a fairly influential watchdog entity over the past few years. This is due in large part to the fact that Pitcavage has fostered extensive contacts with law enforcement personnel throughout North America. He makes detailed information on militia and other right-wing extremists available via a mailing list to roughly 400 select subscribers, many of whom are law enforcement personnel and representatives of other watchdog groups.[127] The attention he received and the credibility he attained with this audience helped Pitcavage establish himself as the research director of State and Local Anti-Terrorist Training Program (SLATT) – a Department of Justice program administered by a private organization, the Institute for Intergovernmental Research, which trains state and local law enforcement personnel from around the country on the topics of terrorism and right-wing extremist groups. Although the program has been extant for only a few years, it has already secured substantial funding, as it received a $2 million grant from the Justice Department's Bureau of Justice Assistance for fiscal year 1999.[128]

Militia Watchdog also interfaces with some of the other watchdog groups, including the Simon Wiesenthal Center, the Center for New Community, the Center for Democratic Renewal, the Northwest Coalition against Malicious Harassment, and Political Research Associates, among others.[129] Despite his humble start in the watchdog community, Pitcavage has established himself as a major player – in fact in September of 2000 he took over the position as the ADL's national fact finding director – one of the most powerful and prestigious of positions in the watchdog movement.

Hatewatch

David Goldman founded Hatewatch in 1995 as a website to counter the proliferation of right-wing extremist sites on the World Wide Web. It examined issues involving online right-wing extremists, and even contained direct links to some of their websites. Goldman believed that this would foster increased public scrutiny on this issue and in doing so, mobilize ordinary people to join the fight against the far right. As Goldman saw it, this exposure, rather than persuading a "silent majority" of angry Whites to join the extremist ranks, had the effect of turning them against the far right.

His detractors however, thought this gave extremist groups valuable publicity. Some on the far right even saw Hatewatch as playing into their hands insofar as web browsers could use the Hatewatch site as a convenient gateway to link to their own websites.

By early 2001, David Goldman believed that his Hatewatch enterprise had proved to be a success. He saw no evidence that the internet turned out to be the Holy Grail recruiting medium for which the far right has long been searching. In his estimation that movement has done a lamentable job in using the internet to increase its membership. As a result, Goldman decided to take Hatewatch offline and close operations. He is now involved in a new project called Paragraph175.org, which he describes as an online "civil rights resource for those concerned about ensuring equality for all."[130]

Miscellaneous: Anti-Racist Action

Anti-Racist Action, ARA, is an outlier in the watchdog community. Whereas virtually all of the other watchdog groups mentioned above (including those with radically left-wing oriented elements on their staff) have attained considerable credibility and good standing with the general public, ARA is often kept at arm's length by its more established counterparts. Moreover, ARA chapters in general do not have the close working relationship with governmental authorities that many of the other watchdog groups enjoy. In fact several boards of education in Canada have designated ARA as a violence-prone organization and have prohibited the organization from trespassing on school grounds.[131] This lack of goodwill with authorities can be explained in large part by the anarchist ethos which permeates the various ARA chapters. This is evident in one of the planks of ARA's "Four Points of Unity," which explicitly discourages cooperation with authorities: "We don't rely on the cops or the courts." What's more, ARA is not loath to take direct action and confront its right-wing adversaries in the streets. This often results in violence on both sides. For example, two ARA members were slain by neo-Nazis near Las Vegas, Nevada in 1998.[132]

According to an unpublished paper on the history of the organization by a member, the first ARA chapter was formed in Minneapolis in 1986, when an anti-racist skinhead gang, the "Baldies" joined forces with a group of self-styled punks, the Revolutionary Anarchist Bowling League (RABL). Together, they began a campaign to rid the twin cities of a racist skinhead gang called the White Knights. They were largely successful and, through working with youth from other cities, the ARA model began to be adopted elsewhere.[133] From there, ARA chapters soon spread throughout the Midwest thanks in large part to an anti-racist network known as "the Syndicate."[134] Today ARA claims to have chapters in over 130 cities and towns in the United States and Canada, and plans on opening new chapters in Mexico, Colombia, and Asia.[135]

ARA is very loosely organized, as it is characterized by an informal, non-bureaucratic, highly decentralized and consensual structure, with no formal positions of authority.[136] ARA resembles the various anarchist "antifa" (short for anti-fascist) groups in Europe insofar as it is willing to confront far-right activists in the streets. Todd Ferguson, a Canadian graduate student in sociology and also an ARA member, explains.

> I think that ARA is different from most other anti-racist groups in two respects. We are very pro-confrontation. Our first Point Of Unity states:
> "WE GO WHERE THEY GO. Wherever racists are organizing or active, we're there ... " Now, that said, it's important to make a distinction between confrontation and violence. We see confrontation as a direct means of enabling the community to respond directly to the people creating problems for the community and, in doing so, preventing them from continuing to create problems. We aren't saying that we physically attack neo-Nazis.
>
> Unfortunately, given how neo-Nazis think and operate, we are sometimes compelled to defend ourselves and others in these situations, as we are legally permitted and morally obligated to. More often than not, however, the bigots back down and run away from us, so we are usually able to impede their efforts without having to defend ourselves physically.
>
> Another key difference between us and other anti-racist groups is summed up in our second point of unity: "WE DON'T RELY ON THE COPS OR THE COURTS." For us, this means that we feel that the community has a right to respond to bigotry directly without going through the channels of official authority. We see this as a more efficient and empowering way of dealing with racism, sexism and homophobia.
>
> These two differences sum up a lot of our strategic thinking about dealing with the extreme right. They are also all what people tend to focus on – but they are only half of the story. ARA also does extensive education work and much work at building an authentic anti-racist youth culture.[137]

Due to its anarchistic nature, ARA avoids cooperation with governmental authorities as much as possible. As Todd Ferguson explained to me, he feels that communities are better able to respond to hate than government bureaucracies are. One controversial tactic that ARA employs is known as "outings" in which ARA members, along with other like-minded activists and sympathizers in the community, demonstrate in front of the homes of known far-right figures.

These demonstrations are often noisy and boisterous and are meant to draw attention to neighbors of the targeted home that extremists are in their midst. Other measures in this regard include putting posters complete with the far-rightist's photo and home address on lampposts and mailboxes.[138] The purpose of these "outings" is to shame the targeted subject among his neighbors and family members in such a way to dissuade him from continuing his extremist activities.[139]

The ARA sees itself as willing to do the dirty work by confronting their opponents directly in the streets. This sets them apart from the more established watchdog groups. Often ARA members are a bit contemptuous of their more established counterparts for this reason. Todd Ferguson explains:

> We cooperate with a host of other anti-racist organizations whenever possible. In the case of the Simon Wiesenthal Center, which characterized the murders of ARA Las Vegas members Dan Shersty and Lin "Spit" Newborn by neo-Nazis not as hate crimes but as being motivated by a fictitious "drug beef" – let's just say we have some particular problems with them!
>
> If we were to cooperate on a project with any of the [watchdogs that] you mentioned, I think a concern ARA would have would be their cozy relationship with the police. All three seem to have a philosophy of avoiding confrontations with racists, "letting the Nazis have the streets," and working with/pressuring law enforcement agencies to solve the problem. That's not our strategic outlook, so it might be difficult to work with each other.
>
> On the other hand, if the SPLC was to offer ARA some of the hundreds of millions of dollars they have locked away, maybe we could work something out! (See, I think, the November 2000 issue of *Harper's Magazine* for a 4-page article on the SPLC's fundraising efforts).[140]

The future of ARA is a bit tenuous. Although it claims to have many chapters, it is often shunned by community leaders and authorities because of its reputation for street confrontations and violence related thereto. Unlike the other watchdog groups, ARA is not well funded. Other than a one-time grant of $8,000 to hold a 1996 conference on anti-racism and youth, ARA remains entirely self-funded by producing and selling ARA-related items such as T-shirts, buttons and patches, etc. What's more, ARA does not even collect membership dues, all of which means that the organization's income is marginal and highly erratic.[141] Despite these limitations, ARA has attracted a number of youth to its organization. What's more, inasmuch as many members are self-styled anarchists, the ARA could conceivably ride on the coattails of a renascent anarchist movement, which has gained momentum in recent years in response to globalization. The ARA's nihilistic orientation is likely to remain attractive to a certain number of younger thrill-seeking activists. In that sense it could serve as a gateway for younger people to get involved in watchdog and other anti-racist activities.

Conclusion

It is hoped that the preceding analysis has demonstrated several characteristics of the watchdog movement, and that some generalizations can now be made. First, it is a highly variegated and nuanced community of organizations, as there appears to be a good deal of diversity in orientation among these groups; however, there is also a high degree of cooperation among them, especially in the area of information sharing.

For the most part, these organizations have attained a great deal of respectability with the general public and community leaders. There are a few exceptions, such as Anti-Racist Action, with which some authorities are reluctant to associate. Furthermore, the watchdogs have considerable access to institutions of influence such as the government, media, and community leaders. As part of their coalition building, several of these watchdog groups work very closely with religious organizations. Thus, ironically, like their far-right adversaries, they also evince a high degree of religiosity, albeit of a more liberal orientation. Several of these groups also control significant resources as they are very well funded. Even the new start-ups, such as the Center for New Community, have secured impressive funding in just a short period of time.

The visibility that some of the watchdog groups have attained has not been without risks. Despite their good standing with the public, their activities have occasionally provoked violent retaliation by right-wing extremists. Although publicly espousing tolerance and condemning hatred is usually a relatively safe and commonplace exercise in the current atmosphere of political correctness, it can entail some risk for those in the watchdog community.

There appears to be a tendency towards vilification of opponents in the watchdog community. Thus much of their analysis that is fed to the public, government officials and law enforcement tends to contain a high degree of bias and should be looked at with a certain degree of skepticism. At times they paint with too broad a brush and label groups and individuals as "violent" and "terrorist" without justification. For example, the US Air Force is reported to have based a military training course called "Dynamics of International Terrorism" on materials supplied by the Southern Poverty Law Center. Included in the materials was information on relatively innocuous groups such as non-violent tax protestors that had nothing to do with terrorism.[142] Furthermore, the watchdogs often seek to conflate non-racist "Patriot" groups with overtly racist groups through links that are often very tenuous.[143]

In sum, the watchdog movement has expanded considerably over the past couple of decades and is now an important fixture in the NGO and interest group landscape. Now that the watchdog community has been examined it is now time to turn our attention to their ideological opponents.

3 Overview of the contemporary American far right

Introduction

The purpose of this chapter is to give the reader a better understanding of the organizations and individuals that populate the contemporary far right. Inasmuch as they are the subjects at whom the various public policy measures examined in this study are directed, it is important to know something about them. Even more so than its watchdog opponents, the far right is a very nuanced movement, consisting of a multitude of different groups, which often disagree on issues. Its diversity notwithstanding, it still has the hallmarks of a larger movement.

As Table 1.1 in Chapter 1 indicated, the contemporary far right is widely dispersed and has organizations in all major regions of the country. This chapter will demonstrate that right-wing extremism has long been a fixture in American history. The contemporary American far right consists of basically three separate movements, although there is some degree of overlap and migration back and forth among them. This chapter provides a typology of the contemporary American far right and identifies the major organizations and individuals that compose it. The sheer number of groups is too great for a comprehensive review and is beyond the scope of this study. Therefore, those highlighted in this chapter were chosen because of their influence in the movement and the degree of attention and opposition that they engender from the government and the watchdog groups.

To put this issue into historical context, this chapter's first section provides a brief historical overview of right-wing extremism in the United States up until the modern era. It is hoped that this first section demonstrates the durability of the far right. Although most far-right movements have been ephemeral and episodic, generally the far right has demonstrated a remarkable capacity to keep reinventing itself through time as it responds to and adapts to the issues of the day.

I then examine the Christian Patriot movement. The various self-styled militia organizations are the most visible and recent manifestation of this particular segment. However, as we shall see, there were some antecedents that provided an ideological seedbed for its development.

The third section of this chapter looks at the racialist right. This segment is often referred to as the "white supremacist" or "white separatist" or "hate" movement. This is the largest and most important segment, and also occasions the fiercest opposition from its watchdog opponents. It is a highly variegated movement and I have further subdivided it into two parts: revolutionary and non-revolutionary.

Before moving on to the next segment, it is worth taking a look at an organization that has been involved in the development and promotion of virtually all of the various orientations of the contemporary far right. It is hoped that this will give the reader a better understanding of how the various orientations fit together in the far-right constellation. Thus the fourth section examines the Liberty Lobby, an institution that could be characterized as the nexus of the movement.

Historical revision, or Holocaust denial as it is sometimes called, is examined in the fifth section of this chapter. Over the years this segment has taken some odd twists and turns and has come to include other issues besides the Holocaust. Although many figures in the movement would deny any affiliation or sympathy with the far right, I shall demonstrate that important representatives of the latter provided the revisionist enterprise with an institutional basis that it did not have on its own. That is not to paint all revisionist historians with a brown brush, as I concede that the motivations for some of them have little to do with furthering a far-right agenda. However, I believe that there are enough significant ties to designate it as part of the far-right constellation.

I conclude the chapter with some generalizations about the contemporary far-right movement in America. It is hoped that by this time the reader will have a better understanding of this movement and will thus be better prepared for the material that will follow.

Historical background

Right-wing extremism has a long tradition in the United States, and there are many studies that have examined the various movements which have punctuated American history. Several historians and observers cite the Anti-Masonic Party of the early nineteenth century as the first right-wing reactionary movement in American politics.[1] The case of the Anti-Masonic Party is important because several commonalties between it and subsequent far-right movements can be discerned.

First, like so many right-wing movements that would follow, the Anti-Masonic Party grew out of the angst amidst economic disruption and transition, in this case from a largely yeoman-based agrarian economy to a more commercially based economy. Accompanying economic change is usually the displacement of status and power of certain segments of the population. Lipset and Rabb see this reaction to displacement as a constant theme in right-wing extremism.[2]

Second, a penchant for conspiracy theories to explain events was evident in the Anti-Masonic movement as well. The Anti-Masons were suspicious of the

Freemasons who figured so prominently in the American establishment during that era. Thus began the search for secret elite cabals, which were alleged to be subverting American society. Anti-Masons saw their enemy as very powerful, which gave them the sense of being an embattled minority, whose mission it was to spread the "truth" that they had uncovered.[3] Like so many far-right organizations that would follow, the Anti-Masonic movement was in large measure a tract society that disseminated literature warning about the perils of its enemy. Related to this was the anti-statist tradition. Anti-Masons believed that the US government was virtually under the sway of Freemasons, an observation not without some merit at the time. Moreover, Freemasons were accused of holding dual loyalties to a belief system outside the framework of the American government.[4] These themes would prove to be enduring elements in the history of American right-wing extremism.

Finally, religion loomed large in the Anti-Masonic movement. Protestant ministers were in the forefront of exposing alleged Masonic machinations and sought to dissuade young men from joining the ranks of Masonry. Ultimately, like several other American far-right movements, the Anti-Masonic Party was of ephemeral nature. Although it attained considerable political clout (it was actually the first American political party to hold a nominating convention), its influence was short-lived. However, it did indeed accomplish much of what it set out to do. Many Freemasons were ousted from governmental positions, and the order went into retreat and never regained the influence that it once had in the upper echelons of American society.[5]

A few decades later the Know-Nothing movement arose as a backlash amidst an influx of largely Irish and Southern German Catholic immigration. Elements of xenophobia and ethnic chauvinism loomed large in its program. Thus emerged in force for the first time a powerful theme in the history of American right-wing extremism: nativism. As David Bennett observed, the Know-Nothing nativists saw the American Eden as imperiled by alien peoples and alien ideas.[6] This theme would recur frequently in subsequent right-wing movements. And once again, Protestant ministers figured prominently in this reactionary movement. What is also significant about the Know-Nothings is that it was the first right-wing movement that engaged in a significant amount of violence. Know-Nothing nativists and Catholic immigrants had some violent clashes, most notably in New Orleans, Louisiana in 1858.[7] Although it enjoyed considerable support for a short time, the Know-Nothing movement imploded over the issues of states' rights and abolitionism.[8]

Shortly after the American Civil War, the fraternal vigilante movement, the Ku Klux Klan, emerged in 1865 in Pulaski, Tennessee. This marked the first instance of large-scale right-wing terrorism in the United States. Their efforts demonstrated that at times terrorism could attain its desired effect; White southerners eventually wrested political control from Blacks and outsiders.[9] Although the original group has long been defunct, it has proved enduring as an inspiration for subsequent far-right groups in the US and abroad. Despite its violent record, the Reconstruction Klan was actually romanticized by some writers (mostly Southern) as a noble order that rescued the South from "carpetbaggers," "scalawags" and Black freemen. Thomas Dixon's novel *The Clansman*, first published in 1905, was emblematic of this sentiment.[10]

By the late nineteenth century yet another movement had appeared, the American Protective Association (APA). The movement enjoyed considerable support and at one point had more than half a million members.[11] Like the Know-Nothing movement a few decades before, the APA targeted foreigners and Catholics. However, much of its animus was also directed at Jews who began to emigrate *en masse* from Eastern Europe and Russia around the turn of the century. Echoing contemporary right-wing anti-globalists, the APA complained that elite capitalists encouraged immigration to drive down the cost of labor, and by doing so, impoverish native laborers. And like contemporary conservatives, the APA chose to operate within the Republican Party. However, like other American far-right movements that preceded it, the APA did not last long and was all but finished by the turn of the century.[12]

In 1915 the release of D. W. Griffith's critically acclaimed feature film *The Birth of a Nation* – which lionized the Reconstruction era Ku Klux Klan – encouraged one William J. Simmons to resurrect the Klan in 1915. Although the Second Era Klan attained great notoriety for its racism, it was in large measure a reaction to a massive influx of Catholic immigrants and a general fear of a diminution in status of native White Anglo-Protestants.[13] And like other right-wing movements that preceded it, the Second Era Klan espoused a platform of moralism as Christian fundamentalists filled much of its ranks. In fact much of the renascent hooded order's harassment was aimed at native Protestants whom they perceived as having morally lapsed.[14] The Second Era Klan's rise was meteoric; it attained an estimated membership of somewhere from 3 to 6 million members. A form of white Anglo-Saxon Protestant nationalism swept the nation, and this sentiment eventually succeeded in greatly curtailing immigration. However, after a series of scandals and internecine squabbles, the group quickly fell into disarray and was a shell of its former self by the end of the 1920s.[15]

The lull in far-right activity did not last long. By the early 1930s the dynamism of fascism in continental Europe inspired similar movements in America, including Gerald Winrod's Defenders of the Christian Faith, William Dudely Pelley's Silvershirts, Fritz Kuhn's German American Bund, the Italian American Fascist League of North America, and Father Coughlin's Christian Front. Despite their numbers, this plethora of groups was never really able to work effectively as a unified movement and ultimately failed to achieve their goals. In fact, Geoffrey Smith argues that their efforts were actually counterproductive, as they played into the hands of President Roosevelt, who exploited their activities as evidence of fifth-columnist subversion which threatened American democracy. According to Smith, this helped President Roosevelt succeed in his effort to involve America directly in World War II.[16] In this instance the far right was little match for its opponents. Moreover, as America slowly marched from isolationism to intervention in World War II, native fascists were increasingly marginalized and found themselves cast as political pariahs, a stigma from which they have yet to completely recover.[17]

The specter of communism in the 1950s provided an opportunity for the far right to return and regain respectability under the banner of McCarthyism. Groups such as the John Birch Society saw communist subversion virtually everywhere, and sought to put liberals and the American left in general on the defensive.[18] It was not long before academics sought to explain the new upsurge in right-wing extremism. In a classic study of that period, *The Radical Right*, Bell, Hofstadter, Lipset and others argued that status deprivation fueled right-wing extremism. Moreover, it was asserted that rightists exhibited dogmatic belief systems and were less tolerant of ambiguity.[19] This was very similar to the analysis of Adorno and members of the so-called Frankfurt School, which sought to pathologize the right wing or "authoritarian personality" and its fears of displacement.[20] In a similar vein, Hofstadter argued, in his classic study *The Paranoid Style in American Politics*, that right-wing extremists had feelings of persecution that were "systematized in grandiose theories of conspiracy."[21] What he felt was determinative in extremism was not so much the truth or falsity of the conspiratorial beliefs, but rather the way in which those ideas were held.[22] Hofstadter acknowledged that conspiracies were indeed part and parcel of politics. However, what distinguished the paranoid style of political extremism was

> not that its exponents see conspiracies or plots here and there in history, but that they regard a "vast" or "gigantic" conspiracy as the *motive force* in historical events. History is conspiracy, set in motion by demonic forces of almost transcendent power and what is felt to be needed to defeat it is not the usual methods of political give-and-take, but an all-out crusade. The paranoid spokesman sees the fate of this conspiracy in apocalyptic terms. ... He is always manning the barricades of civilization. He constantly lives at a turning point: it is now or never in organizing resistance to conspiracy.[23]

The Supreme Court's *Brown v. Topeka Board of Education* decision in 1954 galvanized the racialist right, and the Third Era Ku Klux Klan emerged along with overtly fascist groups such as the National Renaissance Party, the National States' Rights Party, and the American Nazi Party. The Klan in this period enjoyed some regional grassroots support in the South, and even had sympathizers in some positions of local governments.[24] Concomitant with a renascent Klan was the emergence of small neo-fascist groups in Europe and North America. Although these organizations looked to historical fascism for their inspiration, there has been quite a bit of mutation since 1945. Specifically, the post-1945 movements eschew the parochial nationalisms of the inter-war era and instead espouse a pan-Aryan ideology, which seeks to unite all of the various European-derived peoples around the world into a single "racial nationalist" community. Second, although these groups never attracted many followers into their ranks, they were able to draw some very dedicated members who were able to establish some continuity for their movement, and in doing so, keep the flame of their ideology burning to the present day.

Although usually marginalized, far-right movements occasionally garner significant grassroots support, usually at the regional level. George Wallace's bids for the presidency in 1968 and 1972 come to mind here.[25] The previously mentioned Anti-Masonic Party was the first really successful third party in America, and even revolutionized American party politics with the creation of the party-nominating convention.[26] Finally, the Second Era Klan of the 1920s wielded a significant amount of political clout in some local and state governments.[27] However, as Lipset and Raab point out, several characteristics of the American political system seem to inhibit far-right movements from sustaining any kind of enduring political support.[28] Moreover, the American far right is by and large a much stigmatized movement and is seen as beyond the pale of political respectability. As a result, the American far right has been largely a social movement and its various groupings do not field candidates for political office as frequently as their European counterparts.[29]

The opprobrium from the larger society notwithstanding, the far right continues to endure, as evidenced by the numerous anti-statist militia groups, which began to proliferate during the mid-1990s in virtually all regions of the country. With little coordination, these self-styled patriot groups polarized around issues involving opposition to gun control laws, the current trend of globalization, and abuses of federal law enforcement agencies. It is to these and similar groups that compose the Christian Patriots to which we shall now turn our attention.

The Christian Patriot movement

The Christian Patriot or militia movement gained much attention in the aftermath of the Oklahoma City bombing. The main impetus for the militia movement appears to be new gun control laws such as the Brady bill that threaten to weaken the Second Amendment. Also important has been the heavy-handed tactics of federal law enforcement agencies in such fiascos as Ruby Ridge and Waco. However, there were antecedents from which the current movement drew much of its ideological underpinnings.

The John Birch Society

The current militia movement owes much of its worldview to the legendary anti-communist organization, the John Birch Society (JBS). In 1958 a successful candy manufacturer, Robert H. W. Welch Jr, convoked a meeting with like-minded friends in Indianapolis, Indiana to create an organization to counter communist subversion that they saw throughout the US government.[30] The Society was named after John Birch – a young fundamentalist Baptist preacher and intelligence officer who served in China during World War II.[31] Welch developed a tight-knit and disciplined organization, which at its peak in the mid-

1960s reached a membership of approximately 50,000–60,000 members – an astronomical figure by far-right standards.[32]

Welch made significant contributions to the worldview of the radical right by his dissemination of conspiracy theories. Although he was ardently anti-communist, he believed the subversion that he saw actually extended much further back into history than Bolshevism and Karl Marx. Welch propounded the theory that a sinister group, the "Insiders," had been in existence for over two hundred years and was linked to a Bavarian secret society known as the "Illuminati."[33]

The strength and influence of the Birch Society alarmed the ADL. Although the various right-wing organizations of the mid-1960s were by no means unified, they made efforts at coordination and were sufficiently alike in ideology to be considered a coherent movement. The Birch Society was an important nexus and gateway of the radical right during that period. As a result, the ADL issued several reports in the 1960s warning of the danger on the radical right posed by the John Birch Society.[34] At first, this may seem odd insofar as the Birch Society eschewed anti-Semitism and often ousted members who voiced such views. However, earlier research suggested that seemingly innocuous conspiracy theories involving actors such as communists, international bankers, etc., could be quickly transformed into anti-Semitic conspiracy theories.[35] Moreover, there were several examples of members who were, or went on to become, leading anti-Semites.[36]

The John Birch Society's influence waned after reaching its zenith in the mid-1960s. At the time of Welch's death in 1985, the organization was just a shell of its former self. However, in recent years, the Society appears to have rebounded, although it is nowhere near in size and influence that it once was. It operates a website and publishes a periodical called *The New American*. Over the years a virtual "who's who" of the American radical right had at one time or another sojourned in its ranks. One of its members went on to found an organization that resembled in many ways the current militia movement.

The Minutemen

In 1960, a Birch Society member, Robert Bolivar DePugh, founded the Minutemen in Missouri. It was basically an anti-communist group that ironically modeled its organizational structure on a cell system reminiscent of the communist revolutionary models of Lenin and Mao.[37] Eventually, the organization drew considerable attention from government authorities, including Attorney General Robert Kennedy.[38] Consequently the organization was quickly infiltrated and effectively neutralized. For the most part, the organization was more rhetoric than action. However, some members were responsible for blowing up a police station in Redmond, Washington. They also attempted to rob three Seattle banks.[39] One member, Keith Gilbert, was implicated in the theft of 1,400 pounds of TNT, which he allegedly planned to use to bomb an ADL convention.[40] Not surprisingly, the ADL paid close attention to the Minutemen and in 1968 sponsored a critical study of the group.[41]

By 1970 however, the organization was practically defunct as DePugh and another member, Wally Peyson, were finally apprehended after a seventeen-month manhunt and charged with federal firearm violations. Both were convicted and sent to federal prisons. Undaunted, DePugh continued to promote right-wing causes even after his release from prison. Despite the fact that the Minutemen achieved virtually no significant success, its organizational model would hold appeal with subsequent militia activists. Another connection that the Minutemen had with the contemporary far right was that several of its members were early followers of the Christian Identity religion.[42]

The Posse Comitatus

At about the same time that the Minutemen organization was disintegrating, a retired dry-cleaner, Henry L. Beach, and a retired army colonel, William Potter Gale, founded a militia-style organization known as the Posse Comitatus in Portland, Oregon in 1969.[43] The organization espoused a radical decentralization and anti-statism, as exemplified by its title, which translates to mean that there is no legitimate form of government beyond the county level. According to this reasoning, the county sheriff was the supreme law of the land. This extremely loose-knit organization attracted an eclectic assortment of tax protesters, racists and anti-government extremists. Members often fashioned themselves as Constitutional purists and invoked obscure laws to justify their actions. But the organization did not capture much attention until the late 1970s. Capitalizing on the farm crisis, the Posse disseminated numerous conspiracy theories implicating international bankers for this development. These themes resonated with some destitute farmers who were hard hit by the crisis. It was not long before Posse members had confrontations with authorities. On numerous occasions the FBI opened probes on the organization. Usually, the FBI found the allegations leveled against the group to be unfounded.[44] However, there were instances when the threat was real, most notably in the case of Gordon Kahl, a tax protester who in 1983 killed two federal marshals in a shootout in North Dakota. Eventually, a few months later, federal authorities caught up with him. Kahl however, refused to surrender and he and another federal law enforcement officer were killed in a fiery shootout.

Kahl's exploits and defiance earned him martyr status in the annals of the far right. Although, the numerical strength of the Posse had been greatly exaggerated, its influence would extend beyond the life of the organization, as the militia movement of the mid-1990s would pick up much of its ideology.[45]

The contemporary militia movement

The far right is often been described as authoritarian and anti-democratic. However, to the contrary, militia activists more often tend to be Constitutional fundamentalists who believe in the strict letter of the law and never tire of explaining how the Constitution is under threat by an encroaching federal government. In this regard militias espouse a traditional theme of American anti-statism, albeit more shrilly. The contemporary Patriot movement, though, is far from monolithic. Besides the self-styled militia activists, it contains tax protestors, radical libertarians, Second Amendment advocates and a wide array of conspiracy theorists that warn of an impending New World Order. A militia could be defined as "groups of individuals who have formed into paramilitary organizations that stockpile and carry assault-type, military weapons, wear military uniforms, practice military maneuvers, and yet are not part of the military."[46]

The contemporary militia movement came about after a series of events that took place in the early 1990s. First, there was the Ruby Ridge incident, which occurred in 1992 when federal law enforcement officers ambushed the home of Randy Weaver, a White separatist living in the desolate hills of Idaho. Weaver's young son and wife, as well as one Bureau of Alcohol, Tobacco, and Firearms (ATF) agent were killed in what many observers believed was a badly botched operation by the federal government. This was followed by a meeting in Estes Park, Colorado that was convoked by a Christian Identity minister, Pete Peters, in October of that same year. According to some accounts this event laid the groundwork for the contemporary militia movement by urging right-wing activists to organize militias at their local levels.

The Waco incident in 1993 further compounded resentment in the Patriot movement. The final catalyst however, was the Brady Bill, which Congress passed in that same year. Soon after, the Militia of Montana and the Michigan Militia were formed. Amazingly the idea caught on, in large part due to such technology such as facsimile machines and the internet. It was not long before militia-style organizations began appearing around the nation. Just as several of the watchdog organizations were created in response to a perceived crisis, likewise members of the Patriot movement saw the founding of militias as a reactive and defensive measure to perceived federal tyranny. John Trochman, regarded by some as one of the founders of the contemporary militia movement and founding member of the Militia of Montana, expounded on this for me:

> The founding of our nation was done by civilians that primarily said enough is enough to King George and stood up and wouldn't take it anymore. The line in the sand that was drawn way back was, don't come after our guns. And we believe that is the line that has to be drawn, don't mess with our guns. If you recall in early 1994, right after the first part of the Brady Bill, and prior to that we had Waco and Ruby Ridge, so there were several reasons to rally the people. Many people all over the country were looking for us to have a rallying point for them. That's why we picked the name and that's when we picked the name – Clinton and all of the strikes he made against us as far as the Second Amendment is concerned,

has been a tremendous recruiting tool for us. He's done us a wonderful favor.[47]

Norm Olson, a founding member of the Michigan Militia, expressed similar sentiments.

> Our objective of course was to prevent another Waco. Our objective was to put the government on notice that if it were to execute another holocaust like the Mount Carmel tragedy or murder, it would pay dearly. We have interceded whenever there has been a federal siege. We have interceded to let the federals know that if there is bloodshed that there will be a costly, costly butcher's bill to pay.[48]

The notion of a "New World Order" looms large in the discourse of the militia movement. However, there seems to be quite a bit of variation to this theory and the details are often murky. For example, some believe that the New World Order emanates from machinations of the Council on Foreign Relations and the Trilateral Commission. Others point to the United Nations apparatus. Various supra-national organizations (e.g. NATO) and international treaties (e.g. NAFTA) are also cited as part of the New World Order conspiracy. It is worth mentioning that references to the New World Order can be found in establishment organs as well such as the *Wall Street Journal* and the *Economist*. However, whereas the mainstream commentators lean towards a more structuralist theory in which various conditions (e.g. technological and demographic changes) are cited to explain this phenomenon, militia activists are more likely to believe that it is the result of a well coordinated conspiracy directed by a hidden cabal which seeks to undermine national sovereignty and individual liberty. John Trochman gave me his version of the New World Order theory:

> I don't think there's anything new about the New World Order. I think it's an old system that's got a new whitewash or a new face that's called the New World Order. Back in the 1920s a number of nations got together in Moscow including the United States, Britain, China, etc., to create something called the League of Nations. Prior to that it was called the Comintern, which created the League. The American Congress would not accept it at the time. By 1945 they had won over the hearts of Congress enough to vote in this globalization and as I see it, it's a freeway for the corporations. There are no borders for these corporations and they do what they want now all across the planet.[49]

Norm Olson believes that the New World Order conspiracy extends back much further in history:

> The biblical view is the one that I hold to. Students of the Bible or prophecy know that in the end days an unholy trinity will emerge including the false

prophet, the anti-Christ, and the beast signifying the heads of the one world government, the one world economic system, and the one world church.

Last month [August 2000] if you remember, world religious leaders came together. This month world government leaders are coming together and since everything is economic anymore, we can expect a one world economic system here soon between the Eurodollar, trade negotiations and all the rest of it. ... There is an alliance being created and strengthening right now between governments toward a one-world government. You can call it the New World Order if you want to. That's the view that I take. ... The genesis of that goes all the way back to the days of Babel, when they were creating a one-world government. There at that time God confused their languages and ever since then the forces of darkness have been trying to bring together the people of the world to follow Satan and to make war against God.[50]

Militia leaders are sometimes criticized as manipulating credulous members and alarming them with fantastic conspiracy theories, including warnings of Y2K chaos, the use of black helicopters to spy on Americans, the presence of UN troops on American soil, covert detention camps for American dissidents, and weather manipulation by the government, *inter alia*. Olson sought to explain the mindset of some militia members in this regard:

Well, I don't know whether certain people in the militia use fear to motivate people. Morris Dees now, manipulates by fear. He's collecting the money that he has raised. He's doing that by fear. Fear is a very strong motivator. Now some militia leaders are driven by unfounded fear. That is true. And some militia leaders unknowingly will use conspiracy theories unknowingly and people will respond. What we've tried to do, what I've tried to do is to establish the militia much like an encounter group and to talk to people about the things they're frightened of, to find out whether there is a basis for their fears, and to put away their fears if they are spurious without foundation, or if they are real to prepare them to deal with that fear. There are only three responses to fear. You're in denial like the proverbial ostrich with his head in the sand or you run from something that you're frightened of or you face it and you deal with it. We want the latter.[51]

A sense of history suffuses several segments of the American far right. In the case of the contemporary militia movement the American Revolution figures prominently in its mythos and is a source of great inspiration. This idealization of the American founding fathers, though, brings up an interesting paradox. Many of them were practicing Freemasons – an organization that is often cited as a prime player in the New World Order conspiracy! Norman Olson sought to explain this seeming contradiction:

Rather than give a history of Freemasonry, which is readily available elsewhere, perhaps it would be best to look at some of its original principles and characteristics. As it emerged out of the middle ages, the Freemasons became highly structured and rigid:

1 It was a secret oath-bound body.

2 It had secret signs of recognition, rituals, practices, and some rather dramatic remedies for unfaithfulness.

3 It was strongly democratic; and,

4 It was supra-national.

For these reasons, it was feared by strongly authoritarian churches and political tyrants. In fact, the Roman Catholics attempted to suppress it in the 1730s as did the Nazis in the last century.

> But I am not defending Freemasonry, for I oppose it on Scriptural grounds. I do however recognize that the above characteristics were developed over decades even before 1700, and long before either Washington or Jefferson, or even Benjamin Franklin lived. That being the case, I find that Freemasonry DID NOT [emphasis in original] forge the political views of the Founding Fathers, but did encourage and support them ...
>
> I can separate Freemasonry from the vision and courage of the Founding Fathers because I believe these men's characters were formed long before they associated with the lodge. It was BECAUSE [emphasis in original] they had such character that they naturally gravitated to a society of men who shared like viewpoints. Freemasonry did not make them what they were, it merely provided a place where their feelings could be exhibited and reinforced. ...
>
> Bottom line: While there is much, in my humble estimation, wrong with the Freemasons from a scriptural perspective, I can find nothing wrong with them in their political view. But I want to reemphasize that the Freemasons did not create the Founding Fathers any more than the Fraternal Order of Foresters created lumberman. Rather it gave them a place to unify their opinions and build on what they already believed.[52]

In that sense, as expressed above, Olson is able to reconcile his admiration for the Founding Fathers with the suspicion he holds for secret societies and elite globalist organizations.

Critics of the militias often allege that it is a covertly racist movement. However, the racialist right actually derides the militia movement for its diffidence to express overt racism and anti-Semitism. John Trochman's occasional visits to the Aryan Nations compound in Hayden Lake are often cited as the link to the racialist right. For his part Trochman has denied such allegations.[53] It would appear that the charges of racism leveled against the militia movement are greatly exaggerated. In fact there exist a number of minority militia members, including J.J. Johnson, an African-American and founder of the Ohio

Organized Militia; and Clifford Brookings, also an African-American and commander of the Detroit Constitutional Militia. Moreover, many militia groups seek to recruit minority members.[54] Finally, African-Americans have been involved with some of the more radical militia groups, such as the Mountaineer Militia, which allegedly planned to destroy an FBI facility in West Virginia.[55] Norman Olson expressed his views on this issue within the framework of self-determination:

> Now, while we accept racial separatism, we do not accept racial supremacy. We're not imperialists and I will not accept an imperialist philosophy. No race should look down on another race. But if one race wants to remain separate from the others and have, say if a Jew wants his children to marry into the Jewish faith, that's fine. If a German family wants to remain in a German community, fine. If a black wants his child to be wed to another black child, that's fine. And I would certainly agree and endorse that behavior, because that I think is what identity is really all about. But that you see can be skewed and twisted and distorted into imperialism where one group of people looks down on another people as something inferior and that's certainly not what I would do and not what I would endorse. ... Hatred is a strong motivator, [but] hatred has no part in the militia movement that I command.[56]

One notable feature of the militia movement is its proclivity for confrontation with authorities. However, the authorities have demonstrated resolute action in responding to those militia activists who run afoul of the law as evidence by the stiff sentences handed down to members of the Montana Freemen. Moreover, a chief concern of the militia movement – the millennial year 2000 – seems to have come and gone with little incident, thus allaying the sense of urgency that prevailed not long ago. Putting a good spin on this development, Norm Olson cites this as evidence that the movement has successfully fulfilled its mission:

> understand again the militia movement is not an organization or a business that can be judged or measured by terms such as decline or increase. The fact is that we have reached our objective and because we have reached our objective the militia will once again recede into the body politic or into the people to emerge again when there is another threat or danger. Since we do respond to danger, if there's no clear and present danger, we ebb back into or recede into the people again. You can't really look at the militia as in decline. And actually, that's not a negative thing. I mean if they said the militia is in decline I would say that's a pretty good measurement of the pulse beat of what's going on in America. If the militia were to emerge again it would do so because there is a great danger.[57]

Although the militia movement appears to be in sharp retreat, it still retains a core of activists and supporters.[58] Gone are the days however, of sensational coverage from the national media. Most of the militia leaders no longer command the number of weekend warriors that they once did, and much of their energy is directed at the preparedness and gun show circuits at which they sell books, videos, etc. For all practical purposes the movement has lost much of its paramilitary character, perhaps in part due to new anti-paramilitary training statutes enacted by state legislatures (with the encouragement of the watchdog groups), which have dissuaded members from using firearms in an organizational setting.[59] Both the Southern Poverty Law Center and the ADL have also kept close tabs on the movement. They have issued several critical reports and have forwarded information to law enforcement authorities on different occasions.[60] Despite its apparent decline, the movement has on occasion found a sympathetic ear in politics. Congresswoman Helen Chenowith from Idaho and Congressman Steve Stockman from Texas have on occasion voiced support for some of its positions.[61]

Although the Patriot movement and the racialist right do not appear to have a great deal of organizational linkage, there is a degree of overlap in the areas of conspiracy theories, the Christian Identity theology, and opposition to globalization. According to one researcher, the militias can act as a "conveyor belt" in that individuals are initially recruited into them on the basis of issues such as opposition to legislation outlawing firearms, but gradually come to embrace more extremist positions as they are exposed to them in the radical right milieu.[62] Finally, both movements have the same opponents i.e. the watchdogs and the government.

The non-revolutionary racialist right

The racialist right is the more enduring segment of the far right and contains both a revolutionary and a non-revolutionary orientation. Although the race issue looms large in both segments, it is expressed very differently in each camp. Most notably, anti-Semitism figures much more prominently in the revolutionary than it does in the non-revolutionary segment. What also distinguishes the two is that the former holds little hope for achieving political power through conventional political means. Although it may not advocate terrorism or active resistance at the present time, it is generally resigned to that course of action – at least in the abstract – at some time in the future. By contrast, the latter does not advocate violence in either the short term or long term. This section first looks at the non-revolutionary segment, some of whose representatives are known as 'paleo-conservatives'. The second part of this section turns its attention to the revolutionary segment. On occasion this segment resorts to terrorism but that issue will generally be held in abeyance until Chapter 4, which will examine that issue in greater detail.

The Council of Conservative Citizens

The most prominent organization in the non-revolutionary racialist right is the Council of Conservative Citizens (COFCC), most of whose support comes from the South. With a membership of approximately 15,000, it is probably the largest far-right organization in America today.[63] The Council was founded in 1985, when about thirty men, including former members of the defunct Citizens Councils of America, met in Atlanta for the express purpose of creating an organization that would build unity among the more respectable elements of the far right.[64] The Council has tried to keep some of the more radical elements, such as David Duke, at arm's length. Gordon Lee Baum is currently the de facto leader of the organization, whose headquarters are in St Louis, Missouri. Baum described for me the Council in a nutshell:

> The Council of Conservative Citizens is an organization, which was set up to serve as a voice and as an active advocate for the no longer solid conservative majority. It currently has members in every state of the union and seven foreign countries. We have active chapters I believe in twenty-eight states.
> The local chapters constantly run candidates for office and locally elected officials of all sorts – everything from county supervisors to state legislators – come to speak. ... Most of our kind of people are middle-class populist slash social conservative types that probably came more from a Democratic background, with some big exceptions, than from a Republican background.[65]

By far-right standards, the Council has gained considerable access to and endorsements from local, state and national politicians, including most notably Senate Majority Leader Trent Lott, Mississippi Governor Kirk Fordice, and House Representative Bob Barr of Georgia.[66] This has brought the Council considerable publicity and notoriety in the national press. A frequent pattern in the late 1990s was for notable conservative politicians to meet with Council chapters and then quickly repudiate the organization after media scrutiny. Baum recounted some of these instances:

> To give you an example of how some handle it poorly and some handle it well, when Bob Barr spoke to us he made or one of his staffers made some foolish denial and this immediately set the reporters, especially from the *Washington Post*. It perked up their interest because it looked like they were hiding something and they took out after him and it just got worse. The more they deny the worse it looks for them. And this is what happened with Trent Lott, not he himself, both with one of his staffers when he made a foolish comment, "oh he never spoke to them" or something, which was absurd. It was too easily proven. ...
> I don't want to dump on Trent. But Governor Kirk Fordice handled it much more wisely. When they came to Kirk Fordice, and these were both the national and local reporters, he said, "Yes, I spoke to them. They're

lovely people and I'll do it in the future so what? They're constituents. There are a lot of them and I'll continue to speak to a whole variety of people. That's who elected me." That's more or less what he said and with that they kind of went away.[67]

The Council purports to be a conservative organization but has grown increasingly weary of the direction of the Republican Party in recent years. For example, it decries the "Hispanic strategy" of Republican National Committee Chairman Jim Nicholson as a betrayal of the traditional base of the conservative movement (the CofCC strongly opposes liberal immigration policies). Baum expounded on this topic:

> [The Democratic Party] started building a coalition based on the ultra left and minorities. So these people [voters] deserted the Democratic Party in droves. The first one that opened the door to them was [George] Wallace and they found out that they could vote for someone other than a Democrat and God wouldn't strike them deaf and dumb. And so when Reagan came along he pandered to what normally today are called the Reagan Democrats. To be quite frank, the vast majority of Wallace Democrats came into the Republican Party, which was mostly an upper middle class enclave. These people were then and still are quite uncomfortable with them. Well, hot on their heels came the abortion issue, which was materializing in the early 1970s and these people also came into the Republican Party and a lot of them were people that were Catholic and had been Democrats. The overlap between them and the social conservatives, was the Wallacites. These people all came into the Republican Party and in many instances even took over the local clubs, etcetera all over the country. While the Republicans were never comfortable with them, they never understood why these people came over. I've been to Republican functions with old-line Republican big shots and they really honestly think that all of these people came over to them because they had been converted to laissez-faire economics and you know, they want to carry water for big corporations. It's mind boggling. And if you look at what's happening at the Republican convention today, it's obvious they have never caught on. And if these people that breathe life into the Republican party and allow them to become the majority in both the House and the Senate and if you look at where Republicans are coming from, they're from the South and the suburbs around the big cities in which were never really Republican enclaves, but they're about ready to shake them loose. Sam Francis refers to them as the stupid party. They don't grasp that they're about to lose. They've got some vague notion that Hispanics are going to vote for them. And what they're getting is all these old line Hispanics, the ones that been in America for generations out of the southwest and the upper middle class Cubans. But all these new mestizos that are flooding into the country are voting overwhelmingly Democratic because these are people that are in love

with the welfare system. That's why they came here. So really these people are not going to vote Republican. The Republicans don't have the vaguest idea who these people are and instead pander to them by speaking to groups like La Raza like Bush did. They're going to drive off all of these people who built the Republican Party with Reagan.

First, they ought to hold their base. The Democrats are at least smart enough to know that. You got to hold your base. If you don't hold your base, you can't add to it. You're building a weak structure if you take away at your foundation and build on the top.[68]

The Council is very suspicious of neo-conservatives, and has been waging a civil war of sorts in the conservative movement. The Council takes positions on issues involving race but expresses them in a much less offensive way than most other segments of the racialist right. Also, there are no public pronouncements of anti-Semitism.

The notoriety that the Council has received has occasioned criticism from several watchdog groups. ADL national director Abraham Foxman voiced concern in newspaper editorials over the Council's ties to public officials and accused the groups as "cloaking themselves in the mantle of conservatism to underlie their racist agenda."[69] The Southern Poverty Law Center and the Militia Watchdog have featured highly critical articles on the Council, which sought to undercover the group's links and ties with far-right activists and conservative politicians.[70] Although the CofCC is neither violent nor revolutionary in orientation, Mark Potok of the Southern Poverty Law Center went so far as to identify the Council, along with the League of the South (more on that organization below), as the two most serious threats from the far right in America today.[71] Some members of Congress have also denounced the organization and even introduced a resolution condemning it.[72] More moderate conservatives, such as Arianna Huffington and Republican National Committee Chairman Jim Nicholson, have denounced the organization as well.

Despite this criticism, the Council appears to be relatively strong at the present time. It has the semblance of an organization and moderate resources. Moreover, it has managed to attract some of the far right's higher-caliber intellectuals, including Sam Francis, a former syndicated columnist for the *Washington Times*, who writes for the organization's newspaper, the *Citizens Informer*.[73] Another notable Council member, Jared Taylor, leads one of the far right's more highbrow think tanks, known as American Renaissance.

American Renaissance

American Renaissance was founded in 1990 as a far-right think tank that publishes a journal by the same name. It is located in Oakton, Virginia and according to its founder, Jared Taylor, "its purpose is to advance the legitimate group interests of Whites."[74] Taylor does not fit the popular image of the right-wing extremist. For example, he is a graduate of Yale University, speaks fluent

Japanese and French, has established a career as a successful business consultant and has authored a critically acclaimed book on race relations called *Paved with Good Intentions*. In that sense, Taylor exemplifies the more urbane, "button-downed" type of leadership in the "white racial nationalist" movement. He commented on this ongoing change in complexion of the racialist right:

> I think yes, there is increasingly people who are mainstream and quote, respectable, who are becoming active in what for lack of a better term we could call a racial nationalist movement. I think that by and large you do not get more responsible college graduates and high-income type people because most people, by and large, seek honor in their society. They look for success. They want money and most people are cowards. And once the *Zeitgeist* shifted against a certain point of view, most people would prefer to do the safe thing, the thing that will maintain their popularity, the thing that will generate income.
>
> And when I say most people are cowards, I do not exempt myself. I'm a coward in the sense that I'm always having to fight my own cowardice to what I realize is very much against the mainstream. Most people don't like to do that. I don't like to do that. Most people would rather be appreciated, rather than looked down on and be considered a moral inferior. And so people who have the ability to succeed within the mainstream by and large are going to do that rather than to break off and work in an opposite direction to that of the mainstream. I think Joe Sobran once put it rather cleverly. He said, "The purpose of a college education today is to give people the right attitude towards non-Whites and the means to live as far away from them as possible." So whatever attitudes well educated, high income people may have about non-Whites, they're able to insulate themselves from the effects of integration, multiculturalism, cultural enrichment and all these other things that we are supposed to love, but in fact, which we do our best to stay away from. ...
>
> I think more and more mainstream Whites are going to become racial activists because at some point they'll see what the future of the United States will be if they do nothing. More and more Whites, I believe, are going to be prepared to sacrifice this so called respectability and sacrifice at least a certain amount of income as well in order to do what they know is right and to do what they feel will ensure some kind of satisfaction in the United States of America for their children.[75]

Taylor is very outspoken on the race issue and warns that European Americans are committing "unilateral disarmament" if they fail to recognize this issue in an atmosphere in which other racial and ethnic groups assert their group interests, as he explained:

> First of all, race will never lose its salience. Race is a biological fact. I can't think of any society, past or present in which race had no salience. The great

irony in the United States today is that all other racial groups are perfectly well aware of this and they make consistent well-coordinated efforts to advance their interest as a group.

Unilateral disarmament is the term I use to describe the fact that it is Whites, and only Whites, who act as if a nation in which race is not salient is even possible much less desirable … if Whites are the only group that act as though to have racial interests is immoral or wrong, they'll be pushed out and that's precisely what is happening today. Not only physically and demographically, but culturally as well.[76]

Taylor tackles several hot-button issues that are popular in the far right. However, one thing that sets him apart is that he does not impute sinister conspiracies as the motive force behind these issues. For example, speaking on the immigration issue, Taylor remarked:

I don't think there's a deliberate effort to alter the ethnic and racial composition of the population. I think that there are a very small number of people who welcome that. But I think very few people are deliberately setting out to say, "well this was a White majority country. We're going to make it majority non-White." I don't think anyone has that intent. It's simply the fact that if you liberalize immigration today, the people who wish to come to the United States are poor people and the poor countries are generally non-White. I think what we have is a liberal immigration policy, the consequences of which are a demographic transformation. But I think practically no one is consciously and deliberately looking for this kind of reduction of Whites to minority status.[77]

Staples in Taylor's *American Renaissance* magazine include feature stories on issues such as racial differences in IQ testing, immigration, and Black-on-White crime. Towards this end Taylor published a report titled the *Color of Crime* in which he used FBI crime statistics to demonstrate that White are more often the victims in violent interracial crimes involving Blacks and Whites.[78] It is a report that is widely disseminated throughout the far-right movement and was recently the subject of a highly critical article by the SPLC.[79] Abraham Foxman, the ADL national director, also criticized Taylor in a *Washington Post* op-ed column. Taylor asserted that the watchdogs' ulterior motives are not so much to prevent terrorism, but rather to keep certain ideas out of the market place of ideas:

Right-wing terrorism is something that I think is thwarted quite effectively by ordinary law enforcement agencies. They don't need the ADL to arrest people who are throwing bombs. Does the Southern Poverty Law Center and the ADL's constant focus on terrorism and this that and the other help catch these guys and prevent that? I certainly don't see that it has. What their effect mainly is seems to me, is to demonize a certain kind of thinking. Their effect is not to prevent terrorism. It's simply to demonize views with

58 Overview of the contemporary American far right

> which they disagree. And I consider that, well I mean, it's a free country, you can set something up if you want. But I don't see it as an aid to law enforcement. Nor do I see it as a necessary counter-force to terrorism. It's simply a way, and I think somewhat of an underhanded and ungentlemanly way of trying to make points in a debate without actually debating. To call your opponents names is not to refute their arguments. And yet they have chosen such effective names, racist, Nazis, hate mongers, and they so terrorize you that they don't have to debate you.[80]

Although Taylor is very outspoken on the issue of race, he eschews any public expressions of anti-Semitism. In fact, quite a few Jews have spoken at his biennial American Renaissance conferences, including Michael Levin, Robert Weissberg and Rabbi Mayer Schiller.[81] Taylor commented on this:

> I don't suppose we ever had a single conference that did not have Jewish speakers. The first conference, I think nearly half of the speakers were Jewish. I think it is certainly true that Jews have a very considerable influence in the United States and I think it's unquestionable that Jews have often been behind the anti-nationalist movement. Jews have encouraged immigration not just of Jews but of various people from all around the world. On the other hand, I don't think that Jews *qua* Jews are either non-White or some kind of perpetual or inevitable enemy. I think that there are many Jews who feel about these questions much as I do and I'm happy to accept their support and I welcome their participation and any kind of attempt to bring back the kind of United States that I would like.[82]

This makes American Renaissance an outlier in the far-right constellation, and Taylor somewhat of a controversial figure among his peers. Some deride him for this association and even worse, accuse him of being an ADL informant and CIA operative.[83] To his defenders, however, he is a soft-core gateway for those that are curious about the movement. Taylor also has links with and supporters among other racialist organizations, including the Southern heritage movement.

The neo-Confederates

The idea of creating a Southern nationalist secessionist movement is something that far-rightists in the South have experimented with in the past. During the 1980s, there were a couple of attempts at such an enterprise from the revolutionary racialist right, but neither attained any broad-based support among Southerners.[84] However, certain trends such as the advent of the "culture war," the growing salience of multiculturalism, and identity politics seem to have occasioned a demonstration effect among some quarters of the Southern population. If one could mark the specific event that spawned the current Southern Nationalist movement it would be the publication of the book *The South was*

Right! in 1994 by two brothers, James Ronald and Walter Donald Kennedy. Fortunately for the Kennedy brothers, they found a relatively mainstream publisher, Pelican Publishing Company, which has a good distribution network in the Southern region of the country. The book sold well and by 2000 had gone through its eleventh printing. The Kennedy brothers rehashed several Southern apologias including states' rights and the right to secession. It also decried "Yankee atrocities" during the Civil War and minimized the moral failure of slavery.[85] For the neo-Confederates, the "War Between the States" is the backdrop for their mythos.

At the center of the contemporary Southern Nationalist or "neo-Confederate" movement is an organization known as the League of the South. Inspired by *The South was Right!*, a history professor, Dr Michael Hill, the Kennedy brothers, and about forty other people, set out to create an organization that would champion Southern heritage causes. Out of their meeting held in Tuscaloosa, Alabama in 1994 was born the Southern League, later renamed the League of the South. The fledging organization attracted more than a few academics, including Grady McWhiney, Clyde Wilson and Thomas Fleming. At first the organization concentrated on cultural issues and sought to develop, in the Gramscian sense, a cultural "hegemony of ideas" in the South. Over the years it attained a solid organizational footing and has become more overtly political. In 1999 the Southern Party – largely a project of the League of the South – was launched in an effort to compete in elections and gain political power.

There is a multitude of organizations that compose the Southern Nationalist movement and it is far from monolithic. Some individuals and organizations are divided on certain issues, especially race. Essentially there are two competing camps in the League of the South. One is racialist and prefers a Southern nation that is "Anglo-Celtic" in texture, while the other is strictly territorial and favors a "diverse Dixie," in which Southern culture can flourish without regard to race. At times it is difficult to hold these two camps together.

Recent controversies surrounding the display of the Confederate battle flag has had a polarizing effect in the South between its mostly White defenders, who view it as an integral part of their regional identity, and Blacks who view it as a blatant insult and symbol of past servitude. Thus several heated legal battles have come about in recent years. Towards this end, the Southern Legal Resources Center was established to defend the display of Confederate symbols in various institutions. The leader and founder of the Center, attorney Kirk Lyons, has long been a defender of far-right defendants in the courtroom.

What is most significant about the current neo-Confederate movement is that it has substantial grassroots support. For example, the League of the South is estimated to have 9,000 members.[86] Moreover, the League interfaces with a whole network of other Southern heritage organizations such as Sons of Confederate Veterans, Southern Legal Resource Center, Southern Military Institute, the Southern Party, the Confederate Society of America, and the United Daughters of the Confederacy and some of the more respectable far-right groups including the Council of Conservative Citizens, American Renaissance, and the Rockford Institute. Recently the movement was given a shot in the arm with another Pelican publication, R. Gordon Thornton's *The Southern Nation: The New Rise of the Old South*, which expanded on the issues raised in the Kennedy brothers' book. Drawing inspiration from the Eastern European nationalist-independence movements of the late 1980s and early 1990s, he calls for Southern self-determination and secession from the union.[87] In that respect, the neo-Confederates appear imitative of other social movements. For example, in what appears to resemble the current drive for reparations for Blacks because of slavery, the League of the South is at this time planning on petitioning the US Congress for reparations for the damages inflicted on the property of the Southern populace during the Civil War era.[88]

The burgeoning neo-Confederate movement has not gone unnoticed by the watchdogs. The Southern Poverty Law Center recently devoted an entire issue that was highly critical of the movement.[89] And as mentioned earlier, Mark Potok of the Center identified it, along with the CofCC, as comprising the most serious threat from the far right today. Like most of the non-revolutionary racialist right, the neo-Confederate movement eschews any overt expression of anti-Semitism. However, there are some individuals in this segment that do; among the most notable is David Duke.

The European-American Unity and Rights Organization

The European-American Unity and Rights Organization (EURO) was originally founded as the National Organization for European American Rights (NOFEAR) by long time far-right activist David Duke in January 2000. Duke gained national attention in 1988 when he won a seat in the Louisiana state legislature. He went on to place second in senatorial and gubernatorial bids in 1990 and 1991 respectively. Duke, the former Klan leader, has sought to shed his extremist image. To this end he has pattern EURO as a White civil rights organization in the style of the National Association for the Advancement of Colored People (NAACP), LaRaza, and even the Anti-Defamation League (of which he is a vocal critic). EURO seeks to avoid the negative and hateful rhetoric of the more extremist groups, and instead to accentuate positive elements such as racial pride and identity, in short, themes that blend well in the current atmosphere of multiculturalism in which ethnic as opposed to national identity is celebrated. The organization seeks to raise racial awareness among European Americans by concentrating almost exclusively on issues such as affirmative action, non-White immigration, and Black-on-White violent crime. Presently, the organization has its national headquarters in Mandeville, Louisiana. The most active chapter though, is in Richmond, Virginia and is led by a long time activist, Ron Doggett. It has attempted to lobby politicians, although so far it has had little access beyond the local level.[90] Doggett explained some of his efforts in this regard:

[W]e're organized at the local level, we have a lot of activities. We have sought meetings with the governor. We've involved ourselves in local interracial dialogues. These dialogues are nothing new. The political left has had them for years and they issued these reports. Basically, these reports had the same old recommendations by the political left on what needs to be done. So we've involved ourselves in some of these forums and presented our side and now these reports have to be a little more diverse and include our thoughts as well. So we're very active on a local level on a number of issues with a lot of grassroots activity.[91]

Consistent with expressed views of many activists in the racialist right, EURO pronouncements often charge that there is a double-standard, which unfairly deligitimates White racialist groups, while condoning those for non-Whites. Some of EURO's critics go so far as to assert that although the organization purports to be a civil rights organization, in reality it represents the same old bigotry in the style of the Klan in a more respectable garb. For his part, Doggett rejects such allegations:

We don't feel that that's a justifiable charge leveled at us. I honestly and truthfully do believe that we ought to stick up for our rights and I don't mean any animosity towards any other group. But, within those rights we also believe in self-preservation of our race. ... But we believe that's just as much [our] right, self-preservation as a people, as taking on issues of job security and discrimination and things of that nature ...

Clearly there's a double standard and hypocrisy. And it's really one of our better methods, in a way, to break through to the general public. They recognize that there's a double standard and hypocrisy. And nobody likes hypocrisy. And you see these double standards not only in how the different representatives of these groups are treated. Whether it's hate crime or any of these issues. We see the double standard.[92]

Duke frequently points out that European Americans, indeed all European derived peoples around the world, are in danger of being displaced due to such trends as differential birth rates among Whites and non-Whites, and miscegenation.[93] During the late 1980s and early 1990s, Duke appeared to have moderated his positions and repudiated much of his past extremism. However, in 1998 Duke appeared to have rediscovered his roots with the release of his 717-page autobiographical and political manifesto tome, *My Awakening*. In it he covered virtually the whole litany of racialist right staples, including non-White immigration, Holocaust revisionism, racial differences in IQ testing, Jewish influence in the media, etc. The book has sold reasonably well (25,000 copies) and has occasioned criticism from ADL national director Abe Foxman, who referred to it as "a minor league *Mein Kampf*."[94]

At the present time, the future of EURO is uncertain. After a fairly successful start, the organization appears to have stagnated. Until recently, Duke was in self-imposed exile in Russia. In November of 2000 his home, and also headquarters of EURO, was raided by federal authorities on the suspicion that he may have misused funds (gambling) that he solicited for his organization. US Attorney Eddie Johnson had Duke under investigation for nearly two years. Charges have yet to be filed, but taking no chances Duke fled to Russia, where he remained until late 2002. Seeking to make a virtue out of his exile, Duke has published a Russian-language, condensed version of his book and has been disseminating it to Russian sympathizers. He frequently spoke to Russian audiences on the topic of "Jewish supremacism," and seeks to build bridges between the far right in various nations. He has had some moderate success in this area as he has established contacts with French National Front leader Jean-Marie Le Pen, British National Party leader Nick Griffin, the Russian ultra-nationalist Vladimir Zhirnovsky, and retired Soviet General Albert Makashov. This politicking has not gone unnoticed by the ADL, whose office in Moscow urged authorities to open an investigation of Russians that were involved in the publication of Duke's book for possible violations of hate crime laws.[95]

However, by late 2002 Russia's tolerance of Duke appeared to have run out. Rather than face extradition, Duke returned to the US to face charges of mail fraud and tax violations involving the $100,000 sale of a list of Duke supporters to Mike Foster in 1995, a year before Foster became governor of Louisiana. Duke plea-bargained with federal prosecutors in order to avoid trial. However, he faces up to fifteen months in prison and $10,000 in fines.[96] With allegations that he misused donations from such a cash-strapped movement, Duke may have difficulty regaining credibility among his supporters.

Duke has traveled a long road in extremist politics. He first attained national recognition through his membership in the Knights of the Ku Klux Klan, an organization that continues to this day.

The Ku Klux Klan

The Ku Klux Klan has long been a fixture in the American far right. As Table 1.1 in Chapter 1 indicated, the Southern Poverty Law Center identified 138 Klan organizations operating in America in 1999. Despite this seemingly large figure, the Klan movement is organizationally weak, as the vast majority of these groups are "paper tigers," probably consisting of little more than a few members and a post office box. Furthermore, there is no real unity to speak of among the various Klan groups. With the demise of the United Klans of America in 1986 after a civil suit brought by the Southern Poverty Law Center bankrupted the organization, the Klan has virtually ceased to have any organizational foundation. Thus the Klan persists more as an *idea*. And some of those inspired by this idea have harassed and terrorized people by way of assault, murder, vandalism, and cross-burnings.

Throughout much of the Klan's history there have been two general orientations. One is that of the nightriders, who terrorize their opponents. Although the Klan has demonstrated a proclivity for violence in the past, it does not really fit into the revolutionary category. For much of its history it has been the defender of a racial status quo and has not sought to really overthrow or radically change the government.[97] It is for this reason that I have chosen to cover this segment in this section of the chapter. Although there has been somewhat of an internecine debate in Klan circles over the past couple of decades, with one faction calling for revolutionary violence and the other arguing for non-violence, for the most part, the latter seems to have won the debate, at least among the extant Klan organizations.[98] Violent Klan groups do indeed exist, but usually not for long due to vigilant prosecution on the part of authorities.[99]

The other orientation is that of the civic-minded Klan, which seeks to gain respectability among the White general public. This approach has been used frequently throughout the Klan's history. For example, during the 1920s, an organization known as the Women of the Ku Klux Klan, an auxiliary to the parent organization, championed women's issues such as equal pay while contemporaneously espousing racial and religious bigotry.[100] During the 1970s, the mediagenic David Duke eschewed the more offensive rhetoric and depicted his Knights of the Ku Klux Klan as basically a White civil rights organization. More recently, his successor, Thom Robb, has sought to establish the image of a "kinder and gentler" Klan with the public. Some Klan groups have even sought to demonstrate civic mindedness by participating in "adopt a highway" programs, in which members would clean up litter on public roads.[101] Despite its opprobrium in the general public, one asset the Klan does have is its sheer notoriety. This makes the Klan perhaps the most visible and well known type of organization in the far right. Thom Robb explains how this can be useful in recruiting prospective members:

> I think that it's really difficult not to take a little bit of baggage. There are many other organizations in the country that were created for the same purpose and yet they remain very small and we see very little media coverage even though it may be negative so often. We see very little instances because people don't know they exist. We have people all the time contact us through our website who type in "Ku Klux Klan" in a search engine whereas if we had a sign saying "Western Civilization" they wouldn't be able to find us – there's certainly name recognition, and I have found over the years that no matter what name you may call yourself, it isn't that the liberal media hate the name, they hate the ideals that we stand for so we could abandon the name or some other person could create an organization with a totally innocent-sounding name – like Jared Taylor's organization [American Renaissance]. And yet they get media coverage and they're still labeled as haters, monsters, Nazis, and bigots. So no matter what name you use you will be given the same label by our ideological enemies. It's not based upon the name it's based upon the ideals and beliefs of the organization.[102]

Today the various Klan organizations are observed closely by law enforcement authorities and watchdog groups. Since the early 1960s, the FBI has paid close attention to the Klan, as it was a prime target of the bureau's COINTELPRO initiative to disrupt extremist groups. Previously, the ADL has sought to curtail the Klan's activities by sponsoring legislation such as "anti-mask" laws.[103] More recently, the Southern Poverty Law Center has bankrupted several Klan organizations with civil suits. In sum, the Klan is by and large scorned by the general society and has virtually no influence. In fact they are often looked upon with derision by other denizens of the far-right community. Finally, despite its long history, the Klan has done virtually no theorizing or made any serious attempt to produce a body of literature that justifies or rationalizes its views. Its ideology appears to be little more than vigilantism.[104] This is remarkable insofar as the far right is in large measure a tract society in which there is no shortage of books and pamphlets.[105] Despite the generally pathetic condition of the current Klan, the number of groups that use its image as a source of organizational inspiration indicate that it will probably persist for some time.

The revolutionary racialist right

As their critics point out, representatives of the revolutionary racialist right often advocate authoritarian and undemocratic beliefs and espouse a form of anti-statism, but with a twist. Many in this movement principally are not really opposed to the idea of a strong state. In fact most would probably believe that a strong state would be essential to effecting their political and social goals. Instead their anti-statism stems from a belief that the United States government and virtually all other governments of the Western world are under the sway of a Jewish cabal. This notion has been reified in the acronym "ZOG" which stands for Zionist Occupation Government. The importance of this acronym and pervasiveness of anti-Semitism in the movement cannot be overstated. The acronym "ZOG" has attainted great currency in its vernacular as the ZOG discourse travels very well in the international far-right movement and does much to link the disparate groups together.[106] However, as we shall see, there is great variation in this theme. Some have a theological basis while others focus on control over institutions such as the media and international banking. Furthermore, there is a range of intensity with which the belief in ZOG is held. For some it amounts to little more than a popular term of resistance, while for others it is taken quite literally.

It is difficult to pinpoint just when the ZOG acronym was first introduced to the far right's lexicon, but it had become popular by the early 1980s. However, as a concept, ZOG was introduced much earlier. Jeffrey Kaplan asserts that the release of Henry Ford's serial "The International Jew" in the *Dearborn Independent* newspaper marked the start of the ZOG theme in America. According to Kaplan, the serial amounted to an Americanized version of *The Protocols of the Elders of Zion*, the minutes of an alleged meeting of Zionist leaders who plan a fantastic plot to conquer the world and enslave Gentiles.[107] The author of the serial is believed to be one William Cameron, who also helped promote

Christian Identity, a theology popular with many people in the far-right movement.

Christian Identity

If there were one thread that runs through the various far-right movements in American history it would be fundamentalist Christianity. For the contemporary far right, an obscure religious theology, Christian Identity, does much to bind the movement together. Christian Identity has no central body, but rather is a very loose network of individual believers and small congregations. The religion has its origins in nineteenth-century England's "British Israelism," which posited that the peoples of Northwestern Europe were the true descendants of the ten lost tribes of Israel. Originally the British version was philo-Semitic in character, seeking to identify as kindred people with Jews. But eventually this sect found its way to America and metamorphosed into "Christian Identity." There are several variations in beliefs and not all are anti-Semitic.[108] Many variants of this religion do however, demonize Jews and reject their ancestral claim to the Israel of biblical times.

There is no single book or document that is accepted as the authoritative doctrine of this theology. Some subscribe to the so-called "two seeds doctrine," which posits that the biblical character of Adam in the Garden of Eden was preceded by inferior races designated as "pre-Adamic." According to this doctrine, Eve was seduced by the snake (Satan) and procreated with a representative of the pre-Adamic race. Hence was born Cain, the progenitor of the Jews, who would go on to procreate with other pre-Adamic races. The non-White races of today are considered to be the descendents of these pre-Adamic races and are referred to derisively as "mud people." By contrast Abel was putatively born a pure offspring and was the progenitor of the "Aryan" or "White seed." Thus Identity believers trace their conflict with Jews back to the Book of Genesis in the Bible. Other variants of Christian Identity see contemporary Jews as impostors, and claim that they are actually the descendants of a long-lost Eurasian tribe, the Khazars.[109]

According to several versions of Christian Identity, the victory of the righteous and faithful is not assured. That is, it is conceivable that Satan and his minions could actually triumph at Armageddon. Thus there is a sense of desperation that often prevails among Christian Identity believers. Hence the shrill calls for political violence suffused with millenialism. Several observers argue that a millennial ethos is conducive to terrorism, as it loosens the moral and ethical constraints that would normally restrain the more secularly inspired terrorists.[110] This is consistent with previous studies, which indicate that a disproportionate number of those arrested for right-wing terrorism have been followers of this sect.[111]

That said, it is important not to overstate the significance of Christian Identity theology. Although observers of this movement like to expound on its rather elaborate theology and voluminous corpus of literature, it appears often to be more of a rationalization for followers' racism than an actual belief of the heart. As John George, a long time observer of political extremism in America, noted, "[t]he majority probably comprehend little about Identity theology, except that it makes 'whites' God's chosen people, and that is enough for them."[112] Thus Christian Identity is in large part an attempt to provide a theological justification for a political ideology. By doing so, it adds a sense of legitimacy, purpose and ultimacy to their mission.[113] This is not the only instance in which such a project has been undertaken.[114]

The late Wesley Swift is considered to be the single most significant figure in the history of the Christian Identity movement in America. He introduced the theology to Richard Butler, who went on to found the Church of Jesus Christ Christian and its political arm, the Aryan Nations. Some of its more notable leaders today include Thom Robb, Pete Peters, Dan Gayman, Charles A. Weisman and Richard Kelly Hoskins. Its influence also reaches beyond the confines of the revolutionary radical right, as it has gained adherents in the Christian Patriot movement.[115]

Christian Identity has gained much attention from law enforcement authorities, the watchdogs, and even the academic community. It is often referred to as a pseudo-religion by its detractors. Although the theology has served as an important commonality in the far-right underground, its influence appears to be waning. Many of its followers are older, and there seems to be a process of attrition whereby new converts are not replacing fast enough those who are dying.[116] However, the theology has provided a theological and ideological sustenance for the far right over the past couple of decades. Various Christian Identity sects – most notably the Aryan Nations – have on occasion been attracted to National Socialism as well.

National Socialism

National Socialism has a long history in the United States and can be traced to émigré groups such as the German American Bund and the Friends of the New Germany that were active in the 1930s. However, these groups were quickly dissolved as the United States entered World War II. Despite the Axis defeat in 1945, it wasn't long before the National Socialist ideology re-emerged, albeit in mutated form. Although it would retain a great deal of its "Germanic" character, in its postwar guise it has taken on a more "pan-Aryan" orientation, which seeks to unite all of the various European-derived peoples around the world into a single "racial nationalist" community.

Indeed, Hitler and the Third Reich serve as both powerful symbols but also cumbersome baggage for the contemporary racialist. This presents a very serious dilemma for those in the movement, as Jeffrey Kaplan noted:

> The figure of Adolf Hitler … is today the colossus whose legacy for good or ill must be confronted sooner or later by every adherent of the racialist right wing. So great is the burden of history of World War II and the enormity of

the Holocaust that one's attitude toward Hitler and Nazism serves at once as a litmus test of the faith of the far right and as a so-far-unbreachable barrier between the racialist right and mainstream acceptance.[117]

Thus the legacy of Hitler and the Third Reich is ironically both a source of inspiration and an enormous obstacle to reaching out to a larger audience.

The effort to resurrect National Socialism began soon after the Axis defeat in 1945. Several Americans made significant contributions to this effort, the first notable of whom was Francis Parker Yockey. Yockey developed a vast international network of fascists from all over the world, including North America, South America, Europe, the Middle East and even Eastern Europe. He is best known for his turgid 626-page tome *Imperium*, which advanced the notion of a unified Western civilization extending from Ireland to the Ural Mountains. Consistent with this theme was the pseudonym under which Yockey wrote the book – "Ulick Varange" – an Irish first name and a Russian surname. Yockey was an admirer of the German National Socialist regime, and believed that it was a serious attempt to bring about such an "imperium." In fact he dedicated the book to "the hero of the Second World War" (read Adolf Hitler) and waxed eloquently on "the European Revolution of 1933." Drawing on the work of Oswald Spengler, Yockey believed that civilizations went through life phases. He saw National Socialism as a project to renew the vitality of the West.

Although for years the book languished and was distributed primarily to only a small number of the National Socialist faithful in Europe, it eventually was picked up by another American, Willis Carto, who published it and popularized it to an American audience. Although it is one of the most widely distributed books in the far-right movement, it is also one of the least understood, and has thus added to the legend of Yockey, who committed suicide in a San Francisco jail cell in 1960, where he was being held for passport violations.[118] Despite the efforts of Yockey, his writings did not extend much beyond a handful of fanatics. It would take an American, George Lincoln Rockwell, to bring greater exposure to neo-Nazism.

Prior to Rockwell's creation of the American Nazi Party in 1958, there were a few organizations, such as the Columbians and the National Renaissance Party, that adopted some of the symbolic trappings and ideology of Nazism. However, the former quickly ran afoul of the law and was effectively shut down, while the latter remained for the most part a small cult until its dissolution in 1978. George Lincoln Rockwell founded the American Nazi Party in 1958, and it became the first explicitly neo-Nazi party to gain widespread notoriety. Flamboyant and articulate, Rockwell captured much publicity for his cause with his provocative antics. Along with his stormtroopers, Rockwell would visit racial hot spots around the country. Rockwell's "in your face" tactics provoked angry opposition and brought notoriety to his organization, which gave people the perception that it was much larger than it really was (estimates are that it never exceeded two hundred members at any given time). Rockwell tirelessly set about creating a viable party, and established links with like-minded believers, which culminated in the creation of the World Union of National Socialists in Gloucestershire, England in 1960.[119] However, it was not easy for Rockwell to hold his followers together. His organization attracted more than its share of crackpots and provocateurs, and in 1967 a disgruntled member, John Patler, assassinated Rockwell. The government kept close tabs on Rockwell's America Nazi Party, and it was a target of the FBI's COINTELPRO program. The ADL also closely monitored Rockwell, and on at least one occasion persuaded the FBI to open an investigation on him.[120] Despite Rockwell's death the organization actually continues to this day, under the name New Order and under the leadership of Matt Koehl in Wisconsin. However, the organization is really no more than a mail order book distributor. Despite the chaotic conditions of the American Nazi Party's headquarters in Arlington, Virginia, Rockwell influenced several persons who would go on to be key figures in the far right, including one Dr William Pierce.

National Alliance

William Pierce, who earned a Ph.D. in physics, left his position as a university professor in the late 1960s to edit a journal, *National Socialist World*, which was designed to be a highbrow journal for Rockwell's American Nazi Party. By the early 1970s, Pierce had cut off all ties to the organization due to factional disputes with its leader Matt Koehl. In 1974 he founded the National Alliance with several members from another organization, National Youth Alliance, which was effectively a front for Willis Carto of the Liberty Lobby. As Che Guevara was the major theorist for revolution among Latin American revolutionaries, so was Pierce among those in the revolutionary radical right, and at the time of his death in July 2002 he was arguably its most important and influential figure. He was best known for his novel, *The Turner Diaries*, which tells the story of a clandestine terrorist group, "the organization," which seeks to overthrow the US government. Pierce was largely responsible for the creation of a genre of literature in the far right in which a story is told interspersed with ideological digressions, and as some would argue, ideas for carrying out terrorist attacks. The FBI has described *The Turner Diaries* as the "bible" of the racialist right and a "blueprint for revolution."[121] This book will be covered in greater detail in the following chapter, as it has been connected to several serious incidents of right-wing terrorism.

Pierce's National Alliance avoids some of the more overt symbols and accoutrements of Nazism, yet he acknowledges his ideological affinity to it. In an interview with Pierce, I put it to him that he was often characterized as a Nazi, and asked him if he drew much inspiration from German National Socialism. This was his reply:

> Quite a bit, yeah. I mean I don't blindly imitate, and that was my big criticism of Rockwell. Rockwell wasn't doing what he was doing because he was stupid or imitative, but because he wanted an image, which would attract some people to him and get media attention and so on. But I said, Jesus,

there is a big downside to it too. I mean uniforms. Everyone wore uniforms in Germany back in the 1920s. The Catholic Center Party had uniforms. The communists had uniforms. But over here it's just not the tradition, and people think you're some kind of freak if you're seen in around in a uniform with armbands and so on. Especially after Hollywood has ran that into the ground. Most people just don't understand that.

So I have always steered away from this image and tried to look first at the ideas and at the real results, the healthy programs. Hitler was probably the first national leader who wanted to get rid of the evils of smoking cigarettes. But much more than that, the idea was to rebuild a sense of racial, national identity and pride in being German and a sense of selflessness. The German worker was just not working to get the best deal he could get for himself, but he had pride in his contribution to the economy, to the society and so on. And he was in turn rewarded for that with organizations like the KDF and all of the workers' villages and subsidized housing. Volkswagen, the people's car. Hitler wanted every German family to be able to afford their own automobile. So these, at least the way in which they were promoted in Germany, were not just some democratic gimmicks to get votes. It was because he generally believed that this was the way to build a strong, healthy society and it worked. It worked amazingly well. ...

[Hitler] could with an honest vote count go out and get more than 90 per cent of the vote of people, whenever he was putting a proposition to them. He genuinely then had most of the people behind him. ...

I mean the situation in Germany in 1933 when Hitler became chancellor was not really as bad as it is in the United States today. ... And the ideas that the party propagated, well it was really a two-tier thing. Ideas to get votes and there was also the philosophy underlying these ideas, which really was not contradictory to the ideas, but which went much deeper, much more fundamental than just the economic and social ideas that were put forth to get votes. This just wasn't a fringe thing. A very substantial part of the German population agreed with the underlying ideas of National Socialism. So Hitler had an enormous advantage. The disadvantage he had was that the government was in enemy hands. And the forces arrayed against him were very strong. But he and his people were more determined, smarter, and harder working than the people on the other side were and he became chancellor ...

So anyway, yeah, I've been very, very inspired by the thing, not to try to model what I'm doing after that because the strategy has to be quite different in this country than it was in Germany in the 1920s and early 1930s. But the fundamental philosophical ideas I share, the really fundamental philosophical ideas about race, nature, and man's purpose on the earth. Those are the ideas.[122]

Over the years Pierce built his National Alliance into one of the most influential organizations in the far right. Unlike most groups in the far right, the

National Alliance has some real semblance of an organizational structure. Hierarchically organized, Pierce held the position of chairman, below which are regional offices followed by local units, which are comprised of individual members.[123] For most of its years the organization languished and operated on a shoestring budget, and only attracted a very limited number of followers. However, Pierce demonstrated dogged determination and persistence. Always looking for new ways to reach potential followers, he was at the forefront of experiments to gain more attention and notoriety.

As mentioned earlier, there are several versions of the "ZOG" theme in the ideology of the far right. Pierce's version focuses on the centrality of the media. Towards this end, he published a pamphlet titled "Who Rules America?"[124] According to Pierce the media deliberately manipulate the masses and, to use Noam Chomsky's term, "manufacture consent." However, whereas left-wing media critics such as Chomsky and Michael Parenti[125] assert that there is a corporate elite behind this manipulation, Pierce asserted an ethno-religious spin on this theory, i.e. media control by a tight knit Jewish establishment. This led into his critique of democracy as well:

> I do believe in the centrality of the media in determining public policy in the United States today. The whole idea of democracy, the will of the people, is meaningless in the television era simply because most people do not form their own conclusions. They simply accept what they see as fashionable around them. They are lemmings. They really are, most people. So whoever is able to paint the picture of what is fashionable, most of the population will then adopt as their own opinions. If they really believe that all of their neighbors and the Hollywood movie stars, the wise people in Washington, and so on believe certain concepts, they'll adopt those as their own. That's the way people are 98 per cent, probably of the population. ... Most people are not independent thinkers. They do not come to their own opinions. ... And so therefore, whoever controls television and Hollywood and Madison Avenue can determine what the majority of the American people will think. You can shape their attitudes. You can shape their opinions. The politicians are smart enough to figure this out for themselves. Therefore you can control the politicians and you can control public policy. And the whole concept of democracy becomes meaningless.[126]

To Pierce the media were virtually omnipotent in their influence. Consequently he tirelessly sought to develop his own independent media through which he could appeal directly to people. The organization has a publishing arm, National Vanguard Books, which is a major supplier of far-right propaganda throughout the world. The National Alliance also has a shortwave radio and internet broadcast program called "American Dissident Voices," which is listened to by many in the far right.[127] Each week Pierce offered a new broadcast, usually about twenty-five minutes in length. A typical broadcast began with some current event as a launching point and then got "behind the scenes" of the news to uncover alleged machinations of Jewish power. The increasing popularity of his program appeared to coincide with a certain trend in American popular culture in which views are expressed with increasing coarseness. Over the past decade or so the success of television programs such as the *Jerry Springer Show*, *Hardball*, the *No Spin Zone*, and the WWF's *Raw is War* and *Smack Down* seem indicative of a popular demand for discourse and expression that are unencumbered by the constraints of political correctness. Pierce had indeed mastered this style in his broadcasts, as he came across as both cogent and strident to his target audience. Shortly after Pierce's death, Kevin Alfred Strom, who had pioneered American Dissident Voices in the early 1990s, resumed control of the program.

In the years leading up to his death Pierce undertook a project for which he seemed to have big plans: the distribution of White power skinhead music. In 1999 he acquired Resistance Records, the preeminent distributor of such music, from one Todd Blodgett, a former low-level staffer in the Reagan White House and a protegé of Lee Atwater. Under Pierce's direction, Resistance Records appeared to have rebounded and now has potential to be a substantial moneymaker for the organization he founded.[128] However, Pierce saw it as a very important propaganda vehicle to direct at youth as well, as he explained:

> Music is really the first mass medium that we've had. Even to listen to my radio programs, you have to be interested in what I have to say. You deliberately tune in or find it on the internet and you listen to it because you're interested in the message. You're interested in what I have to say about this particular issue. And that's not your average soccer mom. That's not your couch potato. That's not your sports fan. They're not interested in anything except how much beer is in the refrigerator and how much is left on the credit card.
>
> But music is different simply because, for people, music is sort of a background thing and people have become accustomed to certain types of music they actually like. Certain types of rock music for instance. And if I can control the lyrics to that music, then it's really sort of a subliminal thing for a lot of people. People don't listen to Sumner Redstone's propaganda, I mean, they don't watch his propaganda stuff because they want to be indoctrinated that interracial marriage is a good thing. They watch it because they like this lowbrow entertainment that he provides and incidentally they get indoctrinated that sleeping with blacks is very fashionable these days, why don't you try it? It's the same way with Resistance music.[129]

Indicative of the significance to which he assigned to this effort, shortly before his death, Pierce chose Eric Gliebe, the manager of Resistance Records, as his successor in the National Alliance. The thirty-nine year-old Gliebe, a former boxer who fought under the moniker "the Aryan Barbarian," has given high priority to recruiting teenagers into the organization.[130] Furthermore, he has demonstrated a penchant for street activism, which has included several National

Alliance demonstrations at the Israeli embassy in Washington DC to protest American and Israeli policies in the Middle East in 2001–2, and a nationwide distribution of literature to coincide with Jewish holidays and September 11.[131]

The National Alliance has recently sought to capitalize on the growing popularity of violent home video games with the release of "Ethnic Cleansing." The video game plays in the style of such mainstream popular games such as "Wolfenstein." However, in the case of "Ethnic Cleansing," players simulate urban warfare in which White protagonists seek to kill Blacks, Hispanics and Jews. The game is won when the player assassinates a simulated Ariel Sharon.[132]

Much of the attraction of Pierce's propaganda lay in his analysis of the revolutionary right's predicament. He was very cognizant of the opposition arrayed against his movement. He offered no pie-in-the-sky solutions for his followers. Instead he emphasized building a resistance infrastructure in which he could disseminate his message to more people. He had no illusions of successfully confronting "the system" at this particular point in his struggle. He did however, look for opportunities to spread his message and expand his following.

Through his authorship of *The Turner Diaries*, Pierce attained great stature in the far right, was regarded as its elder statesman, and commanded great respect from his followers. And today the National Alliance is the preeminent organization of the racialist right. However, this has also caught the attention of the National Alliance's opponents. The Anti-Defamation League describes it as the "most dangerous hate group in America,"[133] and Pierce was once the target of a civil suit from the Southern Poverty Law Center.[134] Like so many other activists in the far right, Pierce saw the ADL as his most formidable watchdog opponent:

> I think the ADL is the most dangerous group in the country in terms of the First and Second Amendments. Because the ADL is Jewish, they have a hell of a lot more clout than anybody else does. And they are very unscrupulous in the way they go about things. They will do a lot of illegal stuff figuring they can get talk out of it just because they're Jews. ... But they are powerful and dangerous and they got a lot of connections. They have a lot of people in Congress that they can count on to back them regardless of what they do.

However, as evidenced by the following exchange, Pierce also saw somewhat of a symbiotic relationship between himself and his detractors:

G. M. The ADL has often been very critical of you. In fact, I believe that they recently referred to you as the "most dangerous man in America." How does that make you feel?

W. P. I'm very flattered by that. I appreciate that. To be very honest about it the ADL and I have a symbiotic relationship. They raise money by holding me up as a bogeyman. "Send us money and we'll save you from this wicked evil monster Dr No and his machinations, etc." And at the same time, the more the ADL holds me up to be dangerous and successful and effective, the more credibility that I gain with the people I'm trying to reach. So it works both ways.[135]

Finally, the National Alliance has long been under close scrutiny by the FBI, although Pierce managed to keep his organization out of serious legal trouble.[136] In sum, the future of the Alliance is a bit uncertain. Pierce built a dedicated following and his organization is estimated to have approximately 1,500 dues-paying members.[137] However, with the death of Pierce, the long-term viability of the National Alliance is uncertain. Previously, this problem of succession has doomed several organizations in the far right, as they often disintegrate after the passing of their charismatic leaders. The new chairman, Eric Gliebe, has sought to consolidate his hold and has recently removed at least one recalcitrant Alliance leader.[138]

White Aryan Resistance

Tom Metzger founded the White Aryan Resistance, or WAR as it is more popularly known, in 1983. Perhaps more so than any figure, Metzger exemplifies the revolutionary racialist right. Metzger's political odyssey included stints in the John Birch Society, the tax rebellion movement, Second Amendment organizations, the Knights of the Ku Klux Klan, the Christian Identity movement, and at one time in the early 1960s, as a campaign worker for one of Ronald Reagan's gubernatorial bids. However, he eventually became weary of all of these projects and thought them to be too mild for his political tastes. Instead he has promoted a "third way" variant of National Socialism that is highly critical of capitalism. In that sense, Metzger is heir to the Strasser brothers of the Nazi period in Germany, who sought to steer Hitler in a more socialistic, anti-capitalist direction. What's more, Metzger actually draws much inspiration from left-wing icons such as Vladimir Lenin and Jack London. Consistent with his anti-conservative approach, he is willing to make common cause with the political left on certain issues such as US intervention in Latin America. Moreover, he has even sought alliances with Black separatists such as the Nation of Islam. Metzger commented on his thoughts on the political left and some of his efforts to reach out to that movement:

> We have taken a stand since the late 70s early 80s of opposing imperialist activities by what we would call the transnational corporate leadership in this country that we feel pretty much controls what goes on in Washington, DC. So we came out opposing the Cold War because our logic was simple that if there were any kind of nuclear war it would destroy the ancestral homeland of the entire white race. And from there we began to oppose intervention in the problems of Central America and so forth. ... This would cause massive illegal immigration into the United States ...
> We have found that the far left has been just as hard to deal with as many on the so-called far right. I have been quite successful in changing the minds

and reorienting many people from the left. And they have had a great influence on myself. In the area of economics we have a whole lot of agreement. In the area of race we don't have so much agreement. It's very difficult because, immediately once you say that you are a racial separatist, the leadership says, "well, we don't want to talk to you." Whereas, we think that if you have areas of agreement on important objects that you should be able and willing to sit down with people and be willing to discuss them.[139]

Although he is described as a Nazi, Metzger does not shy away from criticizing Hitler and the Third Reich. This makes him somewhat of a "deviationist," which is frowned upon by many neo-Nazis. In fact he sees its legacy as inhibiting the far right's efforts to achieve international unity:

There are things in National Socialism that I think are preferable to capitalism and communism. That is for sure. But the race issue was sort of a mixed-up situation over there. A lot of it was German nationalism that was spoken of as racism. Much of the attitude towards the Slavic people and the whole people of Europe and Eastern Europe was very negative. … Unfortunately, the war took on a sort of Germanic type of thing where 20 million Russians died and I would say probably 19 million of them I would consider white. Fratricidal wars, no matter who starts them, could be stopped. So I fault both sides for something like that. And any kind of fratricidal war where white people are killing white people I'm totally against.

I totally disagree on Operation *Barbarossa*. I think that was a fatal error that still is affecting the world today, the attack on Russia. The hard line right-wing National Socialists say "well the Russians were getting ready to attack Germany." And I say there is no legitimate evidence to base that upon. Just the opposite. Stalin was absolutely crushed and hid in his office for ten days and nobody could get him out to talk to him. He just couldn't believe that Hitler had attacked him.

World War II is at the heart of the problem today because before the war racial separatism was very strong in this country. Eugenic programs were very strong and all kinds of things that I thought were basically good for the race have now been attached to Nazi Germany and called evil. And people say, "We shouldn't do this or that because the Nazis did it."

It is very difficult for people in a country like Russia that had 20 million killed to turn around and say "well we embrace you now." And the Germans also, the many times they have been shafted by England and so forth. And the English being bombed by the *Luftwaffe*. So it takes a long time to heal.

But I believe, and I've said, and I've been really attacked for this, that if they [German Nazis] would have internalized and kept the revolution going in Germany and not allowed it to expand beyond the borders, the world would be a much better place today. The left in Germany had a lot of good ideas. They were buffered by between extreme monopoly capitalism and

Marxism. Both the Strasser brothers and Hitler had good points.[140] But Hitler tended to move towards the industrialists and made a deal with them. And when that happened, the original idea of National Socialism, I believe, went out the window.[141]

Metzger has been in the forefront of the far right's multi-media efforts to disseminate its propaganda to a larger audience. He produces a monthly newspaper, *WAR*, which is one of the most provocative underground publications in the movement and contains articles that advocate the "leaderless resistance" approach to right-wing terrorism. Previous articles have lionized "lone wolf" figures such as Timothy McVeigh, Richard Scott Baumhammers, Joseph Paul Franklin, and John King.[142] He claims to have a prison outreach program and he lists the names and prison addresses of various "POW" White racists who are currently incarcerated.

Metzger was one of the first far-right activists to take advantage of computer technology. He created a computer bulletin board in 1989 that linked together like-minded activists. Other projects include a website, recorded messages on a telephone line, and a television program, *Race and Reason*, which is aired on cable public access stations in scattered towns and cities across America. During the latter half of the 1980s, Metzger, often with his son John, appeared on several major network talk shows such as *Geraldo*, *Oprah*, *The Whoopi Goldberg Show* and *The Morton Downey Show*. This exposure has made the Metzgers among the most visible figures in his movement.

However, this has come at a great cost to them, as they have also caught the attention of the watchdogs and the government, which have mounted serious opposition against their operation. In the past, the FBI has kept close tabs on them.[143] More important however, have been the efforts of the watchdogs. With some assistance from the ADL, the Southern Poverty Law Center prosecuted a successful civil suit against the Metzgers in 1990 and personally bankrupted both of them. Despite this opposition, Metzger, like some other far-right leaders, claims that these groups actually provide him with useful publicity:

> I look a little bit differently on these groups. It's sort of a love-hate relationship in the sense that I almost say well what would we do without the ADL? Because if three or four of us people meet in a telephone booth, they make it sound like it's Nuremberg, 1936. So, in some ways, they have distorted it so badly that it actually works in reverse and a lot of people want to get involved and assume that there is a massive movement.[144]

Tom Metzger, in *WAR*, once even editorialized that the Southern Poverty Law Center actually inadvertently helped the far right insofar as it siphoned off potential dollars from what he perceived as more effective watchdog groups:

> Consider the fact that Sleazy [Morris Dees] has milked millions from those who are our enemies anyway. That may have put him in a better light than

you previously thought. Sleazy has kept millions out of the hands of the Jew ADL and others who actually have a far better oiled apparatus than he. The money would be far more dangerous to the Racist cause in the hands of those Kosher groups. Also, for the most part, those Dees forced out of action were either incompetent or weak.[145]

It is important to keep in mind that the Southern Poverty Law Center defeated Metzger in a civil suit, and thus he probably has some axes to grind. Be that as it may, similar comments are frequently made about Dees in the milieu.

WAR remains undeterred and continues operations, although it has not regained the status it once held in the far right. One of the Metzgers' major initiatives has been to introduce skinheads to the far-right movement, as they view them as potential foot soldiers, although it was this effort that ultimately ensnared him in the civil suit with the Southern Poverty Law Center.

The skinheads

The skinheads first emerged on the American scene in the early 1980s. The subculture was largely imported from Great Britain and revolved around a style of music known as "Oi." A British musician, Ian Stuart, and his band Skrewdriver did much to popularize the skinhead scene with this music. Soon skinhead bands emerged throughout North America and Europe. Today some of the more prominent skinhead organizations are Hammerskin Nation, Outlaw Hammerskins, and Underground Skinhead Action.

Although their numbers are estimated to have only reached a few thousand in the United States, the emergence of the skinheads in the far right was significant for a number of reasons.[146] First, it injected an element of youth into a movement that was aging. Through their music, the skinheads have helped spread their message not only throughout a portion of the far-right movement, but also to rebellious youths who would otherwise not be interested in extremist politics. In this sense their music has served as a recruiting mechanism. Second, and related to that, the skinheads had a radicalizing effect on the rest of the movement. They tended to eschew the more conservative approaches and preferred more direct action. Third, this often led to violence, and skinheads were often involved in confrontations with minorities, law enforcement, and rival anti-racist skinhead gangs. All totaled, at least twenty-five homicides have been attributed to skinheads.[147]

Consequently, the skinheads have come under close attention from authorities. The ADL has also published several critical reports, and has sought to warn law enforcement and educators of the threat that they pose.[148] At the behest of the ADL, the Justice Department created a skinhead task force.[149] Today the skinheads are not as conspicuous as they once were. However, the subculture still lives on in the underground White power music industry, which is by some accounts a potentially profitable enterprise. The skinheads also made common cause with some of the more established organizations of the far right, most notably Dr Pierce's Resistance Records and Tom Metzger's WAR. Unlike the elderly denizens of the movement, who are often staunch Christians, the skinheads are more likely to look towards unconventional sources for religious inspiration, such as neo-paganism.

Odinism

Odinism is a reconstructed neo-pagan religion that has gained popularity primarily with the younger people in the far right.[150] However, the connection between neo-paganism and far-right politics has actually a fairly long pedigree and can be traced back to the late nineteenth century in Austria and Germany, where it is thought by some to have influenced the development of German National Socialism.[151] The Odinists draw their inspiration from the sagas of the old Norse pantheon which includes Odin, Thor, Balder, Frey and Freya. At first thought it seems surprising that Odinism would take hold among the American far right insofar as historically, Christian fundamentalism has figured so prominently in the movement. However, over the past several decades the various Christian denominations have for the most part distanced themselves from racial bigotry and intolerance. Many in the far right began to feel uncomfortable with a Christianity that increasingly condemned their political beliefs.

Odinism must also be placed in the context of identity politics. Some people in the racialist movement sought to discover their primeval pagan roots and search for a mythical golden age unsullied by modern civilization. Thus Odinism appears in many ways to be a manifestation of a White ethnic variant of multiculturalism not unlike Islam as embraced by Black nationalists. Finally, in a milieu in which anti-Semitism looms so large, it is not surprising that some would seek an alternative to Christianity, which has its roots in Judaism.

To this day, Odinism has yet to establish a really firm organizational footing. It is a movement comprised primarily of individual adherents unaffiliated with any formal organization.[152] However, according to some observers it has considerable potential in the far-right community. Although Christian Identity probably still has more followers than does Odinism, the former does not seem to hold much appeal with far-rightists outside of North America, with the exception of a few pockets of followers in England and Sweden. Moreover, even in America, Identity's appeal appears to be limited to people with a Christian fundamentalist background.[153] However, the Odinists on past occasions have been able to collaborate with Christian Identity members, despite holding beliefs that in theory would offend them. On past occasions the two have worked together. A good example is the underground terrorist group, the Order, which included both Odinists and Identity Christians, and which went on a crime spree in the Pacific Northwest in 1983–4. American Odinists do not seem to have a rigid theological dogma that precludes such cooperation. Various far-right groups have no trouble finding common cause with them. In this regard Odinism travels well across different countries. With its loose theology and warrior ethos, Odinism holds appeal with far-right groups in countries in both

North America and Europe, and helps bind them together as part of a larger movement. Herein lies its significance.

What is surprising about the Odinist movement is how little mention the watchdogs and the government have made of it. References to the religion have appeared abundantly in the far-right literature for quite some time now, but for whatever reason the watchdogs and government, up until recently, have basically ignored it. And it's not that there is no ammunition to be used against it. In Norway, Odinists were thought to be responsible for forty-four church arsons during the early 1990s.[154] This had a demonstration effect and was thought to have led to some church burning in Sweden and Germany as well. Thus resurfaced an old form of religious terrorism – iconoclasm – in which the spiritual sanctuaries of one's enemy were targeted. The perpetrators justified their crimes as retaliation against the Christian churches, which they saw as defiling Odin's hallowed ground.[155] Odinism has finally caught the attention of authorities. The FBI's *Project Megiddo Report*, released in the fall of 1999, contained a section on Odinism.[156] Recently, the Southern Poverty Law Center has issued critical reports on Odinism, warning of its spreading popularity among White inmates in the penal system.[157] According to an article in its *Intelligence Report*, Odinism is the religion of the future for the far right.[158] Odinism, however, is not the only religion in the movement to reject Christianity. The Church of the Creator is even more extreme in this regard.

The World Church of the Creator

The Church of the Creator captured much attention in the summer of 1999 when a former member, Benjamin Smith, went on a shooting spree in Illinois and Indiana. The late Ben Klassen founded the Church in 1973, with the release of his book *Nature's Eternal Religion*. Klassen was a moderately successful inventor and businessman, and dabbled in right-wing politics before founding his church. Klassen took issue with the Christian fundamentalists, especially the Identity Christians who figured so prominently in the far right. According to Klassen the Christian Identity religion is misguided. In fact, "Creativity" fully acknowledges the Jewish origins of Christianity. Rather than being a solution to the perceived malaise of the West, Klassen saw it as a major part of the problem. Klassen offers a critique of Christianity in some ways reminiscent of Nietzsche's *Twilight of the Idols* and *The Anti-Christ*, but is much more scathing. According to Klassen's theory, Jews and Whites have been involved in a struggle extending back several millennia. Far from being the white man's salvation, Klassen argued that Christianity was concocted by Jews to confuse him and thus weaken his sense of tribal identity. Thus the universalistic tendencies of Christianity have caused Whites to misplace their altruism away from their racial comrades. The church's current leader, Matt Hale, explains:

> Christianity from its very inception was a Jewish creed, a Jewish philosophy. And we believe that Christianity was fed, so to speak, to the white Romans

in an effort to destroy the white Roman Empire, and has been fed to white people ever since in general to destroy them and to damage their interests worldwide. And we can see it readily by the fact that today you can walk into any Christian church and hear a talk about how all people are equal and God loves us all and racial intermarriage is okay and things of this nature. The religion itself is anti-racist in a sense that it does not talk about the importance of saving the white race or preserving the white race and this has been inculcated in all races. So it is not a racial religion and it is an approach that is contrary to what we believe in. …

I think that any religion that has a Jew, as a savior, is doomed. I think that it is a very troubled religion when you have a Jew as your savior. Now, Christian Identity people say that he was not a Jew after all. But I think that is ridiculous. I mean, Jesus Christ, obviously is not from our people, if he even existed, which we don't believe he did. Even assuming he did exist, he came from the Palestine, of Jewish background. So, basically, Christianity has a seed of destruction for white people within it by virtue of having a Jewish savior.[159]

Creativity rejects all metaphysical beliefs and supernatural deities. Instead it offers an all-encompassing *Weltanschauung* based on the veneration of the White race. In a nutshell, "Creativity" posits that the White race is nature's most gifted creation. Towards this end "Creators" espouse "racial loyalty" and seek to unite the White race in a single global community devoid of all other races. As such, measures should be taken to enhance its health (eugenics) and survival as a distinct racial group (thus there are strictures against miscegenation, and Whites are encouraged to have large families). The Creativity theology seeks to syncretize several disparate themes in history, including Roman classicism, German National Socialism, and the American Western frontier, as Matt Hale explains:

> The Roman Empire was really one of the highlights of our white racial history. … Certainly the Roman Empire accomplished a great many things, everything from roads, to architecture, to art, to language. Certainly the Latin language is a very beautiful language, very organized, and is the basis of many European languages. …
>
> The winning of the west. Well, the winning of the west is really the period in history, which we Creators look most to for inspiration in a sense that when White people came here, they may have been divided by nationality, so to speak. But when they confronted the hostile Indians they forgot that quickly and banded together, and circled the wagons, so to speak, for the white race as whole. And we believe that was a very important event in history. That indeed, is exactly what we have to do today, whether a person

is a German, or a Frenchman, or a Pole, or a Russian, or what have you. We are all White brothers. We have to band together.
National Socialist Germany. Certainly that was an inspiration as well. That Adolf Hitler formed with the German people the first government in history, which was overtly based on race, a concept which we support. Also he showed that the Jews could be exposed and defeated within a country in modern times, which he did. And also we respect Adolf Hitler because he stemmed the tide of communism, which no one had really been able to do, until he came along.[160]

Some critics assert that Creativity is a pseudo-religion, that it is nothing more than a rationale for hatred and bigotry, which seeks to gain legitimacy by cloaking itself in a theological garb. What's more, by its own admission Creativity is atheist. Hale, however, rejects this notion and believes Creativity constitutes a legitimate religion that should have the same legal protection as say Christianity, Islam and Judaism.

The church languished for a few years after Ben Klassen committed suicide in 1993. However, in 1996, a young law student, Matt Hale, revived the church and is recognized today as its leader.[161] He graduated from law school in 1998 and although he passed his Illinois bar examination on his first attempt, he was not granted a law license because a state bar panel deemed that his character was unfit due to his political beliefs. In a rare meeting of minds, the ADL actually issued a press release and criticized the panel's decision.[162] The story took another strange twist when Alan Dershowitz, a high-profile attorney and outspoken member of the Jewish American community, represented Hale for a short time. Dershowitz expressed concern over such a precedent. Consistent with the pragmatism of the Creativity doctrine, Hale saw no compromise on his part in principal in his choice of counsel:

> As far as whether or not my dealings with him were in some ways contradictory to our message, I don't think so. We Creators have always realized that the end justifies the means and whatever tool we have to use in order to accomplish the particular goal at hand, well why not use it? It's kind of like this. If you hand a slingshot or Uzi gun to someone, which should he choose? It is true that one comes from the Jews and one came from white people probably thousands, and thousands, and thousands of years ago. But which is more effective? You have to use the tool that is most effective at that time.[163]

By outward appearances the World Church of the Creator appears to be a modest operation. The church has approximately 300 members and until recently, Reverend Hale's bedroom in his father's house served as the organization's headquarters.[164] However, the church's influence extends far beyond its membership numbers. For example, much of its rhetoric, such as RAHOWA, has gained currency in the vernacular of the far right all over the world.[165]

There was also a very popular, but now defunct, skinhead musical band by the name RAHOWA. Finally, the church has gained notoriety because several of its members have been implicated in violence and terrorism.[166] Consequently, it has come under close attention from both the government and watchdogs. The Southern Poverty Law Center successfully prosecuted a civil suit against the church in 1994. The ADL has issued several reports and press releases against the church, and in 1999 persuaded the Justice Department to open an investigation of the church following the Ben Smith shooting spree.[167] Despite this opposition, the church continues, and attracts new followers in large measure because of it nihilistic appeal to rebellious youth.

As of early 2003 the future of the World Church of the Creator is uncertain. During much of 2002, the church was embroiled in a civil suit with the Te-Ta-Ma Truth Foundation over the latter's trademarked "Church of the Creator" name. Hale argued that his church had existed prior to the Te-Ta-Ma Truth's trademark, and what's more, the "Church of the Creator" name was too generic to be exclusively held by only one organization. Originally, Federal District Judge Joan Humphrey Lefkow ruled in his favor. However, her decision was overturned on appeal. Judge Lefkow was left to enforce the appellate court's decision and ordered that Hale's organization desist using the Church of the Creator name and all of the organization's books, which members consider to be holy texts, were ordered to be destroyed. Angered by the decision, Hale was arrested by an FBI counter-terrorism team in January 2003 on charges that he solicited an unidentified person to kill Judge Lefkow. As of late January 2003 details on the arrest are still incomplete, but according to prosecutors the leader of church's security detail, the White Berets, had been recruited by the FBI to work as an informant since 1999. Prosecutors identified the informant only as " Brother Tony." According to the informant, Hale allegedly requested the address of Judge Lefkow. The informant implied that she should be killed, and although Hale did not directly endorse the plan, neither did he ever instruct the informant not to carry it out. See Bush, Rudolph. "Hale's Security Boss was FBI informer, E-mails, tapes led to arrest, U.S. says." *Chicago Tribune* (January 24, 2003), http://www.chicagotribune.com/news/local/chi0301240295jan24,0,7321287.story. Commenting on Hale's arrest, Mark Potok of the Southern Poverty Law Center did not think the World Church of the Creator would survive its current crisis. Rabbi Abraham Cooper of the Simon Wiesenthal Center opined that if the charges against Hale stick that it would result in "the removal of the most dangerous American racist of [Hale's] generation."[168] Likewise, the ADL also applauded Hale's arrest.[169]

The Liberty Lobby: the nexus of the far right

The Liberty Lobby is one of the most enduring organizations in the far-right constellation, as it has demonstrated amazing continuity over the years largely due to the efforts of its founder, Willis Carto, an enigmatic figure who has been involved in virtually every major effort in the far right. At the Liberty Lobby, virtually all segments of the far right come together. The Lobby publishes a weekly newspaper, the *Spotlight*, which with a circulation of about 50,000, makes it the most widely disseminated organ of the movement. The Liberty Lobby has its headquarters in downtown Washington DC. By appearances the Liberty Lobby and the *Spotlight* seek to appeal to a broad segment of the far right, as it contains themes that would seem to resonate with several different segments of the far right including militias, anti-globalists, conspiracy theorists, and the white racialists. Other far-right organs tend to focus on a narrower readership. In that sense the Liberty Lobby and the *Spotlight* serve as a big tent of sorts under which the disparate elements of the far right can meet. The Liberty Lobby's Mike Piper commented on this aspect of his organization:

> I'm going to answer that by saying we're victims of our own success. We try to reach as many people as possible as what you would describe as far right. A lot of people in the far right don't like the *Spotlight*. Some people in the skinhead movement think the *Spotlight* is too tame, whereas some of the people in the tax protest movement think the *Spotlight* is too radical. They think by not saying Israel or by not doing this or not doing that the ADL will realize they're just good American patriots. Whereas the skinheads come back and say, "Well you don't call the problem for what it is. It's the Jews or this or that or what have you." People even in this internet age tend to section themselves on their own anyway. Each person has his own little segment. ... The *Spotlight* is trying to cover all areas of the far right and try to cover areas of interest for everybody. We've been called a *National Enquirer* of the far right. We do perceive ourselves as a newspaper. We do try to cover the news of what is happening at the national level in a way that is digestible to, not just the far right, but the public as a whole. That's our ideal. Our ideal is to try to be a newspaper that can reach the public and convey a basic point of view.[170]

The Liberty Lobby's founder, Willis Carto, has the reputation of being a shadowy figure and is said to run his organization in an authoritarian fashion, brooking no dissent from his underlings. These leadership traits are at once essential to hold such a fractious and unstable collection of individuals together, yet at the same time have provoked many internecine battles with his former associates. However, the true picture of Carto is probably a bit more complicated than the caricature of an authoritarian egoist with a personality cult. In a movement as fractious as the American far right, it would require someone with considerable diplomacy to foster ties and close working relationships with such a broad number and character-range of activists.

Carto began his career in far-right politics in the 1950s. Like many other activists, he sojourned briefly in the John Birch Society. In 1954 he launched a journal called *Right*, which discussed various conspiracy and racist themes. A major event in his life occurred in 1960, when he visited Francis Parker Yockey in his San Francisco jail cell. Yockey was being held for passport violations and was suspected by the State Department and FBI of being involved in espionage against the United States.[171] Eventually, Yockey committed suicide by swallowing cyanide pills. According to legend, Carto was the last man to see him alive. Yockey left quite an impression on Carto, as he once remarked, "I knew that I was in the presence of a great force," and "I could feel history standing aside me."[172] Carto would go on to publish Yockey's book through his Noontide Press. In doing so, he popularized Yockey in the American far right. Carto offered some of his thoughts on Yockey to me:

> I was instrumental in publishing his work, *Imperium*, which is quite a book. And anybody who has read it, whether he agrees with or not, cannot read the book one time and understand it. It has to be studied. It has some very interesting historical and philosophical ideas. I certainly can't give a lesson on it today, but I can tell you that anyone who is interested can read the book and read my introduction to it.
>
> Do I think his philosophy is still relevant today? Well, that's a hard one, but I'd say probably not because of the complete disintegration of the West. He foresaw a struggle between the West and the Soviet Union. He saw it in Spenglerian terms. I just don't think that things in the interim have, the last forty years, developed in the way that he foresaw. ... I wouldn't say that he was sympathetic towards communism. Anybody who reads his book can see that's preposterous. But he was sympathetic towards the Russian people. Yockey was a nationalist. He believed in nationalism, as I do. Nationalism is an indispensable philosophy for any group of people. Yockey, you might say in current terms, was not a multiculturalist. He knew that multiculturalism could only bring the downfall of all cultures. He knew that multiculturalism would simply reduce all of mankind down to the level of the lowest. And he was opposed to that. He was a very cultured man. I can't say that I agree with all of his thinking, and this was made clear in my introduction. But he was not pro-communist in any way shape or form.[173]

Over the years, Carto has endeavored to build a network with which the disparate segments of the far right could unite; no mean task considering the various contradictions and rivalries between them. However, perhaps more so than any figure, Carto was the man for such a task. His worldview syncretizes numerous conspiracy theories and seemingly contradictory philosophies. For example, the *Spotlight* contains articles with anti-statist themes that are highly critical of big government programs, like Hillary Clinton's proposed national health care plan. This would seem to be at odds with the organic socialism idealized by Yockey and other National Socialists. Carto, though, sees no such contradiction.

> Yes, I can see how these would be an apparent contradiction to people who don't understand what Yockey was talking about. He was talking about an ethical socialism, which really is not Marxism in any way. But as far as the United States of America, Yockey saw, and I saw, that the American nation

has to work out its own destiny within the traditions of American history. And that means representative government and it means the Constitution and it means individual liberty. We've always espoused that. At no time have I said that the United States would have to go to some dictatorship ...

I see no conflict at all with Yockey's international philosophy you might say and historical Spenglerian foundation. But that certainly does not affect the Liberty Lobby's beliefs that since the very beginning the public has to regenerate America and has to put pressure on these guys over here two blocks away [from the Liberty Lobby's HQ in downtown Washington DC] to make them do right. They're not going to do it on their own. They're going to go along with the pressure groups and the big money.[174]

Carto champions a "populist" version of right-wing extremism, which contains many anti-plutocratic and anti-big business themes. Towards this end, Carto edited a book, *Populism vs. Plutocracy: The Universal Struggle*, which highlighted various populists in American history.[175] He shared with me his thoughts on the future of American populism:

The left and right bridge has to be surmounted and it is being surmounted. I mean, I don't have to tell you about the demonstrations all over the world [against the World Trade Organization]. The left is desperately afraid of [globalization], for their own reasons, which really overlaps with our reasons. ... They're against it. We're against it. And we're cooperating with them every way that we can. Of course the left has the image that the ADL has been so successful in [inculcating, and are] trying to scare them away from us from the right. ... Populism has certain ideas, certain values, certain issues that the left and right can both support and they can bridge this gap. If that can happen, or I say, when that happens, because it is going to happen, why this will be a whole different political complexion in this country.[176]

The *Spotlight*'s articles seek to draw attention to the machinations of "globalists" such as the Trilateral Commission, the Council on Foreign Relations, and the Bilderberger Group. These themes appeal to much of the Christian Patriot/militia movement. The *Spotlight* also contains stories that appeal to the racialist right. However, its anti-Semitism is more concealed than in other racialist right organs. Thus, the *Spotlight* is an important bridge between the various segments of the far right, but somewhat unique insofar as the conspiracy theories to which the various segments of the far right subscribe are usually delineated into one of two themes. One theme, popularized by the John Birch Society, decries various globalist organizations such as the CFR, Bilderberger Group, etc., which are seen as inimical to national sovereignty and during the Cold War were thought to have aided and abetted international communism. However, anti-Semitic themes, as a general rule, are not included, and even frowned upon in this style of conspiracy theory. By contrast, the racialist right emphasizes an alleged Zionist or Jewish conspiracy as the guiding hand behind these globalist organizations, and pays little attention to organizations such as the CFR and Bilderberger Group. To some observers this may appear to be opportunism on the part of Carto to blend all these conspiracy themes together in order to appeal to a larger audience. However, Carto's past indicates that he is actually very intellectually eclectic and is able to integrate these seemingly disparate themes into his worldview.

The Liberty Lobby is unique insofar as it has occasionally gained access to elected officials. This is in marked contrast to most of the far right, which either eschews conventional means of politics or is shunned by politicians. The *Spotlight* encourages its readers to contact their elected representatives on public policy issues. On some occasions, Carto dabbles in electoral politics – he worked in George Wallace's 1968 presidential campaign and created the Youth for Wallace organization.[177] In the early 1980s, Carto launched the Populist Party in an effort to establish a political party that would field populist-style candidates in elections. This project was quickly beset with internecine squabbles over its platform and money, and eventually folded.

Over his long career, Carto has fought several pitched battles against his chief nemesis, the ADL. For example, during the 1970s, the ADL worked tirelessly on a successful campaign to dissuade radio stations from carrying the *This is the Liberty Lobby* radio program.[178] On numerous occasions the ADL has issued critical reports on Carto and described him as the "leading anti-Semite in America."[179] However, in recent years, the late Dr Pierce of the National Alliance received that designation. Inasmuch as Willis Carto has fought several pitched battles with the ADL, it is not surprising that he would identify that watchdog organization as his most formidable opponent:

> Oh, I suppose the ADL is the most prominent. They have regional offices all over the country. The ADL has a library, a database on me and they've been inspiring many, many people to be confused and hateful towards me. And really, the people don't know anything about the issues. ... They demonize me just to get people misled who don't want to look behind this hater. ... This is why we don't have a bigger circulation for *Spotlight*. The *Spotlight* is referred to by the ADL over and over and over again as the most anti-Semitic paper in the country. You know, I'm the biggest anti-Semite in the country. ... they can raise a lot of money on me. Morris Dees and the Anti-Defamation League believe me have raised a lot more money demonizing me than I ever raised for the Liberty Lobby. ... They smear me so nobody will pay any attention to me.[180]

Fortunately for Carto, he has managed to avoid serious entanglements with the government, although it has taken notice of the Liberty Lobby on past occasions.[181] One particular project on which Carto has expended much energy, and which has also provoked fierce opposition from the watchdog groups, is Holocaust Revisionism.

The Holocaust/historical revisionist movement

One of the major obstacles that the far right has faced in the postwar era has been the legacy of the Holocaust. The enormity of this event did much to stigmatize postwar fascism and discredit anti-Semitism. Over the past few decades the Holocaust has gained the status of a singularity, unique from other historical events that have occurred. While historians concede that more people may have perished in Stalin's gulags or Mao's Great Cultural Revolution, the cold and methodical way in which the Holocaust was prosecuted is seen by many as the epitome of what Hanna Arendt referred to as the "banality of evil." What's more, the sheer amount of physical evidence and eyewitness accounts would seem to have made the historical occurrence of the Holocaust beyond dispute.

However, various intellectual tendencies that emerged in the 1960s created an atmosphere in which nearly every verity – no matter how seemingly true – could be challenged. This intellectual *Zeitgeist* encouraged skepticism and posits that there are two sides to every story. Nothing in history is off-limits to skeptical inquiry. Seen in this light, Holocaust revisionism is in some ways the far right's answer to deconstructionism.

Holocaust revisionism began shortly after World War II, and its first notable proponent was the Frenchman Paul Rassinier, a former communist and socialist, who also happened to have been interned in the Buchenwald and Dora concentration camps. Over the years a disparate collection of Germanophiles, anti-Zionists, and radical skeptics dabbled in what could be called Holocaust revisionism. However, the movement really achieved notoriety and academic coherence when an engineering professor at Northwestern University, Arthur Butz, published *The Hoax of the Twentieth Century* in 1976. Heretofore, the movement consisted of individuals with no real institutional framework. This changed in 1979 when Willis Carto, the leader of the Liberty Lobby, founded the Institute for Historical Review. Although various individuals in the Holocaust revisionist movement may deny their affiliation or support for the radical right, the fact remains that it was Carto, a scion of the far right, who gave the movement a sound organizational basis.

According to Holocaust scholar Deborah Lipstadt, Holocaust revisionism is an attempt by the radical right to rehabilitate the historical legacy of the Third Reich, and by doing so, make postwar fascism more palatable to the public. Although that assessment may be somewhat over-simplified due to the various ideological tendencies in the movement, there remains a good deal of truth to the assertion.[182] Historical revisionism is important to the far right for another reason as well. For many in the movement, World War II is viewed as a monumental watershed in the course of Western history. As they see it, the direction that cultural and political events of Europe and America have taken in the past fifty years were set in motion during the war and have taken a drastic course for the worse. In short, the war is seen as tragic fratricidal conflict between the various peoples of the West, and therefore that period must be critically reexamined.[183]

The Institute for Historical Review has remained the main purveyor of

Holocaust revisionist material. It publishes a periodical, *The Journal of Historical Review*, that has the accoutrements of scholarship, including articles with footnotes and a board of editors, etc. Many of the IHR's publications are offered for sale in far-right book catalogs. Some of the high-profile Holocaust revisionists, such as David Irving, regularly speak at functions sponsored by far-right organizations.[184]

As is so often the case with Carto's projects, the IHR eventually had a falling out with Carto and split from him and the Liberty Lobby in 1993. The leader of the IHR, Mark Weber, criticized Carto for his racism and reportedly wanted to build a more credible academic think tank untainted by right-wing extremism. Despite Weber's efforts, the IHR is still considered beyond the pale of respectability in most academic quarters. Undeterred, shortly after the split with the IHR, Carto founded the Center for Historical Review, another Holocaust revisionist think tank, which publishes a journal called *Barnes Review*.

What began as Holocaust revisionism has expanded over the years to include many other topics, such as Allied atrocities during and after World War II, the defense of American isolationism and populism, and of course two of its main staples, criticism of Israel and Zionism. Thus, for lack of a better term, the movement is sometimes referred to as historical revisionism, although some mainstream historians may see that as an arrogation and misuse of a legitimate term.

Although the Holocaust revisionists do not appear to have had much success in revising the historiography of the Holocaust, they have been able to generate substantial controversy and publicity. By pushing the envelope to the limit, they have forced Western governments to grapple with various free speech issues. This puts the various Jewish defense organizations in a dilemma. If they do nothing they fear that the revisionists will trivialize the memory of the greatest tragedy in recent Jewish history. However, if they encourage authorities and forums to censor the revisionists they risk falling into the trap of giving the revisionists unnecessary publicity. It appears that the revisionists are well aware of this. A content analysis of the *Journal of Historical Review* revealed that the most frequent theme it covered was not actual review of history, but rather how the revisionists were treated by the media, Jewish defense organizations, the government, and other critics.[185] The Holocaust revisionist movement has indeed occasioned fierce opposition from several quarters. In foreign countries, revisionists are often prosecuted under "hate speech" statutes and receive stiff penalties. The mainstream Jewish defense organizations have sought to keep their publications out of circulation and dissuade institutions from providing them with speaking fora. Finally, revisionists have occasionally come under attack from vigilante-style groups.[186]

In recent years revisionists have sought to use the internet as a medium through which to publicize their message and peculiar historiography. Most notable in this regard is the "Zündelsite," created by one Dr Ingrid Rimland to disseminate materials published by Ernst Zündel, a German expatriate who emigrated to Canada. Zündel has long been active in the revisionist movement and has gained considerable notoriety for his activities in Canada, which resulted in several protracted legal controversies, including a case that went all the way to the Canadian Supreme Court.[187] Dr Rimland recounted the creation of the Zündelsite:

> At the International Revisionist Convention put on by the Institute for Historical Review in 1994, I heard for the first time about a medium called the "internet." I vaguely remember a conversation with Ernst Zündel where he asked me to "look into it." Neither he nor I really knew at the time what its potential was.
>
> I bought some books and started reading, but since I am a techno-dummy, it did not make much sense. It was only after the Zündel-Haus arson in May of 1995 that I became serious about the Net. By then I knew a bit more about Ernst Zündel's struggle and problems with the media, and since I had considerable experience as a writer and PR person, I offered to volunteer my skills for some systematic public relations work.
>
> The Internet seemed a natural, but I was seriously hampered by my lack of computer skills. I took some classes and bought more "how-to" books and very painfully familiarized myself with internet principles such as HTML coding. That summer I bought some web space with an internet company in Santa Cruz, California, called Web Communications, Webcom in short, and laboriously proceeded to put some pages and graphics on the Net.
>
> I called my internet embryo the "Zündelsite" because I wanted it to have a strong "Zündel identity" and be easily recognizable as an entity. It must have been the name that triggered the animosity of a group that called itself "The Nizkor Project" because I was repeatedly and aggressively challenged – "heckled" – is a better term – to join a news group called alt-revisionism and "defend" the accuracy of the documents on the Zündelsite.
>
> The assaults on me and my integrity were quite vicious in that news group and even on my telephone, and I became aware for the first time that there were what Revisionists later called "Internet terrorists" patrolling the World Wide Web whose sole function was to intimidate, ridicule, character assassinate and howl down any opposition to groups and organizations such as the Wiesenthal Center, the ADL, the World Jewish Congress and similar outfits.
>
> A lot of the attacks emanated from what we started calling "Nizkorites" – prominently among them one Ken McVay, ostensibly the owner of Nizkor, and Jamie McCarthy, its webmaster. I was deeply shocked to be so mendaciously attacked, because I had spent a lifetime – first in academia and public schools and later as an educational professional in private practice and writer/lecturer – crafting a respectable professional name for myself,

and no one had ever called me such filthy names and invented so many false stories about me …

I began posting some classic Revisionist documents, among them Richard Harwood's well-known *Did Six Million Really Die?* and Barbara Kulaszka's transcript condensation by the same name of the 1988 Great Holocaust Zündel Trial.

The Wiesenthalers went into a tail spin! I have been told that 2,000 letters went out within hours to university presidents alerting them not to pay any attention to us, and about a week later Telekom, a privatized former state telecommunications outfit in Germany, electronically blackened out the Zündelsite mission statement and shortly thereafter blocked access to some 1,300 websites on Webcom, the world's third largest ISP.

The first cyber war in the history of mankind was on! One of my readers commented that he "felt the planet lurch"! This action caused the "War of the Blue Ribbons" in early 1996 and lasted approximately 4 weeks. Spontaneously, university students and Freedom of Speech activists all over the world took on the Zündelsite cause and created mirror sites of their own in America, Canada, Europe and as far away as Australia. Wherever you see a Blue Ribbon connoting Free Speech in Cyberspace – think Zündelsite![188]

Several important developments have recently occurred in the revisionist movement. First, the IHR won a civil judgment against its former parent organization, the Liberty Lobby and Willis Carto. In the early 1990s, Jean Farrel Edison, an heiress to the Thomas Edison estate, bequeathed a $15 million dollar inheritance to the IHR. Carto claimed to have had control over the IHR when the will was consummated and thus be entitled to the money. However, in December 2000, California Superior Court Judge Runston G. Maino ruled otherwise and ordered the Liberty Lobby to surrender its assets to the IHR.[189] The judge issued a stay of execution until April 2001. However, in July 2001, US bankruptcy Judge S. Martin Teel Jr finally put an end to the complicated eight-year battle as he ordered the Liberty Lobby to surrender its assets to the IHR.[190] Thus in an ironic twist of fate, one of the most longstanding institutions of the far right was forced to close shop, not due to its watchdog opponents, but rather to an internecine feud.[191] The story took a strange twist, as Mark Weber allegedly sought to sell the Liberty Lobby's mailing list to the ADL.[192] Despite this apparent setback, the Liberty Lobby reconstituted itself and its *Spotlight* publication as the *American Free Press* later that year.

A second recent development of import was a scheduled conference on "Revisionism and Zionism," which was scheduled for late March of 2001 in Beirut, Lebanon. Although the event was cancelled at the last minute, it demonstrates a growing cooperation between the Western revisionists and Islamic sympathizers. The Institute for Historical Review and the Swiss-based Verité et Justice had planned the conference, which was to include lectures in English, French, and Arabic. The Swiss organizer, Jürgen Graf, had recently fled to Iran – a country reportedly where other revisionists have received a warm welcome –

after his appeals of a 1998 Swiss conviction for hate speech violations had been denied. The scheduled event had occasioned fierce opposition from the Jewish defense watchdog groups. The Simon Wiesenthal Center took the lead in a lobbying effort that also included the Anti-Defamation League and the World Jewish Congress in putting pressure on the Lebanese government to cancel the event. The US State Department also put pressure on the Lebanese government. After a cabinet meeting on the subject, Lebanese Prime Minister Rafik Hairi announced that the conference would be cancelled. Not to be deterred, the conference was ultimately held, albeit in a scaled-down version, in Amman, Jordan.

There would seem to be a meeting of minds between the far right and some anti-Zionist extremists. The conference held in 2001 could presage future cooperation between the two camps. According to the ADL, Holocaust revisionism has gained considerable currency in the media of several Middle East countries, including Egypt, Iran, Syria, Lebanon, Qatar, as well as in that of the Palestinian Authority.[193] Thus the Holocaust revisionists may find a receptive audience among some quarters in the Middle East.

Conclusion

Presently the American far right is in a state of flux. It appears that the Patriot/militia movement is in rapid retreat. However, other segments in the racialist right, most notably the Southern heritage movement, appear to be gaining ground. The Council of Conservative Citizens has demonstrated viability in recent years in several ways, such as gaining more members and access to elected officials.

The Christian Patriot and racialist right are really two distinct movements. Although various watchdog groups have attempted to link the two, for the most part the former eschews the latter's racism. However, there is some overlap and meeting of the minds between the two in the areas of the Christian Identity theology, conspiracy theories, and strong criticism of the federal government.

The National Alliance also appears to be strengthening, and according to the ADL is now the most dangerous hate group. A large part of the preceding discussion has dealt with the National Socialist segment, of which the National Alliance is the most significant organization. Although Nazism is arguably the most hated ideology in America, and although the hard core segment has always been small, it has had an influence far beyond what its membership numbers would suggest. While it's true that this segment is notorious for attracting more than its share of crackpots, it has also attracted a number of very dedicated and literate individuals who have done considerable theorizing on the predicament of the far right *vis-à-vis* the larger society. Leaders such as George Lincoln Rockwell, Matt Koehl, Joseph Tomassi, Martin Kerr, Harold Covington, Pövl Riis-Knudsen, Colin Jordan and William Pierce have been keenly aware of the *Zeitgeist* and have continually strategized for ways to effect their political and social goals. This has given their ideology an enduring quality, as it is frequently refined to reflect current conditions. Over the years, the National Socialists have established somewhat of a "hegemony of ideas" in the far-right movement, as they have heavily influenced other segments such as the skinheads, Christian Identity, and the Ku Klux Klan.[194] What's more, the National Socialists have been among the most internationally oriented, and have built alliances, albeit modest ones, with like-minded activists in other countries.

As much of the preceding discussion illustrates, the far-right groups could be characterized as, according to Seymour Martin Lipset's term, "preservatist."[195] In that sense many are backward-looking and idealize a mythic golden age, as one observer explained:

> Many groups on the far right are extremely fond of developing their own rituals, especially rites of passage, and of re-telling and re-tooling history until it verges on the status of myth. … Participants in the sub-cultures of the far right also seldom tire of reviewing American history, generally in order to pinpoint where things went wrong and by implication to identify the golden age to which we should all aspire to return.[196]

However, there is quite a degree of variation in this theme. For instance, the Patriot movement looks to the American Revolution for inspiration, while the neo-Confederates look to the Civil War. The Odinists idealize the Viking era, while the National Socialists and many of the historical revisionists admire Hitler's Third Reich. The Church of the Creator idealizes not only the Third Reich, but also the Roman Empire and the American Western frontier of the nineteenth century. And Christian Identity followers identify with the lost tribes of Israel. History thus appears to loom much larger in the far right than in the political left, which tends to be more forward-looking.

As the above comments from some of the far-right activists have made clear, there are really only two watchdog groups that matter: the Anti-Defamation League and the Southern Poverty Law Center. The far right is virtually oblivious to all other watchdog groups. This is no surprise insofar as these are the two watchdog groups that are most likely to directly impinge on the activities of far-right organizations through such measures as civil suits, surveillance and legislation. Generally speaking, there is a grudging respect for the ADL among the denizens of the far right. It is viewed as a formidable opponent – indeed the embodiment of ZOG. By contrast, Morris Dees and the Southern Poverty Law Center are seen as opportunistic and as exploiting the far right for their own personal enrichment. There is obviously much hostility between the watchdogs and their right-wing ideological adversaries, and little prospect for dialogue between the two sides. Each camp tends to see the other in terms of absolutes.

As Walter Laqueur observed, the American right-wing extremist groups are defensive in nature.[197] The racialist right sees itself under siege by aliens that threaten to undermine its traditions. The movement often couches its slogans in terms of racial survival. Likewise, the Patriot movement sees its liberties threatened by an increasingly intrusive and tyrannical federal government. As an FBI report noted, militias are generally reactive as opposed to proactive. They are more inclined to sit back and wait for things to happen.[198] Overall, both movements remain relatively small, disunited and organizationally weak, as they do not command a great deal of resources.[199] Still another problem they face is age. Some of their most prominent leaders are in their sixties and seventies, which could present a problem of continuity in upcoming years. What's more, by and large the far right is a very stigmatized movement, with neither significant grassroots nor elite support. This is in marked contrast to its watchdog opponents, who are much better financed and enjoy a good deal of respectability. Despite this asymmetry between the two sides, the American far right has demonstrated a dogged persistence and a remarkable capacity to continually reinvent itself.

Its weakness and lack of broad-based support notwithstanding, many of those in the far right believe that in a sense, history is on their side. They are generally very pessimistic about the future of America, and forecast that conditions will one day change in their favor. Their various magazines, newspapers and newsletters are filled with lurid stories of the consequences of such trends as crime, racial integration, immigration and globalization – stories that would, as one observer noted, do the supermarket tabloids proud.[200] Moreover, they draw selectively from various corpuses of mainstream literature to support their prognostications.[201] More recently, the incidence of ethnic conflict in many regions around the world, such as in the Balkans and in Rwanda, is invoked to give credence to their warnings of the consequences of multiculturalism in America. Finally, a frequent theme invoked is one of economic cataclysm, which will usher in a revolutionary period and radicalize Whites out of their complacency. In this sense, their analysis is Marxian, as they presage the demise of contemporary capitalism.[202]

Several factors militate against any significant electoral strategy for the American far right. First, as mentioned above, the movement is weak and does not really command the resources to create a viable party. Second, the American winner-takes-all electoral system discourages third parties. This is in contrast to the countries of continental Europe which have adopted the system of proportional representation. Thus it is no surprise that it is in those countries in which the far right has enjoyed the most electoral success. Finally, the changing demographics in America, whereby it is projected that over half of the population will be non-White by mid-century, makes a racial exclusionist party unfeasible at the national level. For these and other reasons, some elements of the far right have decided that a strategy of revolution and terrorism is the only viable alternative to effect their political and social goals. It is to that topic which we shall now turn.

4 The far right and terrorism

Introduction

Terrorism and other forms of political and social violence have long been associated with the far right. During the mid-nineteenth century, members of the reactionary Know-Nothing movement were occasionally involved in violent confrontations with Catholics and immigrants, most notably in the riot in New Orleans, Louisiana in 1858.[1] Right-wing violence in America reached its highwater mark during the Reconstruction Era Ku Klux Klan's reign of terror in the aftermath of the Civil War. The total amount of carnage that the hooded order perpetrated during that period is difficult to quantify, but it is estimated that in the state of Louisiana alone it was responsible for at least 2,000 killed, wounded or injured in the few weeks preceding the presidential election of 1868. In addition other estimates of violence for that period include seventy-five killings reported in Georgia, 109 in Alabama, and more than 150 for one single county in Georgia.[2] The primary victims were Black freedmen, "scalawags," "carpetbaggers" and Radical Republicans. The Klan's membership is estimated to have reached 555,000 during the Reconstruction period.[3] The Second Era Ku Klux Klan, which reached its zenith in the 1920s, had more than its share of violent episodes as it targeted primarily Blacks, Catholics and "morally lapsed" White Anglo-Saxon Protestants. According to one estimate there have been 245 incidents of right-wing terrorism since 1978.[4] Although other forms of organized violence have punctuated American history, such as episodes from the political left and organized labor, right-wing violence appears to have a longer history and a more enduring quality.

This chapter looks at right-wing terrorism and violence in America. The first section examines the recent patterns of right-wing terrorism. The second section examines some of the more noteworthy episodes of right-wing terrorism. The third section explains the theorizing that has gone on within the far-right movement on the subject of terrorism, including various strategies and their feasibility. Lastly, the conclusion presents some final comments on this topic.

Patterns of right-wing terrorism

It is very difficult to quantify with precision the incidence of terrorism in the United States. The American criminal justice system treats terrorism as a crime. When caught, terrorists are tried in regular courts as there is no special classification for the crime of "terrorism." The FBI has endeavored to classify and collate terrorist incidents in America. However, much of its data on domestic terrorism are inconsistent and unreliable due to changing classifications of terrorist incidents.[5] What's more, as a 1976 government report demonstrated, the sheer number of violent incidents of a political or quasi-political nature make this effort all the more cumbersome.[6] Finally, due to the wide range in the severity of violent incidents – ranging from scuffles with police and minor injuries to bombings and homicides – it is difficult to ascertain and operationalize an overall level of seriousness or threat posed from a particular variant of political extremism in comparison to others.

Chris Hewitt made a significant contribution towards this effort by collating the number of fatalities in America by different categories of terrorists for the period 1955–98. By focusing on fatalities, researchers now have a good database by which to measure and compare different variants of terrorism. This section draws upon Hewitt's research to discern recent patterns of domestic right-wing terrorism. Table 4.1 presents the statistics for right-wing terrorism taken from Hewitt's study. His data omit the fatalities connected with the 1995 Oklahoma City bombing.

Table 4.1 Terrorist fatality victims classified by type

Victim type	Far-right wave I Percentage	Number	Far-right wave II Percentage	Number	Total Percentage	Number
Politicians/ officials	0.0	0	1.7	2	1.2	2
Police/ military	0.0	0	7.5	9	5.1	9
Factional	1.8	1	2.5	3	2.3	4
Enemy activists	44.6	25	8.3	10	19.9	35
Hate crimes/ random	50.0	28	70.8	85	64.2	113
Informers	3.6	2	5.8	7	5.1	9
Robbery	0.0	0	0.8	1	0.5	1
Accidental	0.0	0	0.8	1	0.5	1
Total	100	56	100	120	100	176

Source: Hewitt, Christopher. "Patterns of American Terrorism 1955 - 1998: An Historical Perspective on Terrorism-Related Fatalities 1955 - 1998." *Terrorism and Political Violence* 12 (1), pp.1-14 (2000).

According to Hewitt, since 1955 right-wing terrorism has occurred in two distinct waves. The first wave began in the early years of the Civil Rights era in the 1950s, and ended in the early 1970s. By his calculation, there were fifty-six fatalities attributed to right-wing violence during that period. Most of the terrorist fatalities occurred in the South (forty-six deaths or 82 per cent).[7] Those targeted by right-wing terrorists fell into just a few distinct categories. Fifty per cent of the victims (twenty-eight) were targeted for no other reason than some ascriptive characteristic such as race or ethnicity. This was followed closely by "enemy activists," in this case usually civil rights workers (twenty-five deaths or 44.6 per cent). Suspected informants and factional disputes accounted for two and one deaths respectively. The second wave of right-wing terrorism commenced in 1978 and still continues. According to the Israeli political scientist, Ehud Sprinzak, right-wing terrorism is characterized by a process of "split-delegitimation," in which not only the "outsider" (e.g. foreigners, ethnic and religious minorities, reds, and gays) is targeted but contemporaneously, the very state itself, which is seen as ineffective, or worse yet, under the actual sway of the outsiders. This theoretically leads to an evolution of right-wing terrorism. At first the terrorists usually avoid confrontations with authorities and their animus is directed at the "outsider." However, eventually they convince themselves that the government is not doing enough to protect the "original community" and the state also becomes a target.[8] On an ideological level Sprinzak's theory holds up well, as those in the revolutionary racialist right view their governments as under the heel of "ZOG."

On an empirical level, Hewitt's data lend support to the applicability of Sprinzak's theory to American domestic right-wing terrorism. For his identified second wave of right-wing terrorism, there is evidence to support the proposition that representatives of the state have been targeted with increasing frequency. Although the vast majority of victims of right-wing violence still fall into the "hate crime/random" category (eighty-five deaths or 70.8 per cent), also targeted were politicians and representatives of the police, none of whom were killed in the first wave. As Hewitt's data demonstrate, during the Civil Rights era various Ku Klux Klan groups targeted almost exclusively blacks and civil rights workers. Government officials were not targeted. To the contrary, on some occasions local law enforcement officials were bona fide Klan members or worked hand-in-glove with the group.[9] However, in the second wave, right-wing terrorists were extremely hostile to the police and killed several of them (nine deaths or 7.5 per cent). Whereas two politicians were also killed during this wave, none were killed in the first. Several episodes during the 1990s, in which members of the Patriot movement targeted state facilities and government representatives, also support Sprinzak's theory.[10]

Other victims listed by Hewitt included "enemy activists" (ten deaths or 8.3 per cent), "informers" (seven deaths or 5.8 per cent), "factional" and "robbery" (both categories claimed three victims or 2.5 per cent each), and "accidental (one death or 0.8 per cent). All totaled, 120 fatalities were counted in the second

96 *The far right and terrorism*

wave. The second wave differed in two ways. First, whereas the vast majority of terrorist activity was confined to the South in the first wave (82 per cent), in the second wave the majority of activity (64 per cent) occurred outside of the South.

Second, the various Klan organizations played a much lesser role in the second wave.[11] The vigilance of the FBI effectively quelled the Klan of the Civil Rights era, and serious right-wing violence for the most part dissipated. However, by the late 1970s a new pattern of right-wing terrorism emerged, characterized by organizational fragmentation and a new revolutionary orientation. The next section highlights the more significant episodes of right-wing violence that have punctuated the current wave.

Significant episodes of right-wing terrorism

The Greensboro Massacre

If one had to pinpoint a particular incident that really marked the genesis of the revolutionary orientation of the far right, it would be the Greensboro Massacre in 1979. On November 3 of that year, members of a neo-Nazi party, the National Socialist Party of America, and a local Ku Klux Klan organization clashed with demonstrators led by members of the Communist Workers Party in a "Death to the Klan" rally. The confrontation had been a culmination in a series of disputes between the two sides. At the demonstration a shootout between the two sides ensued, in which five members of the Communist Workers Party were fatally wounded. The Klansmen and Neo-Nazis suffered no serious casualties.

The shootout in Greensboro raised some nagging questions about the use of police informants in investigating extremist groups. According to some accounts, a police informant, Edward Dawson, instigated the confrontation.[12] The incident also brought attention to an intriguing figure in the far right, one Harold Covington, who at that time was the leader of the NSPA. Over the years he has earned a very controversial reputation in the far right. Highly literate and articulate, he has done a significant amount of writing and theorizing on strategy.[13] However, he has also been involved in some very bitter internecine feuds that have led some activists to impugn his propriety and credentials in the movement. Covington was a principal organizer of the demonstration, but was conspicuously absent from the actual event. Rumors surfaced among both left- and right-wing activists that he was an informant and agent provocateur for the FBI, BATF and CIA. For his part, Covington denies these allegations:

> The allegations come from a book entitled *Code Name Greenkil*, written by a leftist lesbian named Elizabeth Wheaton who was, and for all I know still is, employed by an old CPUSA front group called the Institute for Southern Studies and its magazine, *Southern Exposure*, which may or may not be

defunct by now. There is little I can say, except that Wheaton is a politically motivated liar with a transparent agenda. ... I have always found it wryly amusing that people who claim to hate leftists and lesbian perverts suddenly decide that on this one subject – Harold Covington – a carpet-munching Commie speaks with ex-cathedra infallibility.[14]

In two subsequent trials – one local and one federal – juries acquitted all of the defendants.[15] The juries were convinced by the self-defense arguments put forth by the defense counsels. This clash was significant because it was the first high-profile incident of right-wing violence since the Civil Rights era. Moreover, it demonstrated that Klansmen and neo-Nazis could cooperate. Previously, Klansmen looked askance at the foreign and un-American orientation of the neo-Nazis. Henceforth, neo-Nazism would have a significant influence on the ideology of a much broader portion of the racialist right. For many in the movement, Greensboro was seen as an event equal in symbolic significance to Lexington and Concord. This event would also be the catalyst for the creation of a progressive-oriented watchdog group, the National Anti-Klan Network, which would go on to become the Center for Democratic Renewal.

Gordon Kahl and the Posse Comitatus

The farm crisis of the mid-1980s provided a seedbed for right-wing extremism in America's heartland. One of the more prominent organizations in that area of the country was the Posse Comitatus. Despite its sometimes bombastic rhetoric, the Posse posed only a minor irritant to authorities. However, that changed on February 13, 1983, when a Posse affiliate and radical tax protestor, Gordon Kahl, got embroiled in a confrontation with federal authorities in Medina, North Dakota. A group of lawmen sought to serve Kahl a warrant for tax violations. Extremely distrustful of authorities, Kahl refused to be served and a shootout ensued in which two marshals died and four others were wounded, including Kahl's son Yorie. Amazingly, Kahl a sixty-three-year-old farmer and World War II veteran, had single-handedly caused the authorities to retreat.

Kahl evaded authorities for about four months, but on June 3, 1983, they finally caught up with him in Lawrence County, Arkansas. Still defiant, Kahl managed to mortally wound a local sheriff, who also happened to fire a fatal shot which struck Kahl in the head. Not realizing that Kahl was dead, the lawmen attempted to force Kahl outside of his bunker dwelling by pouring fuel down the chimney. The place went up in flames and sparked rumors that the FBI had summarily executed Kahl then incinerated his corpse and murdered the slain sheriff to cover up the truth.[16] As a result, Kahl entered the far right's pantheon of martyrs. His death also became the catalyst and a call to arms of an underground right-wing terrorist group, the Order.

The Order

Shortly after the death of Gordon Kahl, an annual Aryan Nations Congress was held at the compound in Hayden Lake, Idaho in the summer of 1983. At that meeting a young charismatic member of the National Alliance, Robert Jay Matthews, hatched the idea that an underground resistance group ought to be created to avenge the death of Kahl. Matthews had considerable powers of persuasion and was able to ultimately draw nearly fifty members into his clandestine terrorist group, "the Order."[17] It went on a crime spree in the early 1980s, which included several armored car heists, robberies, bombings, and at least five homicides.[18]

Matthews reportedly drew much inspiration for his organization from a novel, *The Turner Diaries*, written by his ideological mentor Dr William Pierce (under the pseudonym Andrew Macdonald), the chairman of the National Alliance, who died in 2002. Reportedly Matthews made the novel required reading for all members. It is perhaps the most widely read book in the subterranean world of the far right, and has sold approximately 350,000 copies – an amazing figure for an underground book.[19] Inasmuch as the book is thought to have been an inspiration for the Order and has been connected to several significant episodes of right-wing terrorism, it is worth a brief examination.[20]

Cleverly written as a novel, it tells the story of a cellular White-supremacist revolutionary group, which conducts a terrorist campaign against the US government, which it regards as merely a front for a Jewish cabal working from behind the scenes. According to the editor in the preface of the book, it is the year 100 in the New Era, 100 years after the Great Revolution, which culminated in 1999. A recent excavation of the ruins of Washington DC has unearthed the diaries of one "Earl Turner," a resistance fighter in the "Great Revolution." The rest of the novel is supposed to be his account of a race war that convulsed the world at the close of the twentieth century. According to the story, the character Turner was an important yet relatively low-level figure who belonged to a resistance movement known as the "Organization," which had waged a war against the "System." The Organization's exploits include armed robbery to procure the necessary funds to carry out its struggle. Government buildings and other important institutions are targeted. The objective is to weaken the "System" and also to polarize the population.

A struggle of apocalyptic proportions ensues as American society implodes under the weight of racial strife. The book contains numerous episodes of very graphic violence interspersed with ideological digressions. A veritable race war leads to ethnic cleansing writ large, which degenerates into the most bestial behavior, including cannibalism. In a grisly orgy of retribution, the Organization punishes so-called race-traitors in a spectacle called "the Day of the Rope," in which tens of thousands are strung up on lampposts, power poles and trees throughout southern California. Eventually the Organization acquires nuclear weapons and a global atomic war ensues involving America, the Soviet Union and Israel. For his service, Turner is inducted into a quasi-monastic inner circle of the Organization known as "the Order." His final mission is to fly a small crop duster plane equipped with a nuclear bomb on a kamikaze mission to destroy the Pentagon. Turner selflessly agrees and succeeds, thus dealing the system its fatal blow. From that point the Organization gains the upper hand and by 1999 "just 110 years after the birth of the great one" (read Adolf Hitler) victory is clearly in sight.[21] After victory in America, the revolution spreads throughout the rest of the world. The book closes with a millennial tone. From the ashes of devastation the West experiences a civilizational renewal and is once again master of its own destiny.

There has been much speculation on what Pierce's true intentions were when he wrote the book. Many of his critics, and indeed some of his admirers, contend that it is a blueprint for a revolution and terrorism campaign. For his part, Pierce attributed other reasons for writing the book. I put it to him that his critics, and some of his supporters for that matter, say that his novel the *Turner Diaries* is a blueprint for a revolution. Did he agree with this assessment? This was his reply:

> Well, in a word, no. In 1975, I was commiserating with a friend who was a professor in classics at the Urbana campus at the University of Illinois [Revilio P. Oliver] and I said, "look I got seventy-five news racks spread all over downtown DC. I talk about issues that are earthshakingly important. These are vital issues. It's the survival of our race, the survival of our civilization, the survival of America, and people aren't paying any attention. They're just going about their business. They're not interested. What the hell is the matter with this country?" And he said, "Well, do you expect people to read anything serious these days? They've been raised on television. If you want to reach the general public with the printed word rather than television and animated cartoons or whatever, it's got to be fiction. It has to be recreational. It's got to be the kind of stuff that they can sit down and relax with." And we talked more about it – fiction – and how it could have an effect, like *Uncle Tom's Cabin* and these types of things.
>
> So I thought about it and I thought well, it's worth a try. I was editing and publishing the tabloid *Attack!* [The title of a National Alliance periodical that went on to become the National Vanguard; it is currently not in print]. I didn't want it to look like a one-man band so I thought I would try writing an adventure story and serializing it one chapter each issue, so I used a pseudonym Andrew MacDonald. So anyway, I sort of roughed out things in my head in 1975 and then I made up the details as I went along. I just did one chapter each month.
>
> There are certain rules that the writer must follow. Something exciting and violent had to happen in every chapter to keep up the interest. So anyway, I did it. It took three years to finish it and as I went along I was amazed at the response to the thing, because, I mean really, the interest really picked up in the tabloid and it was because of the *Turner Diaries*. I never intended it to be a book; it was just a tabloid serial. I started the serial-

ization in 1975 and it ran for three years. But, by the time I approached the end of the thing, I realized was, Jesus, I got so much attention in the thing I got to reissue it as a book. So I did in June or July of 1978. And the rest is history. But it was not intended from the start to be anything except an experiment in getting people to absorb ideas through this recreational reading. They won't read a serious editorial or a serious historical feature. They will read an adventure story, and so you slip the ideas into the adventure story in the dialogue.[22]

The Turner Diaries contains elements that appeal to a broad segment of the far right. For example, for Second Amendment activists, there is part of the story that tells of a government effort to confiscate guns under a new piece of legislation called the "Cohen Act." The millennial themes of apocalypse resonate with many in the Christian Identity movement. It is primarily the revolutionary racialist right to which the book appeals. It also contains what many observers have said are ideas for carrying out acts of terrorism. In fact the FBI has referred to it as a blueprint for revolution.[23] However, Pierce denied this characterization, and instead claimed that he wrote the book merely as means to spread his ideology and attract more supporters.[24]

Like the "Organization" in *The Turner Diaries*, Robert Jay Matthews endeavored to build a clandestine resistance group. His group went on a crime spree and a terrorist campaign that gained nationwide notoriety. Its activities included counterfeiting, armored car heists, bank robberies, and four homicides. In a milieu in which terrorists often resemble more the gang that couldn't shoot straight than professional terrorists, the exploits of the Order were, in a word, electrifying. One armored car heist took in a whopping $3.6 million – which at that time in 1984 set the record for the highest amount of money ever stolen in such a robbery.

Although, the Order was racist and anti-Semitic in orientation, consistent with Sprinzak's theory of split deligitimation, it gave its highest priority to targets such as the state and other institutions. Matthews instructed Order members to avoid petty conflicts with racial minorities, as that would distract the group from its primary mission. A list of prominent enemies marked for assassination was compiled, which included the leader of the Southern Poverty Law Center, Morris Dees, the former Secretary of State, Henry Kissinger, banker David Rockefeller, television producer Norman Lear, and international financier Baron Elie de Rothschild.[25] Despite such lofty intentions, the Order settled for a Denver-based Jewish disc jockey, Alan Berg, as its first target of assassination. Berg was an acerbic talk radio host and occasionally berated far-right callers on his radio program.

The Order's exploits soon caught the attention of authorities and the FBI identified the group as the most serious domestic terrorist threat in the country.[26] Ultimately, the counterfeiting operation led to the group's demise, as one of its recruits, though not an official member, Tom Martinez, agreed to become an informant for the FBI after his arrest for passing counterfeit money that the

Order had printed. He set up two of his colleagues, including Matthews, in a sting operation at a hotel. A shootout ensued, and amazingly Matthews escaped after wounding an officer. He remained undaunted and issued a "Declaration of War" against the United States government, which he sent to several newspapers. Finally, authorities caught up with Matthews at Whidbey Island in Washington state. Matthews, however, refused to be taken alive, and a standoff which lasted a couple of days followed. He single-handedly engaged in several shootouts with SWAT teams. Eventually, the authorities lost their patience and on December 8, 1984, dropped white phosphorous illumination flares onto the roof of the house in which Matthews had barricaded himself. This set off a fire that engulfed the structure and Matthews perished in dramatic fashion. A concerted effort by federal, state, and local law enforcement agencies eventually crushed the Order, and many of its members are now serving lengthy prison sentences.

The Order's campaign caught many in the radical right by surprise. Some criticized their exploits as ineffectual and quixotic, while others lionized them as exemplary "Aryan warriors." Pierce offered his assessment and recollections of the Order when I asked him what were his thoughts on the Order's campaign, and whether he thought that it had been counterproductive:

> No, I don't think it was counterproductive. Although when I got some inkling that Bob had something in mind like this, I told him that I thought that he was misjudging the tempo of the times. He gave a talk called the "Call to Arms." He gives this speech at the 1983 annual convention of the National Alliance and it was based on his experiences with his neighbors and people that he had met in the Pacific Northwest. He talked to a lot of truck drivers, who I guess, were hurting economically. A lot of farms were being repossessed because the farmers couldn't pay their bank debts. Matthews based on this very atypical sampling of the population concluded that the country was in a revolutionary ferment. I said, "Bob that's not true. If you stay here in Washington, DC for a while and talk to the people around here they're fat and happy. I mean they're unhappy about some things that are going on, but they're comfortable. The country will not rise up unless they feel threatened and they have been made to suffer for a while."
>
> But anyway, he had already made up his mind that he was going to do something drastic. And so he did. So my judgment of the thing afterwards was that Bob made a miscalculation about how people would respond. He thought that if he set an example, maybe not from the general public, that he could recruit a lot of people and it would snowball, that it would grow. And partly I was aware because word was getting back to me from various people during all the time that this was going on. He would show up at a city, Atlanta or somewhere, at a place that they would call a safe house based on I guess CIA terminology, and they would put a bunch of guns and piles of money, hand grenades and copies of the *Turner Diaries* out on the

table and they would have a list of names they had gotten of people that ought to be sympathetic. They would get these people over the so-called safe house and show them all the money and they would tell them, "The revolution has started, comrade. Are you with us or not?" [Laughs] And of course they would relate the stories of bank robberies and so on. Typically what would happen is that it would just blow the guy's mind and he would say, "My god, I have to think about this. Let me get back to you tomorrow." And they'd say, "Okay, but don't take too long because, you know, things are moving along now." And so he would get out of there and the first thing he would do is get on the telephone and tell all of his friends and say, "My god, do you know what I just saw?" I don't know how he [Matthews] stayed ahead of the FBI for as long as he did. I mean, it was a crazy way to run an underground operation.

I liked Bob. I had a lot of respect for him because he had some personal qualities that I really think were excellent. Bob Martinez [an associate of Matthews' who informed on him and provided information, which ultimately led to the capture of members of the Order] was a gutter rat. I kicked him out of the Alliance a year or a year and a half before Matthews started his thing because of the things that he had done that I told him not to do. And I thought that maybe the fact that he had been kicked out – publicly expelled – that people would stay away from him. Bob Matthews thought that I was being to rough on him because he [Martinez] was a salt of the earth, redneck, street person type who basically had a good heart. But he was a gutter rat. I know gutter rats when I see them. And Martinez was strictly a no-good. But Matthews recruited him and gave him some counterfeit money to distribute. So what does Martinez do? He goes and buys a couple of cases of beer and gives the guy a one hundred-dollar bill and gets change. And he goes back to the same beer place the next day to buy more beer [laughs]. That's how he got caught. And this is just stupid, absolutely stupid. But that's sort of typical of this, you know, right-wing movement. And so Martinez gets caught and like a typical rat that is cornered he says, "What can I give you if you'll ease up on me?" He told them everything he knew about Matthews and said, "Look I'll make a deal with you. I didn't make the money. I was just distributing it. I was hard up and I didn't think about it. But, I'll take you to the people who are making it." And then he set Matthews up and there was a big shootout at a hotel, but Matthews shot his way out of there. Mr Martinez got caught and agreed to work for the other side if they would go easy on him. I could have predicted that.[27]

Although the Order tactically did not really achieve much, it was significant insofar as it marked a change in the orientation of the far right. The United States government was now seen as the enemy and the far right began to take on a more revolutionary posture. No longer did it seek to preserve the status quo. Rather it sought the overthrow of the US government, which it reasoned was now under the heel of ZOG. The Order has been lionized by the far right and its incarcerated members are regarded as POWs to others in the movement.[28] Thus, on a symbolic level, the Order's campaign was important, as George Eric Hawthorne, a one-time leading figure in the skinhead movement, explained:

> Although their precise actions mean little in the greater scheme of things, the fact that they ACTED [emphasis in original] – acted with unprecedented selflessness and sacrifice – means everything to this movement today[29] – Tactically speaking, Alan Berg was a bad choice – The physical act of killing Alan Berg was about as meaningless as assassinating the White House gardener – But historically speaking, in the wider context of things, it was of unfathomable significance. It marked the transition from conservatism to radicalism. It marks the beginning of the Second American Revolution, a revolution that shall strike into the heart of everything diseased that America has become.[30]

Subsequent underground groups inspired by the Order have attempted to model their organizational structure on it, and even appropriated its name. Shortly after the demise of the Order, a new group emerged calling itself the *Brüder Schweigen Strikeforce II* or Order II. It was however, quickly crushed by authorities.[31] More recently, in 1998, the FBI arrested members of a group, the New Order, which drew inspiration from the original organization. The members allegedly planned on attacking the Southern Poverty Law Center facility and ADL offices.[32]

On a more instrumental level, the Order distributed much of its stolen money to "above ground" far-right organizations around the country. It was hoped that the stolen money could be used as "mortar" to cement the fragmented elements of the racialist right.[33] For example, Robert Jay Matthews disbursed $200,000 to Glen Miller for his White Patriot Party that was active in North Carolina during the 1980s. He is also alleged to have donated $250,000 to Tom Metzger and WAR.[34] More important, it is strongly suspected that Matthews also gave Dr Pierce a substantial amount of money. Looked at in hindsight, remarks that Pierce made in a 1984 speech to the National Alliance in which he unveiled plans to move his organization's headquarters to West Virginia, would seem to suggest this transfer of money may have occured:

> We've been able to acquire this land only because a few of us, a relative handful, have had the vision, the commitment to our goal, and the spirit of self-sacrifice which eventually everyone who remains a part of our community must have...
>
> I'll say it again: We have this land because of the sacrifices of a relevant few. They're people who did not sit back and hold on tight to what they had, thinking that when the times comes that we are really making great strides forward, then they'll give us a little boost. No. These were people who have had the faith and the selflessness to put everything they had on the line for us now, when we're still almost nothing compared to what we will be one

day. And some of the names of these great-hearted few cannot even be told until our goal has been reached, perhaps in anothe r generation.

Pierce, William Dr., " White Zion, part 2: Our Community." American Dissident Voices, November, 30, 2002.

If this is the case, then it enabled Pierce to establish his National Alliance on a solid footing and relocate to West Virginia. Thus the Order would have significantly contributed to the success of arguably the most important organization in the revolutionary right today.[35] Another organization to which the Order had a more direct connection was the Covenant, Sword, and the Arm of the Lord.

The Covenant, Sword, and the Arm of the Lord.

In the late 1970s a Christian Identity minister, Jim Ellison, founded a community in Arkansas known as the Covenant, Sword and Arm of the Lord (CSA). Over the years it took on a paramilitary orientation, as members believed that eventually their enemies would one day besiege their compound, which in a sense they did. Ellison stockpiled many weapons and trained members how to use them in a mock village called "Silhouette City."[36] Furthermore, the compound came to be seen as a safe haven for those in the far-right underground who sought to evade authorities.

Ellison interfaced with others in the movement and attended the 1983 Aryan Nations Congress. Expressing anger over the death of Gordon Kahl, he declared himself the White resistance leader of the American heartland.[37] Previously, Ellison provided paramilitary training to several persons who went on to become members of the Order. He also provided sanctuary to some of its fugitive members when authorities were pursuing them.[38]

The CSA was linked to several episodes of terrorism. For example, Ellison and another member, Richard Wayne Snell, firebombed a Jewish community center in Bloomington, Indiana, and a gay church in Springfield, Missouri.[39] In another incident, Snell fatally shot a pawnbroker in Texarkana, Arkansas. Finally, during a routine traffic stop, Snell opened fire on an Arkansas state trooper and fatally wounded him. The CSA also planned several other serious terrorist attacks but failed to successfully carry them out.[40]

The violence and terrorism emanating from the CSA compound eventually captured the attention of federal authorities. Once authorities had implicated the CSA in these offenses, the FBI's elite anti-terrorist unit, the Hostage Rescue Team, quickly surrounded its compound. Although the CSA demonstrated a proclivity for violence, after some negotiation, Ellison surrendered to authorities without incident. He eventually cooperated with authorities and turned state's evidence against some members of the Order in a trial at Fort Smith, Arkansas in 1988.

The rise of "leaderless resistance"

After the demise of the CSA and the Order, the revolutionary right went into a period of retrenchment and did some soul-searching on the topic of revolutionary strategy. From this interlude emerged a change in the tactics of right-wing terrorists. Terrorism expert Bruce Hoffman argues that terrorist groups learn from past mistakes and adjust their tactics accordingly.[41] The lessons drawn were that when a terrorist organization grew to the size of the Order, it would eventually fall prey to infiltration and eventually be crushed. The CSA demonstrated that it was not feasible for terrorist groups to congregate in a compound that could easily be identified and surrounded by authorities.[42]

Having learned from the mistakes of the Order and the CSA, the violence-prone far right now employs an approach known as "leaderless resistance," a kind of lone wolf operation in which an individual, or a very small cohesive group, engages in acts of anti-statist violence independent of any official movement, leader or network of support.[43] Inasmuch as the contemporary far right is organizationally fragmented, leaderless resistance makes a virtue out of necessity. Moreover, this notion dovetails well with the new internet technology.[44] However, a word of caution is in order. Although right-wing advocates of the leaderless approach have theorized extensively on the concept, it remains in large part a construct of academic scholars and journalists. That is to say, it is a somewhat facile way of attributing the often unorganized and sporadic nature of right-wing violence to some larger operational plan. There is anecdotal evidence which suggests that several perpetrators who appear to have employed this approach, were psychopaths with little ideological sophistication. That said, the leaderless resistance concept should not be completely dismissed as merely a topic for abnormal psychology. As one observer noted:

> Terrorism is almost always linked to a wider social movement. Klan terrorism in the South was part of a broader pattern of white resistance to the civil rights struggle. Black terrorism was associated with the rise of the black power movement. Leftist terrorism emerged in the context of widespread student opposition to the Vietnam War. Therefore, in order to understand the current upsurge in terrorism, it must be located within its political and social context.[45]

Leaderless resistance arises in large measure because of the failure of organized right-wing terrorism. Despite the seemingly desperate nature of this approach, some of the most lethal incidents of right-wing violence in America fall under this category, as the following examples illustrate:

- Over a period of time in September of 1980, an Army private and far-right sympathizer, Joseph Christopher, killed at least thirteen Blacks and Hispanics in the Buffalo area of New York state.[46]
- Joseph Paul Franklin affiliated with neo-Nazi groups, but eventually severed his ties shortly before embarking on a campaign of murder that is believed

to have begun in 1980 and ended in 1982. Franklin targeted interracial couples and is alleged to have killed at least thirteen people, but the actual number is unknown.[47] He also wounded a high-profile African-American attorney, Vernon Jordan, and paralyzed Larry Flynt, publisher of the pornographic magazine *Hustler*, with a gunshot wound.

- Frank Spisak, a neo-Nazi, wandered the back streets of Cleveland and killed at least three Blacks over the period 1980–3.[48]
- In 1984, James Olive Huberty walked into a McDonalds fast food restaurant in San Diego and shot twenty-one people to death, most of whom were racial minorities. Rather than submit to arrest, Huberty shot himself to death before he could be captured. Although, his motives are not entirely clear, the police discovered right-wing racist literature among his personal effects in a search of his home after the incident.[49]
- In December of 1990, Walter Leroy Moody is alleged to have conducted a mail bomb campaign, which took the lives of US Appeals Judge Robert Vance and Robert Robinson, a Black city alderman in Savannah, Georgia. Judge Vance had rendered some controversial decisions in desegregation cases. Other bombs were sent to the 11th Circuit Court of Appeals in Atlanta and an NAACP office in Jacksonville, Florida, but were defused.[50]
- On Christmas Eve in 1985 in Seattle, David Lewis Rice murdered a family of four because he thought that they were Jewish and communists. Rice was obsessed with communists and other patriot themes such as the Federal Reserve, international bankers, and the belief that foreign troops were preparing to invade the United States.[51]
- Eric Rudolph is suspected to have bombed several abortion clinics and gay bars in 1997 and 1998. In addition, he is suspected of planting the bomb in the Centennial Park at the 1996 summer Olympic games in Atlanta, Georgia. He is thought to be a believer in the Christian Identity theology. So far he has eluded a team of up to 200 agents equipped with bloodhounds, helicopters, and heat-seeking sensors. And despite a $1 million reward, no one has come forward with information leading to his arrest.[52]
- On July 4 weekend of 1999, Benjamin Smith, a former member of the World Church of the Creator who had recently resigned from the organization, embarked on a shooting spree in Illinois and Indiana that left two dead and several injured.[53]
- In August of 1999, Buford Furrow, a former security guard for the Aryan Nations compound, terrorized a Jewish day care center in Los Angeles, injured several people and shot dead an Asian-American postal carrier.[54]
- In April of 2000, Richard Baumhammers, an immigration attorney and founder of a miniscule right-wing organization, the Free Market Party, killed five people – his Jewish neighbor, three Asian-Americans, and one Black – in a shooting rampage near Pittsburgh, Pennsylvania.[55]

Several of the terrorists mentioned above had histories of mental illness, and it is difficult to tell with any certainty if their right-wing beliefs were determinative in their decisions to carry out their attacks. Although a sign of desperation, the notion of leaderless resistance should not be taken lightly.[56] According to the government's own prosecution case, the most lethal act of domestic terrorism – the Oklahoma City bombing – appears to fit in the leaderless resistance category.

The Oklahoma City bombing

On April 19, 1995, two years to the day of the culmination of the Waco tragedy, the Murrah federal building in Oklahoma City was bombed, leaving at least 168 dead and many others wounded. This attack was the most lethal act of domestic terrorism ever perpetrated on American soil. The subsequent investigation would implicate Timothy McVeigh as the chief culprit of the attack. He also had some accomplices including Terry Nichols and Michael Fortier; however, the scope of their involvement is still uncertain. In the FBI's own description, "one of its most extensive investigations" failed to turn up a significant militia connection to the bombing. McVeigh and Nichols are reported to have attended meetings of the Michigan Militia, but the group did not welcome them. To the contrary, members of the group thought they were loose cannons and should not be granted membership.[57]

Although McVeigh may not have had any formal affiliation with extremist groups, there is evidence to suggest that he was a denizen of the subterranean world of the far right. McVeigh appears to have found several reasons to carry out his attack. During the 1993 siege of the Branch Davidians, McVeigh made a pilgrimage to Mount Carmel. He was reported to have been extremely upset over how the government handled the situation. He was also angered by the government's siege at Ruby Ridge, Idaho at which federal agents shot and killed Randy Weaver's wife Vicki and their son Samuel. McVeigh had chosen the Murrah federal building in particular, because he wanted to punish the BATF and the FBI, both of which were involved in the two incidents mentioned above.[58] In his personal letters and statements, McVeigh echoed many of the Constitutionalist themes that are popular in the Christian Patriot/Militia movement. He absorbed much of the anti-government propaganda of the Patriot movement at various gun shows that he often attended. Although he did not usually evince a visceral racism, he actively explored the propaganda of the racialist right. At one time, he obtained a trial membership of a Ku Klux Klan organization based in North Carolina. However, according to McVeigh he declined to renew his membership because he felt that the Klan was "manipulative to young people." Moreover, he felt that the government, and not racial minorities, was his enemy.[59]

McVeigh was also enamored of Dr Pierce's *Turner Diaries*, distributed it among his Army buddies, and even went so far as to sell the book at a loss at gun shows.[60] However, the anti-gun control theme, not the racism, is what seems to have resonated with McVeigh. This is somewhat surprising since the Second Amendment theme is really incidental to the book; racism is the leitmotif. However, the gun laws are presented in the book as links in a chain which ulti-

108 *The far right and terrorism*

mately results in the loss of individual rights. McVeigh seems to have identified with the protagonist in the book, Earl Turner, and when he was arrested, the police found photocopied pages of the book in an envelope in his car. McVeigh even highlighted the following sentences:

> The real value of our attacks today lies in the psychological impact, not in the immediate casualties. More important, though, is what we taught the politicians and the bureaucrats. They learned this afternoon that not one of them is beyond our reach.[61]

Shortly after the bombing, observers were quick to point out the parallels between that attack and an incident in the novel. The character Earl Turner blows up an FBI building with a fuel oil and fertilizer bomb concealed in a truck. In the novel, the blast takes place at 9:15 a.m. The Oklahoma City bomb detonated at 9:02 a.m.

McVeigh was obviously aware of Pierce's National Alliance. According to phone records, he called an Arizona chapter's recorded phone message line several times.[62] McVeigh also ran advertisements in the *Spotlight* newspaper. Thus McVeigh seems to have been familiar with much of the subterranean world of both the Patriot movement and the racialist right. Dr Pierce gave me his thoughts on Timothy McVeigh in the following exchange:

G. M. Several observers speculate that *The Turner Diaries* inspired Mr McVeigh to bomb the federal building in Oklahoma City. Do you have any thoughts on that?

W. P. He may have been enamored of the *Turner Diaries*. It was my understanding that he recommended it to a lot of people when he was in the Army and so on. But did it inspire him to bomb the federal building in Oklahoma City? That's really not true because what inspired him to do that was Janet Reno's massacre of all of those women and children down in Waco. While the siege was going on he went down there and he was very upset. He thought that the government had no business doing what they were doing. And then, when the fire burned all of those people up he was really pissed and he certainly made a decision that he was going to send a message to the government that if the government terrorizes the people, then they were going to get a dose of their own medicine. And this is essentially what he said at the sentencing in court later. It's clear that it was Waco that inspired him to do his thing in Oklahoma City.

People have said that the bombing of the FBI headquarters, the fictionalized bombing [in the *Turner Diaries*] that Earl Turner did was the blueprint for Timothy McVeigh. But that's not true. I talked at length with Steven Jones, the defense attorney for Timothy McVeigh, about this to help him prepare opening statements because I knew what the government was going to do. They were going to use the *Turner Diaries*, because that's what the media were doing. … The media had been saying over and over again this is where

The far right and terrorism 109

he [McVeigh] got the idea. This is where he got the recipe for the bomb. I knew that this prick, this guy in the wheel chair –

G. M. The prosecutor Joseph Hartzler?

W. P. Yeah, so I talked with Jones about that and pointed that out to him. I don't know how conversant he was with chemistry. McVeigh's bomb was constructed with entirely different ingredients. I mean he may have gotten the recipe from somewhere but it couldn't have been *The Turner Diaries*, because it was a bomb made out of nitro-methane and ammonium nitrate and set off with a detonating cord. My bomb was ammonium nitrate and fuel oil and set off with a dynamite booster. Anyway, I wanted Jones to be able to point that out in his opening statements. And also to point out that clearly McVeigh had different motives because the motive for the bombing of the FBI headquarters was spelled out in the *Turner Diaries*. McVeigh had bombed the building to send the government a message. They [the terrorist characters in the *Turner Diaries*] bombed the FBI headquarters because they were concerned about an internal passport system, which was going to be administered from some basement in the FBI headquarters, where they had a bunch of super computers that would keep track of everybody all over the country and so on. And they wanted to destroy this computer bank.

G. M. So you're suggesting that it was done for tactical reasons, not really symbolic reasons like McVeigh's bomb.

W. P. That's right. For specific tactical reasons and it's spelled out in there in *The Turner Diaries*. So it's not that McVeigh had the same motive and got the idea and so on. If you want to blow up a big target you use a truck bomb. You can't carry a bomb in a backpack. What are you going to do? You have to use a car or a truck. It's history. I mean that's what everybody does. For example, the 1983 bombing of the Marine barracks in Lebanon. The bombing of the US embassy in Beirut was another truck bomb and so anyway anytime you want to blow up something that requires more explosives than you can carry on your back, you get a truck.[63]

According to statements made by McVeigh in a new book, *The Turner Diaries* did indeed have a profound influence on him and was instrumental in his choice of target.[64]

After the bombing Pierce downplayed the connection between McVeigh and *The Turner Diaries* and disavowed the attack, mostly for tactical reasons, by asserting that it served no real purpose at this particular state of "resistance." In an interview with Robert Griffin, Pierce elaborated on this:

If one is waging a war against the government, civilians are going to be killed. But you have to look at the bigger picture. … Under a circumstance like that, if it were part of a war, then a bombing of the Oklahoma City sort is morally justified. But if you are going to engage in a war you have to meet certain requirements. One of them is you have to have a plausible strategy, a plan that can be reasonably argued will get you what you want to achieve. If

McVeigh was throwing a single punch to send a message, then its moral justification is debatable. You might well say that this was an overly expensive message in that case.[65]

Timothy McVeigh remains an enigmatic figure. By some accounts he would appear to be the veritable paradigm of the leaderless resistance concept.[66] Some of his letters suggest that he favored a mass uprising, not lone wolf operations. However, they also evince a strong sense of despair and desperation in short themes that lend themselves well to the leaderless resistance concept.[67] Commenting on the leaderless approach, Dr Mark Pitcavage, the ADL's chief fact finder, gave me his analysis:

> By the very nature of being extreme, no matter what the ideology is, whether it's left wing or right wing or single issue, people can be motivated to commit criminal acts. Either by striking out against a target they don't like or perhaps even to get money to finance their activities. But generally speaking, the larger the group is, the less likely it will be motivated to act in that way. The smaller a group is, the more likely that for psychological or other reasons the members may be motivated to act that way.
> And so most of the actual terrorism or criminal extremism has tended to come from small groups or from individuals who have splintered off from groups, generally because they were disappointed that those groups were not taking action. They tend to refer to groups like that as the eat, meet, and retreat crowd. I think McVeigh is sort of a more example of that. ... We know that he dabbled with several different groups and that he even thought about starting a group of his own in Arizona. But in the end he never stuck with any group. And it kind of matched his sort of peripatetic nature. He was always traveling around, going from place to place, and he really sort of epitomizes the person who doesn't join groups but is nevertheless part of the movement and will act violently in support of goals of the movement.[68]

There were many coincidences about the Oklahoma City bombing that suggested there was a larger conspiracy at work than in the government's version of the case. For example, there was some speculation that McVeigh had connections with some of the remnants of the Covenant, Sword and the Arm of the Lord. Not long before the bombing, McVeigh placed a phone call to Elohim City, an encampment where some former members of the CSA now live. Its leader, Robert Millar, was the spiritual advisor of Richard Wayne Snell, the CSA member responsible for at least two homicides. Coincidentally, Snell was executed on the same day as the attack. Just hours before his execution Snell saw news of the bombing on television and is reported to have remarked, "[Arkansas] Governor Tucker, look over your shoulder. I wouldn't trade places with any of you or any of your political cronies. Hell has victory. I'm at peace."[69] To add further mystery to the story, the CSA's former leader, James Ellison, testified in 1988 that in 1983 he and

Snell had visited the building and talked about blowing it up.[70] A former leading CSA member who has since repudiated his extremist views, Kerry Noble, said that he was convinced that McVeigh followed the plot hatched by Snell and Ellison.[71]

However, according to recent statements by McVeigh, he called Elohim City in an effort to search for a prospective hideout and not to enlist the help of others in the commission of his terrorist act. The person for whom he was calling was not there at the times that the calls were made.[72] Thus McVeigh was not able to convey his request. Furthermore, he asserts that members of the community had no foreknowledge of the bombing.

In addition to the theory linking the bombing to the CSA, there are other theories that purport there was an Islamic connection to the incident. Stephen Jones, McVeigh's defense attorney, was one of the main purveyors of this theory.[73] However, McVeigh recently said that this theory was "nonsense" and a "red herring."[74] According to McVeigh's recent statements, there was no larger conspiracy and the government's version was correct after all. Still, there remains the chance that he may be covering for accomplices and thus might not be entirely truthful about what happened.

It is interesting to note how the radical right responded to the Oklahoma City bombing. Although McVeigh was usually depicted as a fellow traveler of the Militia movement, I know of not one instance where a militia leader has publicly condoned the attack. Just the opposite is true. Quite often militia leaders blamed the attack on a government conspiracy. For example, Norm Olson from the Michigan Militia at first blamed the Japanese government. He claimed that it was in retaliation for the 1995 Tokyo subway attacks, which he believed the United States government, and not the *Aum Shinrikyo* cult, had perpetrated.[75] A view held by many in the Militia movement is that the government deliberately orchestrated the attack and tried to implicate the militias so that it would create a crisis atmosphere in which it could pass new anti-terrorist legislation and allow a witch hunt against the far right.[76] This sentiment was given a veneer of credibility after the release of a report by a retired Air Force Brigadier General, Benton Partin. Partin had been responsible for the testing and design of many non-nuclear weapon devices used by the Air Force. His report concluded that the single bomb allegedly used could not have caused such destruction. Instead, he asserted that the destruction was caused in the main by several "demolition charges attached to supporting column bases, at locations not accessible from the street, to supplement the truck bomb damage."[77] Moreover, Partin believed that a "classic cover-up" followed the incident.[78]

By contrast, the racialist right seemed much less likely to ascribe the attack to some larger conspiracy involving the government or unknown others. Dr Pierce dismissed such theories:

> Well, this is the theory that the government did it to themselves to give them an excuse for a crack down on the far right. ... [But] I'm convinced that McVeigh essentially did this by himself. He may have had somebody besides

Nichols who helped him get the materials together and helped him mix it up. But it certainly didn't involve the government. I mean if you deal with the government you know the type of people they have. They're bureaucrats. They're cover your ass type of people. They don't have the balls to do something like that. I mean, imagine, suppose the damn thing would unravel. These are not people to take chances like that. These are clockwatchers. It's just inconceivable to me that a bunch of FBI and CIA types would have blown up the federal building just to blame it on somebody else. No, it didn't happen.[79]

Like their militia counterparts, most leaders in the racialist right did not condone the attack, but more so on its tactical efficacy rather than a sense of moral revulsion. However, some of the more radical proponents of the leaderless resistance approach did condone the bombing, including Alex Curtis, who designated McVeigh as the "lone wolf of the century," and Tom Metzger, who commented in an editorial in his newspaper *WAR*:

> WAR will break with most other Race Separatist groups on this issue and take the unpopular position at the moment. WAR will not try to deflect the sword by blaming an Iron Heel [the US Government] conspiracy to destroy the Iron Heel Federal building in Oklahoma City. WAR will not sidestep *The Turner Diaries* issue even when its own author tends to side-step his handy work [*sic*]. WAR will not criticize or pick apart the actions of Timothy McVeigh – Timothy McVeigh has gone farther than any Aryan thus far in striking back at the beast.[80]

In an interview, Metzger clarified his position:

> I believe that Timothy McVeigh's symbolic act in Oklahoma City was a legitimate legal target. It's unfortunate that the government saw fit and was arrogant enough to put child daycare centers in these government installations because in any kind of civil upheaval in every country, government buildings can become targets. And so in studying Timothy McVeigh and his way of thinking, I see that he came back from Iraq disillusioned that we were killing hundreds of thousands of people over there virtually for nothing and burying them alive in trenches and everything, his mind began to change about the American government the same as mine had changed.[81]

The Aryan Republican Army

Around the same time of the Oklahoma City bombing, a six-man group of bandits, which called itself the "Aryan Republican Army," was making headlines in the Midwest for a series of bank robberies that confounded authorities. Its members included Peter Langan, the putative leaders, as well as Richard Lee

Guthrie Jr, Scott Anthony Stedeford, Kevin William McCarthy, Michael William Bresica and Mark Thomas. All totaled, the Aryan Republican Army is reported to have been responsible for robbing twenty-two banks and netting some $250,000 in cash. Although the goals of these renegades are still murky, they are alleged to have consorted with some of the more notorious figures in the far-right underground, including the residents of Elohim City, Dennis Mahon, and possibly even Timothy McVeigh. One author goes so far as to theorize that the money stolen was used to fund the terrorist attack on the Murrah federal building in Oklahoma City.[82]

Authorities eventually closed in on the Aryan Republican Army and put an end to its campaign. Although its significance is disputable, it could presage a pattern in other countries beset by terrorism, where criminal enterprises use their ill-gotten gains to fund terrorist and revolutionary movements.

The events of the mid-1990s, most notably the Oklahoma City bombing, sent shock waves through the far right and accentuated an ongoing debate on the best course of resistance and terrorism. It is to that debate to which we shall now turn.

The development of the far right's theoretical approach to terrorism

Until recently not much attention was paid to the strategic approaches adopted by American right-wing terrorists. By contrast, the exegeses of the proponents of left-wing terrorism and guerrilla warfare have received quite a bit of attention and critical analysis.[83] However, there has been a good deal of theorizing on the topic of terrorism in the far-right underground. This section reviews the major approaches to terrorism that the far right has employed and advocated.

As mentioned earlier, the far right is a relatively small and heavily stigmatized movement that does not enjoy broad-based support from the public. Most in the movement realize that the forces arrayed against them – the government and the watchdog organizations – are collectively vastly more powerful than they are. Consequently, there has always been a conservative majority in the far right that believed that it would be foolhardy to prematurely engage in revolutionary violence. Such an approach would almost certainly lead to organizational suicide. Thus the more conservative elements advocated a strategy that would concentrate on utilizing propaganda to build a revolutionary majority. This came to be known as the theory of mass action.[84]

A leading proponent of this approach was George Lincoln Rockwell, the founder of the American Nazi Party that was active in the 1960s. Rockwell believed that events such as racial integration, school busing, the Vietnam War, race riots and rising crime would engender urban mayhem and thus create favorable conditions for his party. He entertained the idea that his party could actually win national power by 1972. However, Rockwell fell to an assassin's bullet in 1967, and with his departure some elements of the far right became disillusioned with the conservative approach.

Joseph Tomassi, a member of Rockwell's successor organization, eventually departed and founded the National Socialist Liberation Front (NSLF), a neo-Nazi organization that patterned itself on the left-wing models of the Weathermen and the Symbionese Liberation Army. Tomassi correctly saw that in the early 1970s, the idea of creating a Nazi-style party that would win support of a majority of the population was futile. However, he believed that it was still possible to strike blows against "the system," provided that revolutionaries were prepared to act resolutely and alone. Whereas the state demonstrated over and over again that it could infiltrate and effectively neutralize any right-wing organization, it had yet to develop the capability of thwarting the actions of individuals or small groups acting alone. However, the NSLF campaign was reckless and its revolutionary arm was quickly crushed. Like Rockwell, Tomassi was also killed by a disgruntled member. Although the organization never succeeded in striking a serious blow against "the system," according to one observer its "contribution to the leaderless resistance concept [was] incalculable."[85] Thus was born the concept of leaderless resistance in the far right. However, the approach had still not been given a name and the idea would languish for the most part among the far-right theorists until the early 1990s.

Another resistance approach occasionally used by the far right has been the cellular model. The far right's version of this approach can be traced back to an anonymous tract titled *The John Franklin Letters*, which was popularized by the John Birch Society in 1959.[86] The John Birch Society promoted the book as a call to resistance in the wake of a communist takeover, which the group believed was always just around the corner. Although the Birch Society organizationally patterned itself on the cellular model, it was loath to engage in any political violence.

The Minutemen, as discussed in Chapter 3, also adopted the cellular structure with a centralized command structure, and some of its members were implicated in violence. Its leader, Robert DePugh, published a manual for activists, *Blueprint for Victory*, which gave advice on political, military, economic and psychological warfare.[87] The Minutemen tried to maintain the semblance of a centralized command structure, and discouraged individual initiative, leaderless-resistance types of operation. A former member, R. N. Taylor explained:

> The Minutemen never advocated leaderless resistance "per se." In fact where such did occur, where an individual or small group, did in fact take some action on their own, it was generally a cause for concern and created trouble for the National organization. We did our very best to maintain a certain discipline among the members.[88]

Despite these efforts, some members of the Minutemen ran afoul of the authorities and the organization was effectively shut down after some episodes of violence. The popularity of the cellular model reached its zenith with the campaign of the Order. The Order carried out various missions in small groups, and there were plans on splitting the organization into interlocking separate cells. Despite some spectacular moments, it was resoundingly quashed after a concerted effort by government authorities. The crushing defeat of the Order and the CSA ushered in a debate on the best strategy of "resistance" to employ in the far-right movement. Thus the concept of leaderless resistance was reexamined and updated for current conditions.

Jeffrey Kaplan observes that the movement's discourse became increasingly chiliastic by the late 1980s.[89] The mass action theories of previous generations were seen as unrealistic. The cellular model had been discredited with the demise of the Order. A period of despair and hopelessness seemed to settle over the movement. However, two events, first the ambush of Randy Weaver's home in Ruby Ridge in 1992, and second, the siege at Waco in 1993, once again galvanized a broad segment of the far right. Previously isolated voices calling for resistance found their messages being heard by a more receptive audience.

Leaderless resistance had several proponents during the 1980s, but the concept was truly crystallized and gained currency as a result of the October 1992 meeting in Estes Park, Colorado convoked by Christian Identity minister Pastor Pete Peters. This event provided a forum for the articulation of a new leaderless resistance approach. Whereas prior to the meeting the concept was only vaguely recognized by some, it was now given a name and disseminated to a much larger audience. This event, more than any other, popularized the notion in the far-right community.

One of the speakers at the conference was Louis Beam, a firebrand orator and a longstanding far-right activist. Previously, Beam was a leader of a Klan organization and was at one time the Aryan Nations' "ambassador at large." Pastor Peters included Beam's essay on leaderless resistance in a published report on the meeting.[90] In his essay, Beam identifies the late Colonel Ulius Louis Amoss as the source of inspiration for his theory. Amoss had written about mounting resistance in the event that the United States was taken over by communists during the Cold War. According to Beam, an organized approach is untenable under current conditions. The government is too powerful and will not allow the existence of any potentially serious oppositional organizations. The leaderless resistance model proffered by Beam rejects the pyramid structure in which the leadership is located at the top and the mass of followers at the bottom. Beam reasons that in a technologically advanced society such as contemporary America, the government, through means such as electronic surveillance, can without too much difficulty penetrate the structure and reveal its chain of command. From there the organization can be effectively neutralized from within by infiltrators and agents provocateurs.

Beam also studied the communist cell system, but argued that it was inappropriate for the contemporary American far right because it could not presently avail itself of the resources that the communist cells had, i.e. central direction, outside support and adequate funding.

As a strategic alternative, Beam invokes the "phantom cell" model of organization as described by Colonel Amoss. This approach draws upon the "Sons of

Liberty" or the "Committees of Correspondence" – the Revolutionary War patriots who resisted British colonial rule – as a strategic basis of resistance for the contemporary far right. According to Beam's historical interpretation of this movement, it operated in small cells independently of the others with no central command or direction. Applying this model, Beam argues that it becomes the responsibility of the individual to acquire the necessary skills and information to carry out what is to be done. Members take action when and where they see fit. Organs of information such as newspapers, leaflets, and now the internet, enable each person to keep informed of events. Beam concedes that leaderless resistance is a "child of necessity," but argues that all other alternatives are either unworkable or impractical. Furthermore, he points out that this approach presents an intelligence nightmare for authorities insofar as it is much more difficult to infiltrate "a thousand different small phantom cells opposing them."[91]

Prior to his "Leaderless Resistance" essay, Beam made another contribution to the concept. In two essays titled "Understanding the Struggle Part I" and "Understanding the Struggle Part II," Beam created a point system for potential terrorists to achieve the status of "Aryan warrior." Beam advances a nine-level schematic chart to explain his version of a conspiratorial cabal that he sees ruling the United States. At the first level is the control center at which a "Satanic anti-Christ Conspiracy for control of the world" formulates policy and decision making. These policies are handed down to lower level echelons in the conspiracy scheme, including "opinion makers," "federal government," "bureaucrats," "Jewish and White secondary leaders of subordinate level pressure groups" (e.g. ADL, Republican Party) and "street people" (e.g. leftist demonstrators), among others. More credit is given for the assassination of representatives of the highest levels than for the lower levels.[92] This essay was disseminated through computer networks, of which Beam was a pioneer in exploiting during the 1980s.

In essence, Beam synthesized the cellular and leaderless resistance models. His idea quickly caught on and ushered in a period of theorizing and debate on the topics of resistance and terrorism within the far-right movement. Moreover, the government and watchdog groups were quick to take notice, and saw this as evidence of the development of a loose but widespread far-right terrorist network.[93]

Richard Kelly Hoskins, a Christian Identity minister from Lynchburg, Virginia, also popularized the leaderless resistance approach with the publication of his book, *Vigilantes of Christendom*. In his book, Hoskins offers his bizarre interpretation of historical events. According to Hoskins, throughout history righteous "Phineas Priests" have fulfilled a sacred role by assassinating those who have transgressed God's law.[94] He cites some diverse historical examples including Robin Hood, St George, Beowulf, King Arthur, John Wilkes Booth, Jesse James, Gordon Kahl (the late radical tax protester and member of the Posse Comitatus), and Robert Jay Matthews (the late leader of the Order). Not long after the first publication of the book, several right-wing terrorists identified themselves as Phineas Priests, and have engaged in criminal acts including robbery and terrorism. For example, in 1996 a White separatist cell calling themselves Phineas Priests committed a string of bombings and bank robberies in Washington state.[95] Other right-wing extremists have also used the name; however, the name appears to denote more of a "state of the mind" fellowship than a formal organization.[96]

Perhaps unintentionally, Dr Pierce of the National Alliance contributed to the popularity of leaderless resistance with his publication of a novel titled *Hunter*, which is in some ways the sequel to *The Turner Diaries*. *Hunter* tells the story of a lone wolf assassin, Oscar Yeager, a Vietnam veteran and a contractor who does work for the Defense Department in the Washington DC area. The story begins with Yeager as a racist, yet not an anti-Semite. At first he murders inter-racial couples. However, eventually he meets a rogue FBI agent and a local leader of a right-wing organization, the National League (read National Alliance), who lecture him on the "Jewish question." More so than *The Turner Diaries*, *Hunter* includes ideological digressions in the dialogue between its characters. After discussion with his new found colleagues, Yeager becomes a full-blown anti-Semite. At the behest of the rogue FBI agent, Yeager wages a one-man terror campaign against politicians and politically liberal activists, among others. His goal is to demonstrate the weakness of the "system" and ultimately provoke a race war.

For his part, Pierce claimed that ideological propagandizing, and not a call for terrorism, was the intention of the book. I pointed out to Pierce that in his novel *Hunter*, the protagonist, Oscar Yeager, is a lone wolf who employs the notion of leaderless resistance; moreover, that the author had dedicated the book to Joseph Paul Franklin, who would seem to have exemplified this approach. Was *Hunter* meant to be read as an advocacy of the leaderless resistance approach? Pierce replied:

> No it's not. In the first place when I wrote the book, I might have heard the term leaderless resistance, but it's nowhere mentioned in the book, and I certainly was not advocating that. The big difference between *Hunter* and *The Turner Diaries* is that I hope I learned something from the reaction to *The Turner Diaries*. As I said, I never intended for it to be a book, but it turned out to be a book simply because is was so popular as a tabloid series and then I got thinking, why did this have so much more effect than the serious stuff that I had been writing? And I came to understand it. I mean, fiction, drama, generally is powerful because the reader or the viewer puts himself into the position inside the skin, inside the head of the protagonist if he can identify with the protagonist. Then he not only experiences vicariously the action as it's taking place but he observes the world through the eyes of the protagonist. He hears the thoughts of the protagonist. You know you have a lot of long monologues both in the *Turner Diaries* and in *Hunter*. ...you see the *Turner Diaries* had no character development. Earl Turner sprang full-blown into the world in the beginning of the story and he didn't change

throughout the whole novel. So I said, Jesus, this could be a teaching experience because what I'll do is I'll have the protagonist learn as he goes along, change his ideas. I'm going to have the protagonist start off as a typical idiot conservative who can see the niggers but cannot see the Jews, because the Jews are much less visible. Oscar Yeager had his experiences with blacks in the military and in his experiences with the Vietnam War. So he came back to civilian life in Washington, DC with some very definite racial ideas. But he had never been interested in politics. He had never done much reading on that sort of thing. He never thought about the Jewish angle. He didn't understand the influence that the Jews had. He didn't understand Jewish strategies and so forth. So he learns as he goes. And the idea is that maybe the reader of the book will learn as he goes too by identifying with Oscar Yeager. So anyway, that was the idea, to have some character development, which hopefully would help the education of the reader.

But no, it's hardly an advocacy of leaderless resistance. I mean, Oscar Yeager was a lone wolf when he started but he changed fairly early in the book and came to the conclusion that, that their was no way to get things done. It was therapeutic for him. He was doing this for selfish reasons. But if you really wanted to have an effect it would have to be in an organizational context and that's completely contrary to the leaderless resistance thesis.[97]

Regardless of Pierce's true intentions, *Hunter* fitted well into the far right's *Zeitgeist* of the 1990s in which the leaderless resistance approach was very popular.[98]

Another contribution to the theory of leaderless resistance comes from David Lane, the most celebrated of the imprisoned members of the Order. Since his incarceration, Lane has immersed himself in reading, and ironically has come to be seen as a Nelson Mandela of sorts to those in the White separatist movement. When put on trial for the last time in 1987, he defended his beliefs in his closing arguments before the jury.[99] He is perhaps known for his "14 Words" motto that he coined, which is a popular salutation in the discourse of the movement.[100] Furthermore, he writes tracts on revolutionary tactics from his prison cell. In his essay "Wotan," Lane distinguished between two arms of the resistance movement. The first is the "above ground" or political arm, which concerns itself mostly with the dissemination of propaganda. The underground, or "Wotan,"[101] is recruited from the ranks of the political arm. However, when an activist decides to enter this realm, he is advised to sever all ties with the political arm, lest he compromise it to prosecution and persecution by authorities. Wotan is encouraged to develop a "totally revolutionary mentality" and not concern himself with the ethical implications of terrorism, as "those who do not share his cause are expendable and those who oppose his cause are targets."[102] One interesting trend that can be discerned from Lane's essay is an increasing preoccupation with anonymity and the idea that the recommended number of terrorists that comprise a cell should be drastically reduced: "Wotan are small autonomous cells, one-man cells if possible. No one, not wife, brother, parent or friend, knows the identity or actions of Wotan."[103] Increasingly, proponents of leaderless resistance advise that only one-man operations are proper for current conditions in America.

Up until recently, the most vociferous advocate of the one-man approach to leaderless resistance has been Alex Curtis, a young man who operated the *Nationalist Observer* website out of San Diego, California. Like Beam, Curtis reasons that at the present time the far right is too easily infiltrated to mount any kind of organized campaign of resistance. Moreover, those organizations that suggest such actions even in an abstract way could possibly be slapped with a civil suit for "vicarious liability," in which they are blamed for influencing the violent actions of others. Thus Curtis instructs his readers and listeners that they must act entirely alone.

Like Lane, Curtis envisages a two-tiered resistance organization structure with an above ground propaganda arm and a second tier of lone wolves. The propaganda arm concentrates solely on just that, disseminating propaganda. Curtis advises against formal memberships and meetings as they offer opportunities for authorities and watchdog groups to identify and gather information on activists and sympathizers. For his part, Curtis in 1998 created an internet site that includes an audio "update" program that reviews and critiques recent episodes of right-wing violence. Also he sends out regular email messages to an estimated 800 subscribers.[104] In these media, he points out mistakes and offers suggestions on how they could be avoided. He counsels lone wolves not to cooperate with authorities, and only respond to them with "the five words," i.e. "I have nothing to say." In addition, he produced a "security issue," which instructs readers on how to avoid detection by authorities and what to do if arrested.

Curtis has become the far right's most vitriolic advocate of terrorism. Each month he would designate someone "Aryan of the Month." Previously he has bestowed this recognition on lone wolves such as Benjamin Smith, Scott Baumhammers, and David Copeland.[105] He also has no compunctions about the most lethal methods of terrorism. A recent issue of his bi-monthly periodical, *The Nationalist Observer,* contained an article which described various biological toxins that could be used for weapons of mass destruction, including the type-A bubonic and typhoid toxins.[106]

Essentially, Curtis sees leaderless resistance as a means by which to provoke a strategy of tension that would polarize the population along racial lines. He welcomes measures such as hate crime laws, because he believes that they are selectively used against Whites and will thus engender hostility among them. Although random hate crimes would appear to have little tactical value, Curtis sees them as a means by which to foment a revolutionary atmosphere:

> When you want to initiate change you want people to be seething with hate. Hate is an emotion that causes people and institutions to take actions against one another and create change. We should encourage niggers to hate us and Jews to hate us and increase the hatred they feel for us.[107]

Not surprisingly, Curtis' violent rhetoric caught the attention of authorities and the watchdog organizations. In November of 2000 the ADL issued a critical report on Curtis entitled "Alex Curtis: Lone Wolf of Hate Prowls the Internet." About a week later he was arrested along with two other individuals for various alleged civil rights violations. The arrests were the culmination of an an extensive two-year joint investigation by the FBI and the San Diego Police Department dubbed "Operation Lone Wolf." Failing to follow his own advice, Curtis allegedly acted with others to harass several prominent figures in the San Diego area, including Congressman Bob Filner, La Mesa Mayor Art Madrid, regional ADL director Morris Casuto, and the Director of the Heartland Human Relations and Fair Housing Association, Clara Harris.[108] Despite the amateurish characteristics of the alleged offenses, the authorities have taken Curtis and his accomplices seriously, as they remain in prison without bail to this day.

Over the past decade the leaderless approach has indeed gained much popularity in the far right. Indeed, even the geriatric-oriented Liberty Lobby recently released a publication on the subject.[109] However, the far right has not unanimously endorsed this approach. In light of some of the recent putative examples of leaderless resistance, some critics find it futile and counterproductive, as it often engenders a great deal of negative publicity and unwanted attention from authorities. Some elements of the far right now call for a more gradualist approach. Ironically, those advocating this new approach are from the National Alliance, the organization whose propaganda has been associated with many incidents of right-wing violence.

Writing under the pseudonym "Eric Hollyoak," Steven Barry wrote a scathing critique called "The Fallacy of Leaderless Resistance" in *Resistance* magazine, the organ of the late Dr Pierce's Resistance Records.[110] Barry is a retired Army Special Forces sergeant, and claims to have had much experience in counter-insurgency warfare during his twenty-five-year military career.[111] He took issue with the amateurish approach of leaderless resistance and could find no historical examples where it had been applied successfully. In his view, it amounts to little more than anarchy that degenerates into banditry. He sees no operational utility and believes that the approach is fundamentally flawed. According to Barry, leaderless resistance appeals to the "lowest (or most psychotic) common denominator" within any given organization. Moreover, it plays right into "the enemy's hands" insofar as organizations can be held accountable under the application of vicarious liability lawsuits initiated by watchdog groups such as the Southern Poverty Law Center.

Barry argues that armed resistance is just a subset of a larger strategy of political warfare, which also includes ideological warfare, organizational warfare, psychological warfare, intelligence warfare, and mass warfare. In the main, Barry sees the leaderless resistance approach as organized backwards. He believes that careful planning and organization must precede armed resistance. In order to successfully accomplish the preceding tasks, a policy making body is necessary with a centralized chain of command through which it can issue orders. Furthermore, Barry points out that no resistance underground is capable of sustaining itself without some kind of support system – friends and accomplices who provide intelligence, safe houses, escape routes and supplies – virtually all of which the far right currently does not have. Barry's recommendations are reminiscent of the strategic approach used by the Shining Path movement in Peru, which spent ten years creating a clandestine organizational structure before embarking on a campaign of violence in the 1980s.[112]

In sum, Barry was very critical of armed right-wing violence, and not even the Order escaped his caustic pen. According to his analysis, the Order's campaign was doomed to failure because it had no real network of support. Barry saw this kind of "grassroots" style of resistance as hopelessly futile.

Barry's article sparked a hailstorm of controversy in the revolutionary right. For many, the exploits of the Order were seen as beyond reproach. The most vociferous proponents of leaderless resistance, including Alex Curtis and Tom Metzger, harshly criticized Barry for what they saw as heresy. Former Order members Richard Scutari, Gary Lee Yarbough and Randy Duey also took issue with Barry and pointed out that Dr Pierce had no reservations about accepting largesse from the Order. Those such as Curtis and Metzger retorted that this approach was not meant to be a permanent strategy, but rather the most viable approach at the present point in time. According to their reasoning, a societal breakdown will eventually come about, at which time an organized resistance infrastructure will naturally develop. For his part, Barry remained unapologetic:

> [I]t is not up to me to mend fences with those who persist in their error. WAR, the Order, etc., immediately began a campaign of backbiting and mudslinging, some of which I've read with amusement, the vast bulk of which I simply ignore. But in no way did any of the responses posit a single historical example of "leaderless resistance," let alone justify the notion's operational or strategic utility. Leaderless resistance, stripped of all its rather ill considered appeals to "tactical independence," is nothing but anarchy. I don't know if you've noticed, but the whole "far-right movement" is wallowing in incompetence.
>
> A month after the leaderless resistance article appeared, Dr Pierce went to some effort to "correct" those parts of the article dealing with the Order. His corrections may or may not have been more accurate than my descriptions; I got my information from books and published articles. There has been some acrimony between Pierce and Metzger. I do not know the origin, and I really don't care. I don't get involved in any of the Peyton Place squabbles on the right.[113]

Just where Dr Pierce stood on the issue of resistance and terrorism has been a topic of great speculation among those who study the subject. Pierce's opinion on this topic could appear ambiguous. In some of his broadcasts he gave veiled praise for Islamic terrorists who had carried out dramatic acts of terrorism. Some saw Pierce as a cheerleader on the sidelines, one who "built bombers, not bombs" and instigated others to commit acts of terrorism. However, if one examines his pronouncements closely, it is apparent that he actually favored a more gradualist approach. He had criticized random acts of violence, such as the attacks by Benjamin Smith and Buford Furrow, not for moral reasons, but because he believed that such acts would give his opponents reason to crack down on the far right before it was in a position to mount effective resistance. Instead he believed that such "resistance" must be properly directed in a disciplined manner. He stressed the need to build a revolutionary infrastructure before the far right can physically oppose "the system." Pierce elaborated on his position in an interview:

W. P. My view of the matter is that we can't afford any kind of systematic illegal activity. By that, I mean any scheme to raise money illegally or not pay our taxes, rob banks or assassinate people. We can't do that because certainly if we did we would get caught and lose. I don't have any experience with that sort of thing. I have other things to do. I just believe that eventually we would wreck the whole operation if we tried to operate illegally. So we have to work within the law at this stage. It just doesn't make sense for us to be illegal. What's to be gained by being illegal?

G. M. Do you see yourself permanently playing the role of a propagandist, or do you think that someday, if conditions allowed for it, that your organization could transform itself into a group that actually physically confronts the system, if you will?

W. P. We do what seems to me makes sense to do at any given time. We can not win ultimately unless we are able to communicate with the people much more effectively than we are now.

So all of our efforts have been aimed at building up a communications infrastructure, multi-media infrastructure. If ten years from now, the Jews are successful in outlawing the First and Second Amendments, we may have to do other things. We may be forced to be much more confrontational than we are now. I just hope that the timing is such that we are not forced into a position where we can't win.

G. M. In your own words, your opponents have done a pretty good job in marginalizing you. If your organization were to obtain a certain critical mass of strength and influence, do you really think that the government and your watchdog opponents would let it continue? By that, I mean there seems to be a kind of self-limiting aspect to the far right. If it gets a little too strong, it seems engender opposition that contains it from expanding.

W. P. Well, you know you got to constantly keep your eye on what's happening. Sometimes the government, our enemy, may have a plan. "Well, we're not going to let these boys get too big. You know, if they start getting too big, we're going to slap them down." But maybe, when the time comes and they think now we've got to stop them that they have lost a little bit of the ability to do that. History has a habit of catching people by surprise. Catching people who thought that they had everything under control by surprise. ... And it happened over and over and over again that the established regime, which should have been able to maintain control, loses control because it was overwhelmed and events snowballed on them. They weren't able to keep up with what happened, what happened too fast and caught them by surprise.

I don't know what's going to happen. I really don't. I'm just doing what I have to do now because we can't win without being able to communicate with the people. So that's what I'm trying to do. When we can do that a lot more effectively than we're doing now, we'll think about what we're going to do next.[114]

Repeatedly, Pierce would maintain that conventional politics was futile for his movement and that armed struggle was inevitable. However, Pierce had no illusions of the extent of his influence and power, and warned that any premature resistance or terrorism would only provoke his opponents into repressive measures that the far right is currently unable to counter. Thus at this present time, the late Dr Pierce's National Alliance is concentrating on building a multimedia propaganda network. Pierce commanded great respect in the far-right movement. However, especially since his death, there probably remain a number of loose cannons who will ignore those admonitions of restraint for the present time. Although there is virtually no organized right-wing terrorism at this time, lone wolf terrorists will more than likely continue to cause sporadic havoc.

Conclusion

It is hoped that the preceding analysis has demonstrated that right-wing terrorism and violence has a long history in America. In recent years observers have noted a shift in terrorism from the political left to the political right.[115] FBI data do much to lend credence to this assertion.[116] In Europe, large migrations from the Third World have occasioned an often-violent xenophobic backlash from right-wing extremists and skinhead hooligans.

However, its significance should not be overstated. Relative to the size of America's large population, right-wing terrorism is not substantial. Excluding the Oklahoma City bombing, Hewitt's data indicate that 176 people were killed as a result of right-wing violence during the period from 1958 through 1998.[117] Not to trivialize the victims, these figures are relative and can be compared to other forms of violence to be put in proper perspective. In one year alone (1991), in just one American city, Los Angeles, there were over 700 deaths related to intergang violence.[118] What's more, most right-wing terrorist activities in the United States have been short-lived, in large part because the groups had very little public support.[119] There are some distinguishing characteristics about right-wing terrorism that make it unique.

According to Hewitt's analysis, more so than any other type of political extremism, right-wing violence targets individuals because of ascriptive characteristics such as race. Whereas other terrorists are more likely to strike at the state and other institutions, right-wing terrorists are more likely to target individuals in attacks that appear as "hate crimes."[120] This pattern still holds, despite a shift in recent years in which right-wing terrorists have increasingly targeted the state. The political and social goals of right-wing terrorists resemble in some ways those of ethnic-nationalist terrorists insofar as both often seek to create a territorial community that is ethnically or racially homogeneous. However, in another analysis by Hewitt, which included case studies of ethnic nationalist terrorist campaigns in Greece, Northern Ireland and Spain, the percentage of victims targeted because of their ethnic background was still substantially lower than it was for American right-wing extremists.[121] In this sense, right-wing violence appears "non-strategic" and lacking purpose or direction, and violence often appears as an end in itself.[122] This would suggest that one of the reasons watchdog groups figure so prominently in the area of right-wing terrorism is because this particular variant of terrorism, more so than others, tends to be directed more at *personal* targets such as members of racial and religious minorities rather than *impersonal* targets such as the state and other institutions. Variants of terrorism that tend to target the state (e.g. left-wing terrorism) by and large do not arouse the level of visceral fear among segments of the population, other than, perhaps, representatives of the state. It is thus understandable that right-wing terrorism – which frequently targets specific population groups – would engender greater intervention by private organizations composed of representatives that are targeted both violently and rhetorically by extremists. This development would be consistent with Truman's theory of interest group formation, i.e. that organizations often come about to protect the group's welfare and safety from rival groups.[123]

Since the demise of the Order, there has not really been any organized threat of terrorism and violence emanating from the racialist right. Virtually all violence has been perpetrated by individuals or "lone wolves," who act on their own initiative without any directive from the extremist groups with which they are sometimes affiliated. Those right-wing extremists who tend to associate with the revolutionary segment of the racialist right – most notably adherents of the Christian Identity theology and the skinheads – seem to have the greatest propensity towards violence.[124] The incidence of the Christian Identity religion among so many right-wing terrorists is consistent with a larger global phenomenon, i.e. a tendency for contemporary terrorists to draw upon religious inspiration to justify and rationalize their violence. In recent years, several observers have argued that religious fanaticism is conducive to terrorism insofar as it loosens the moral and ethical constraints that would normally restrain the more secularly inspired terrorists. Although this may sound a bit counter-intuitive, according to this theory, those terrorists who believe that God is on their side are more self-assured in their mission and hence have fewer compunctions about using violence.[125] The lethality of religiously inspired terrorism during the 1990s lends credence to this theory.[126]

The *modus operandi* of right-wing terrorists has undergone some change over the past decade or so. The primacy of leaderless resistance in the racialist right presents a challenge for authorities insofar as it is difficult to predict from where a threat may come. It is much easier to infiltrate an organization rather than a clique of a few individuals, or to read the mind of one lone wolf. It is important to keep in mind that the prominence of leaderless resistance is symptomatic of the organizational and financial weakness of right-wing terrorists. No real terrorist infrastructure as such exists in the far-right milieu. What is more, as James Adams has pointed out, the *sine qua non* for the development of such an infrastructure is money.[127] Generally speaking, right-wing terrorists have neither garnered support from state sponsors nor developed adequate means of self-financing.

In recent years organized groups in the Militia movement (e.g. the Montana Freemen and the Republic of Texas) have been a problem for authorities. However, the outlaws in this segment appear to concentrate their illegal activities primarily on "paper terrorism" (e.g. issuing phony checks and filing illegal liens) rather than political violence.

One obvious concern is the potentially greater lethality of instruments of terrorism. Changes in technology have enabled terrorists to inflict potentially greater damage. The Oklahoma City bombing demonstrated the potential lethality of "terrorism on the cheap" conducted by just a few individuals. Indeed, more so than the terrorists of the previous decades, contemporary terrorists appear more intent on punishing their targets. Buck Revell, a former assistant director of the FBI, explains:

> Domestically the change has been in the extreme right-wing groups that are also willing to inflict mass casualties. They want to punish not the United States per se, but the government of the United States that they view as the enemy. They base this in many instances on religious fervor. Their religious tenets, whether it's the Aryan Nations or any of them, they base it around the so called Christian Identity movement, which is obviously a terrible revision of any true Christianity. But again, they justify the taking of lives on the basis of their religious tenets, and it also has one other thing. It empowers individuals, and in fact emboldens individuals, to act within the context of attacking the government. So therefore coming out of this you have essentially very small groups or perhaps one or two individuals who feel empowered to act and punish the government for the things that they perceive to be governmental abuse, whether it be a Ruby Ridge or a Waco or whatever particular event that they use to take issue with. They demonstrate a willingness and intent to punish and to inflict mass casualties.
>
> The other big difference is that today terrorist organizations, whether they're international or domestic, have C3I capability. That is Command, Control, Communications and Intelligence. Any group today with the communications capability of cyber technology has access to all kinds of information on the internet, including on a mobile basis, and the ability to

126 *The far right and terrorism*

use it *vis-à-vis* both their cyber and internet communication capabilities. ... So very small and not well funded groups today have the capability of nation states only ten years ago because of the rapid evolution of technology and the availability of that technology ...

[This terrorism is] very cheap for a magnified result. Essentially the truck bomb that McVeigh built was less than $500 and he would have damn near knocked down the whole building with better placement. ... The change in philosophy, the change in lethality, the change in technology, and the change in intent to commit mass casualties. Although there may be fewer incidents, the incidents that we do have are really magnified by the expansion of capability and the very draconian philosophical approach of both the domestic right-wing extremists and the international religious based terrorist groups.[128]

Elements of the American far right have demonstrated on at least one previous occasion that they would not be averse to such tactics. For example, the CSA allegedly planned to poison water supplies, and recently a militia group, Southeastern States Alliance, allegedly planned on destroying a nuclear power plant. Fortunately, these examples never made it beyond the planning stages.

Another ominous trend is the targeting of vital parts of infrastructure that could potentially paralyze or do great damage to the day-to-day lives of many people. The following examples illustrate this potential hazard:

- In 1996 the FBI arrested eight members of the Washington State Militia for manufacturing and possessing explosive devices. They discussed plans on using them to destroy a radio tower, a bridge and a train tunnel.[129]
- In 1997, members of the True Knights of the Ku Klux Klan were arrested for having planned the bombing of a natural gas processing and storage facility, which could have released deadly hydrogen sulfide into the air.[130]
- In 1995, a twelve-car Amtrak train was derailed near Hyder, Arizona. The crash killed one person and seriously injured twelve others. Although the perpetrators were never caught, they left behind a message that mentioned the Bureau of Alcohol, Tobacco, and Firearms, the FBI, Ruby Ridge and Waco. These themes suggest that an anti-government right-wing group may have perpetrated the attack. Finally, they signed the letter "Sons of Gestapo."[131]
- Members of a Florida-based militia group, the Southeastern States Alliance, were arrested in 1999 for planning to steal explosives from National Guard armories to be used in attacks to blow up power lines, a nuclear plant and government offices.[132]

Finally, bio-terrorism, such as an anthrax attack, is one more measure that terrorists could employ. There are some ominous indications that this approach may have been already considered:

- In 1998 the FBI arrested two men for allegedly possessing anthrax. The FBI later dropped the charges. "As it transpired that they only possessed a harmless strain used in veterinary vaccines." One of the defendants, Larry Wayne Harris, was reported to have been affiliated with the Aryan Nations. Prior to that incident, Harris had pled guilty to illegally obtaining bubonic plague bacteria through the mail. Harris had also authored an underground book called *Bacteriological Warfare: A Major Threat to North America*.[133]
- In 1995 the FBI arrested members of the Patriot's Council, a Minnesota-based tax protest group, for allegedly manufacturing and planning to use ricin, a highly toxic biological substance.[134]

Despite the potential for greater lethality, terrorist expert Bruce Hoffman observed that traditionally the weapons of choice for the secularly inspired terrorists were basically guns and bombs. These terrorists were reluctant to use the more lethal measures because they hoped to gain a measure of sympathy from their audience. As Brian Jenkins once pointed out, "terrorists want a lot of people watching and a lot of people listening and not a lot of people dead."[135] However, the religiously inspired terrorists – into which category many in the far right would fit – demonstrate a willingness to use weapons of greater lethality, and appear to have less compunction over inflicting heavy casualties.[136] Ariel Merara has argued, however, that the increasing availability of weapons of potential greater lethality notwithstanding, terrorists have been loath to use them for a variety of reasons, including the psychological, social, and political context within which terrorists operate. The most important factor limiting the use of weapons of mass destruction (or 'WMD'), as he sees it, is the organizational feature of terrorism, which requires terrorist organizations to maintain clandestineness, which in turn dictates a compartmentalized organizational structure, which therefore limits the capabilities for carrying out terrorist attacks. Terrorist groups employing WMD would need a high level of organizational complexity and members with considerable skills. The clandestine nature of terrorism, however, militates against this development, except in the case of state sponsored terrorism. But as Merara points out, state sponsors would be loath to enable terrorists with such capability for fear that the former could be held accountable and would thus bear the brunt of retribution by the aggrieved state.[137] Finally, as another observer noted, the commission of mass acts of destructive terrorism would require a long period of training and conditioning in a closed environment impervious to outside standards of morality. Such insular environments are harder and harder to maintain in the increasingly interconnected and globalized world of today. As a result, early warning signs are more likely to be made available to law enforcement and intelligence authorities long before serious threats can be carried out.[138]

During his tenure as FBI Director, Louis Freeh has stated that the threat of domestic terrorism comes from three primary categories: right-wing extremists, Puerto Rican extremists, and special interest extremists.[139] However, there are now indications that another force is becoming the chief focus of the government's attention in this area, one which regularly disrupts cities which host meetings and conferences by supra-national organizations. For example, a disparate coalition of anti-globalist protestors seriously disrupted the World Trade Organization (WTO) meeting in Seattle, Washington in the fall of 1999. More recently, protestors caused considerable havoc during the April 2000 World Bank and International Monetary Fund (IMF) conference in Washington DC, which resulted in a partial government shutdown. Consequently, anti-globalist anarchists appear to be displacing right-wing extremists as the government's focus of attention with regard to political extremism and terrorism.[140] Some watchdog groups that normally monitor the far right have also taken notice. For example, recently the Southern Poverty Law Center expressed concern over a possible link-up between anti-globalist elements of the far right and the far left. According to one of its reports, elements of the radical right were attempting to infiltrate and direct the fledgling opposition to the WTO. The SPLC warns that these far-rightists might make common cause with left-leaning anarchist demonstrators.[141] Likewise the ADL helped the Philadelphia City Council craft an ordinance that would make it illegal for protestors to wear masks.[142] This was based on similar statutes that the ADL had crafted that were directed against the Ku Klux Klan.

But the far right continues to capture the attention of authorities, especially given its proclivity for violence throughout its history. The federal government has responded to the far right in several different ways over the years. It is that topic to which we shall now turn.

5 The US government's response to right-wing extremism

Introduction

Terrorism poses a special problem to democratic governments. As Walter Laqueur noted, the constitutional constraints they place on themselves make it more difficult to combat terrorism. Furthermore, if these governments fail to effectively combat terrorism, they are subject to ridicule and contempt by the press. Finally, if they adopt stringent measures, they leave themselves open to charges of oppression and violation of human rights.[1] However, one principal advantage that democratic governments generally have is that they enjoy legitimacy among most of their populations. Thus they can usually depend upon their sustained support in efforts to suppress terrorism.[2]

As mentioned in previous chapters, episodes of right-wing extremism and violence have punctuated American history almost from the founding of the republic. Consequently, the government has had to deal with this development on many past occasions. This chapter examines various ways in which the US government has responded to right-wing terrorism and extremism.

The first section provides some historic background on this topic. The Reconstruction Era Klan presented the government with its first major challenge of containing right-wing violence on a large scale. Other major periods of government involvement in this area include the "Brown Scare" from the late 1930s to mid-1940s, and the Civil Rights Era of the 1950s and 1960s.

Subsequent sections examine and identify the chief government agencies which deal with the public policy issue, and explain how they are organized to do so. The second section looks at the Federal Bureau of Investigation (FBI). Inasmuch as the FBI is the chief agency that is responsible for investigating and preventing domestic terrorism, it warrants close examination.

The third section looks at the Congress. On several past occasions both chambers of Congress have concerned themselves with right-wing extremism. For example, the erstwhile House Un-American Activities Committee investigated both extreme left- and right-wing groups and issued reports on its findings. In more recent years, the Senate Judiciary Subcommittee on Terrorism and Government Technology has held hearings on subjects related to this issue, including the militias and Ruby Ridge.

The fourth section examines how the Department of Defense (DOD) has grappled with this issue. Inasmuch as the military is an important arm of the government, the political leadership is obviously concerned about insuring the loyalty and discipline of its soldiers.

The United States is unique among most other countries insofar as it has a tradition of, and codified protections for, free speech. This gives extremist groups much more latitude in propagating their ideas. The fifth section of this chapter examines how the Supreme Court of the United States has handled First Amendment issues dealing with the far right.

The sixth section takes a look at international cooperation between the United States and German governments in dealing with right-wing extremism. Finally, there are conclusions and some final observations on this topic.

Historical background

The Reconstruction Era Ku Klux Klan

The first significant campaign of right-wing terrorism that provoked a serious government response occurred during the 1860s and 1870s with the emergence of the Reconstruction Era Ku Klux Klan. As mentioned in Chapter 4, right-wing terrorism reached its apogee in America during the Reconstruction's Klan's reign of terror in the aftermath of the Civil War. By 1868, the Klan had spread from its original environs of Tennessee to other states in the South. It henceforth became a national problem.

The federalist system presented an obstacle for authorities in dealing with the Klan. The crimes the Klan perpetrated were state offenses and as such the federal government technically did not have jurisdiction over most of them.[3] However, all of this occurred in the aftermath of the Civil War – hitherto the greatest military conflict the country had experienced. Thus the occupying Union forces were in place to help deal with the problem. Consequently, up until 1871, the federal government relied on the military to quell the violence of the Klan.

Klan violence was widespread and presented legal challenges to the Union Army. General Ulysses S. Grant wanted to avoid the appearance of military despotism, and was reluctant to order military trials in times of peace when civilian courts were open. According to one historian, the Union commanders genuinely detested the Klan and sympathized with its victims; however, the local authorities were loath to prosecute Klan offenders and most were released without prosecution.[4]

Word of Klan terrorism eventually reached Congress, which was by 1870 compelled to act on the crisis. In that year it passed the Enforcement Act, which empowered Congress to enforce the provisions of the recently ratified Fifteenth Amendment.[5] Section 6 of the new law made it a felony offense for two or more persons to conspire together or go in disguise with the intent of depriving someone of any privilege of citizenship, or to punish him afterward for having exercised it.[6] This section was intended to be used as the basis for federal indictments brought against the Klan.

However, federal authorities seldom used the new law. It was thought that the new law's presence alone would act as a deterrent against further terrorism. But violence continued and both the President and the Congress were deluged with reports of these outrages along with appeals, often from Southern Republicans, for help. In 1871, Congress formed a committee to investigate the Klan. A report was issued, which concluded that the Klan was in large part political in nature and used various unlawful measures including intimidation, whipping and murder on behalf of the Democratic Party in the South.[7] Violence was particularly pronounced in South Carolina, where Governor Robert K. Scott and the state legislature were crying out for federal assistance. To meet this challenge, Congress passed the Ku Klux Klan Act in 1871. The new law sought to enforce the Fourteenth Amendment and proscribed conspiracy and the use of disguises to deprive someone of his equal protection of the law. Furthermore, it allowed the President to use the armed forces as a last resort to suppress conspiracies that violated the new civil rights laws. Finally, the new law empowered the President to suspend the writ of habeas corpus if he saw fit to do so.

The new Klan Act was a highly partisan measure, with Republicans supporting it and Democrats opposing it, and it became somewhat of a political hot potato.[8] The War Department and newly created Justice Department each believed that the other should initiate proceedings against the Klan. One particular challenge the government faced was securing evidence against the clandestine hooded order. Thus the federal government for the first time made wide use of informants. Under the direction of H. C. Whitley, the head of the Secret Service, many informants infiltrated the Klan by posing as businessmen or laborers seeking economic opportunities.[9] The informant program proved effective, and at long last the arrests and prosecutions of Klansmen were underway.

Federal prosecution was not without significant problems, however. So many arrests were made that the federal courts became clogged with Klan cases involving serious crimes. The number of federal prosecutors, judges and clerks were not adequate to handle the tremendous workload, and consequently many serious cases were not brought to trial. As a result a carrot was used in conjunction with the stick. For example, in Mississippi, federal authorities expedited the problem by offering suspended sentences in exchange for pleas of guilty.

These difficulties notwithstanding, the federal government's diligence eventually proved to be effective. Klan violence so quickly dissipated by the end of 1871 that by the time of the presidential election in 1872, the federal government did not deign it necessary to employ extraordinary means to preserve order. Although Klan violence greatly decreased, members and fellow travelers remained vocal in their threats of retribution against Republicans, which the latter took quite seriously. Eventually, a *modus vivendi* of sorts was reached between the recalcitrant elements in the South and the federal government. Prosecutions against Klansmen continued to fall off and many pardons were granted. In 1876, the Supreme Court in its *US v. Reese* decision, eviscerated much of the 1870 Enforcement Act by ruling that the federal government could protect civil rights against abridgement only by states and not private citizens.[10] What's more, the public in the North grew tired of enforcing order and fair elections in the South. Finally, when Rutherford B. Hayes became president in 1877, he declared Reconstruction over. Soon thereafter, newly elected Democrats in South Carolina came to a mutual agreement with federal officials to drop all legal charges of a political nature.

The federal government's campaign ultimately defeated the Klan, but arguably the organization achieved its primary objectives. It demoralized the Republican Party in the South, which enabled the Democratic Party to regain political power. Furthermore, it did much to prevent the full enfranchisement of Black freedmen, which consigned them to second class status for a long time. The Confederate General, Nathan Bedford Forrest, the Invisible Empire's first Grand Wizard and national leader, eventually ordered the organization to disband, which initiated a long lull in right-wing violence. But the Klan idea proved to be resilient, and was resurrected at Stone Mountain, Georgia in 1915.

The Second Era Ku Klux Klan

The Second Era Klan reached its zenith in the 1920s, and is estimated to have reached a membership of between 2 and 5 million.[11] This is an impressive figure when one considers that membership was restricted to White, Protestant, native-born Americans. Moreover, the new Klan exerted considerable political influence during that period. Many Klansmen and sympathizers were elected to state and local political offices, and even such prominent political figures as Supreme Court Justices Hugo Black and Edward White were once members before taking office. Despite its veneer of respectability, the Second Era Klan was often violent, so much so that calls were made to curb its activities. For the most part however, responsibility was left to the state and local governments to handle the Klan, as the federal government was loath to get involved. There were exceptions, however. In 1924, the Justice Department's Bureau of Investigation (the precursor of the FBI) used the Mann Act[12] to successfully prosecute the "Imperial Kleagle" of Louisiana.[13] Generally though, both the executive and legislative branches were disinclined to take action against the Klan.

The Anti-Defamation League stepped forward to fill this void and drew up model legislation aimed at exposing Klan membership. One such bill, the "Anti-Intolerance Act," was introduced into Congress, but died in committee. However, similar ADL-crafted statutes were passed in several states including New York, Iowa, Minnesota and Michigan.[14] In its *Bryant v. Zimmermann* (1928) decision, the Supreme Court upheld the New York state law, which outlawed parading with masks and required the public registration of certain "oathbound" organizations.[15]

Ultimately, the Second Era Klan imploded due to various internecine battles and scandals. Moreover, the promiscuity in its selection of targets, which included not only Blacks, but also Jews, unions, communists, Catholics, and "morally lapsed" White Anglo-Saxon Protestants, made too many Americans feel at risk.[16] By the late 1920s, Klan affiliation became a political liability. However, remnants of the Second Era Klan would soldier on until the mid-1940s, whereupon the US Bureau of Revenue finally administered the coup de grace in 1944. The Bureau filed a lien of $685,000 in back taxes on profits made during the 1920s. The Klan could not pay its tax bill and was forced to dissolve.[17]

The Brown Scare

The Great Depression was a severe trauma for many Americans, and was a watershed period in American history. Political realignments were afoot as Franklin D. Roosevelt forged a broad coalition to win the presidency. The far right also changed, and its focus shifted away from Nativism and anti-Catholicism to anti-Semitism and anti-communism.

A variety of measures were used to counter right-wing extremism during this period. There were already anti-subversive laws on the books that federal government and state legislatures had passed during the "Red Scare" of the 1920s. More were added in the 1930s and 1940s.

The German American Bund was one of the principal and most visible far-right organizations during that period. It grew out of another organization, the Friends of the New Germany, in 1936. At its height it reached a membership of somewhere between 20,000 and 25,000.[18] Not surprisingly, both the government and the watchdogs targeted the Bund. It came under close scrutiny by the FBI, and some of its members were subpoenaed to testify before various congressional committees which investigated subversive activities. For its part, the ADL managed to infiltrate the Bund, placing several undercover investigators into the organization, one of whom was the personal chauffeur of the Bund's leader Fritz Kuhn.[19] Through these efforts, the ADL was able to expose Americans who supported the Bund.

Efforts were made at the state level to curtail the activities of right-wing extremists. The Bund was very active in New York, which was the home state of Representative Samuel Dickstein, one of the Bund's most dogged critics. Several Bundists testified before his McCormack-Dickstein Committee, which he co-chaired. During the hearings, some Bundists reported that they were National Guardsmen. This alarmed Dickstein and he initiated an inquiry into the Guard's citizenship requirements. In March 1938, New York Governor Herbert Lehman ordered the dismissal of all aliens, and soon thereafter Congress followed his lead.[20] Right-wing extremists gathered much attention in New York City, where young members of the Christian Front and other rightist groups disseminated provocative literature and occasionally fought street scuffles with Jews. To meet this challenge, Mayor LaGuardia created an anti-subversive unit in the New York City Police in September 1939 to keep tabs on right-wing extremists in the city.[21] Another measure was passed by the New York State legislature in 1939, which forbade persons from wearing uniforms or other military-style attire in public that resembled uniforms from a foreign nation.[22] The bill was aimed at members of the German American Bund, whose uniforms resembled those of German SA stormtroopers.

Ultimately it was New York authorities that were responsible for breaking up the Bund. Its leader, Fritz Kuhn, was charged and convicted of misappropriation of his organization's funds and sent to jail in 1939.[23] The organization soldiered on for two more years, but decided to dissolve itself on December 8, 1941, just after the Japanese attack on Pearl Harbor. Despite charges that the Bundists were agents of a foreign power, the German government disavowed connections with the organization.[24] Furthermore, in 1938, the Attorney General released the report of an FBI investigation, which cleared the Bund of any federal wrongdoing.[25]

Action was taken to combat right-wing extremism at the federal level as well. By 1936, President Franklin D. Roosevelt was concerned that potentially hostile fascist and communist governments might have an influence on domestic extremist groups. Far left organizations, such as the Communist Party USA (CPUSA), also recruited many members during that period.[26] To meet this potential challenge, Roosevelt conferred with FBI Director J. Edgar Hoover in a private meeting to discuss the problem. Roosevelt instructed Hoover to develop an intelligence apparatus to gather information on extremist groups.[27] Inasmuch as it was not illegal to belong to an extremist organization, technically the FBI had no legal authority to investigate such matters. However, Roosevelt found a loophole to circumvent this technicality. Under the Appropriations Act, the FBI was authorized to conduct such investigations at the request of the Secretary of State. To make the operation legitimate, Roosevelt convoked another secret meeting, which included himself, Hoover, and Secretary of State Gordon Hull. According to Hoover's account, Hull complied with Roosevelt's request. Thus the bureau was authorized to gather domestic intelligence, in this case by presidential directive rather than by statute. The program was kept secret, and neither the Congress nor the Judiciary was apprised of it. Attorney General Homer Cummings was told only after the fact.[28]

To implement the program, the FBI created a file-classification system for managing intelligence. A nationwide informant plan was designed and developed, which aimed at infiltrating extremist groups. Hoover coordinated this information with intelligence officials in the military and the State Department. Funding for the FBI increased substantially.[29] Civil liberties were sacrificed in part to wartime exigencies, as intrusive and unregulated investigative techniques developed during that period.[30] By 1938 the FBI began to compile information on German aliens, and also assumed responsibility for investigating espionage and acts of sabotage.[31] Towards this end the FBI created the Plant Informant Program in 1940, to gather information on potential saboteurs working in defense facilities. In the same year the FBI initiated the American Legion Contact Program, which used local legion posts to investigate and report incidents of suspected espionage and subversive activities.[32]

Other private groups augmented these efforts. The Non-Sectarian Anti-Nazi League, led by Samuel Untermeyer, made efforts to counter domestic extremists by alerting the public and demanding investigation of their activities. An affiliated organization, The World Anti-Nazi Council, spearheaded an economic boycott against Germany, which drew criticism from some domestic right-wing extremists.[33]

Both the ADL and the American Jewish Committee worked closely with, and provided information to, government authorities including congressional committees, Army and Navy Intelligence, and the FBI.[34] According to a claim by Arnold Forster, an important member of the ADL's fact-finding division during that period, most of the data on pro-Nazi propaganda that federal agencies possessed came from ADL field investigators and other private organizations.[35] The ADL often employed agents from outside investigative agencies who operated as independent contractors. Many were retired federal government investigators.[36]

The results of these investigations were often funneled to sympathetic journalists, who wrote stories and editorials against the threat of native fascism and fifth-column subversion.[37] For example, Dillard Stokes of the *Washington Post* wrote articles that exposed the activities of extremists, and even assisted materially in collecting evidence for the Great Sedition Trial of 1944.[38] One important ADL contact was the famous journalist Walter Winchell, who by-lined one of the most popular columns of the day. Winchell yielded considerable influence, not only in journalism but also in politics, and was a friend of President Roosevelt. The ADL's Forster devoted much time to supplying Winchell with information on right-wing extremists and fascist sympathizers that the journalist used for his popular exposés.[39] Forster also occasionally fed material to another high-profile journalist, Drew Pearson.[40]

One of the most significant works of anti-extremist journalism came from Avendis Derounian, who under the pseudonym of John Roy Carlson, wrote a book called *Under Cover*. The book sold over 800,000 copies and was the top non-fiction bestseller of 1944.[41] Carlson posed as pro-fascist Italian-American in order to infiltrate American far-right groups during the late 1930s. Some watchdog organizations had a hand in this effort, as the ADL and Friends of Democracy supported Carlson during his undercover investigations.[42] His book read like an adventure story as he skillfully exploited the exposé formula and depicted himself as an intrepid undercover agent. Ultimately he came to be on friendly terms with many prominent individuals in the American far right, including eighteen defendants in the Great Sedition Trial (see below). Using a "links and ties" technique, Carlson sought to demonstrate that there was an intricate conspiracy involving the German government, representatives of the far right, and isolationist members of Congress (e.g. Senators Wheeler, Nye and Taft, and Representatives Fish and Hoffman). To make his point, Carlson cited interlocking letterheads and chains of associations – some of which required Carlson as an essential link – which allegedly tied these individuals into a subversive conspiracy. One weakness of this method was that many of these individuals had never even met one another.[43]

Carlson's book did much to shape the public's perception of domestic right-wing extremism during that period. His thesis also dovetailed nicely with President Roosevelt's efforts to silence his isolationist opponents in the Congress. Even before the attack on Pearl Harbor, Roosevelt had been pressuring the Justice Department to round up some of his more outspoken and disreputable critics and put them on trial. According to the historian Richard Gid Powers, Roosevelt seemed to have in mind a mass trial that would link domestic extremists with his congressional critics.[44] In that respect, Carlson's book furthered Roosevelt's aim by giving credence to such a theory. Powers goes so far as to assert that Carlson's book ultimately persuaded the government to pursue the Great Sedition Trial of 1944.[45] Several defendants and critics of this trial also believed that the prosecution was based in large part on Carlson's thesis.[46]

The Brown Scare culminated in the Great Sedition Trial of 1944 (formally *US v. McWilliams*). Thirty American rightists and foreign nationals, including Lawrence Dennis, Gerald Winrod, Elizabeth Dilling, William Dudley Pelley and George Sylvester Viereck, were charged with sedition. Several members of the German American Bund were included among those indicted, as the prosecution argued that the defendants were part of a German government network of subversion. The specific charge was a violation of the Smith Act of 1940, which prohibited the advocacy of insubordination, disloyalty, mutiny or refusal of duty in the military or naval forces of the United States, as well as the advocacy of the overthrow or destruction of any government in the United States by use of force or violence. Many of the defendants had published literature that was highly critical of FDR, the New Deal and US intervention overseas while lauding American rightists and isolationists, European fascists and the Japanese. The prosecutor, O. J. Rogge, argued that the defendants were part of a worldwide Nazi conspiracy by virtue of their beliefs and goals. He went so far as to name Adolf Hitler and his lieutenants as co-conspirators. The prosecution claimed that it could prove that the defendants had received funds and instructions from the German government.

The defendants were in fact, however, a disparate collection of rightists. Some admired European fascism, while others favored traditional versions of American populism and nationalism and looked askance at any form of totalitarianism. Rogge's thesis raised more than a few eyebrows, as many critics found it highly implausible that such a disparate collection could be part of some well-oiled conspiracy.

Rogge used the Laswell method of propaganda analysis as part of his prosecution strategy, by which he sought to demonstrate consistencies between the American rightists' and German Nazi propaganda. According to one critic, Rogge's thesis was a *Protocols*-style conspiracy theory in reverse.[47] Precisely how involved the various watchdog groups of that period were in this case is difficult to determine due to its sensitive nature. As mentioned earlier, various private groups and individuals had supplied intelligence information to the Justice Department prior to the trial. One of the defense counsels, James J. Laughlin, caused quite a stir in the courtroom when he requested the impounding of the ADL's files as part of the discovery process. He conjectured that much of the prosecution's evidence was based on the ADL's intelligence, and argued that it would be necessary to determine precisely what had been provided in order to mount an effective defense for his client. However, the presiding judge, Edward C. Eicher, denied the request.[48]

The trial dragged on for seven months until Judge Eicher died suddenly of a heart attack and his successor declared a mistrial. However, the government did not officially drop the indictment until two years later. The sedition trial had many critics, including prominent isolationist members of Congress such as Senators Burton K. Wheeler (MT), Gerald Nye (ND) and William Langer (ND), Representatives Hamilton Fish (NY), Claire Hoffman (MI) and even the Attorney General Francis Biddle.[49] Contemporary historians of this subject generally concede that the defendants were not part of a subversive conspiracy.[50] That many of the defendants admired Hitler, Mussolini and European fascism and advocated a fascistic style of government for the US was not in doubt. However, the activities of most of the American rightists were legal, and although unpopular, what they wrote and spoke were within the bounds of First Amendment protection. However, the fact that the government ceased prosecution and released most of those caught in the government's dragnet before or shortly after the end of hostilities, illustrates the American legal commitment to free speech. Conspicuously absent from the trial, the American Civil Liberties Union (ACLU) offered no support to the defendants, nor did it issue any statement against the government's prosecution of their speech.[51]

By the end of World War II the American far right was demoralized and imploding. However, events in the 1950s allowed it to rebound.

The Third Era Ku Klux Klan

A renascent Klan emerged in the aftermath of the *Brown v. Topeka Board of Education* Supreme Court decision in 1954. The new terrorist Klan organizations added a new weapon to their arsenal – dynamite. According to one estimate, over 130 targets were bombed in the South for the period 1956–63.[52] The 1963 bomb attack on the 16th Street Church in Birmingham, Alabama, which claimed the lives of four schoolgirls, shook the conscience of the nation. At first, federal authorities were loath to get involved in the Klan terrorist campaign in the South. FBI Director J. Edgar Hoover thought that a heavy-handed response would exacerbate tension in the region.[53]

The Civil Rights Act of 1964 added a new sense of urgency to the Klan's campaign of terror. During July, August and September of that year, twenty-seven black churches were burned to the ground, and Klan membership is estimated to have reached 14,000 at that time.[54] The murder of three civil rights workers in Mississippi that same year – James Chaney, Michael Schwerner and Andrew Goodman – finally provoked a response from the Justice Department. When Attorney General Robert Kennedy insisted on an aggressive response to this incident, Hoover complied and launched a sweeping crusade against the Klan, most notably in Mississippi. A field office was established in Jackson, Mississippi in July 1964 to handle the crisis. At the center of the conspiracy was Sam Bowers, the leader of an extremely violent Klan organization, the White Knights of the Ku Klux Klan. Eventually eighteen men, including local law enforcement personnel, went on trial for conspiring to violate the civil rights of the three civil rights workers. Outside federal intervention was essential in stemming the Klan's violence. As one observer noted, the Klan concentrated its violence in areas in which popular and police sentiment granted them a high degree of local immunity.[55] Extensive investigations by the FBI began to take their toll on the Klan and its membership dropped precipitously.

As in previous epochs of right-wing violence, private actors played a role in its suppression. For example, during the Civil Rights Era, journalists such as Walter Winchell and Drew Pearson drew the public's attention to the Klan.[56] The most notable instance of collusion between private actors and the government, however, occurred in 1967 in response to bombings of Jewish homes and synagogues in the South. The White Knights of the Ku Klux Klan, led by Sam Bowers, launched a campaign against Jewish targets after some representatives of the Southern Jewish community had voiced support for the Civil Rights movement. The new attacks alarmed the local Jewish community. This most recent rash of Klan violence, now aimed at Jewish targets, prompted a swift and resolute response from J. Edgar Hoover.[57] To handle the crisis local Jewish leaders, along with the local police and the FBI, worked together to devise a plan to stop the violence. A. I. Botnick, the regional director of the ADL in New Orleans, Louisiana, took the lead in raising reward money to solve the case of a synagogue bombing, and raised roughly $36,000 for this effort.[58] The money was to be used to enlist the help of informants who would lead authorities to the perpetrators. Two Klansmen, brothers Alton and Raymond Roberts, were employed in this effort and were paid with the money that had been raised. The FBI strongly encouraged the ADL's Botnick to participate in the planning, and together they decided to fight fire with fire. Local law enforcement, the FBI and the ADL's Botnick eventually came up with a plan to set up the perpetrators in what amounted to a death trap. The chief culprit behind the bombings was thought to be Thomas A. Tarrants III, a young, fanatical racist linked to Bowers' organization. Another Klansman, Danny Joe Hawkins, was thought to be his accomplice. Eventually a trap was set for them as they, with the connivance of the two informants, planned a bomb attack on a Jewish leader's home. In effect, it was a plan to lead the attackers into an ambush. However, as a last minute replacement, Kathy Ainsworth, a respectable married woman, a grade school teacher by day and right-wing radical by night, replaced Hawkins as Tarrants' accomplice. The two traveled to the residence of a prominent member of the Jewish community, where they planned to plant a bomb. However, the would-be attackers fell into a trap and were met with a fusillade of shots. Ainsworth was killed and Tarrants was struck numerous times but somehow managed to survive.[59] Tarrants fired back and miraculously managed to flee before being apprehended not far from the scene.

According to investigative reporter Jack Nelson, the FBI and the Meridian Police Department had in effect used money raised by the ADL to pay the two informants to arrange for two Klansmen to attempt a bombing so that the police could execute them during the commission of the crime.[60] The attack proved effective, as it finally broke the back of the Klan violence in Mississippi. However, neither the FBI nor the ADL wished to claim responsibility for the incident. Jack Nelson broke the story in 1970, but generally the public was not alarmed, as it was loath to sympathize with Klan terrorists. However, liberal organizations such as the American Civil Liberties Union and the American Friends Service Committee called for an official investigation.[61] As we shall see in the next chapter, such tactics were not uncommon during that period. Violent repression was also visited upon extremists from the political left, most notably the Black Nationalist movement. Much of this political repression was conducted under the rubric of COINTELPRO, which sought to disrupt extremist groups. This program was aimed mostly at the far left in large part, because it was more robust than its right-wing counterpart during that era. However, the FBI also targeted far-right organizations under the aegis of this program.

COINTELPRO: White hate groups

On March 8, 1956, FBI Director J. Edgar Hoover received authorization to launch the Counter Intelligence Program, which came to be known by the acronym COINTELPRO. COINTELPRO sought to disrupt extremist and dissident groups through a variety of methods including infiltration, psychological warfare, legal harassment, and occasional extralegal force and violence.[62] All totaled, the FBI admitted to 2,370 officially approved COINTELPRO actions from 1956 through 1971.[63] The major COINTELPRO operations fell into five major categories:

- CPUSA
- Socialist Workers Party Disruption Program
- "Klan-White hate groups"
- "Black nationalist hate groups"
- "New left"

It was in the year 1964 that the FBI decided to add the Klan and various "White hate groups" to the list of targets under COINTELPRO. According to the 1964 FBI memorandum that initiated this effort:

The purpose of this program is to expose, disrupt and otherwise neutralize the activities of the various Klans and hate organizations, their leadership and adherents. The activities of these groups must be followed on a continuous basis so we may take advantage of all opportunities for counterintelligence and also inspire action in instances where circumstances warrant. The devious maneuvers and duplicity of these groups must be exposed to public scrutiny through cooperation of reliable new media sources, both locally and at the Seat of Government. We must frustrate any effort of the groups to consolidate their forces or to recruit new or youthful adherents. In every instance, consideration should be given to disrupting the organized activity of these groups and no opportunity should be missed to capitalize upon organizational and personal conflicts of their leadership.[64]

Initially, seventeen Klan organizations and nine "hate" organizations were targeted under the COINTELPRO "Disruption of White Hate Groups" effort.[65] The program had the approval and support of Attorney General Nicholas Katzenbach.[66] In that same year the FBI's internal supervision of Klan activities was transferred from the General Investigations Division to the bureau's Domestic Intelligence Division. Thus the Klan investigation was moved from the criminal to the intelligence division.[67] What was unique about this particular COINTELPRO operation was that it was the first one whose targets had no connections in any way to a foreign intelligence movement or international revolutionary organization. All totaled, 289 different programs of action were approved and used against various Klan and far-right organizations under COINTELPRO.[68]

A variety of methods were employed to disrupt far-right groups under COINTELPRO. The bureau used approximately 2,000 informants in this effort, and according to one estimate, 15 per cent of the Klan's membership was comprised of informants.[69] A favorite technique was to spread rumors by sending anonymous or fictitious materials to members of these organizations. Examples included letters that were sent to Klansmen's wives alerting them to their husbands' infidelities. Letters were sent to their employers, which often resulted in their termination from employment. Another highly effective measure was the "snitch-jacket" technique, by which an impression was created that a Klan member was actually a police informant. The bureau also scoured right-wing publications for scuttlebutt, and would reprint embarrassing stories about far-right leaders and disseminate them to their followers.[70] Taken together, these measures undercut what the Klansmen thought was one of their greatest strengths – secrecy.

COINTELPRO often sought to cause animosity between far-right organizations such as the United Klans of America (UKA) and the American Nazi Party.[71] Derogatory cartoons on postcards that suggested internal organizational scandals were sent to members to foster suspicion and undermine morale. On occasion the bureau created completely notional organizations, such as the National Committee for Domestic Tranquility (NCDT), which positioned itself as a reasonable patriotic organization that would criticize the extremist approach of the Klan. In the FBI's words, the NCDT "was founded on the basis that it [would] be an effective counterintelligence tool against Klan and other hate group activities."[72] In another instance, the bureau created a rival Klan organization to siphon off members from a Klan organization that it sought to neutralize, the United Klans of America, led by Robert J. Shelton, which was the largest and most influential Klan organization during this period. The notional Klan under the bureau's direction attracted 250 members.[73]

The Bureau also sought to collect information on these various hate groups from private organizations.[74] The bureau occasionally fed information to media outlets that would be used for critical stories on the Klan and other radical rightwing groups. The *Saturday Evening Post* was often used as part of this effort.[75]

One of the most controversial features of the COINTELPRO initiative directed against the Klan was the Bureau's use of informants, who some claim often amounted to agents provocateurs. One in particular was Gary Thomas Rowe, who was recruited in 1960. During congressional hearings, Rowe testified that he had actually instigated incidents of violence, and had done so with the approval of J. Edgar Hoover.[76] He was present at the incident in which a civil rights worker, Viola Liuzzo, was murdered. There was speculation that Rowe may have even fired the shot that killed Mrs Liuzzo.[77]

Cumulatively, these COINTELPRO measures had a devastating effect on the morale of right-wing extremist groups. So much suspicion was created among members that they were extremely loath to initiate violence in any kind of organizational setting. By 1971, membership in the Klan had plummeted from its high of 14,000 members in 1964, to 4,300 members.[78] In this regard, COINTELPRO was a resounding success.

The FBI in the contemporary era

The Levi Guidelines

Violations of civil liberties notwithstanding, COINTELPRO was an effective means by which to counter extremism. However, in 1971, a small group of burglars calling themselves the "Citizens' Commission to Investigate the FBI" broke into an FBI office in Media, Pennsylvania and removed files on the program. Eventually, the files were leaked to the press and the public got wind of the program. The revelations of misconduct ultimately led to congressional investigations in the Senate and House Select Committees on Intelligence Activities, headed by Senator Frank Church and Representative Otis Pike. The negative publicity surrounding the program pressured the Justice Department to make changes to the law enforcement and investigative policies of the FBI. Increasingly the FBI was seen as a political police agency. Hence the Levy Guidelines were adopted on April 5, 1976 in an attempt to de-politicize the FBI.[79] According to the new guidelines, in order to commence an investigation of a dissident group, evidence of a criminal predicate[80] was required. An investigation could not be opened solely on activities protected by the First Amendment. The guidelines marked a significant departure from traditional policy, in that it moved federal law enforcement away from its preventive functions. This measure was not without its critics, as one observer opined "it means every terrorist gets one free blast."[81]

These guidelines divided investigations into three levels (preliminary, limited and full) and specified the type of investigative techniques appropriate to each level.[82] Furthermore, in 1976 FBI Director Clarence Kelley transferred responsibility for investigating terrorist organizations from the Intelligence Division to the General Investigative Division. The upshot was that terrorism cases would henceforth be treated as traditional crimes, without a clearly defined preventive strategy.[83] Furthermore, the Privacy Act of 1974 attempted to stop the FBI from spying on people because of their political beliefs. The overall result of these changes was dramatic. The number of domestic intelligence cases initiated dropped from 1,454 in 1975 to only ninety-five in 1977.[84]

Despite these changes in policy, the FBI still kept tabs on the far right. For example, in 1981, it was revealed that the leader of the most militant Klan organizations in the country, Bill Wilkinson, had been an FBI informant since 1974.[85] Private investigators did their part as well. For example, in 1979, investigative reporter Jerry Thompson began an eighteen-month undercover infiltration of a Klan organization in Alabama. His story received much publicity in the national press and television in 1981.[86]

The pendulum in bureau policy began to swing in the opposite direction not long after Ronald Reagan assumed the presidency in 1981. Some members of Congress, such as Representative Joseph Early (MA) and Senator Jeremiah Denton (AL), were critical of the low priority accorded to domestic security. However, FBI Director William Webster resisted Republican efforts to expand the scope of domestic terrorism investigation for fear of embroiling the bureau once again in the issue of political policing.[87] Webster eventually relented, and by the fall of 1981 policy changes were made. The impetus for the changes came from renewed left-wing terrorism.[88] Consequently public support for stronger FBI intervention in terrorism increased. In 1982 President Reagan designated the FBI as the chief agency responsible for responding to acts of domestic terrorism and monitoring terrorist groups.[89] In 1983 Attorney General William French Smith revised the guidelines for domestic security, and by doing so granted greater flexibility to FBI field offices in conducting domestic terrorism investigations. In effect, the predication threshold for investigation was lowered so that the FBI no longer had to "wait for blood in the streets" before it could investigate a potential terrorist group, as the new guidelines made clear: "[i]n its efforts to anticipate or prevent crimes, the FBI must at times initiate investigations in advance of criminal conduct."[90] According to these guidelines, the FBI is now permitted to investigate domestic extremist groups when three elements exist: "a threat or advocacy of force; apparent ability to carry out the proclaimed act; and the potential violation of a federal law."[91] Furthermore, there is nothing in the guidelines which precludes the FBI from opening an investigation based on information received from private groups such as the Southern Poverty Law Center or ADL. In some ways, these changes move in the direction of the Smith Act, which prevailed in the earlier part of this century. Under that law the FBI could open an investigation based on the advocacy of violence alone. Finally, the FBI elevated its counter-terrorism program from a Priority 3 program to Priority 1 – its highest level investigative priority.[92] In sum, these changes indicated that the government was once again taking the threat of domestic terrorism very seriously.

The Hostage Rescue Team

By the early 1980s terrorism had become a salient issue in the public mind. Several high-profile acts of international terrorism against US personnel overseas compelled the government to take measures to protect American territory from such eventualities. Unlike many other countries at that time, the United States did not have an elite anti-terrorist unit in the style of the British SAS, or the German GSG-9, or the Italian GIS. Moreover, the upcoming Olympic Games to be held in Los Angeles added a sense of urgency to the creation of such a unit. In late 1983, Oliver Buck Revell, then the head of the FBI's Criminal Investigative Division, persuaded FBI Director William Webster to authorize the creation of an elite anti-terrorist division in the FBI. Webster agreed, and Special Agent Danny O. Coulson was made the first commander of the Hostage Rescue Team – an elite squad of fifty agents who could be deployed at a moment's notice to handle such emergencies.[93]

The first major deployment of the new unit occurred in 1985 when it was called upon to arrest members of the Covenant, Sword, and the Arm of the Lord (CSA) at the group's compound in Arkansas. The operation was a stunning success as the violence-prone CSA, and fugitive members of the Order that had sought sanctuary there, surrendered without incident after a couple of days of negotiations with HRT Commander Coulson.[94] Increasingly the activities of the radical right caught the attention of federal authorities, and a concerted effort was made to stymie them.

Operation Clean Sweep

To counter the threat of renascent right-wing terrorism, in 1985 the FBI, the IRS Security Division, the Justice Department, and the BATF joined forces in one of the largest joint efforts in law enforcement history known as "Operation Clean Sweep" to investigate leaders of the movement.[95] It was, however, primarily a Department of the Treasury initiative and was allegedly the brainchild of an Assistant US Attorney, Steven Snyder.[96]

From the perspective of right-wing terrorists, their timing could not have been worse. These new anti-terrorist measures were put in place just as the Order set out for its "war in 84." As one observer noted, the right-wing terrorist groups never knew what hit them.[97] Their members found themselves criminally prosecuted under the 1970 Racketeer Influenced and Corrupt Organizations (RICO) statutes, which were presumably enacted to target organized crime syndicates.

The watchdogs also played a role in this effort, as evidenced by the case of Glen Miller. During the mid-1980s, Miller's White Patriot Party gained a considerable following in North Carolina. He organized street parades and rallies that could gather up to 500 marchers, and at its peak, membership was estimated at 5,000.[98] Miller also received $200,000 in cash from the money that the Order had stolen. It was not long however, before the authorities and watchdogs were on to Miller. First, Morris Dees from the Southern Poverty Law Center initiated a civil suit against Miller and his organization. However, there was not enough evidence against Miller so Dees settled for an agreement, which, *inter alia*, forbade Miller's party from conducting paramilitary training. Dees later accused Miller and his organization of violating the terms of this agreement. In a highly unusual development, a federal court appointed Dees as a special prosecutor and he won a criminal contempt of court case against Miller and his organization.[99] Soon after the verdict, Miller decided to go underground, but was later apprehended and cooperated with authorities.

Operation Clean Sweep culminated in the Fort Smith sedition trial of 1988, in which a who's who of some of the most radical elements of the far right were prosecuted for conspiring to overthrow the United States government. James Ellison, the former leader of the CSA, turned state's evidence and was the government's star witness at the trial. Despite great effort on the part of federal prosecutors and the ADL, an Arkansas jury acquitted all of the defendants and the far right enjoyed a rare upset victory.[100]

The defense effort owed much of its success to a young attorney, Kirk Lyons, a William Kunstler of sorts for far-right causes. Lyons originally took on the case to represent Louis Beam, a personal friend and also defendant in the trial. Eventually however, Lyons emerged as de facto chief counsel for all of the defendants. Ultimately he was able to convince the jury to find his clients not guilty. He gave his thoughts on the trial:

> Steve Snyder basically cooked up this idea, why don't we dust off the sedition trial laws and indict the leaders of the right wing along with the guys we just put in jail from the Order and the guys we put in jail from the Covenant, the Sword, and the Arm of the Lord. Let's bring all of them together in one big conspiracy and basically give the *coup de grace* to the right wing. And even if we lose we still bankrupt them. …
>
> But essentially I went there and worked on behalf of all the defendants. We were able to create a team that beat the Feds. We were able to unite the defendants with the appointed attorneys with the retained attorneys and we had some very strict rules and we won. The government spent $10 million and lost. They had a great big celebration planned. They had all the goodies piled up in the clerk's office, champagne, and food. They were ready for a

party. And I still think that it was the height of bad manners that they didn't give it to us once they didn't need it.[101]

The FBI's Buck Revell gave his comments on the trial as well:

> I think the government probably misplayed its hand. Sedition is a difficult crime to prove. They probably should have been tried on substantive violations, whether they be armed robbery or other various conspiracy violations and so forth. I'm not sure that the government had the best legal team there. Frankly, it was again primarily an ATF US attorney process. I didn't follow it as closely as I would have had it been an FBI investigation, but some of the people there definitely needed to be prosecuted. It's just a matter of how they were prosecuted. I think that could have been better.
>
> I think they wanted to make a point that this group was engaged in seditious activities. I think it was more of a philosophical issue and I really think they should have focused on their specific criminal act and not gotten into the sort of esoteric issues of sedition. Now obviously, there's a crime of sedition, but there are also other crimes that really should have been focused on. I think when you really start arguing before a jury is this sedition, or, is this an exercise in First Amendment rights, it becomes really confusing. Instead of trying to make a point through the trial, if they had really focused on the criminal conduct that is understood by the layperson, they very likely would have done a better job of convincing the jury that these people were guilty of crimes.
>
> So in hindsight it's easy to say that, but at that time we were concerned within the bureau about the use of these seditious conspiracy process. I would say it was a concern that that was not the right tactic. It always better to go after the specific criminal acts than it is to argue for a sort of global conspiratorial process.[102]

Despite this legal victory, at this stage the radical right was in disarray and the domestic terrorist threat from both the left and the right had largely evaporated by the mid-1980s. However, this lull in activity would prove to be short-lived. The 1990s would witness several high profile confrontations between political and religious extremists and law enforcement authorities.

Ruby Ridge

Inasmuch as the radical right has a penchant for firearms, it is not surprising that the Department of Treasury's Bureau of Alcohol, Tobacco and Firearms (BATF) would often take notice of their activities. In 1989, Randy Weaver, a reclusive White separatist who lived with his family in the hills of Idaho, sold two sawed-off shotguns to a BATF informant.[103] Weaver had on occasion visited the Aryan Nations compound at Hayden Lake. BATF authorities offered Weaver a deal if he would agree to inform on right-wing extremists and suspected firearms-law violators in exchange for a light penalty for his alleged offenses. Weaver, however, refused the offer. Thus began a protracted and very costly investigation. In 1990 a Boise grand jury indicted Weaver for making and possessing an unregistered firearm. A mistake was made on the court docket and Weaver appeared on the wrong date for his preliminary hearing, at which point he decided to retreat to the mountains and ignore the authorities. Federal judge Harold Ryan in Boise issued a warrant for his arrest, and US Attorney Maurice Ellsworth indicted Weaver for failing to appear at his hearing. The US Marshals Service (USMS) assumed the responsibility of serving the arrest warrant.[104] In a remarkable operation, the USMS spent sixteen months surveilling Weaver's home, but did not make any attempt at a traditional arrest.[105]

The Weaver saga captured much attention in the local area. Television talk show host Geraldo Rivera even sent a crew to Idaho to do a story on Weaver. All of this publicity was an embarrassment to authorities, and pressure was building to apprehend Weaver. Finally, on August 21, 1992, four deputy US marshals drove out to Ruby Ridge to conduct a reconnaissance of Weaver's property. Things soon got out of control as a marshal shot and killed the pet dog of Sammy Weaver, Randy's son. This set off an exchange of gunfire, and Deputy Marshal Bill Degan was shot and killed by Kevin Harris, a friend of the Weavers who had been living on their property. Other marshals fired back and Sammy Weaver was killed.

Once a federal agent had been slain, the FBI assumed responsibility for the incident and the Hostage Rescue Team was deployed. The FBI had received what amounted to hyperbolic assessments of Weaver. They were told of Weaver's military background as an ex-Green Beret, and that he was thought by some to have booby-trapped the grounds on which he and his family lived. Moreover, the BATF authorities claimed they believed that Weaver had access to explosives, grenades and automatic weapons.[106] In short, because of this the FBI exaggerated the threat posed by Randy Weaver.[107] To meet this supposed hazard, Larry Potts, the FBI supervisor of the Ruby Ridge siege, altered the agency's rules of engagement and deadly force policies. Potts' directive stated that any armed adult seen outside of the Weaver cabin or on the grounds of Ruby Ridge should be considered an immediate threat and could be subject to deadly force.[108] Tragically, Lon Horiuchi, a Hostage Rescue Team marksman, fired a fatal shot at Vicki Weaver as she held her infant daughter. Eventually, Bo Gritz, a highly decorated Vietnam veteran and popular figure of the Patriot movement, helped negotiate an end to the standoff. The esteemed attorney Gerry Spence represented Weaver and Harris, who were charged with conspiracy to commit murder and murder respectively. Spence got his clients acquitted of all of the most serious charges and the jury fined the federal government for withholding evidence and for lying. Moreover, it concluded that the federal government had acted with a "callous disregard for the rights of the defendants and the interests of justice."[109] Weaver filed a $20 million civil suit against the government. The government eventually settled and paid $3.1 million to Weaver and his surviving children in exchange for him dropping the suit. In sum, the incident had a devastating effect on the morale of the FBI, as several agents with stellar service records effectively had their careers ruined.

Although the Randy Weaver fiasco captured only a limited amount of attention when it occurred, other incidents soon followed on its heels that would later magnify the significance of the original ambush at Ruby Ridge. Just a few months later, the siege at Waco would lay bare the consequences of faulty planning in responding to dissident groups.

Waco

On February 28, 1993, the BATF sent seventy-six agents to storm the Mount Carmel Center near Waco, Texas, for the express purpose of arresting persons on suspected firearms violations. The compound was the home of the Branch Davidians, a religious sect led by David Koresh. The raid was badly botched, as the BATF never had an element of surprise.[110] A shootout ensued, and four BATF agents were killed and twenty-eight others were seriously injured. Five Branch Davidian members were also killed, and four others, including Koresh, were injured.[111] As a result of the fatalities of federal agents, the FBI's Hostage Rescue Team was once again called in to assume responsibility and take direction of the operation. They would also receive assistance from the US Army.[112]

The initial raid was followed by a 51-day standoff. The authorities handled the crisis very poorly, as they repeatedly violated fundamental principles of hostage and barricade protocol. A campaign of psychological warfare was unleashed that heightened the defiance of the cult members. Loud noise was blared at the barricaded compound. Helicopters flew at low altitude over the building and high-intensity stadium lights were focused on the compound.[113] Attempts at constructive dialogue went nowhere as FBI negotiators derided Koresh's pronouncements as "Bible babble" and called him a "self-centered liar," "coward," "phony messiah," "child molester," and a litany of other epithets.[114] The confrontational approach exacerbated tensions and had a polarizing effect on the two parties. In short, pressure was applied not as a way of furthering negotiations, but rather as a device for inducing the Davidians to surrender.[115] Little regard was given to the eschatology of the sect, which had prepared them for an apocalyptic *dénouement*.

Finally, on April 19, the FBI raided the center using an armored car, which rammed holes into the structure in order to pump CS chemical gas warfare agent, despite the fact that its manufacturers warned against its use indoors.[116] Soon after a conflagration broke out, which killed most of the persons inside. A subsequent investigation determined that seventy-five people died in the fire and two more, including Koresh, were killed by gunfire.[117] It was the largest armed entry into an American home, resulting in the largest number of fatalities of law enforcement officers and civilians.[118] One of the chief problems with the FBI's approach was that the children in the compound were regarded as hostages. As such, the approach used obviously imperiled them and was ill advised.

The legal reason for the BATF's involvement was to see if Koresh had been manufacturing machine guns illegally there.[119] The Mount Carmel estate was also suspected of accumulating a heavy arsenal of weapons, including nearly 300 assault rifles with hundreds of thousands of rounds of ammunition.[120] Finally, included in the BATF's arrest warrant application were allegations of child abuse involving members of the cult, including Koresh.[121] Much of this information was later determined to be faulty and supplied by an anti-cult watchdog group.

The FBI relied on various watchdogs for advice during the siege. Most important was the Cult Awareness Network (CAN), a controversial organization that specialized in "deprogramming" youths who had joined cults. CAN occasionally monitored right-wing extremist groups as well.[122] Subsequent investigations revealed that it was one Rick Ross, a deprogrammer working for CAN, who first went to the BATF with stories of alleged sexual child abuse and firearms law violations among Branch Davidians. Ross had elicited this information from a former Davidian member whom he had deprogrammed in 1992.[123] Ross consulted with both BATF and the FBI throughout the affair.[124] He was far from an unbiased source of expertise. An FBI report for the Department of Justice stated that Ross had "a personal hatred for all religious cults" and would help any law enforcement effort "to destroy a cult."[125] The ADL also supplied information on the Davidian cult to authorities, but little is known of its contents or what effect it may have had on decisions made.[126]

There was much fallout from the Waco disaster. For years the FBI maintained that during the final assault of the Davidian compound, it did not use any materials that were capable of starting fires. However, subsequent investigations revealed that some pyrotechnic gas was used during the assault.[127] This finding prompted Attorney General Janet Reno in September 1999 to appoint John Danforth as a special counsel to investigate further. Eventually he issued a report, which cleared the government of any wrongdoing, but the appearance of misconduct has not gone away.

The Waco siege occurred contemporaneously with the trial of Randy Weaver, and the similarity of the two events was not lost on the denizens of the far right. At first it may seem very odd that Waco became such a *cause célèbre* to those in the movement. After all, the Branch Davidian sect was multi-racial and generally philo-Semitic. Moreover, the lurid accusations of child abuse and the licentious lifestyle of Koresh would seem to do little to gain sympathy among the far right. However, two factors seem to have propelled Waco into the conscience of the movement: historical context and the conspiratorialism that inheres in radical right-wing ideologies.[128] Several confrontations with authorities had preceded Waco, including Gordon Kahl, the CSA, and Ruby Ridge. From the perspective of the far right, the events at Waco were seen as the logical culmination of government actions that sought to liquidate the state's enemies. In that sense Waco was the breaking point for hopes of compromise with the system.[129] The lesson learned in the far-right movement was that the government had determined to eliminate them one by one.[130]

This event galvanized the far right as the Militia movement spread throughout many states. What's more, it provoked Timothy McVeigh to strike out against the government in revenge.

The Oklahoma City bombing and its aftermath

The April 19, 1993 bombing of the Murrah federal building in Oklahoma City killed 168 people and was the most lethal act of terrorism committed on American soil. It did not take the authorities long to find the suspects. The mastermind of the bombing, Timothy McVeigh, was apprehended on the same day of the attack and ultimately sentenced to death for the crime. His accomplice, Terry Nichols, was sentenced to life in prison. A third defendant, Michael Fortier, plea bargained with authorities, and received a sentence of twelve years in exchange for cooperating with the prosecution.[131] With Fortier, the FBI invoked rarely used statutes forbidding "misprision of felony" (i.e. concealing evidence of a felony) to induce him to cooperate with the prosecution. As Philip Heyman, a former Deputy US Attorney General, observed, this tactic was contrary to the Anglo-Saxon legal traditions of England and the United States.[132] However, the exigencies of this horrific act of terrorism called for serious measures to solve and prosecute the case. In this instance, the United States appears to have moved in the direction of European countries that are willing to sacrifice a certain amount of civil liberties to more effectively combat terrorism.

Prior to the bombing, the FBI did not pay much attention to the Militia movement. Furthermore, one of its most extensive investigations failed to turn up a significant militia connection to the bombing. However, after this attack, the association between the two stuck in the public mind and the FBI began to monitor the militias and other far-right organizations much more closely. In the aftermath there were many calls to alter and expand counter-terrorism policy. This event, more than any other factor, was the impetus behind the expansion of counter-terrorism programs.

For starters, FBI Director Louis Free loosened the Attorney General's guidelines for investigating extremist groups.[133] He also formed the Executive Working Group on Domestic Terrorism, which meets every two weeks to share intelligence and plan strategy. Not even a year after its founding, FBI militia investigations had increased fourfold.[134] As a result of these policy changes, the number of politically oriented domestic surveillance operations increased substantially. Just prior to the Oklahoma City bombing the FBI was working on roughly 100 terrorist investigations. This figure jumped to about 900 two years after the bombing.[135]

The FBI also began an outreach program to militia organizations, which was intended to allay suspicion on both sides.[136] This initiative gives the FBI an idea of which organizations are actually criminally prone. The FBI's Buck Revell commented on the program:

150 *The government's response*

> I think it's almost on an organizational specific basis. Essentially it tries to de-demonize, I guess you could say. It's much harder to deal in a violent fashion with people that you have dialogue. As long as you think that you are a target, it is very easy to visualize brutalities that would preempt cooperation. But if we say, "look, we don't agree with what you're saying. We don't agree with your beliefs, but in America you have First Amendment rights and as long as you don't step over those rights or violate other people's rights or violate the law, you can say and do whatever you feel like doing. … If you sit down and just discuss with them that we're not going to try to usurp their rights including their exercise of the First Amendment. We're not going to go out and try to stop you from collecting legal weapons irrespective of what the Second Amendment really says. But just open up a dialogue. …
>
> I think that's a useful tactic to use and also I think it's the right thing to do. They are American citizens and as long as they haven't violated the law, I think that we, the United States collectively, have an obligation to try to reach them. Now that doesn't mean you negotiate with terrorists. Once they cross the line and commit violent acts you deal with them vigorously and forcefully to exercise your responsibility. The more dialogue that you can have, the more you can dissipate their concerns that are so far fetched and nonsensical, but to them are very real. The better chance you have to, essentially, if not neutralize, but to de-escalate the situation. And I think that's an important initiative to have.[137]

John Trochman, the leader of the Militia of Montana, has participated in this program. He offered his comments:

> We have a good working relationship with the FBI, people that we feel are genuine Americans in the FBI. I don't like us to be divided from our government. We're probably the reason it was started because of a situation we had arranged with an FBI agent here. We set the pace for that to happen because of an open communications link between them and us. If they had a problem, they'd come and contact us. If we had a problem, we'd contact them. And we explain away our differences and we've had a good working relationship because of that.[138]

Norman Olson, a former leader of the Michigan Militia, was more suspicious of the program and refused to participate:

> We call them the coffee and donut sit-downs. No I haven't [participated] and I warned militia groups around the country not to sit down and partake and break bread with the FBI. What they're really doing, and it's not to build bridges of understanding, what they're really doing is profiling. The staff people or the people that show up for these sit-downs include psychologists and they are profiling behavior. That's all it is. … Remember the FBI

people are tasked by higher-ups to do this. It's not something they take on their own initiative and say, "well I think I'll just go out and make friends with the militia this afternoon." They're told to do this. And part of that of course is profiling. It's the same way that they created these sieges and then they measure the reaction of the local community as to how much and how far they can go before the local community raises objections. ... We saw that up in Montana with the Freemen siege. They're very clever about that. They're doing training and taking measurements and documenting.[139]

Another important initiative began in 1994 when the FBI created a Critical Incident Response Group (CIRG) to deal more thoroughly with domestic hostage taking, barricade, and terrorist situations. The CIRG deploys resources to FBI field offices that are responsible for handling such crises. It is broken into two branches. The Tactical Support branch contains the Hostage Rescue Team and an Operational Training Section. The Special Investigation branch contains the following: Crisis Management Unit; Crisis Negotiations Unit; Aviation and Special Operations Unit; National Center for the Analysis of Violent Crime; and the Domestic Emergency Support Team (DEST).[140] As a result of these new measures, the FBI was better prepared to deal with its next major confrontation with right-wing extremists.

The standoff with the Montana Freemen

After the fiascos of Ruby Ridge and Waco, the federal government began responding to right-wing extremists more gingerly, but also resolutely. The 1996 siege of the Montana Freemen at their "Justus Township" estate in Jordan, Montana was a success story in this regard. Members of the Freemen were accused of committing a variety of acts of "paper terrorism" in the Midwest region, such as printing billions of dollars of phony checks and issuing illegal property liens against their enemies. In 1995 the FBI infiltrated the Freemen with a husband and wife team of civilian informants, and was thus able to keep close tabs on the group.[141] The FBI enlisted the support of high-profile figures in the Patriot movement to help negotiate an end to the standoff. Kirk Lyons, an attorney who has represented many far-right clients, played a role in the negotiations. He offered his account of the incident:

> Well it showed that the FBI was at least willing to change its tactics to avoid the public relations nightmare that Waco was. ... The initial capture of the Freemen was peaceful. That made it very difficult for them to escalate it into a violent response and most of the Patriot movement abandoned them. ... If we hadn't gotten those people out of there, the Hostage Rescue Team was going in. But it was quite a thing for the FBI to bring us in. They were pissed off at us. They were not happy about our lawsuit at Waco [Lyons was part of the legal team that represented survivors of the Waco tragedy that brought a civil suit against the government]. The negotiation team basically

told us very frankly, "we screwed up at Waco, but we learned our lesson as you're seeing here." So it was interesting. ...

The problem with the Freemen is that they've got a really unrealistic attitude of what they're facing, the forces arrayed against them and an unrealistic attitude of how to fight the thing. They're living in a fairy world of unreality and they think that courts will respect the stuff that they file. ... They think if they wave this magic talisman of the common law that the judge will grant their freedom. They assume that the courts actually read this stuff. They don't. They throw it away. It's called frivolous. ...

Once they got to jail and found out that all of that gobbledygook that they bought didn't work, they then felt that they had to blame somebody. ... These Freemen started saying that this Lyons guy must have sold us out because our common law magic gobbledygook isn't working and something else must be to blame.[142]

Lyons' reputation suffered in the Patriot community after the Freemen affair, as rumors spread that he was a government plant. In a sense he was banished from the Patriot movement after his participation in ending the Freemen standoff. These rumors appear, however, to be unfounded. Since, then Lyons has concentrated on Southern heritage issues.

John Trochman from the Militia of Montana also helped in the negotiations. Like Lyons, his reputation was tarnished, at least temporarily, and he was criticized by some of his peers for cooperating with authorities.[143]

After an eighty-one-day standoff, the Freemen eventually surrendered without incident. Ultimately, the leaders of the Freemen received very stiff penalties. The ringleader, Leroy Schweitzer, was sentenced to 22½ years on conspiracy charges involving, *inter alia*, bank fraud, threatening a federal judge, and illegal possession of firearms.[144] If one could point to a specific incident that started the decline of the Militia movement, it would probably be the conclusion of the Freemen standoff. No dramatic Lexington and Concord clash with authorities ensued. The Freemen were seen more as opportunistic profiteers than genuine patriots. Finally, the reputations of some high-profile Patriot figures who helped in the negotiations were damaged, perhaps unfairly from their perspective. After 1996, the Militia movement went into rapid retreat and today is only a shell of its former self. In this regard, the FBI's efforts at Justus Township were doubly successful. The standoff ended peacefully, and its ensuing fallout in the Patriot community led to the dissipation of a movement that the FBI had identified as a serious threat to domestic security.

New initiatives

The confluence of several factors during the mid-to-late 1990s put domestic terrorism close to the top of President Clinton's national policy agenda. Just prior to the Oklahoma City bombing, the Japanese *Aum Shinrikyo* cult attacked a subway in Tokyo. Members of Congress were alarmed when they discovered that the FBI had not been tracking the terrorist group because technically under the guidelines at that time, it did not have the authority to do so insofar as *Aum Shinrikyo* was not suspected of committing a crime in the United States. Consequently, a new wave of counter-terrorism policies and measures were initiated.

President Clinton issued Presidential Decision Directive (PDD) 39 in 1995, which designated the FBI as the chief government agency responsible for investigating and preventing domestic terrorism. It was the first directive to make terrorism a national top priority, and also concluded the United States was threatened from within. This policy further articulates and defines the roles of members of the US counter-terrorism community. Pursuant to PDD 39, a specialized interagency team – Domestic Emergency Support Team (DEST) – was created to provide expert advice and guidance to the FBI on scene commander and coordinate response measures.[145]

Soon thereafter new legislation was passed, including the Anti-Terrorism and Effective Death Penalty Act of 1996. This law contained the most thoroughgoing measures heretofore aimed at combating terrorism. The various new laws and initiatives nearly doubled the amount of money spent on counter-terrorism to $11 billion a year. Much of the money went to the FBI, whose anti-terrorism budget jumped from $78 million to $609 million a year.[146] Some of the new initiatives created since 1995 include the following:

The FBI's Counter-terrorism Center was established in 1995 to better coordinate strategies among federal agencies. The center encompasses the operation of the FBI's International Terrorism Operations Section as well as the Domestic Terrorism Operations Section. Eighteen federal agencies maintain a regular presence at the center and participate in its daily operations. At the field operational level, the FBI sponsors eighteen Joint Terrorism Task Forces in major cities, which brings together federal, state and local law enforcement personnel to work on interagency cooperation and coordination.[147]

The National Infrastructure Protection Center (NIPC) was established by the FBI in 1998. This office integrates personnel from state and local public safety agencies and representatives of the private sector to prevent, deter and investigate attacks on the nation's critical infrastructure.[148]

The National Domestic Preparedness Office was created by the US Department of Justice in 1998 – a multi-agency center composed of representatives from various federal agencies, as well as state and local law enforcement and public safety agencies. Its primary mission is to serve as a clearinghouse of information to state and local officials on how to develop preparedness strategies for their communities, especially with issues concerning weapons of mass destruction (WMD).[149]

154   *The government's response*

The Counter-terrorism Division   consolidates all FBI counter-terrorism activities into one division under one senior FBI executive. Its creation was announced in November of 1999 by FBI Director Louis Freeh.[150]

The Oklahoma City National Memorial Institute for the Prevention of Terrorism (MIPT)   was created by the Justice Department in 2000. The institute hosts conferences on the topic of terrorism and seeks to draw upon the expertise of experts working in the fields of counter-terrorism and academia. It receives substantial funding as Congress has awarded it a $15 million annual budget. MIPT's activities are also intended to complement those of the National Domestic Preparedness Office. Its current director is retired Army Chief of Staff General Dennis Reimer.[151]

The United States Government Interagency Domestic Terrorism Concept of Operations Plan (CONPLAN)   was created in 2001 to provide overall guidance to federal, state and local agencies on how the federal government would respond to terrorist threats and attacks involving WMD. The primary agencies involved in CONPLAN include the Department of Justice, the Federal Emergency Management Agency, the Department of Defense, the Department of Energy, the Environmental Protection Agency, and the Department of Health and Human Services.[152]

Many factors have contributed to this flurry of new counter-terrorist measures over the past few years. Although experts generally see international terrorists as posing the most serious terrorist threat, it was perhaps domestic right-wing extremists, more than any others, who made counter-terrorism a salient issue and put it on the public policy agenda. Both government authorities and watchdog organizations have taken them very seriously. For about the last decade and a half, right-wing terrorists have preoccupied counter-terrorist personnel working in the area of domestic terrorism.

Just prior to the turn of the century in the fall of 1999, the FBI released a report, *Project Megiddo*, which alerted various chiefs of police around the country to the potential violence that groups holding millenarian beliefs could perpetrate. The report noted that the nature of the terrorist group had changed. It had become less well defined as it disavowed the traditional hierarchical organizational structures. In short, leaderless resistance was cited as the expected *modus operandi* for terrorists in the early part of the twenty-first century. The report placed much significance on Dr Pierce's *Turner Diaries*, as it outlines both a revolutionary takeover of the government and a race war.[153]

The report came under fire from not only the far right but also some respectable conservatives and civil libertarians, who saw it as a modern-day inquisition that sought to stigmatize certain viewpoints.[154] The report focused almost exclusively on the political right, and tended to paint with a broad brush by conflating terrorists with those who are not violence-prone. It was also highly suspected that both the ADL and the Southern Poverty Law Center had a hand in the preparation of the report. For its part, the FBI denied any such collusion.[155] But fueling suspicion was the coincidence that the ADL issued a report, *Y2K Paranoia: Extremists Confront the Millenium*, at the same conference – the International Association of Chiefs of Police in Charlotte, North Carolina – at which the FBI released its report.

Now that we have examined the FBI's role in this area of policy, it is time to see how other branches of government have dealt with this problem.

Congress

On past occasions, the US Congress has been dealt with the issue of right-wing extremism. Its chief involvement in this area has been through investigation of extremist groups. Both chambers have held hearings on the subject and have issued reports relating to it. As mentioned earlier in the chapter, Congress investigated the Reconstruction Klan during the early 1870s and issued a detailed report.[156] Congress also passed numerous laws to curtail Klan terrorism in the South.

The House Un-American Activities Committee (HUAC)

Due to the lull in right-wing extremist activity, Congress did not pay much attention to the issue again until the 1930s. The impetus for an investigative committee at this time, however, was left-wing radicalism. In 1930 the House of Representatives created a committee to investigate communist propaganda in the United States. Representative Hamilton Fish chaired the committee. A "Special Committee on Un-American Activities Authorized to Investigate Nazi Propaganda and Certain Other Propaganda Activities" – more commonly known as the McCormack-Dickstein Committee – succeeded Fish's committee in 1934. John McCormack (MA) was the chairman but it was Samuel Dickstein (NY), the vice-chairman, who directed the investigation. Dickstein aggressively sought to expose native fascists and prove a link between them and the Nazi government in Germany. The committee reported its findings in 1935 and focused primarily on the Friends of the New Germany (a precursor to the German American Bund) and the Silvershirts, a quasi-fascist organization led by William Dudley Pelley.[157] One tangible piece of legislation – the 1938 Foreign Agents Registration Act – ultimately came out of the committee's work. Two years later, Dickstein introduced a congressional resolution to launch a more ambitious investigation of subversive activities. In order to accomplish this he garnered bipartisan support by agreeing to investigate extremists from both the left and the right. His resolution failed, but Representative Martin Dies (TX) introduced a similar resolution that was passed with Dickstein's support. Dies became chairman of the new Special Committee on Un-American Propaganda, but to the dismay of Dickstein, shifted the body's focus away from exposing native fascists to communists and their fellow travelers.[158] In 1945, that body was succeeded by the House Committee on Un-American Activities (HUAC).

Throughout its existence the HUAC focused overwhelmingly on left-wing extremism. Inasmuch as some communist-style organizations in America held ideological allegiance to the Soviet Union, this is understandable. Moreover there is evidence that the CPUSA received material support from the Soviet government.[159] On occasion, however, the HUAC investigated extreme right-wing organizations as well. For example, in 1956, the committee released its *Preliminary Report on Neo-Fascist and Hate Groups*. Indicative of the anemic condition of the racialist right at that time, the report focused on the miniscule National Renaissance Party, which was little more that an odd-ball cult around the figure of one James H. Madole in New York City, and a publication entitled *Common Sense*, which was published by Conde J. McGinley.[160]

A more thoroughgoing HUAC investigation of the Klan was conducted in 1965. Soon after the slaying of civil rights worker Viola Liuzzo, President Lyndon B. Johnson and Georgia Congressman Charles L. Weltner called for a congressional probe of the Klan.[161] The committee estimated that there were at least seventeen separate Klan organizations with approximately 16,000 members attached to various local units (klaverns).[162] However, the investigation centered principally on one organization, the United Klans of America, led by Robert Shelton. The committee subpoenaed Shelton to testify, and ordered him and other Klan leaders to release their membership records. They refused and were charged with contempt for Congress. Eventually the charges were dropped against most of the defendants, but Shelton and South Carolina Klan leader Robert Scoggin each spent a year in prison.[163]

The committee found evidence that the Klan had infiltrated into positions of public trust. In several instances the committee uncovered Klansmen in elected and appointed positions in state and local government as well as positions in law enforcement agencies.[164] Finally, the committee found that Klan leaders had incited acts of violence.[165] The Klan's activities, though, were almost exclusively confined to the South at that time.

Recent investigations

The HUAC continued for over a decade after its investigation of the Klan, but was finally dissolved in 1975. However, Congress still on occasion investigates episodes of right-wing extremism or issues related thereto. For example, in October of 1995 the Senate Judiciary Subcommittee on Terrorism, Technology and Government Information investigated the siege at Ruby Ridge. Randy Weaver testified and received a remarkably sympathetic hearing. FBI Director Louis Freeh also testified, and acknowledged that his agency had made several misjudgments during the siege.[166]

That same year the Committee on Government Reform and Oversight of the House of Representatives investigated the Waco incident. The investigation lasted over a year, and in August 1996 the committee issued a report. Although the committee found that David Koresh and other Branch Davidians were ultimately responsible for the tragedy, the report was scathingly critical of the BATF, the Justice Department and the FBI. The majority report made several recommendations the chief, among them being:

- Federal law enforcement agencies should take steps to foster understanding of their targets under investigation.
- Congress should conduct greater oversight of the BATF in the future.
- The FBI should expand the size of its Hostage Rescue Team.[167]

After the Oklahoma City bombing in 1995, the previously obscure Militia movement had become well known throughout the United States. On June 15 of that year, Senator Arlen Specter (PA) held hearings on the movement in the Senate Judiciary Subcommittee on Terrorism, Technology and Government Information, which he chaired. Several militia leaders from around the country were invited to attend the hearings and five testified, including John Trochman and Bob Fletcher from the Militia of Montana; James Johnson, an African-American leader of the Ohio Unorganized Militia; and Norm Olson and Ken Adams from the Michigan Militia. Representatives of law enforcement agencies also testified, as well as representatives from the Simon Wiesenthal Center.[168] According to Specter, he hoped that by holding the hearings the militias would lose credibility. As he put it, the militia leaders' beliefs would "fall on their own weight" once they were made public.[169]

The militia leaders regaled the committee with their conspiracy theories and criticisms of the government in Washington. However, they also denounced the Oklahoma City bombing. Specter, who chaired the hearing, was alternately patient and testy throughout their testimony. At times he and Michigan Militia leader Norm Olson verbally sparred. While the other militia leaders attended the hearing in business suit attire, Olson defiantly wore his camouflage uniform and refused to take off his hat in a display of contempt for his senatorial hosts. John Trochman and Senator Diane Feinstein (CA) traded barbed comments as well.

The hearing was broadcast by C-SPAN on four occasions and thus gave significant exposure to the militia leaders, who emerged from it feeling that they had achieved a public relations victory. Some people were critical of Specter's decision to hold the hearings. For example, Representative Charles Schumer (NY) opined that the hearing was a cheap publicity stunt and that it had turned into a "soapbox for the radical right."[170]

The watchdogs have not been without their occasional critics in Congress. For example, in 1949 Representative John E. Rankin of Mississippi called upon the House Committee on Un-American Activities to investigate the ADL. He also introduced a bill that would have made it unlawful for an individual to be a member of the organization, punishable with a year in prison and a $10,000 fine. His bill, however, died in committee.[171] During the late 1940s, at the state level, Senator Jack B. Tenney, chairman of the California Legislature's Joint Fact-Finding Committee on Un-American Activities, made numerous statements against the ADL in the California Senate, and also issued critical reports on the group.[172]

Department of Defense

The United States military has dealt with the issue of political extremism on several occasions throughout its history. As mentioned earlier in this chapter, the Great Sedition Trial of 1944 centered on the allegation that native fascists had violated the Smith Act of 1940, which prohibited insubordination in the armed forces. The military is obviously one of the nation's most important institutions insofar as it is responsible for safeguarding its security not only from external enemies, but potentially from internal turmoil as well. Inasmuch as the military controls the nation's most lethal weaponry, it is imperative that the political leadership maintains the loyalty of, and discipline over, its soldiers. Perhaps the most serious threat that extremist groups pose is that they could cause internal disharmony and potentially create a conflict of loyalties in that the values of the extremist group may be at odds with the policies or actions of the military and the US government.[173] Furthermore, groups that espouse racially exclusionist and supremacist views could be all the more disruptive in an institution as racially and ethnically diverse as the contemporary military.[174] This section highlights the chief instances in which the military has dealt with the issue of political extremism with special focus on the far right. It also examines the Department of Defense's evolving policy in this area.

Military investigators occasionally discover that some armed forces members are involved in far-right groups, and this has sometimes led to their discharge from military service.[175] The Department of Defense formalized an extremism policy in 1974 with the issuance of Executive Order 11785. For the first time the DoD used the terms "knowing membership" and "active participation" to determine polices toward individuals involved in extremist organizations. This terminology or concept was henceforth included in several subsequent regulations.[176] However, the policy in this area still remained vague and was thus clarified in 1986.

Weinberger's restrictions in the armed forces

In 1986 Defense Secretary Caspar Weinberger announced new restrictions on extremist activity in the US armed forces. The revised DoD Directive mandated that military personnel must reject participation in organizations that: (a) espouse supremacist causes; (b) attempt to create illegal discrimination based on race, creed, color, sex, religion or national origin; or (c) advocate the use of force or violence, or otherwise engage in efforts to deprive individuals of their civil rights.[177]

This new policy raised important First Amendment issues insofar as the federal government has the authority to determine what constitutes a hate group. This in effect abridges the associational rights of some service members who choose to affiliate themselves with groups which espouse unpopular beliefs. However, the US Supreme Court has traditionally deferred to military authorities on such controversial issues. Moreover, the leadership of the US armed forces has demonstrated a strong commitment to promoting racial equality and harmony within its ranks. Despite these restrictions, the new policy distinguished between "active" participation, which was proscribed, and "passive" participation, which was permitted but discouraged. Examples of "active participation" include directly participating in rallies and demonstrations involving extremist groups; raising funds; distributing literature; and recruiting members. Examples of "passive participation" include mere membership; attendance at an event; and receiving literature in the mail. Despite the fact that passive participation is not explicitly forbidden, commanders are charged to take "positive actions when soldiers in their units are identified as members of extremist groups and/or when they engage in extremist group activity."[178] The commander's options range from informal counseling to formal disciplinary action.

Defending American values

The military reviewed its policy again in 1995. Soon after the Oklahoma City bombing, the Army issued guidance on the issue in a message entitled "Extremist Activity," on May 3, 1995.[179] Later that same year, on December 7, three soldiers of the 82nd Airborne were accused of murdering an African-American couple in Fayetteville, North Carolina. The House of Representatives National Security Committee decided to hold hearings on extremist activities in the military shortly after the homicides. This event was the catalyst for a renewed examination of policies regarding extremism in the armed forces. The Army took the lead in this endeavor. First, an internal investigation was conducted at Fort Bragg, which revealed that a total of twenty-six soldiers at that installation had at one time been involved to some extent in an extremist group.[180] Second, on December 12 of that year, Secretary of the Army, Togo West, announced the creation of a task force to investigate the influence of extremist organizations in the Army. Various private groups, including the ADL, the Southern Poverty Law Center, the NAACP and the Simon Wiesenthal Center, encouraged and assisted in this effort.[181]

Major General Larry R. Jordan chaired the task force, which released its findings in a document entitled *Defending American Values* in March 1996. The depth of the report was remarkable in that it was completed in the span of just three months. The task force conducted 1,681 individual interviews with military leaders and 5,957 interviews with soldiers and DoD civilian employees in group settings at twenty-eight Army installations in the United States, Germany and Korea. This was augmented by 17,080 additional confidential questionnaires administered by the Army Research Institute at these same installations. The major findings were the following:

- Only an infinitesimal percentage (0.52) of those interviewed claimed that they knew of a soldier or Army civilian employee who was active in an extremist group. Moreover, only 0.98 per cent of the respondents reported ever coming into contact with representatives of extremist groups on or near Army installations. Most commanders, leaders and soldiers perceive that extremist activity is minimal in the active Army.
- Although very few extremists were identified in the Army, leaders believed that the former could have a dysfunctional effect on unit cohesion.
- Gang-related activities appear to be more pervasive than extremist activities, and were seen as a much greater security concern for soldiers.[182]

The task force made twelve recommendations, the chief among them being:

- The Army expand its regulations on extremist activity.
- The development of a reporting system on extremist activities.
- The dissemination of information on extremist activities throughout the Army; and a review of human relations training to raise awareness on the issue of extremism.[183]

Secretary Caldera's policy on extremist activities for Army civilian employees

In March of 2000, Secretary of the Army Louis Caldera issued a Policy on Extremist Activities for Department of the Army Civilian Employees. Previous policy had been aimed at the uniformed segments of the Department of Defense (i.e. active duty, reserve component and National Guard). This policy sought to bring Army civilian employees under the same associational limitations as the uniformed services. The policy is somewhat ambiguous. It proscribes specific activities during duty time, including attending extremist meetings, recruiting, fundraising, etc. However, it implies that even passive membership activities, such as the receipt of extremist literature or attendance at an extremist meeting during off-duty time, could also be grounds for disciplinary action.[184]

The thrust of the recent policy efforts has been to curtail "passive" participation in extremist groups, such as joining membership organizations and subscribing to extremist publications. The DoD also plans to step up sensitivity training to its members and to dissuade them from extremist activities. Furthermore, there are plans to improve the monitoring and reporting methods of extremist activities on DoD facilities and their surrounding areas. Other measures seek to proscribe the display of symbols and various styles of clothing or tattoos that convey or connote extremist messages. These measures have been recommended and applauded by watchdog groups. For instance, Joe Roy of the Southern Poverty Law Center, testifying before the House of Representatives National Security Committee in June 1995, recommended that the military proscribe both active and passive participation in extremist groups. Roy believed that even "mere members" should be discharged from military service.[185]

The Special Forces Underground

As mentioned earlier, extremist infiltration of the armed forces is a major concern for several reasons. One concern is that military members could provide pilfered weapons from military arsenals to violence-prone extremist groups. Related to that, the training soldiers receive during their military service could conceivably be put to use for extremist activities. In the postwar era, many prominent individuals and leaders in the far right were also military veterans.[186] Furthermore, on some previous occasions, military personnel participated in paramilitary training with right-wing extremists.[187] Two more reasons why the military is so important is that it controls the nation's most lethal weapons and is conceivably in a position from which it could seize the key positions of the government. Although it is extremely unlikely at the present time in America that extremist factions could engineer a coup, it is an eventuality that must always be guarded against. In fact, as Walter Laqueur noted, military coups could become the normal form of political change in most parts of the world.[188] Thus it is not surprising that the DoD would take seriously any faction that would question its authority or the legitimacy of the current government. Those fears were realized when revelations of a covert group known as the Special Forces Underground (SFU) surfaced in 1995.

On April 30, 1995, the CBS television news program *60 Minutes* ran a story on the putative organization. Not surprisingly, when word of the existence of the SFU leaked out, it caused considerable consternation among the Army's leadership. At first the Army denied the group's existence.[189] However, an investigation into the organization was eventually launched, with Command Sergeant Major William H. Rambo Jr leading the effort. Eventually, it transpired that Steven Barry, a Sergeant First Class in the Special Forces, was the founder and leader of the organization.

According to Barry, the impetus for the creation of the SFU was the Ruby Ridge and Waco incidents.[190] According to some reports, during the Army's deployment in Haiti to help reinstall the deposed Jean Bertrand Aristide as president, Barry and some members of his SFU helped certain anti-Aristide Haitian military and paramilitary forces hide weapons in direct defiance of official US and UN efforts to disarm them.[191]

Eventually the Army's Criminal Investigation Division (CID) caught up with Barry and identified him as the leader of the SFU. However, Barry was careful to closely follow the letter of regulations and there was technically little authorities could do to him under the Uniform Code of Military Justice (UCMJ) laws. Ultimately Barry was given a reprimand and had his security clearance revoked. He was however, allowed to complete his military service and retire.

The SFU publishes a newsletter called *The Resister*, which started out humbly as a short mimeographed newsletter. Technically, the publication did not violate Army policy as long as it was published off-base and contained no disclosure of classified information. Be that as it may, the publication remained a major embarrassment to the Army. Timothy McVeigh is reported to have had a copy of the newsletter in his car when he was arrested shortly after the Oklahoma City bombing.[192]

Barry appears to have moved in a more extremist direction in recent years as well. In addition to his own publication, he occasionally writes for the late Dr William Pierce's *Resistance* magazine under the pseudonyms Eric Hollyoak and Joachim Peiper. As mentioned in the previous chapter, he wrote a highly controversial critique of the leaderless resistance approach in one issue. In another, he advised skinheads to join the Army and volunteer for light infantry training in order to obtain the requisite fighting skills in a future American race war.[193]

In recent years Barry has cultivated ties with both the revolutionary and non-revolutionary segments of the far right. For example, his friend John Pate, editor of *Soldier of Fortune* magazine, helped give the SFU good publicity in its early years. Barry has also spoken at conferences of American Renaissance and the Council of Conservative Citizens. Finally, he is reported to have been a close associate of the late Dr Pierce, and to be presently the "military advisor" of the National Alliance. Thus Barry has become a fairly well known, albeit controversial figure in the far-right movement. It is difficult to say with certainty, however, how much influence his SFU really has. According to Barry, and some of his watchdog critics, it is a covert right-wing organization composed of some of the most highly trained personnel in the area of insurgency warfare, and thus a potentially serious threat to the government. However, the possibility remains that the SFU could basically be a very small operation whose significance the watchdogs (and to a lesser extent Barry) have exaggerated for their own ends.

The Supreme Court

On occasion the US Supreme Court has rendered decisions in cases involving issues of political extremism, most notably in the realm of the First Amendment. This section reviews some of the more significant cases in this area.

State v. Klapprott

During the 1930s, a few state legislatures passed group libel and defamation bills which sought to curtail the provocative speech of native-fascist groups. For example, the New Jersey legislature passed a "race hatred" law in 1935, which in 1940 was used against August Klapprott and eight other members of the German American Bund. Authorities raided the group's Camp Nordland and seized anti-Semitic literature. The New Jersey Supreme Court invoked two permissible limitations on speech that it believed applied to this case. First, citing several US Supreme Court sedition cases from the World War I era, it held that it could proscribe speech that "menaces the state itself." Second, and concomitant with the first requirement, the state had to prove that the speech in question constituted a "clear and present danger" to a substantial interest of the state. The US Supreme Court, however, disagreed and struck down the law the following year. The high court ruled that the Klapprott case involved speech that offended private citizens and not the state. As such, the court argued that offensive attacks on individuals could be handled through civil remedies such as libel and slander actions.[194]

This case was a landmark decision in the area of group defamation. The Bundists found allies in the American Civil Liberties Union, who defended them in this case. In retrospect, it is remarkable that the high court would be so lenient to a seemingly subversive group just when the nation stood on the brink of war.

Terminiello v. Chicago

In 1949 the Supreme Court rendered its *Terminiello v. Chicago* decision, which centered on Arthur Terminiello, a defrocked Catholic priest who was an active anti-Semite and quasi-fascist organizer in Chicago. Terminiello had been arrested by authorities for disturbing the peace as a result of a speech he gave in Chicago, which drew about a thousand angry demonstrators. He was convicted on the ground that his speech was of a kind that "stirs the public to anger, invites disputes, brings about a condition of unrest, or creates a disturbance."[195]

In a decision that would set the course for the development of free speech over the next several decades, the Supreme Court overturned the Illinois court's decision. Speaking for the majority, Justice William O. Douglas remarked that the "function of free speech under our system of government is to invite dispute."[196] He added that provocative speech should not be just reluctantly tolerated but encouraged because it can spur people to think about controversial issues: "It may indeed best serve its high purpose when it induces a condition of unrest, creates dissatisfaction with conditions as they are, or even stirs people to anger."[197] Twenty years later, an incident involving a right-wing extremist would once again prompt the high court to examine the issue of free speech.

Brandenburg v. Ohio

Clarence Brandenburg was the leader of an Ohio-based Ku Klux Klan organization in the 1950s. During a rally, which was filmed by reporters, Mr Brandenburg expressed his desire to expel Jewish-Americans and African-Americans to Israel and Africa respectively. Moreover, several of his fellow Klansmen were shown to be armed with firearms. Based on this film, Ohio authorities charged Brandenburg with violating the Ohio Syndicalism law enacted in 1919, which forbade the spread of unpatriotic views and the advocacy of criminal syndicalism. In *Whitney v. California* (1927) and *Dennis v. United States* (1951), the Supreme Court upheld the right of the state to proscribe the advocacy of violent means to effect political change. However, in *Brandenburg* (1969) the Court sought to distinguish between the abstract advocacy of the use of force or law violation on the one hand, and the actual planning of an illegal act that was likely to result in its fulfillment on the other. In doing so the Court overruled *Whitney v. California* (1927) by deciding that the mere abstract advocacy of an illegal act that was not likely to incite or produce an illegal action was protected by the First and Fourteenth Amendments of the Constitution. In the Court's view, Brandenburg's actions did not constitute a "clear and present danger."

Twelve years earlier, in *Yates v. United States* (1957) the Court ruled that advocating and teaching the forcible overthrow of the government is immune from prosecution under the First Amendment, so long that it is expressed in the abstract. Taken together, these two decisions cut the ground from under the Smith Act and form what is commonly referred to as the "speech plus" doctrine, i.e. some evidence of action beyond words must exist to justify a criminal prosecution. These rulings would serve as ammunition for ACLU attorneys in the Skokie case.[198]

The Skokie case

Perhaps the most controversial free speech case in American history was *Skokie v. Illinois* (1978). This controversy began when a small neo-Nazi organization was denied a permit to demonstrate in Marquette Park, Illinois. Marquette Park was the site of racial tensions between its White residents and their African-American neighbors residing in an adjoining community. The National Socialist Party of America (NSPA), an offshoot of George Lincoln Rockwell's American Nazi Party, considered Marquette Park a stronghold for its activities. When denied a permit, the group retaliated by requesting a permit to demonstrate in the town of Skokie, Illinois, a community in which many Holocaust survivors resided. The town of Skokie passed several local ordinances to prohibit the demonstration. The NSPA challenged these ordinances and its leader Frank Collin filed a suit.[199] The ACLU interceded on behalf of the NSPA and argued that these ordinances amounted to a "prior restraint" of speech. The ADL, the American Jewish Committee and the American Jewish Congress joined the town of Skokie in fighting the NSPA's challenge, arguing that allowing the NSPA stormtroopers to march in full regalia, including swastikas, would amount to "fighting words" and thus engender "menticide," i.e. such a strong emotional discomfort as to warrant its proscription.[200]

The "fighting words" doctrine originated in the 1942 Supreme Court case *Chaplinsky v. New Hampshire* (1942). The ACLU argued that fighting words must be directed at an individual. The proposed demonstration was not directed at any particular individual, but rather was an expressive act warranting First Amendment protection. The ACLU invoked the Supreme Court's decision in *Gooding v. Wilson* (1972), in which it ruled that the "fighting words" restriction could not be used to punish insults directed against large groups of people. A potentially volatile situation was brewing, as many angry people and groups, including the Jewish Defense League, were planning to counter-demonstrate. The town of Skokie sought to require an insurance indemnity from the NSPA in the event of damage stemming from the demonstration. However, such an indemnity would be exorbitant for such a small organization. Moreover, virtually no insurance company would cover such a proposition. The Court ruled that this amounted to a "heckler's veto" and was an unconstitutional impediment to free speech. Eventually the Supreme Court ruled in favor of the NSPA, and in doing so largely eviscerated the "fighting words" restriction. However, a couple of months before the scheduled event the NSPA held a demonstration in St Louis and was met by a large group of hostile counter-demonstrators. This incident gave the NSPA second thoughts about the proposed Skokie march.

Eventually the Community Relations Division of the Justice Department brokered a face-saving maneuver for both sides. The NSPA received permission to march in Daly Plaza in Chicago, which it did, and the controversy finally came to a close. In the end Skokie was a Pyrrhic victory for the far right as it did much to mobilize the "counter-hate movement."[201] Harold Covington, a member of the NSPA at the time of the *Skokie* decision, offered his comments on the controversy:

> First off, it was NEVER [emphasis in original] our intention to march in Skokie; what we wanted was our legal right to rally in the parks in Chicago restored, which we eventually obtained. If we did end up marching in Skokie, one thing I suggested to Collin was that rather than a "full" demonstration of all 30-odd of us, we carry out a token act of freedom of speech, i.e., one man, fully uniformed, march out and stand on the town hall steps at attention holding a Swastika banner and stand there for half an hour as a symbolic act. And yes, I volunteered to be that individual. Eventually the deal Collin worked with the city fathers in Chicago was to restore our access to the parks in exchange for having our "victory rally" on Daly Plaza. The Supreme Court decision officially covering the Swastika and political uniforms as constitutionally protected speech was almost an unintentional by-product of the central issue, which was to restore our right to rally in the parks. That decision is for all practical purposes a dead letter since enemies the of racial struggle, such as Morris Dees, have discovered the abuse of the civil courts and civil litigation in order to do an end run around the First Amendment and harass and annoy people who dare to speak aloud certain unpalatable truths, but for what good it does anyone, it's still there. The "counter-demonstrators" in St. Louis were the tail end of a St. Patrick's Day parade and were basically a bunch of drunken yahoos who thought they were Irish and were willing to throw beer bottles at pretty much anyone.[202]

Although the Supreme Court expanded the scope of protected speech in this case, the decision alienated many erstwhile free speech advocates. For example, the major Jewish defense organizations, which had previously been strong advocates of the First Amendment, had supported the "prior restraint" provisions of the local ordinances enacted to prohibit the Skokie march. At least for a brief period anyway, the free speech coalition was severely fractured and the ACLU was strongly criticized for its "First Amendment *über Alles*" position.[203]

R.A.V. v. St Paul

R.A.V. v. St Paul arose from an incident in 1990 in which a small wooden cross was burned on the lawn of an African-American family in St Paul, Minnesota. A juvenile, Robert Anthony Viktora, was charged in connection with this incident. Although he did not formally belong to an extremist organization, Viktora told a reporter that he had written and visited several far-right groups, including the White Christian Patriots League and White Aryan Resistance.[204] Viktora could have been charged with numerous violations, including disorderly conduct, trespassing and terroristic threats, but the county chose to prosecute him under a hate crime ordinance. In effect, Viktora was being prosecuted more for his expression and motive than the actual act itself.

Although the US Supreme Court expressed abhorrence to Viktora's actions, it ruled that the St Paul ordinance was under-inclusive in that it punished only "fighting words" that caused distress on the basis of race, color, creed, religion or gender. Words that upset groups based on other characteristics were not prohibited by this law. Also at issue was the so-called overbreadth doctrine. In essence, this refers to laws which can be used selectively to prosecute, on a discriminatory basis, individuals whose views are in disfavor with the state. Thus the overbreadth nature of such a law would deter free expression, hence producing a "chilling effect" on unpopular speech. Critics of the court's decision had a difficult time disabusing themselves of the false notion that the decision legally permitted the burning of a cross on a targeted minority's lawn. The county could have availed itself of several laws with which to prosecute the act, but instead chose what was later deemed an unconstitutional ordinance.[205] As the aforementioned Supreme Court decisions show, the far right has played an important part in the development of free speech law in the United States. The United States is exceptional in comparison to other Western democratic governments, in that it allows right-wing extremists such a great degree of latitude to express their views. Over the past few decades many democratic states have taken measures to restrict the speech and activities of the far right by creating laws against group defamation, incitement to violence, and propagation of false history, all of which have often been labeled under the rubric of "hate speech." What is surprising from an American perspective is the ease with which these laws have been enacted. Supporters of these laws have encountered very little opposition.

The American model of free speech was most poignantly expressed by Justice Oliver Wendell Holmes' "market place of ideas" metaphor. The argument goes that people should have unfettered access to a variety of ideas, even those which are very unpopular. Open debate inclusive of all views will determine which ideas have merit. This argument assumes that government should be neutral to all ideas and only ensure a level playing field, or to use the economics metaphor, a non-monopolistic, perfectly competitive market place of ideas. Any government sanction of speech, even if unpopular, runs the risk of a slide down a slippery slope in which more and more abridgments of expression could be made.

Critics of the American model occasionally cite the example of Weimar Germany as paradigmatic of what can happen if there are no prohibitions against certain forms of speech – especially that which denigrates and scapegoats minorities.[206] The fledging National Socialist German Workers Party (NSDAP) had several organs to propagate its views, including the *Völkisch Beobachter*, and Julius Streicher's *Der Stürmer*. The NSDAP eventually won a plurality in the Reichstag, and the aging President Hindenburg appointed Adolf Hitler as Chancellor. All of this was achieved by legal means. This experience may well have influenced the limits of free speech protection in many of the post-Holocaust constitutions, including those of Canada and many countries in Europe.

The First Amendment scholar Samuel Walker argues that the strong tradition of free speech in America came about from a series of choices and was not pre-determined by the original Constitution. What he sees as determinative in shaping free speech law is the influence of advocacy groups. In his view, free speech has triumphed in large part because it has had an effective advocate. Conversely, as Walker sees it, there has never been a strong advocate for restricting free speech. Hence, the free speech battle has been "terribly one-sided."[207]

Thus public policy involving right-wing extremism has been unique in the area of the First Amendment. The watchdogs have played a much more cautious role in this regard. Walker points out that several of the Jewish defense organizations, including the American Jewish Congress and the National Jewish Community Relations Advisory Council, have usually pursued a strategy of education and "quarantine" to deal with right-wing extremists.[208] What's more, these organizations made common cause on the free speech issue with both libertarian and civil rights groups. The major civil rights groups abandoned the idea of restrictive speech laws, such as group libel, because they believed that these could pose a threat to their efforts to attain equal rights. They calculated that their principal strategy for advancing group rights could best be achieved through the expansion of constitutionally protected individual rights.[209] As Walker points out, "provocative speech was a crucial weapon for the civil rights movement and the struggle for racial equality."[210]

In that sense, the watchdogs have not played the same adversary role *vis-à-vis* the far right in this area of policy to the same degree as they have in others. However, as I shall demonstrate in Chapter 6, several of the watchdog groups have endeavored to restrict the far right from the market place of ideas through other measures.

International cooperation

American authorities have on occasion cooperated with foreign governments to combat right-wing extremism. The most notable examples of such cooperation have been between the United States and Germany. In a speech at the Berlin City Hall in 1994, FBI Director Louis Freeh went so far as to identify hate crimes as one of the top crime problems facing Europe and the United States.[211] Reportedly, Freeh consulted with the German authorities on this issue and urged international cooperation between the two governments.

The most publicized case in this area involved an American, Gerhard Lauck, the leader of the NSDAP-AO,[212] a neo-Nazi organization based in Lincoln, Nebraska. His organization was one of the major suppliers of neo-Nazi propaganda to Germany, and published a journal, *New Order*, in about ten different European languages. Because of First Amendment protections in the United States, Lauck's organization had become one of the most important propaganda mills for the "neo-Fascist International" in Europe. Lauck had been arrested in Germany in 1974 for giving a pro-Nazi speech and spent four months in prison for this offense, after which he was deported and banned for life from entering Germany.[213] Lauck is a vocal critic of the German government, and advocates lifting the government's ban on overtly Nazi organizations. The notoriety stemming from this case was an embarrassment to American officials. According to an Associated Press Report, Freeh told German authorities in 1994 that he might be able to legally supply them with the addresses to which Lauck was sending his organization's propaganda materials.[214]

In 1995, Lauck was arrested in Denmark on an international arrest warrant for violating German hate speech laws. A German court convicted Lauck in 1996 and he was sentenced to four years in prison. The US government offered no protest to Lauck's conviction, despite the fact that he was arrested in a third country for activities which were protected by the American Constitution.[215]

A similar case involved Hans Schmidt, a naturalized American citizen of German origin. Schmidt publishes a right-wing newsletter, *GANPAC [German-American National Public Action Committee] Brief*, which has subscribers in Germany. While on a visit to Germany in 1995, Schmidt was arrested for *Volkverhetzung* or "incitement to hate," because of an offensive letter he sent to a German state legislator. Schmidt alleges that the US Embassy in Germany actually provided erroneous information to German authorities to assist in their prosecution against him.[216] Schmidt eventually received bail in 1996 and quickly departed Germany and returned to the United States to avoid any further prosecution.

The most recent example of cooperation between German and American authorities occurred in August 2000, when the US Marshals Service, at the request of the German Federal Ministry of Justice, arrested a German national, Hendrik Albert Viktor Moebus, for violation of his parole in Germany. In 1994, Moebus had been convicted as a minor, along with two accomplices, of the homicide of a German youth in the previous year. He was paroled in 1998, but as part of his release agreement he was prohibited from participating in extremist activities. Soon thereafter, Moebus was reported to have violated these terms by making extremist public comments and organizing far-right groups. To evade prosecution, Moebus left for America in 1999 and eventually found his way to Dr Pierce's National Alliance encampment in West Virginia. While there,

Moebus did work for Pierce's Resistance Records. Eventually, the US Marshals caught up with him and he was arrested near Lewisburg, West Virginia, about twenty miles from the National Alliance headquarters. The German embassy applauded the arrest and a spokesman commented, "[w]e have very close cooperation with the US authorities regarding fighting right-wing extremism."[217]

Moebus was an important figure in the skinhead "White power" music industry in Europe, and Pierce reportedly had big plans for Moebus at his record company.[218] Moebus' case became a *cause célèbre* for National Alliance supporters, who mounted a "Free Hendrick Moebus" campaign that included picketing the German embassy in Washington DC. Pierce framed the affair as a free speech case and expended much effort in an attempt to secure Moebus' release from prison. National Alliance attorney Victor Gerhard argued that Moebus' remarks and activities in Germany would have received First Amendment protection had they been committed in the United States. As he saw it, Moebus faced criminal prosecution if he returned to Germany for no other reason than his political beliefs, and thus should be granted political refugee status in the United States. Immigration authorities decided otherwise, and as it now stands, American authorities are preparing to extradite Moebus to Germany.

In the above cases, the subjects violated German speech laws, but such actions, one could argue, would technically come under the protection of the First Amendment and hence would not constitute criminal offenses in the United States. This would seem to put the US government in a dilemma. However, these arrests occasioned virtually no protest outside of the radical right; thus the US government had considerable room to maneuver without much fear of criticism.

Conclusion

As the preceding discussion illustrates, the American government has long grappled with the issue of right-wing extremism. This issue has frequently impelled the federal government to create and change public policy to meet the challenges that it presents to American society. First, the various episodes of right-wing violence that have punctuated American history have greatly influenced public policy in the area of counter-terrorism. Second, and related to this, Congress has often played a supervisory role over federal law enforcement in this area. Futhermore, Congress has on occasion investigated extremist groups to determine their impact on American society. Third, the prospect that right-wing extremists could enter the ranks of the military has prompted the Department of Defense to address this issue. Finally, First Amendment issues involving right-wing extremists have compelled the Supreme Court to define the permissible boundaries of free speech.

Various watchdog organizations have frequently worked closely with authorities in dealing with right-wing extremism. During the 1920s, the ADL spearheaded these efforts by sponsoring legislation to curtail the activities of the Second Era Ku Klux Klan. The most important area of cooperation has been intelligence sharing, which was first widely used during the Brown Scare and continues up to the present time. Law enforcement authorities should, however, exercise great caution in this area. The Waco tragedy, in which the Cult Awareness Network played an advisory role, demonstrated the pitfalls of relying on erroneous information. Thus intelligence sharing must be done with great caution, for two reasons. First, to avoid another conflagration like Waco. As two observers noted, when "watchdog groups are lobbying for a maximum response policy in order to make examples out of 'hate groups,' disaster is often just around the corner."[219] The second reason is to maintain the appearance of propriety. It could be potentially embarrassing for both the government and watchdog groups if it appears that outside actors unduly influence sensitive areas of policy such as law enforcement and criminal justice.

The next chapter examines in greater detail the various methods NGOs have employed to counter the far right.

6 The watchdogs' response to the far right

Introduction

The watchdog groups take a multifaceted approach to countering right-wing terrorism and extremism. Several of these efforts have already been covered in previous chapters. This chapter reviews some of the more important initiatives in greater detail. The first section looks at measures aimed at militia-style organizations. The second section examines hate crime legislation. The third section discusses the use of civil suits to silence far-right organizations. The fourth section looks at efforts to combat the far right on the internet. The fifth section covers various training and educational programs. The sixth section examines intelligence sharing. The seventh section highlights some examples of NGO-driven prosecutions. The eighth section discusses efforts to keep the far right out of the market place of ideas. Finally, some concluding observationss are offered.

Measures aimed at militias

Anti-paramilitary training statutes

One obvious concern to both watchdogs and government alike is paramilitary training by extremist groups. Even prior to the contemporary Militia movement, other segments of the far right have occasionally gained notoriety for this type of activity. For example, during the 1980s, Louis Beam's Texas Knights of the Ku Klux Klan, Glen Miller's North Carolina-based White Patriots Party and the Illinois-based Christian Patriots Defense League gained notoriety for their occasional paramilitary training drills.

These activities quickly caught the attention of watchdog groups, who wasted no time in looking for ways to curb this trend. The ADL took the lead in this effort by crafting legislation which proscribed paramilitary training by unauthorized groups. The Southern Poverty Law Center followed suit and introduced its sponsored legislation as well. When the contemporary Militia movement surfaced in 1994, more attention was brought to this issue. The watchdogs were ready to respond with a media campaign to heighten public awareness of the fledgling movement and its potential for danger. In 1994 the ADL issued a highly critical report entitled *Armed and Dangerous: Militias Take Aim at America*. A renewed legislative initiative to ban paramilitary training in all states of the country followed. The campaign has proven to be very successful, as twenty-four states have enacted such statutes, thirteen of which are based on the ADL's model.[1] The thrust of the legislation is to make it illegal to operate paramilitary camps. According to the ADL, the model bill is guided by three primary objectives:

- First, the statute *must not be violative of any constitutional guarantees* [emphasis in original], particularly the First Amendment freedoms of speech and association. A statute which is susceptible to being struck down as unconstitutional by the courts is of no value.
- Second, the statute *must deal directly with the problem of paramilitary training camps* [emphasis in original]. Such a statute would have a greater impact on public awareness than would a statute which dealt with the problem only indirectly or peripherally.
- Third, the statute *must be drafted narrowly so that it clearly does not prohibit legitimate lawful activities* [emphasis in original], such as rifle ranges and karate clubs. This is important in minimizing opposition to the bill by powerful special interest groups.[2]

Although paramilitary laws are seldom enforced, the SPLC has on occasion used civil law to curtail the paramilitary training activities of far-right groups.[3] In a celebrated case, the SPLC initiated a lawsuit against Louis Beam's Texas Knights of the Ku Klux Klan to stop the group from conducting paramilitary training, which some members used as part of a campaign to harass Vietnamese immigrant fishermen in the Galveston Bay area of Texas.[4]

Common law courts

Another measure aimed largely at the Militia movement is ADL-sponsored legislation which proscribes so-called "common law courts." These pseudo-legal venues became popular with some militia groups during the mid-1990s. The common law courts are set up as parallel courts under the direction of "freemen" who claim that there are two types of citizenship. The first, called "state citizenship," is considered a natural and organic type of citizenship that predates the ratification of the Fourteenth Amendment. The second type of citizenship is considered inferior in nature and is supposedly conferred by the federal government via the Fourteenth Amendment. According to this logic, citizens can re-assert their sovereignty by renouncing their agreements with the federal government. However, by doing so they are obliged to follow the unwritten and age-old practices of "common law."[5]

These common law courts render judgments that include property liens, criminal indictments, and other forms of "paper terrorism" against their enemies and state authorities whom they believe have violated the Constitution and the public's trust. On balance, the common law courts would seem more like a laughable nuisance than any kind of serious grassroots challenge to authority. However, one study, which surveyed 426 judges, mostly from the Western part of the United States, found that 55 per cent of them had reported common law challenges to their authority over the course of the previous year. Furthermore, 30 per cent of those judges who encountered challenges were subsequently sued by their challengers in established federal or state or local courts. Finally, and most disturbing, these legal challenges appear to have upset a considerable number of these judges, as 30 per cent consciously took measures to enhance their security after these experiences.[6]

To meet this challenge, in 1996 the ADL's Legal Affairs Department drafted a model statute that criminalizes the practice of common law courts, and introduced this legislation into state legislatures.[7] What's more, the federal government too has focused more attention on the issue, as evidenced by the FBI's *Terrorism in the United States 1997* report on domestic terrorism, which carried a story on the problem.[8] These combined efforts appear to have had a deterrent effect on those "patriots" who would otherwise consider such pseudo-legal shenanigans, as the reported number of these courts has dwindled substantially over the past couple of years.[9] The current trend of hate crime legislation could have even greater potential in countering the far right, in that it makes expressions of racial and ethnic hostility potentially very costly.

Hate crime legislation

Hate crime laws are occasionally used to prosecute perpetrators of right-wing violence. Essentially a "hate" or "bias" crime is one that is directed against a victim because of some immutable attribute such as race, ethnicity or some affiliation (religion) or particular lifestyle (gay and lesbian, interracial marriage). As explained in greater detail in Chapter 4, right-wing terrorists very often choose targets they perceive as "outsiders" for no other reason than some ascriptive characteristic as mentioned above. Moreover, because of the organizational fragmentation of the American far right, the distinction between terrorism and hate crime is often blurred. The notion of leaderless resistance, as discussed earlier, is in effect a call for those in the movement to act on individual initiative and commit acts of terrorism as they see fit. Such acts, divorced from any direct involvement of an organization, more often resemble hate crimes than acts of terrorism. And although very few right-wing groups regularly commit terrorism, some advocate violence, and can presumably influence the lone wolves that do.[10] Thus hate crime laws can be used to counter right-wing violence. Most offenders arrested for hate crimes do not formally belong to organized far-right groups, and even those that do belong to such groups usually act independently without any directive from their organizations.[11] Be that as it may, watchdog groups have done much to link organized far-right groups with the issue.

The hate crime legislative drive consists primarily of two categories of criminal law. First, are hate crime reporting statutes. In 1990 the US Congress enacted the Hate Crime Statistics Reporting Act, which directed the Attorney General to collect data and issue annual reports on predicate crimes that demonstrate "manifest evidence of prejudice based on race, religion, sexual orientation, or ethnicity."[12] The law also instructed the Attorney General to establish guidelines for data collection and the necessary evidence and criteria for determining bias. The FBI's Uniform Crime Reports (UCR) Section now has responsibility for this program. Several private groups, most notably the ADL, the SPLC and the National Gay and Lesbian Task Force Policy Institute, also release data and research reports on the topic. Public officials often prevail upon them for their expertise in this area of public policy.

Advocates of hate crime legislation argue that data reporting highlights important trends in hate crimes and gives law enforcement agencies and public policy makers important information to help them deal with this problem. Although many supporters of these laws assert that there is a growing hate crime wave, there is little empirical evidence to support such claims. As Table 6.1 illustrates, the number of reported hate crimes has remained very steady throughout the 1990s.[13] What's more, as Table 6.2 indicates, the percentage of the American population victimized by hate crimes is extremely low. This is not to trivialize the problem, but rather to point out that it remains fortunately a relatively rare occurrence, in that around one in every 20,000 persons is victimized in the United States each year. Americans are far more likely to be victims of serious offenses other than hate crimes.[14]

Table 6.1 Hate crime incidents in the United States (1992–9)

	'92	'93	'94	'95	'96	'97	'98	'99
Total hate crime incidents reported	6,623	7,587	5,932	7,947	8,759	8,049	7,755	7,876
Percentage of population covered by hate crime statistics	51	58	58	75	84	83	80	85

Source: FBI Hate Crime Statistics.

The second area of hate crime legislation is sentence enhancement. This legal measure in effect redefines conduct that is already criminal as an aggravated form of an existing crime.[15] In effect, "enhancement legislation" seeks to increase the punishment of those crimes for which there is a biased motive. The rationale for the enhanced penalty is that the whole group to which the victim belongs suffers from the hate crime insofar as it is intended to cause the entire group fear and intimidation. Moreover, such crimes are said to undermine communal harmony and could possibly lead to retaliatory attacks on the part of

Table 6.2 Number of hate crime victims in the United States and their percentage of the population (1996–9)

	1996	1997	1998	1999
Total number of hate crime victims	11,039	10,255	9,722	9,802
Estimated US population covered by hate crime reporting statistics	223,000,000	223,000,000	216,000,000	233,000,000
Percentage of population victimized by hate crime statistics	0.0050	0.0046	0.0045	0.0042

Source: FBI Hate Crime Statistics.

members of the group to which the victim belongs. Finally, there is evidence to

indicate that on average, hate crimes tend to be more violent than other criminal incidents.[16]

However, there is little evidence that this legislation has had the intended effect of promoting inter-group harmony. In fact just the opposite could be true, insofar as such legislation creates "protected classes," excluding certain types of victim, and encourages people to view crimes from the perspective of group identity. As Jakes and Potter argue, hate crime legislation, far from fostering improved inter-group relations, often encourages the opposite effect by emphasizing group differences and grievances. As they see it, the main purpose of such legislation is symbolic, not substantive. By redefining such crimes as an aspect of inter-group conflict, such laws encourage groups to identify themselves as victimized and besieged. This can lead to a status competition of sorts between victim groups, and in doing so increase each group's sense of resentment.[17] Moreover, it is often suspected that the laws are often enforced selectively – as one observer noted, "racially motivated" is a euphemism "for a crime by White (and not Black) racists. It creates the anomaly of a White youth receiving a stiffer sentence for mere graffiti on a Black business than a Black youth might receive for the burglary of its owner!"[18]

When used selectively, such laws could conceivably contravene the equal protection clause of the Fourteenth Amendment. However, there are now indications that these statutes are actually being used to prosecute African-Americans at an increasing rate. This has caused some minority leaders and libertarian activists to reconsider these laws.[19]

The ADL has been by far the most important advocate of hate crime legislation, and began lobbying for it in the 1970s. Its model statute, or a close facsimile, has been adopted in all but nine states.[20] Watchdog groups have been effective in influencing public opinion through the reports and expert testimony that they provide to the media, educators, legislators and law enforcement officials. Some local police departments have developed close working relationships with them in this area.[21] Many politicians at the local, state and national levels are now eager to champion such measures in the cause of combating bigotry and promoting greater inter-group tolerance. For example, in 1997 President Clinton held a White House Conference on Hate Crimes. In 2000, Senator Edward Kennedy introduced a hate crime law that passed the Senate, but did not receive approval in the House of Representatives. And speaking before an ADL conference that same year, Vice-President Al Gore called for a national hate crime law.[22]

The FBI has also given increasing attention to this issue. In 1996 the bureau created a Civil Rights Division, which investigates, among other things, hate crimes.[23] This office offers assistance to local police departments which lack the resources to adequately investigate hate crimes on their own. Recently, in April 2001, the US Department of Justice's Office of Juvenile Justice and Delinquency Prevention, together with the US Department of Education, awarded a million-dollar grant for a hate crime prevention plan to be administered by the Partners Against Hate – a coalition including the ADL, the Leadership Conference Education Fund, and the Center for the Prevention of Hate Violence.[24] As these initiatives demonstrate, the watchdogs have succeeded in bringing greater attention to the issue of hate crimes. This is consistent with Ken Kollman's findings that interest groups influence public opinion effectively through increasing the salience of issues.[25]

Although the perpetrators of hate crimes are usually juveniles or young adults, and without much wealth, the SPLC has on occasion used civil suits to hold far-right organizations responsible for the actions of their law-breaking members. This novel and controversial use of the civil suit has effectively put some right-wing organizations out of business.

The use of the civil suit to silence the far right

As discussed in Chapter 5, the US Supreme Court has demonstrated a strong commitment to free speech, even in its decisions involving hate speech and the far right. Lacking criminal laws with which to silence the far right, some opponents have turned to the civil suit to effect the same result. In essence, this novel approach seeks to hold leaders of far-right organizations vicariously liable for the actions of their members, even in some instances where there is no evidence of any directive to commit an illegal act. The SPLC has effectively used this tactic against far-right groups on many occasions.

In 1987 Morris Dees won a civil suit against the United Klans of America (UKA) and two of its members responsible for the 1981 slaying of African-American teenager, Michael McDonald. At issue in the trial was the liability of the UKA for the acts of its members. Although there was no evidence to indicate that the UKA's leadership had sanctioned the homicide, Dees had demonstrated that during the 1960s, the UKA had been involved in several serious episodes of racist violence.[26] In that sense, he argued, the UKA was a violence-prone organization. The ADL supplied some evidentiary information to support the SPLC's efforts, including a copy of a 1979 edition of the UKA's organ, *The Fiery Cross*, which carried a racist cartoon on its cover that depicted the lynching of a Black man. Dees argued that this amounted to incitement to murder. The jury agreed and awarded a $7 million judgment to the victim's mother. The UKA was forced to relinquish its assets to Mrs Beulah McDonald and consequently dissolved.

In another case, the SPLC, working in concert with the ADL, brought a suit against Tom Metzger, his son John and their organization, White Aryan Resistance (WAR). This suit arose out of the 1988 assault and death of a young Ethiopian immigrant, Mulageta Seraw, who, along with two friends, was attacked by three skinheads in Portland, Oregon. The skinheads responsible had never met either one of the Metzgers; however, they occasionally consorted with Daniel Mazella, a loose associate of the Metzgers who was neither involved in nor present at the assault. Dees argued that the Metzgers were responsible for the conduct of their associate Mazella, who had allegedly influenced the racist beliefs of the skinheads involved in the assault. A jury agreed with Dees, and in 1990 Seraw's family was awarded $12.5 million in damages.[27] However, the Metzgers remain undeterred, as WAR continues its operations to this day.

The SPLC's most recent civil suit victory came against the Aryan Nations in September 2000. A jury returned a $6.3 million judgment against the organization and its leader, Pastor Richard Butler. The jury found the Aryan Nations responsible for the 1998 assault on a Native American woman and her son by two of the compound's security guards.[28]

Other SPLC civil suit victories include the following:

- In 1981 members of Louis Beam's Texas Knights of the Ku Klux Klan were enjoined from harassing Vietnamese fishermen in the Galveston Bay area of Texas.
- In 1990 members of the Invisible Empire Ku Klux Klan were ordered to pay damages and perform community service for a 1979 attack on civil rights workers in Decatur, Alabama.
- The SPLC won a default judgment against the Church of the Creator (COTC) in 1994 for the slaying of a Black man by one of its members in 1991. A subsequent suit was initiated against William Pierce and his National Alliance. The SPLC argued that the COTC had transferred some of its assets to the National Alliance prior to the judgment, in an effort to hide them from the court. In 1996 a North Carolina court ruled in the SPLC's favor and Pierce was forced to pay $85,000 to the victim's family.
- In 1998 a federal jury awarded nearly $1 million in damages against two Klan organizations for harassing civil rights marchers in Forsyth County, Georgia in 1987.
- In 1998 the largest ever judgment against a hate group ($37 million) was levied against the Christian Knights of the Ku Klux Klan and four of its members for their roles in a conspiracy to burn a Black church in 1995.

Although it was not proven that the Klan organization had authorized the arson, it was held responsible for influencing the perpetrators to commit the arson.

- In 2000 an administrative law judge awarded $1.167 million to a Reading, Pennsylvania fair housing advocate who had received threats on a right-wing website, ALPHA HQ. The site had labeled the plaintiff, Mrs Bonnie Johari, a "race traitor" and displayed an animated picture of her office exploding. The SPLC represented the plaintiff.[29]

These civil suits have occasioned criticism from some civil libertarians who believe that they have a chilling effect on free speech for a number of reasons. First, the rules of evidence are much looser in civil as opposed to criminal cases; in the latter there are more restrictions on what is admissible in a trial. Second, in civil cases the plaintiff need only demonstrate a preponderance of evidence, rather than the guilt beyond a reasonable doubt standard of criminal cases. Finally, unlike in criminal cases, defendants are not guaranteed legal counsel if they cannot afford to pay for it. As a result, civil suits are in large part a contest favoring the side with the most resources. What is more, insofar as far-right groups are usually poorly financed and unpopular with much of the general public, it is all the easier to prevail over them in civil suits, or as one former SPLC intern commented, it "is kind of like shooting fish in a barrel."[30] Ray Jenkins, a writer for the *Baltimore Sun*, criticized Morris Dees for "convert[ing] the civil law, whose basic purpose is to settle disputes between individuals, into an arm of the criminal law."[31] Laird Wilcox, a keen observer of extremist politics and a left-wing libertarian, noted:

> Had this doctrine that organizations are responsible for the acts of their members been established as a legal precedent in the 1960s, it would have decimated the early civil rights movement and would have bankrupted the NAACP and CORE. ... Even the labor movement and the anti-war movement could have been crippled by lawsuits arising from the violent acts of some of their participants. Suppose a Black activist group was hit with a $7 million judgment because one of its members killed someone in the Watts riots? This sounds far-fetched, but had the Dees precedent existed then it could have happened.[32]

Some of the SPLC's detractors assert that the center is opportunistic in that it supposedly takes advantage of some of its clients for its own personal gain. The argument usually goes that although the plaintiffs might be awarded huge multi-million dollar judgments, they actually see very little of that money because these right-wing organizations are usually poorly financed. What's more, critics charge that the SPLC exploits these high-profile cases in fundraising campaigns, which bring in substantial sums of money for the center. The SPLC counters that its aim is not so much to make money for its clients from damage awards, but rather to bankrupt the organizations and individuals responsible for crimes and effectively put them out of business.[33] Mark Potok of the SPLC defends this practice and believes that it deters right-wing groups from violence:

> No one here thinks these groups have millions of dollars. Nor do they think so when they go into these suits. So these suits are not filed with the thought that the plaintiffs are going to become multi-millionaires. That's not the point. ... I think that what these suits do by and large is they make these groups very reluctant to get close to criminal violence if they can avoid it. So I think there's some utility in that. Well, I can only say anecdotally, but it seems fairly clear that you see less and less violence directly from these groups.[34]

Combating the far right on the internet

The ever-expanding internet medium presents the opportunity for groups and individuals that would otherwise not have access to the market place of ideas a chance to have their views heard. The far right has enthusiastically taken advantage of the new medium, and sees it as a powerful vehicle through which to spread its message. David Duke waxed exuberant about the internet, and goes so far to assert that it will eventually bring victory for his cause:

> The Internet serves the truth like no other medium in the history of the world. ...[35] I told him [Dr William Shockley, the inventor of the silicon chip transistor, which made possible the computer revolution] that he had given us the most powerful weapon the world has ever seen: the power of the truth unleashed. ... Dr Shockley forged for the truth, an electronic Excalibur that we shall wield unto victory. ...[36] Internet proficiency is as important to our cause as was learning to use a sword in the Middle Ages or a long rifle in the American Revolution.[37]

The Aryan Nations was one of the first far-right organizations to enter cyberspace. In the early 1980s it launched the "Aryan Nations Liberty Net," which was a computerized bulletin board network of like-minded groups and individuals. For the most part these bulletin boards were unsophisticated and did not reach many people. However, that changed in 1995 when Don Black, a close associate of David Duke, created Stormfront.[38] Over the years, Stormfront has come to host many right-wing websites, and serves as an important entry point for those curious web surfers who seek them out. Many extremist websites now proliferate the Web; by 1998, their number was estimated to have reached somewhere between 600 and 800 worldwide.[39]

Not surprisingly, use of the internet by right-wing extremists has caused much consternation among the watchdog groups. As mentioned in Chapter 2, several of them were specifically created to counter the far right on the World Wide Web (e.g. HateWatch, Nizkor Project and Militia Watchdog). Several of the more established watchdog groups have also dealt with this issue. The Simon Wiesenthal Center produces a CD-ROM called Digital Hate 2000, which lists extremist sites that it finds offensive.[40] Since 1985, the ADL has released several reports on the topic.[41] Moreover, on at least one occasion the ADL has testified before the Senate on the issue.[42] In 1999, the ADL created HateFilter® – a software program that blocks access to far-right websites. The program also has a "redirect" feature, which allows users who try to access a blocked site the chance to link directly to the ADL or a related watchdog site, to access educational material. HateFilter® runs on Mattel's CyberPatrol®, a software-blocking program that has been distributed to approximately 15,000 private and public libraries, schools and universities.[43] Surprisingly, the SPLC does not support this effort, because in its opinion filters simply do not work.[44] Somewhat related to this issue, pressure is occasionally exerted on internet service providers to prohibit offensive discourse on bulletin boards and dissuade various dot.com merchants to restrict the sale of items with extremist themes.[45]

The government has begun to address the issue as well. ADL officials met with both President Clinton and Vice President Gore in 1999 to make their pitch for the HateFilter® software program. Both were impressed and agreed to support its distribution.[46] Furthermore, Senators John McCain (R-AZ), Ernest Hollings (D-SC), Dan Coats (R-IN) and Patty Murray (D-WA) introduced the "Children's Internet Protection Act," which would require libraries and schools that receive federal funding to install filter programs that would, among other things, block access to certain extremist websites. Finally, Senator Diane Feinstein (D-CA) sought to introduce legislation via an amendment to another bill that would have prohibited the dissemination of materials related to bomb-making on the internet.

Training and educational programs

Training and educational programs are important vehicles for the watchdog groups to influence public policy towards extremism. For quite some time, the ADL has been active in this area. For example, it periodically presents lectures on extremism at the FBI academy in Quantico, Virginia.[47] In 1980 the US Commission on Civil Rights (USCCR) contracted with and paid the ADL $20,000 to produce a report on far-right groups entitled *Hate Groups in America*.[48] More recently, in June of 2000, the ADL and the US Holocaust Museum started a training program for FBI recruits.[49] In April 2002, the ADL announced that it was distributing a CD-ROM called *Extremism in America: A Guide to Law Enforcement Officials across the Country*.[50] And in May 2002, the ADL and the FBI co-sponsored a day-long conference in Quantico, Virginia on "Extremist and Terrorist Threats: Protecting America After 9/11." Representatives from over 500 federal, state and local law enforcement agencies attended.[51] Other watchdog groups have also joined in this effort, and offer similar programs of their own, which they conduct for both government agencies and private organizations.

The Simon Wiesenthal Center's National Institutes Against Hate Crimes conduct four-day training courses on hate crimes and right-wing extremist groups. The program's purpose is to bring together teams of criminal justice professionals in leadership positions to formulate strategies to confront the issues of hate crime and extremism. Each institute typically hosts three to five teams. Each team has six members: one judge or other member of the judiciary, one prosecuting attorney, one public defender, one probation officer and two law enforcement personnel.[52] The Simon Wiesenthal Center also periodically presents high-profile conferences and symposia on the subjects of terrorism, extremism, and hate crime.[53]

Perhaps the most significant training program is the State and Local Anti-Terrorism Training (SLATT) course, which up until recently was administered by Dr Mark Pitcavage, the founder of the Militia Watchdog and current head of the ADL's Fact-Finding Division. SLATT is a joint program between the FBI and a private organization, the Institute for Intergovernmental Research. It is funded through a grant from the Department of Justice's Bureau of Justice Assistance.[54] The SLATT program is conducted by the FBI's National Security Division Training Unit, and is designed to foster "pre-incident awareness" and "pre-incident preparation," and interdiction training to state and local law enforcement personnel in the areas of domestic anti-terrorism and extremist criminal behavior. Since its inception, the SLATT program has trained more than 10,000 law enforcement personnel in ninety workshops. These workshops can run for four hours to three days. The training staff is composed of law enforcement and research personnel who specialize in the area of extremism.[55] According to Pitcavage, the program was formed as a result of the Oklahoma City bombing. But, unlike other programs, this one was designed to help prevent such events from ever taking place. In sum, the main idea behind the program is to provide extensive training on criminal extremism to state and local police officers, because they are almost invariably the first on the scene to handle such incidents.[56]

Some of SLATT's detractors assert that the course smacks of political profiling that selectively targets the political right. Moreover, the program's emphasis on preemptive screening of so-called extremists in their view unfairly stigmatizes some people for no other reason than for expressing views that are protected by the First Amendment.[57]

Intelligence sharing

The most effective effort in countering the far right has been in the area of intelligence sharing. Once again the ADL has taken the lead in this field. More recently, the SPLC has moved into this area, and as Morris Dees put it, his organization "has long shared intelligence with law enforcement agencies."[58] The SPLC is thought to have one of the most comprehensive databases on right-wing extremism. Its researchers and investigators are reported to clip about 1,000 newspaper articles a week and read 150 far-right magazines, which it receives through disguised addresses.[59] Furthermore, the SPLC reportedly monitors approximately 500 extremist websites daily to alert researchers to any changes.[60] Both the ADL and SPLC regularly issue newsletters and research reports to law enforcement agencies on the activities of far-right groups.

FBI documents obtained under the Freedom of Information Act (FOIA) indicate that the ADL has made considerable efforts to cultivate a close working relationship with the FBI.[61] However, early efforts to encourage cooperation were not wholly successful. The late J. Edgar Hoover, for instance, kept the ADL at arm's length and resisted its blandishments for further cooperation.[62] However, when William Webster became FBI director in 1978, cooperation between the two agencies expanded. And in 1985 the ADL won a remarkable coup when the FBI issued a memorandum instructing its field offices to "contact each [ADL] Regional Office to establish a liaison and line of communication."[63]

Former FBI Assistant Director Buck Revell expounded on the legal limitations on intelligence sharing imposed on the FBI, and how the agency occasionally prevails upon the watchdogs for information:

> We received all the reports and we certainly reviewed and looked at the reports, but we couldn't accept them at face value. In other words, if we were going to use any information, we had to independently access and then establish the origins of the information if we were going to use it as evidence. But because of restrictions of the Privacy Act and the Attorney General's guidelines, the FBI is prohibited from collecting ambient intelligence. Unless there is an open case, you can't collect information. In order to have an open case you have to have a criminal predicate, unless it is within the foreign intelligence guidelines.
>
> So essentially everything that occurs out there that the Southern Poverty Law Center or the Anti-Defamation League collects, the bureau is prohibited from collecting, unless is happens to be an open and pending case against some entity that is being investigated …
>
> So in that sense they provide a sort of an early warning system if something really presents perhaps a cataclysmic circumstance. It doesn't mean that they can short-circuit the requirement. But at least if there is something that does indeed trip the criminal predicate, there's information that can be pulled into the process and independently verified so you don't start at ground zero. So they don't act as agents of, or surrogates for the FBI. But the FBI at the appropriate time can utilize their research if it fits within the guidelines as far as initiating an investigation.[64]

Some critics believe that the intelligence sharing between the FBI and the watchdog groups constitutes a circumvention of the Attorney General's Guidelines, in that the former can prevail upon the latter's files when it sees fit to do so. Moreover, watchdog groups do not have to concern themselves with strict civil liberties restrictions to which the FBI must adhere when gathering information on its subjects of investigation. Finally, another area of concern is the circulation of personnel between law enforcement and watchdog groups. For example, Neil Herman, a retired high-ranking FBI official who once led the agency's Joint Terrorist Task Force,[65] became head of the ADL's Fact-Finding Division upon his retirement from the bureau in 1999. Not long after assuming this position, he lobbied senior Justice Department officials to relax the constraints that inhibit the FBI from investigating extremist groups.[66] He resigned from this position in 2000. For his part, the current ADL chief fact-finder, Dr Mark Pitcavage, saw nothing untoward in its relationship with the FBI and other law enforcement agencies.

> In the first place there's no sort of on-going collusion. There's no sort of on-going cooperation with any of these groups and say, the FBI. There might be times when for instance, the FBI has opened a criminal investigation on Joe Blow. They might then go to say, the Southern Poverty Law Center, and say "Look, you know, we think that Joe Blow may be involved in some criminal activity. Do you guys have any information on it?" And so nothing like that has indicated that there was already a criminal predicate. And so it doesn't bend or nullify the spirit of the letter of the privacy laws or Attorney General guidelines.[67]

Related to the issue of intelligence sharing is the use of informants. On many occasions watchdog groups have sponsored informants who have infiltrated right-wing organizations. As mentioned in Chapters 2 and 5, private informants were widely used to infiltrate various native-fascist and far-right groups during the 1930s and 1940s. During the late 1940s and early 1950s, a journalist and southeast research director for the ADL, Stetson Kennedy, infiltrated a Klan organization in the South. He published a rather sensationalist account of his experience in a book titled *Southern Exposure*. His investigative work did much to build opposition to the Klan, and even persuaded US Attorney General Tom Clark to place the organization on his "subversives list."[68]

During the 1980s, the ADL sponsored an informant named James Mitchell Rosenberg. Rosenberg's activities were so provocative that he drew criticism from another watchdog organization, People Against Racist Terror, which was alarmed by his extreme-right organizing and advocacy of racist violence.[69] In another instance, the ADL sponsored one Andy Oakely, who infiltrated neo-Nazi and Klan organizations in the Midwest. He later wrote a book based on his experiences, *"88": An Undercover News Reporter's Exposé*.[70] The most controversial use of informants, however, relates to the so-called ADL San Francisco Spy Scandal.

The ADL San Francisco Spy Scandal

Around January 1993 rumors began to surface in San Francisco that its police department had illegally leaked confidential information on numerous political activists and organizations in the state of California. A few months later, on April 8, 1993, the San Francisco Police Department carried out a five-hour raid on the ADL's San Francisco and Los Angeles regional offices because of information received that the ADL had received some of this information, and seized ten boxes of documents. At the center of the controversy was one Roy "Cal" Bullock, an informant who had worked for the ADL since 1960.[71] Bullock infiltrated numerous political organizations, and all totaled, his files contained information on 12,000 individuals and over 950 groups of all political orientations.[72] He divided his files into four categories: "Right Wing," "Pinkos," "Arab" and "Skins" (for skinhead groups). The investigation revealed that he had passed his information on to the San Francisco regional ADL office. Surprisingly, the groups on which he spied were not confined to the far right, but also included many progressive, left-wing and anti-Apartheid organizations. In fact most of the groups on which he spied could be counted in the "progressive" category – groups with which the ADL had on numerous previous occasions formed alliances. Not surprisingly, Arab-American organizations were also targeted. One observer speculated that the ADL monitored many of its seemingly like-minded organizations because it feared the emergence of an alliance between Black and progressive organizations on the one hand, with the Palestinian cause in Israel on the other, which in his estimation resembles the plight of Blacks during the American Civil Rights era.[73]

Bullock is alleged to have received much of his information from San Francisco Police Detective Tom Gerard, with whom he began working in 1987. Gerard had extensive experience in the field of intelligence, and during the early 1980s worked for the CIA in El Salvador.[74] He supplied Bullock with numerous confidential police records on various left-wing, right-wing and civic organizations in California. What's more, Gerard and Bullock sold information on anti-Apartheid activists and the Arab-American community to the governments of South Africa and Israel.[75] To avoid prosecution, Gerard fled to the Philippines in November 1993.

The scandal nearly developed into a major disaster for the ADL. The *San Francisco Observer* newspaper ran many critical articles on the scandal, one of which reported that investigators had found evidence of similar illicit contacts with twenty other law enforcement agencies nationwide. The story quoted one police official as saying "This Gerard-Bullock thing is the tip of the iceberg – this is going nationwide."[76] However, the ADL was ultimately able to conduct masterful damage control. It reached an agreement with the San Francisco District Attorney's Office to avoid prosecution. As part of the agreement, the ADL denied any wrongdoing, but paid a $75,000 fine, which went to a hate crime prevention program. A civil suit initiated by those on whom Bullock spied dragged on for several years. The plaintiffs sought to uncover the secret files as part of the discovery process of a civil suit, but the ADL resisted such requests. In a controversial ruling, a California State Court of Appeal decided in 1998 that the ADL did not have to turn over the impounded records to the plaintiffs because it had "journalistic privilege" as a news-gathering organization, and as such did not have to reveal information even if this had been obtained under illegal circumstances.[77] This decision occasioned criticism from some civil libertarians. Commenting on the ADL's use of "shield" laws that protect the press from revealing its sources, Laird Wilcox opined:

> In no sense, however, is the ADL on a par with the *New York Times* or *Time Magazine*, nor is it even remotely related to the working press. Its publications are designed to support the ideological agenda of the organization and its constituency, and not to provide "news."[78]

Likewise Robert Friedman commented:

> for the most part, journalists don't share their files with domestic police agencies. The ADL has no such inhibitions. Because many of its files are not open to public scrutiny, false information collected by ideologically biased researchers cannot be corrected.[79]

In September 1999, US District Court Judge Richard Paez ordered the ADL to permanently refrain from illegally gathering information on the plaintiffs. The City of San Francisco also eventually reached an agreement with plaintiffs. The police department disbanded its counterintelligence unit after the scandal, and revised it policies for monitoring political groups.[80]

From the perspective of the ADL, it appeared to have weathered what appeared to be a potential major crisis without much of a setback. News of the story did not reach far beyond the environs of San Francisco. The whole affair did, however, severely damage its standing with the American left. Prior to the scandal, the far left – including its civil libertarians – for the most part ignored the ADL's spying on the far right. However, many were shocked and dismayed to discover that the ADL had compiled dossiers on them as well. Robert Friedman wrote a highly critical account of the affair in the left-wing magazine *Village Voice*.[81] Daniel Levitas, a former executive director of the Center for Democratic Renewal, commented that the scandal "had completely tainted the ADL's credibility and reputation with regard to its objectivity."[82] Perhaps the most vociferous left-wing critic was Chip Berlet of Political Research Associates. He recalled a meeting in the mid-1980s that he and another researcher, Russ Bellant, had with the late Irwin Suall, the ADL's chief fact-finder until the late 1990s. Berlet was flabbergasted to discover that the ADL had been monitoring the American left:

> [W]e introduce ourselves, say what we are up to and Suall leans back in his chair and basically runs down a dossier on each of us: about what our political activities are, who we work with, what organizations we belong to. … We were just sitting there with our mouths open feeling very uncomfortable. … And then he leans forward and says, "The right wing isn't the problem. The left wing is the problem. The Soviet Union is the biggest problem in the world for Jews. It's the American left that is the biggest threat to American

Jews. You're on the wrong track. You're part of the problem." We were stunned. I was basically in tears. ... We stumbled out of there in a daze.[83]

Since the scandal broke, Berlet has strongly criticized the ADL's intelligence gathering methods (see Chapter 2 for more details).

NGO-driven prosecutions

As mentioned in Chapter 5, NGOs have on occasion assisted government authorities in prosecuting right-wing extremists. For example, the historian Richard Gid Powers suggests that authorities built much of their prosecution of native fascists in the Great Sedition Trial on information from private groups and individuals such as the ADL and John Roy Carlson. In another example, a federal court appointed the SPLC's Morris Dees as a special prosecutor in a case involving Glen Miller.

More recently, in August of 2001, the SPLC sought to persuade the US Department of Justice to prosecute one Mark Coterill, the leader of the now defunct American Friends of the British National Party (AF-BNP), for allegedly violating the Foreign Agents Registration Act. Coterill had founded the AF-BNP in early 1999 as a vehicle through which to raise money for the parent organization, the British National Party, in England. He would hold meetings in the Northern Virginia area, at which many notable far-rightists including Dr William Pierce, David Duke, Kirk Lyons, Nick Griffin (the chairman of the BNP), Roy Armstrong (of the German National Democratic Party), Don Black and Richard Kelly Hoskins, among others, would give speeches, and after which Coterill would take up collections for the AF-BNP. In this sense, Coterill endeavored to not only build solidarity among far-rightists in America, but also cement ties with like-minded activists overseas.

Not surprisingly, the appearance of so many high-profile far-rightists at the AF-BNP's venues eventually caught the attention of the watchdogs. In August of 2001, Mark Potok of the SPLC wrote a letter to the Attorney General requesting that Coterill be prosecuted for allegedly violating the FARA. Potok claimed that the AF-BNP had raised at least $85,000 since 1999.[84] For his part, Coterill contends that the Department of Justice had actually known of his activities since 1999, and that he had in fact met with DOJ representatives who told him that it was not necessary to register as a foreign agent. However, after the SPLC's inquiries into the matter, the Department of Justice has opened an investigation and the major media have taken notice as well.[85]

Countering the far right in the market place of ideas

As discussed in Chapter 5, the watchdog groups have tended to confront right-wing extremism more gingerly in the area of free speech and the First Amendment. What's more, efforts to legally exclude extremist views from the market place of ideas have not been very effective in the United States.

Consequently, some watchdog groups have sought to use other means to effect the same result.

On numerous occasions watchdog groups have filed formal complaints with the Federal Communications Commission (FCC) against radio stations that air extremist programs. They argued that these programs served no public interest and thus should not have access to the airwaves. The pattern appears to be that the FCC usually declines to take action in these cases on First Amendment grounds and defers to the local community to decide what action is appropriate.[86] As a result the watchdogs have had to look for other ways to curtail extremists' use of the mass media. One method that has proved effective is applying pressure directly on media outlets and dissuading them from disseminating extremist views.

A good example of this was the case of the Liberty Lobby, which began airing a program called *This is Liberty Lobby* over scattered radio stations in 1973. The program expressed views that were highly critical of Israel and Zionism. Consequently, the ADL took an interest and sought to dissuade radio stations from carrying the program. To meet this challenge the ADL chief fact-finder at the time, Irwin Suall, sent a directive to ADL regional offices with recommendations for action against the Liberty Lobby radio program. Regional directors were instructed to communicate directly with station managers and discourage them from airing the program.

For a while, the Liberty Lobby enjoyed some success, as it was able to find nearly 200 stations to carry its program.[87] And by 1974, the Liberty Lobby appeared to have pulled off a major coup in that it had signed a contract with the Mutual Broadcasting System to carry the program on its extensive network of 600 stations. However, the ADL mounted an intense campaign and ultimately the Mutual Broadcasting Network cancelled the contract.[88] The Liberty Lobby countered by filing a suit in a federal court against the ADL and the Mutual Broadcasting System, charging that two had conspired to restrain trade in violation of federal anti-trust laws. The court dismissed the case in 1976. The Liberty Lobby appealed, but in 1978 the US Court of Appeals for the Fifth District unanimously affirmed the district court's decision.[89]

The SPLC has on occasion made efforts to restrict the far right from the mainstream media as well. In 1996 National Alliance chairman Dr William Pierce found a book publisher with a national distribution network to publish his book *The Turner Diaries*. The book (discussed in previous chapters above) had gained considerable notoriety the previous year because of its connection to Oklahoma City bombing perpetrator Timothy McVeigh. Thus there was a potential market of curious readers. Lyle Stuart, the publishing company's owner, was a left-wing maverick and had previously published controversial books.[90]

The SPLC sought to discourage booksellers from carrying Pierce's book by mounting a letter-writing campaign. Dees asked the country's major book distributors to refrain from selling the book, arguing that sales would help fill Pierce's coffers.[91] Dees' advice notwithstanding, some dealers decided to carry

The Turner Diaries anyway. However, the publisher was forced out of business not long after the book's release, and Pierce was back to selling the book on his own again.[92]

Conclusion

The cumulative effect of the various efforts discussed above has done much to neutralize the far right in America. First, the watchdogs have been successful in lobbying for legislation that can be used against far-right groups, such as anti-paramilitary training, laws that proscribe common law courts, and hate crime statutes. Second, various civil suits have bankrupted extremist groups and probably have discouraged others from engaging in violence. Third, training and educational programs that the watchdogs have sponsored have raised awareness on the topic of right-wing extremism among law enforcement and other public and private agencies. Fourth, the watchdogs have maintained intelligence files on right-wing extremists that are occasionally shared with law enforcement. This information can be used to thwart criminal conspiracies in their seminal stages, and can also be used by authorities if they decide to prosecute extremist lawbreakers. Fifth, the watchdogs have succeeded on previous occasions in keeping extremists out of the mainstream market place of ideas. Finally, as discussed in Chapter 5, some of the watchdogs occasionally worked directly with authorities to counter the far right. Examples include Morris Dees being appointed as a special prosecutor by a federal court, and the ADL's working relationship with authorities in Operation Clean Sweep. Finally, Chapter 2 mentioned some of the more confrontational methods that groups such as Anti-Racist Action employ, such as street fights and counter-protests.

Admittedly, it is very speculative to say just how influential and/or dangerous the American far right would be in the absence of their watchdog opponents. However, it is virtually inconceivable that a right-wing terrorist group could emerge in the United States on the scale of the *Aum Shinrikyo* organization in Japan. Watchdog groups would almost undoubtedly have alerted authorities to such a development and persuaded them to take resolute action. Previously, some right-wing extremist groups (such as the Order) have demonstrated revolutionary and other violent ambitions. It is not unreasonable to assume that they would have had a much better chance of effecting their goals in the absence of the watchdog organizations. As in other areas of public policy, the government is more likely to act resolutely when prodded by interest groups. What is unique about the response to right-wing extremism, however, is the preeminent role that watchdog groups have played.

It is generally believed that the number of private groups, which seek to counter the political left and other variants of extremism, is much lower than those arrayed against the political right. In fact, a recent study estimated that there currently are approximately 300 such groups nationwide that seek to counter the far right.[93] What is more, the watchdog groups that oppose the far right tend to have considerably more resources. Furthermore, virtually all of the watchdog organizations that have targeted the political left have been very ephemeral in nature, or at least have not involved themselves in that particular issue for very long. By contrast, as previous chapters have sought to demonstrate, those watchdog groups arrayed against the far right employ a much broader scope of activities than those groups that have periodically countered other variants of extremism. The latter have confined their efforts primarily to issuing reports and occasionally providing information to authorities, but to my knowledge there is no evidence to indicate that authorities reciprocated and *shared* information with them on a regular basis. It appears to have been basically a one-way street in that regard, in contrast to the anti-right watchdogs. Furthermore, the anti-left watchdogs were relatively few in number, transitory, and did not command the resources of their counterparts who oppose the far right. Chapter 7 seeks to explain, among other things, why the anti-right NGOs have been so successful in this area of public policy.

7 Conclusion

Introduction

This chapter offers some final comments on the topics discussed in the preceding chapters. The first section seeks to explain why NGOs have been so effective in this field of public policy. The second section addresses some of the civil liberties implications of the collaboration between the government and NGOs. The third section offers some public policy recommendations. The fourth section speculates on the significance of the far right in the future. And finally, the impact of 9/11 on this issue is discussed.

Why have the NGOs been so influential?

Why have watchdog groups been able to set so much of the agenda in this field of public policy? First, unlike other public policy issues, this area of public policy is basically a no-lose proposition for lawmakers. By supporting policies such as hate crime legislation, anti-paramilitary training statutes, and tougher counter-terrorist measures, lawmakers send symbolic messages that they are taking a tough stand against bigotry and support law and order. By doing so, they gain the approval of the interest groups that advocate these policies. Furthermore, with the exception of some of the new counter-terrorist initiatives, these policy measures usually do not involve significant fiscal costs, and hence they do not really raise issues of tax increases or sacrificing money from other programs to implement them.[1]

Second, there really is not much competition or countervailing power on the other side of this issue. The far right, although it episodically experiences spurts of growth, is still small, organizationally fragmented, and has little popular support. And overall the movement is considered to be beyond the pale in American society. Thus there is a feeling of mutual suspicion between both the far right and the larger society in which it finds itself. Jeffrey Kaplan referred to this development as "mutual delegitimation," which posits that

> not only is the nascent dissident group engaged in a process of stripping the regime of its claim to legitimacy, but either simultaneously or more often as

a precondition for the radicalization of the right-wing group, the dominant culture at both state and non-state levels has anathematized the discourse of the radical right.[2]

Thus the contemporary far right finds itself with very few friends outside of its movement, as even the American Civil Liberties Union now seems to be less enthusiastic in supporting unpopular causes associated with the movement as it was in the past. Table 7.1 below lists the most recent available financial data on assets and annual income of the eight most important NGOs in this area of policy. As these data indicate, the top eight NGOs collectively command assets of over $309 million and collectively receive an annual income of over $154 million. By comparison, virtually all far-right organizations are poorly financed. Furthermore, the success of interest groups depends largely on their position in the social structure and their access to powerful political institutions.[3] As explained in Chapter 2, several of the watchdog groups – most notably the ADL, the Simon Wiesenthal Center and the Southern Poverty Law Center – have received access to and support from high-level public figures including politicians, celebrities and other influential opinion makers. Because of this

Table 7.1 Financial assets and annual income of top three watchdog groups (FY2000), US$

	Assets	Annual income
Jewish defense organizations		
Anti-Defamation League	17,737,259	48,693,379
American Jewish Committee	70,055,959	39,793,811
Civil litigation watchdog group		
Southern Poverty Law Center	147,441,903	32,520,416
Progressive-oriented watchdog groups		
Center for Democratic Renewal	102,290	543,282
Political Research Associates	737,022	708,556
Regional watchdog groups		
Northwest Coalition Against Malicious Harassment	142,124	442,710
Center for New Community	507,450	256,886
Total	309,300,033	154,578,433

Source: guidestar.org.

imbalance, watchdog groups dominate this area of public policy unimpeded by strong opponents.

By contrast, virtually all far-right organizations are poorly financed. Even the most affluent of them would probably not be on a financial par with the second-level watchdogs such as the Center for Democratic Renewal, Political Research

192 *Conclusion*

Associates, the Northwest Coalition Against Malicious Harassment and the Center for New Community.[4] In those areas of public policy in which there are fewer powerful opponents, the lobbyists' influence tends to be greater.[5] As one observer explained, the strength of an interest group is measured in part "by the strength or weakness of the other political forces and institutions which [it] encounters."[6] And the far right is much weaker than the various groups arrayed against it.

Third, as Malecki and Mahood have pointed out, one way that interest groups can enhance their success is by framing their concerns as part of the larger national interest.[7] Watchdog groups have effectively persuaded much of the American public and policy makers that their agenda is consistent with the national interest. Representatives from the ADL and SPLC are often called upon to give expert testimony and advice on such issues as terrorism and hate crime legislation. By doing so, they have raised the salience of these issues about which they feel strongly, and have influenced public opinion.[8] Watchdogs have done much to brand the far right as beyond the bounds of acceptability in American society, and to depict them as a threat to be contained. The anti-terrorist measures advocated by these NGOs are seen as dovetailing with domestic security. Slighting the civil liberties of unpopular groups is seen as an acceptable price for increased national security.

Civil liberties implications

The efforts of both NGOs and the government have done much to stymie the threat from the far right in America. However, their tactics are sometimes overzealous and at times have proven counterproductive. The Ruby Ridge siege and Waco conflagration come to mind here. The resentment resulting from the way in which the government handled these events did much to fuel the Militia movement in the mid-1990s, and so angered Timothy McVeigh that he perpetrated the most horrific act of domestic terrorism as a retaliatory act.

As discussed in Chapter 5, there is evidence to suggest that the government responded injudiciously to the Branch Davidian cult in Waco largely on account of spurious information received from the Cult Awareness Network watchdog group. Waco illustrates the consequences resulting from ideologically driven advocates trying to persuade law enforcement agencies to fight their enemies for them.[9]

What are the implications of such cooperation between the government and NGOs in this area of public policy? First, it raises some civil liberties issues. For instance, some NGOs provide to law enforcement agencies, information on citizens and groups that they consider extremist. However, the vast majority of extremist groups are usually law abiding; they just espouse unpopular opinions. Those that do otherwise risk organizational suicide because they are often closely monitored. What is more, many groups and individuals in the far right do not even publicly advocate revolutionary goals and ambitions. Organizations such as American Renaissance, the League of the South, and the Council of

Conservative Citizens display characteristics that are not unlike analogous minority organizations that are concerned with identity politics. An obvious double-standard would seem to be present in this situation, whereby analogous left-wing and minority organizations do not face the same level of scrutiny by authorities, at least at the present time.

Second, the activities of undercover informants are sometimes questionable. The frequent incidence of such informants in far-right organizations, especially those that do not espouse violent and revolutionary ambitions, would seem to indicate that at least the spirit of the Attorney General's guidelines is not always upheld. Arguably, the use of informants not officially affiliated with the government, but working for private watchdog groups, would seem to circumvent the guidelines when information is regularly fed back to government authorities. One study found that 35 per cent of 223 individuals arrested on charges related to right-wing terrorism had not actually consummated any terrorist act. This suggests, according to the author of the study, that "there is an undeniable agent provocateur aspect in many of these cases."[10]

Public policy recommendations

Responding to political extremism does indeed present a conundrum to authorities. An inescapable fact is that intelligence gathered through the use of informants is an indispensable part of law enforcement and criminal investigation, without which it would be nearly impossible to solve many serious crimes.[11]

Table 7.2 Most important factors involved in the capture of terrorists

Informants and infiltrators	43.4%
Surveillance	32.1%
Caught in the Act	27.7%
Investigation	16.5%
Information from public	8.4%
Routine patrolling	7.6%

Note: The data used to derive these figures included information on 249 individuals that were captured.
Because many cases involved more than one factor, the percentages sum to more than 100 percent.

Source: Hewitt, Christopher, 'Understanding Terrorism in America: From the Klan to Al Qaeda' p.90 (Routledge, 2003).

In fact, a study by Chris Hewitt found that the use of informants was the single most important factor leading to the capture of terrorists (see below Table 7.2).

Thus intelligence gathering and sharing must be done gingerly for a number of reasons. First, to avoid overreaction, authorities must have some mechanism in place by which to ascertain the veracity and accuracy of the information that they receive. The second reason is to maintain the appearance of propriety. It could be potentially embarrassing for both the government and watchdog groups if it appeared that outside actors were unduly influencing sensitive areas of policy such as law enforcement and criminal justice. Third, intelligence abuses run the risk of undermining public support for counter-terrorism efforts. This is no trivial concern, as this is exactly what happened after revelations regarding COINTELPRO surfaced in the early 1970s. As a result of this controversy, the nation's counter-terrorist and domestic intelligence apparatus was substantially scaled down. Moreover, this kind of a backlash can have a deleterious effect on the morale of those personnel responsible for these functions.[12] Finally, law enforcement and intelligence agencies must work with limited resources. They are not well served if they receive hyperbolic threat assessments from NGOs without corroboration. For most of the 1990s, right-wing terrorists have preoccupied government counter-terrorism analysts. Perhaps, in some ways, this attention was misdirected, as more focus should have been placed on the better organized, more disciplined and well financed international terrorists, namely those radical Islamic terrorists that compose Al-Qaeda.[13] Clearly, the first World Trade Center attack of 1993, the bombings of US targets in Saudi Arabia in the mid-1990s, the bombings of the US embassies in Kenya and Tanzania, and the attack on the *USS Cole* clearly demonstrated the serious capabilities and intentions of this terrorist network. Despite these red flags, the FBI continued to shift the agency's counter-terrorism efforts to combating right-wing extremist groups. According to a retired FBI official, this pattern held all the way up to September 11, 2001.[14] A number of factors may have contributed to this development. For example, President Clinton exploited the Oklahoma City bombing by drawing parallels between anti-government militias and a resurgent Republican Party that advocated small government. Political correctness probably had a part in this oversight as well. The FBI's much heralded report on possible Y2K terrorism, *Project Megiddo*, made no mention of the threat from Islamic terrorists. In fact the only serious terrorist threat surrounding the landmark date involved an Al-Qaeda operative, Ahmed Ressam. Similarly, a Commerce Department official in charge of security went so far as to expurgate all references to Islamic extremists in a Y2K report on potential terrorist threats.[15]

The Ruby Ridge and Waco incidents underscored the tensions between the BATF and the FBI. A good deal of friction between the two agencies has been detectable in the past. Several prominent officials in the FBI and Justice Department have criticized current policy, which often leads to mixed jurisdiction between the two agencies. Former Hostage Rescue Team Commander, Danny O. Coulson, perceived that the whole affair was misguided from the start and blamed the BATF for the fiasco:

> Here was a guy [Randy Weaver] holed up in the mountain, waiting for the Tribulation, charged with what I believe to be a thoroughly insignificant offense. He was arrested by the ATF in front of his wife. He was pressured

to become an ATF informant. A bunch of guys in camouflage showed up and killed the family dog in front of his son. There was a firefight in which his only son was killed. …

But what had started this crazy business? A lousy ATF case involving two guns that had nothing to do with crime in the United States. A bench warrant for nonappearance. What was the point? At the same time that we were trying to find more FBI agents to send into high-crime areas to reclaim our streets, we had a federal agency chasing after a mountain man who had produced a couple of shotguns.[16]

Buck Revell sees the bifurcation of law enforcement duties between the BATF and the FBI as problematic:

One of the difficulties is that you have the ATF out there enforcing gun laws and many times that will transcend over into some of the domestic security type issues. Frankly, I'm of the belief that you should only have one agency involved in this area. That way you can have guidelines and proper control. Both Ruby Ridge and Waco were ATF operations from the start that got the bureau into a situation that was no fault of the bureau. I think the ATF has outlived its usefulness. The taxing part ought to be turned over to the IRS and the investigation and law enforcement parts ought to come to the FBI. That way you would have a consistent and focused effort. The ATF doesn't operate under the Attorney General's guidelines. The FBI does and I think anything dealing with domestic security issues ought to be under the same guidelines.[17]

Former Attorney General Ed Meese saw difficulties arising from this arrangement as well:

Waco and Ruby Ridge were both unfortunate situations, particularly when the bureau was the one that got the black eye. In both cases the situation had been caused by the BATF, with I think some serious errors of judgement on the part of engaging in the events that led to these two situations. …

[T]here would really be no reason for coordination [between the BATF and the FBI] if these were BATF enterprises that they conducted on their own. The only reason the FBI got into them was because of the mistakes of the BATF. Federal officers were killed, which made it automatically an FBI case. …

[T]he BATF has jurisdiction over certain fields related to terrorism that are there by historical accident. As you probably know, up until, I'd say the 1960s, there was a general feeling that the federal government had no authority to get involved in a lot of these, what you might call normal crimes, regular crimes, including the possession of firearms. And so the only way in the 1930s, when there were a lot of machineguns being used in bank robberies, there was a big cry for the federal government to do something, and the only thing they could think of constitutionally was to tax machine-guns. And that's how the BATF got that responsibility. It was the same outfit that taxed liquor and cigarettes, which is how you got alcohol, tobacco, and firearms. Firearms were added to the alcohol and tobacco tax section of the Treasury Department. And so then, over the years, guns became much more of a matter of federal cognizance. ... And because the BATF had the enforcement responsibility, gradually somehow, explosives got added to the firearms responsibility. So you have now the BATF having almost concurrent jurisdiction with the FBI on a lot of these things related to firearms and explosives and being the lead agency in many of the investigations.[18]

Several confrontations between the BATF and right-wing extremists have escalated into major fiascos, which have seriously damaged the credibility of federal law enforcement. Besides Ruby Ridge and Waco, the BATF was also thought to have played a major role in the investigation of the extremist groups involved in the Greensboro Massacre mentioned in Chapter 4.[19] In light of these incidents, it appears that it would be advisable for the BATF to operate under the same guidelines to which the FBI adheres when investigating extremist groups. Another policy recommendation would be to re-examine the respective roles of the BATF and the FBI in this area of counter-terrorism. The current bifurcation of jurisdiction appears to be problematic. Perhaps it would be advisable for the BATF to hand over a greater share of its investigations involving potential terrorist groups to the FBI, the agency that appears to be better equipped to handle such cases.

Another recommendation would be for the FBI to expand its outreach program that it currently has for Militia/Patriot groups to other segments of the far right.[20] Although many may find their views and ideologies distasteful, this program could work to allay suspicion on both sides of the issue. Since the subjects of this program would voluntarily participate, it would not be a violation of their First Amendment rights. Furthermore, it would allow authorities to better judge the information that they receive from private sources such as the watchdog groups. Authorities must have a means by which to better judge the veracity and accuracy of the intelligence they receive. By engaging in non-confrontational dialogue, both sides may be able to moderate the negative stereotypes that they hold for the other. What's more, these contacts could reduce anxiety and the potential for misunderstanding. Finally, in the event of a crisis, established contacts would keep open a line of communication between the two sides.[21]

As regards the watchdog organizations, these could bolster their credibility by increasing the transparency and accountability of their operations. As mentioned earlier, it is not uncommon for governments to rely on NGOs for expertise when developing public policy. That said, it is reasonable to expect private organizations to be held to an equivalent set of standards when they work closely with the government on such important issues as law enforcement and counter-terrorism. Anything less could damage the credibility of the government and the NGOs upon whom it relies, as an observer explained:

> Many of these groups possess expertise that governments find valuable in developing their policies. Public consultation has become the new mantra in public management as governments have reached out to civil society for help in dealing with public problems. Such groups will also find that they are increasingly subject to the kinds of scrutiny usually reserved for governments and bureaucracies, and will also have to ensure legitimacy and credibility by paying more attention to accountability and openness, as well as ensuring the reliability of their information sources. …
>
> The private sector can become a partner in counter-terrorism and crisis management, provided that the same standards applied to governments and states apply: accountability, respect for the rule of law, and openness (if not during a crisis, then afterwards).[22]

It may also be prudent for the watchdog organizations to develop a better division and specialization of duties between them. For instance, some watchdogs, such as the ADL and the SPLC, appear to be doing too many activities for one organization. They may actually be better served by separating some of their functions among other groups. It raises some ethical questions if an organization engages in surveillance on its ideological opponents and provides intelligence on them to law enforcement agencies lobbies while it contemporaneously lobbies for special political causes and specific policies against the same. If these functions were separated and carried out by different organizations it would do much to remove, first, any potential conflict of interests; and second, the appearance of ethical impropriety that occasionally surfaces.[23]

The significance of the far right

Compared to other forms of violence in America, domestic terrorism remains, fortunately, a relatively uncommon occurrence. In fact, the total number of deaths attributed to inter-gang violence in Los Angeles for just one year alone (1991) was greater than the estimated number of all terrorist fatalities in the United States from 1958 through 1998.[24] According to a 1996 Center for Democratic Renewal estimate mentioned in Chapter 1, there are roughly 25,000 "hard core" members of right-wing extremist organizations and another 150,000 to 175,000 active "sympathizers" who buy literature, make contributions, and periodically attend meetings.[25] With a total national population that now exceeds 280 million, that works out to about one far-right member and/or sympathizer for every 1,400–1,500 persons. Thus, relative to the size of America's large population, the estimated membership of right-wing extremist groups is not significant.

As Lipset and Raab point out, several characteristics endemic to the American political system seem to inhibit far-right movements from sustaining any kind of enduring significant support. First, owing to the nature of the American political party system, the mainstream political parties are able to co-opt the issues that fuel right-wing extremism. Second, the first-past-the-post, or plurality, electoral system militates against the development of both fringe right and left political parties. What's more, in plurality systems, the larger the constituency, the less likely it is for minor parties to compete successfully in elections. Third, the two-party system in a nation as large and diverse as the United States encourages political moderation.[26] Finally, the wide availability, and the character of, education in America has fostered a high level of "democratic restraint."[27]

Thus it would seem that, despite all the attention the far right has received, its threat has been somewhat exaggerated. In fact one of the most distinguishing characteristics of the movement is its weakness. And currently the far right poses no threat whatsoever to the state system in the United States. In its current guise one would be hard pressed to call it more than a nuisance. Does such a minimal threat warrant such attention? Recent trends in Western countries could conceivably presage a change in fortunes for the far right and increase the potential for terrorism therefrom. It should be kept in mind that the possible consequences of these trends listed here are highly speculative.

One interesting development of recent years is the convergence of ideas among various right-wing groups, not only in the United States but also other nations of the Western world.[28] Likewise, Cas Mudde found that the extreme right parties of Europe, their national and ethnic particularism notwithstanding, generally share the idea that those of European descent are linked by a common meta-culture.[29] Kaplan and Weinberg posit that this convergence has come about largely for two reasons: (a) a similarity of conditions in the various countries of the Western world (e.g. the transition to multicultural societies, third world immigration, low native fertility rates, and declining life chances for many native youths); and (b) new internet technology that enables far-right groups to communicate with one another across national borders unencumbered by national hate speech laws.[30] Although this is not the first time this has occurred, the ties are now much more developed and widespread. One consequence of this is that right-wing terrorists have the potential to draw upon support from a greater number of sources, and conceivably have more foreign sanctuaries available to which they could flee in order to evade prosecution. However, this process of convergence should not be overstated. It is primarily on an ideological plane – success at organizational convergence has been less forthcoming. The far right is notorious for its internecine squabbles and backbiting, and its members often have a difficult time cooperating with one another. Thus a monolithic global movement seems highly improbable, at least for the near future.

As mentioned earlier, anti-Semitism looms large in many quarters of the far-right movement and, if anything, has intensified since the heyday of historical fascism. Likewise, many Islamic extremists hold a similar worldview, known as anti-Zionism. Moreover, the far right often champions the Palestinian cause in its literature. Thus there is clearly a meeting of minds between the two political movements. Further, recent terrorists attacks orchestrated by the likes of Osama bin Laden demonstrate a more reckless abandon than the more secularly inspired PLO terrorism of the 1970s and 1980s. Thus the potential for a new terrorist alliance exists: well funded Middle Eastern terrorists working with domestic right-wing terrorists. Collusion between the far right on the one hand and Arab and Islamic extremists on the other has occurred in the past, but with little effectiveness.[31] This is in large part because traditionally, groups such as the PLO favored fostering ties with radical left-wing groups (e.g. the erstwhile West German Red Army Faction). However, with the retreat of left-wing radicalism, a new coalition based on the maxim of "an enemy of my enemy is a friend of mine" could develop. The religiously inspired Islamic extremists seem to have less compunction about their choice of targets and the lethality of their attacks, and might consider working with domestic right-wing terrorists who also see the US government as the enemy.

Increasingly the two movements offer very similar critiques with regard to several prominent issues that challenge the world today, including globalization, modernity, secularization, and American foreign policy in the Middle East. Both movements see the US government as hopelessly under the control of Jews or Zionists. Furthermore, both movements see this government as pursuing policies which are at cross purposes to their interests. The comments of Osama bin Laden in a 1998 interview sound strikingly similar to those of someone like Dr William Pierce of the far-right National Alliance:

> I say that the American people gave leadership to a traitorous leadership. ...
> The American government is an agent that represents Israel in America. If we look at sensitive departments in the present government like the defense department or the state department, or sensitive security departments like the CIA and others, we find that Jews have the first word in the American government, which is how they use America to carry out their plans in the world and especially the Muslim world.
> The presence of Americans in the Holy Land supports the Jews and gives them a safe back. ...
> So, we tell the Americans as a people, and we tell the mothers of soldiers, and American mothers in general, if they value their lives and those of their children, find a nationalistic government that will look after interests and not the interests of the Jews.[32]

However, this threat should also not be overstated. In the United States there is no real far-right terrorist infrastructure to speak of; leaderless resistance – actually a sign of desperation – predominates. Thus, even if Middle Eastern terrorists were willing to collaborate with native right-wing terrorists, they would be hard pressed to find a viable terrorist network already in place. What's more, it is unlikely that the Militia/Patriot movement, with its reverence for American traditions, would be comfortable cooperating with anti-American Islamic extremists. Many in the racialist right also would probably have some qualms over such an arrangement, but for different reasons, as the FBI's Buck Revell explained:

> [I]n the past the American extreme right has looked at that [Muslims] as being one of the outside groups, as being quote "mud people" and so forth. They have been very derisive towards the Muslim population. It's almost like a circle at which it joins in some of their beliefs such as, take the American government's concern with Israel and the hatred of Jews. They come together even though they are at the extreme opposites of the pole. So there is overlap and you may find on the margins some cooperative activities. But, I don't think that will last very long. They're too different in their goals and objectives. I don't think they'll find much common ground other than the common hatred towards the United States government and for the Zionist movement and the nation of Israel.[33]

The comments of one Pövl. H. Riis-Knudsen, a long-time Danish neo-Nazi ideologist (and who is rumored to have once been romantically involved with a Palestinian woman), would tend to lend credence to Revell's assessment:

> Sure I sympathize with the Palestinians. Islamic activists are oriented towards Islam – a religion for which I have no sympathy. In the short term, the Zionist issue could form some common ground, but it is worth remembering that the Arabs and Islam have nothing against Jews – except for the fact that the Jews have occupied Palestine. And the spread of Islam around the world – and of Arab money and influence – is every bit as dangerous as Jewish money and influence, and maybe even more, because there are so many more Arabs than there are Jews. However, the bottom line is: it is difficult to cooperate with Muslims in the West when, at the same time, you want to expel these very same Muslims, who are doing Allah's work by Islamizing the West. The controversy over Ahmed Rami in Sweden (the well-known revisionist) is symptomatic of this.[34]

Finally, virtually all Western countries are in the process of ethnic transformation. Previously homogeneous societies are evolving into multicultural societies. The 1990s began with great optimism, as the democratic model gained popularity around the world. Francis Fukuyama went so far as to proclaim that we had reached the end of history in that, as he saw it, all of the major ideological conflicts that caused so much damage in the twentieth century had finally run their course. The democratic model, which included representative government and protection of civil rights, was seen as the culmination of man's ideological development.[35] Not long after, however, other voices expressed a less sanguine view of global politics and saw other trends contemporaneous with democratization, namely the return of tribalism. For example, in 1993 Patrick Moynihan, the long-time observer of ethnic politics, saw the specter of violent ethnic conflict afflict nations, thus leading to "pandemonium" in many parts of the world.[36] That same year, the eminent Harvard professor Samuel Huntington propounded his "clash of civilizations" paradigm, in which he asserted that conflict in the twenty-first century would be most pronounced along civilizational fault lines. According to Huntington, the very elements that inhere in democratic systems, i.e. democratic governance, majority rule and political campaigns, tend to be exploited by populist demagogues as they often appeal to constituents on the basis of group identities such as ethnicity, culture, and religion. Huntington warned of possible civilizational conflicts of truly apocalyptic proportions.[37] The United States and the rest of the Western world are experiencing massive immigration from the Third World. As a result, the "fault line" conflicts about which Huntington warned, also have the potential to manifest themselves not only between the West and other civilizations, but also within Western countries themselves.[38]

The American republic has indeed always been diverse, and racial, ethnic and religious antagonisms have long bedeviled the country. The perspicacious French observer of the early republic, Alexis de Tocqueville, went so far to predict that race war would ultimately engulf the nation.[39] However, assimilation has proven to be a powerful centripetal force in American history. But with the rise of multiculturalism, the assimilationist paradigm has lost much of its normative appeal as more and more people opt for a racial or ethnic as opposed to national identity. And history has demonstrated that multinational states can be vulnerable when they are divided along racial, ethnic and religious lines. Political extremism can flourish and sporadic terrorism can become more frequent, and even worse, develop into full-blown guerilla warfare in which the very existence of the state is put in jeopardy. It is in such a polarized environment that the greatest potential for the far right lies. As mentioned in Chapter 3, many in the racialist right believe that America will implode under the weight of ethnic and racial strife sometime in the not-so-distant future. A popular underground book in the movement is *Civil War Two: The Coming Breakup of America*, which concludes that the ethnic and racial heterogeneity of the population has reached critical mass and that the country is now on a slow march to a Balkans scenario writ large.[40] This potentially somber scenario has not gone unnoticed by those outside the movement, including those in the watchdog organizations. Chris Freeman, from the Center for Democratic Renewal, expressed a more sanguine view of this development:

> I definitely think that the United States is undergoing some drastic changes right now. And it's not limited to the United States. I think the world is undergoing a lot of changes. But one thing I've seen is encouraging is that you have people that can come together at the protests in Seattle or DC or all around the world protesting the World Trade Organization from very diverse and different backgrounds. Workers, environmentalists, women's

rights advocates. People came together under one banner. I think that sort of speaks for itself.[41]

Only the future can tell if the American experiment will continue and develop into a truly multicultural society. Regardless, it is this transformation to a multicultural society that seems to be fueling the far right around the world, as candidates such as Jean-Marie Le Pen and Jörg Haider make political capital by playing on the xenophobic fears of voters, and young skinhead hooligans target foreigners. Thus concern over right-wing terrorism in America in not unwarranted, though it is still relatively infrequent.

To conclude, the US response to the far right is qualitatively different than the response to other variants of extremism and terrorism, inasmuch as NGOs participate to a much greater degree and influence much of the public policy agenda. In effect, the response to right-wing terrorism and extremism is a joint effort by private watchdog groups and the government. This cooperation, however, raises some civil liberties issues.

Currently right-wing terrorism is sporadic and poses no serious threat. However, future trends could presage an atmosphere in which right-wing violence could become more widespread and lethal.

September 11 and after

The September 11 attacks on the World Trade Center and Pentagon brought home the issue of terrorism like no other previous attack in America's history. The government was strongly criticized in many quarters for its failure to anticipate and prepare for such a horrific eventuality. This perception notwithstanding, the Clinton administration had given high priority to the issue of terrorism on its policy agenda. Its approach, however, was incremental and not sweeping. As discussed earlier, much of the impetus for these efforts actually came from the perceived threat of domestic right-wing extremists and self-styled citizens' militias. Some of President Clinton's more notable policy initiatives were in the area of counter-terrorism, on which current homeland security and counter-terrorism can build.

In the aftermath of the September 11 attack, the federal government, with support from the American public and US Congress, called for more vigilant measures to root out potential terrorists at home and abroad.[42] To meet the exigencies of the new terrorist threat, Congress passed the US Patriot Act, which was signed into law by President Bush on October 26. The thrust of the new law was to give authorities more options for surveillance with less judicial supervision.[43] It contains several features that should help authorities combat terrorism. First, it authorizes the use of so-called "roving wiretaps" to tap any phone lines that a suspected terrorist may be using. Second, it permits surveillance of a suspect's internet activity and gives the FBI greater latitude in conducting secret searches of suspects' homes. Third, it allows for greater sharing of information among grand juries, prosecutors and intelligence agencies. Fourth, it expands the powers of the Immigration and Naturalization Services (INS) to detain immigrants suspected of terrorist activities. Fifth, it gives the government greater power to penetrate banks suspected of being involved in the financing of terrorist groups and activities. And finally, the new law statutorily creates new crimes, enhances penalties, and increases the length of statutes of limitation for certain crimes. These new measures were welcomed by the ADL.[44]

President Bush also approved the use of special military tribunals to streamline the trials of suspected foreign terrorists, as these allow for greater secrecy and faster trials than do ordinary criminal courts. The ADL endorsed this new measure, and issued a press release praising the new guidelines as "a significant step forward in efforts to balance national security interests with traditional rights accorded criminal suspects in American courts."[45] The United States has not convened such tribunals since the Second World War, when suspected German saboteurs were secretly tried by the US military.

The fact that all nineteen perpetrators of the 9/11 attacks were of Arab descent and were Muslims was not lost on the American public. Some people feared that the presence of a large number of immigrants constituted a potential fifth-column threat to America, while others took it upon themselves to strike out in "revenge" against the Arab and Muslim communities. In the aftermath of the attacks there was a marked increase in the number of bias crimes, including assaults and vandalism against Muslim-Americans, Arab-Americans, and even those who were mistakenly identified as such because of their physical appearance. To counter this trend, many political leaders, including President Bush and New York Mayor Rudy Giuliani, exhorted Americans not to succumb to bigotry and blame Muslim Americans for the atrocity. The Department of Justice directed its Civil Rights Division's National Origin Working Group to help counter violations of civil rights laws against individuals "perceived to be Arab American, Muslim American, Sikh American, or South-Asian American."[46] Furthermore, the DOJ's Community Relations Service sponsored a meeting with Arab and Muslim leaders to brief them on the USA Patriot Act. The meeting was an effort to respond to the concerns of the Arab and Muslim communities related to issues surrounding 9/11 and the response thereto.[47] Moreover, some NGOs have also decried the bias crime "revenge" attacks against Muslim Americans, and have made efforts to reach out to this community.[48]

The various NGOs opposed to right-wing extremism – most notably the Jewish defense organizations – have also responded to the 9/11 challenge. The ADL has been monitoring the response to this crisis from Arab, Muslim and right-wing extremists. Its internet website features a section entitled "What They are Saying," where the comments of extremists regarding 9/11 are posted. The ADL has also sought to debunk various rumors circulating on the internet to the effect that the Israeli government, specifically its secret service agency Mossad, was complicit in the September 11 attack.[49] The Simon Wiesenthal Center has also made efforts in this area.[50] Recent events have caused the Jewish defense organizations to take greater notice of the potential threat posed by militant

Islam. Consequently, Islamic extremism may come to preoccupy them in the future, as ADL National Director Abraham Foxman commented:

> The old right-wing anti-Semites exist. The skinheads exist and the right-wing fascist anti-Semites exist. They are not as significant today but they're there. ...
>
> Today the alarming danger comes from Moslem anti-Semitism. It is more intense. It is more angry [sic.]. It is more violent. It is tied to a political conflict. It operates in a totalitarian environment. ... The same message can be reinforced from the mosque, to the media to government. They all play the same tune. There is no voice of dissent.[51]

The far right's reaction to the September 11 attack was mixed. In some quarters, most notably in Europe, the far right expressed a palpable degree of *Schadenfreude* over the terrorist attack. For example, Horst Mahler, the erstwhile left-wing radical turned right-wing extremist, went so far as to proclaim that the attack marked the beginning of the end of the "Judeo-American" "empire."[52] Others in the far right were less sanguine about the current state of affairs and feared that the American government's war on terror could spill over into a witch hunt against domestic extremists as well, as David Duke opined:

> My fellow Americans, please open your eyes! Bush's first action after September 11 was to fund the creation of the biggest Secret Police apparatus in the history of the world. ... When the billions of appropriated monies work its way, the size of our "secret police" will make the former KGB look like a kite next to a Jumbo Jet. Americans will have about as much privacy as one would have in a glass outhouse.[53]

Many in the movement also expressed feelings of vindication, insofar as many of the issues about which they feel strongly featured prominently in the attack. Inasmuch as all nineteen hijackers were immigrants, this underscored the potential problems of America's liberal immigration policy. The most articulate critic in this respect was probably Jared Taylor of American Renaissance, who warned of the possibility of more terrorist attacks in his article "Will America Learn its Lessons?"[54]

The most frequent refrain however, was that the terrorist attack was visited upon America because of the government's unstinting support for Israel. Many in the far right derided President Bush's explanation that the terrorists had attacked America because of its freedom and democracy. For example, Jared Taylor sarcastically commented:

> Does President Bush really imagine Osama bin Laden saying to his men: "Those Americans are just too damn free; they've got too much opportunity. Let's kill as many as we can?" The idea is absurd. Islamic militants have a grudge against us because of our attacks on Afghanistan, Libya, Iraq, and

Sudan. But the main reason they hate us and want to kill us is that we support Israel.[55]

The most vitriolic in this regard was the late Dr William Pierce of the National Alliance. Repeatedly since 9/11, Pierce used his weekly radio broadcasts, *American Dissident Voices*, to propagandize against American foreign policy vis-à-vis the Middle East. Other far-right organizations and figures, including the World Church of the Creator, the Institute for Historical Review, Bo Gritz, Aryan Nations, Posse Comitatus, and various neo-Nazi groups, have expressed virtually identical sentiments.

The Jewish defense organizations have worked hard to counteract this perception. For example, the ADL conducted surveys to determine if the American public blamed the attack on the United States' close relationship with Israel. According to the study, 63 per cent of those surveyed rejected the notion.[56] The American Jewish Committee issued briefings that argued that Islamic extremism predates the state of Israel and is thus a side issue to the current terrorist campaign.[57] Finally, the Simon Wiesenthal Center announced a two-prong strategy, consisting of an expansion of its worldwide monitoring coupled with increased sharing of this information with government officials, the media, and other important international figures.[58]

The potential for collaboration between right-wing and Islamic extremists has not gone unnoticed by the government. Homeland Security Director Tom Ridge announced through a spokesman that the FBI had stepped up its efforts to monitor groups in light of such an eventuality.[59] Adding credence to these suspicions was the case of Ahmed Huber, a seventy-four-year-old Swiss national, who was reputed to be the liaison between European right-wing extremists and Islamic extremists. Huber, a convert to Islam, sits on the board of Al Taqwa, a financial firm, which allegedly helps fund the Al-Qaeda organization. What's more, the spate of anthrax-laden letter attacks heightened suspicion that right-wing terrorists might be coordinating their efforts with those of foreign terrorists. According to one account, some top CIA and FBI officials suspected that domestic extremists were responsible for the anthrax attacks.[60]

However, at the present time there appears to be cooperation primarily on a rhetorical level, as there does seem to be a potential for synergy between the two movements in the area of propaganda. Internet technology has done much to cement such alliances among seemingly disparate groups across national borders and different cultures. Abraham Foxman, the National Director of the ADL, commented on how the internet can facilitate this "globalization of hate":

> Today a sermon in Cairo travels across the globe within minutes, through the network, the internet, e-mail, and Al Jazeera. This globalization facilitates the incitement and hate that makes the message of anti-Semitism more potent and very real. It is now out there everywhere – this technology has

given anti-Semitism, hate and incitement a strength and a power of seduction that it has never had in history before.[61]

Not all representatives of the far right, however, sympathized with the Al-Qaeda terrorists. Norman Olson, a militia leader in Michigan, offered the services of the militia to President Bush in fighting terrorism on the home front. Nick Griffin, leader of the British National Party, publicly supported British military action against Bin Laden and his terrorist network. However, he tempered this support by demanding that efforts be made to eradicate the root causes of terrorism, i.e. to end support for Israeli aggression against Palestinians, and to end the blockade of Iraq, which has resulted in human suffering in that country.[62] In a strange twist to this story, the BNP launched a joint anti-Islam campaign with Sikhs and Hindus residing in Britain. Among the aims of this campaign was to counter the "politically correct lie that Islam is a religion of peace."[63]

Not long before the September 11 attacks, the American far right appeared to have suffered several setbacks. Just one year earlier, the Aryan Nations lost a $6.3 million civil suit filed by the Southern Poverty Law Center. In November 2000, the FBI arrested Alex Curtis, and in doing so silenced the most strident advocate of the leaderless resistance approach. Finally, in the summer of 2000 one of the most important and enduring institutions of the American far right, the Liberty Lobby, was forced to shut down as a result of a civil judgment awarded to its erstwhile subsidiary, the Institute for Historical Review. However, the September 11 attack appears to have reinvigorated the American far right, and more importantly, increased the salience of the issues about which it feels strongly. It is conceivable that the far right could exploit the current crisis as a way to call attention to its critique of America. If the war on terror should falter, public support could shift in favor of the far right. The government has also been galvanized by the crisis and appears to be more vigilant in combating terrorism. These efforts could also conceivably spill over into the area of domestic extremism. Finally, the NGOs are keeping a close watch on the current crisis as it unfolds, and responding accordingly. As a result, these various developments presage added potential for confrontation in the future.

Notes

1 Introduction

1 Some of the new laws and measures include the 1996 Anti-Terrorism and Effective Death Penalty Act, Presidential Decision Directives on counter-terrorism (PDD-62) and infrastructure protection (PDD-63). Defense Secretary William Cohen obtained presidential approval to create a permanent task force headed by a general officer, to coordinate the military's response to a domestic chemical or biological attack. See "Pentagon Plans Domestic Terrorism Team," *Washington Post*, February 1, 1999, A2, p. 2. The FBI called 1995 the "year of the terrorist" and hired an additional fifty analysts to study both international and domestic terrorism. See Bureau of Justice Assistance, *A Policymaker's Guide to Hate Crimes* (Washington DC: Bureau of Justice Assistance, 1997) p. 23. Annual funding for the FBI's counter-terrorism program has grown from $78.5 million in 1993 to $301.2 million in 1999. Moreover, the number of agents funded for counter-terrorism investigations has grown from 550 in 1993 to 1,383 in 1999. Freeh, Louis, "The Threat to the United States Posed by Terrorists," testimony before the US Senate Committee on Appropriations, February 4, 1999.

2 FBI data indicate that from 1993 to 1996 right-wing terrorists were responsible for the majority of domestic terrorists incidents in the United States (Federal Bureau of Investigation, *Terrorism in the United States 1996* [Washington DC: FBI, 1996]). However, FBI data on domestic terrorism are notoriously inconsistent and unreliable due to changing classifications of terrorist incidents. There is often a high degree of arbitrariness in which acts are labeled "terrorist" by the government, academia and the media. For a critical examination of the FBI's data collection on domestic terrorism see Hamm, Mark S., *Terrorism, Hate Crime, and Anti-Government Violence: A Preliminary Review of the Research* (Indiana: Indiana State University, 1996). According to Chris Hewitt's calculations, domestic right-wing terrorists (he refers to them as 'white racist') were responsible for more terrorist killings than any other category of terrorism in the United States. See Hewitt, Christopher, "Patterns of American Terrorism 1955–1998: An Historical Perspective on Terrorism-Related Fatalities 1955–98," *Terrorism and Political Violence*, 12 (1), p. 5 (2000).

3 I compiled this table using data from the Southern Poverty Law Center's website (www.splcenter.org). It is important to keep in mind that although this is a list of "far right" groups it does not necessarily follow that they are terrorist. However, terrorists often come from the ranks of extremist groups. This table lists only the number of groups and is not comprehensive. It says nothing about the membership totals of the groups. It should be kept in mind that they are usually small. Furthermore, the SPLC counts all the various chapters of an organization, e.g. the Council of Conservative Citizens, as separate organizations for its compilation.

4 Center for Democratic Renewal, *The Changing Face of White Supremacy* (Atlanta GA: CDR, 1996).

5 For more on the German government's response to political extremism see Groenwold, Kurt, "The German Federal Republic's Response and Civil Liberties," *Terrorism and Political Violence*, 9 (4), pp. 136–50 (1997).
6 For more on the Israeli approach to responding to right-wing extremism see Cohen-Almagor, Raphael, "Combating Right-Wing Political Extremism in Israel: Critical Appraisal," *Terrorism and Political Violence*, 9 (4), pp. 16–23 (1997).
7 In this instance, Walter Laqueur was referring to the fascist variant of right-wing extremism. Laqueur, Walter, *Fascism: Past, Present, and Future* (New York: Oxford University Press, 1996) p. 6.
8 Berlet, Chip and Matthew N. Lyons, *Right-Wing Populism in America: Too Close for Comfort* (New York: The Guilford Press, 2000) pp. 1–17.
9 Roger Griffin originally outlined his definition of fascism as the embodiment of an ultra-nationalist paligenetic myth in Griffin, Roger, *The Nature of Fascism* (New York: Routledge, 1993). He later buttressed his theory using the paligenetic myth as the leitmotif of an anthology of essays, which he edited, with contributions from both fascists and observers of fascism. See Griffin, Roger, *Fascism*, Oxford Readers (Oxford: Oxford University Press, 1995).
10 See for example Canovan, Margaret, "Populism," in Berlet and Lyons, *Right-Wing Populism in America* (New York: Harcourt Brace Jovanovich, 1981) pp. 289, 293, 294.
11 Lipset and Raab use this term to characterize extreme right-wing movements in their study *The Politics of Unreason: Right Wing Extremism in America, 1790–1970* (New York: Harper and Row, 1970).
12 Kaplan, Jeffrey, *The Encyclopedia of White Power: A Sourcebook on the Radical Racist Right* (New York: AltaMira Press, 2000) pp. xxii–xxiii.
13 Mudde, Cas, *The Ideology of the Extreme Right* (Manchester: Manchester University Press, 2000) p. 11.
14 Mudde, *The Ideology of the Extreme Right*.
15 Laqueur explains this change in thinking in Laqueur, Walter, *The New Terrorism: Fanaticism and the Arms of Mass Destruction* (New York: Oxford, 1999) p. 9.
16 FBI, *Terrorism in the United States 1998* (Washington DC: FBI, 1999) p. i.
17 FBI, *Terrorism in the United States 1998*, p. ii.

2 Who are the watchdogs?

1 This University of Florida study is cited in Padilla, Maria T., "Race Violence Leads to Rise in Anti-Racism Groups," *Salt Lake Tribune* August 22, 1999, http://www.sltrib.com/1999/aug/08221999/nation_w/17231.htm. It is worth mentioning that like their far-right opponents, most of these organizations are small. However, there are several that have substantial resources and political clout (e.g. Anti-Defamation League, American Jewish Committee, Simon Wiesenthal Center, and Southern Poverty Law Center).
2 The disturbance theory was propounded by Truman and Wilson. For a synopsis of their theory see Wilson, James Q., *Political Organizations* (New York: Basic Books, 1973) p. 97.
3 A 1990 study by the Hudson Institute found that seven out of ten Americans belong to at least one association and one out of four belongs to four or more associations. The 1996 edition of *The Encyclopedia of Associations* enumerated more than 22,000 national non-profit organizations in the United States. See Hrebenar, Ronald J., *Interest Group Politics in America, Third Edition* (New York: M. E. Sharpe, 1997) p. 14.
4 This is his how David Truman defined interest groups in his classic study *The Government Process*. Truman, David B., *The Governmental Process: Political Interests and Public Opinion*, 2nd edn (Berkeley CA: Institute of Governmental Studies, 1993). Non-governmental organizations (NGOs) usually have a non-profit connotation but can

also constitute as interest groups in some situations. For purposes of this book I shall use the terms NGOs, pressure groups, and interest groups interchangeably.
5 Tocqueville, Alexis de, *Democracy in America* (New York: Harper Perennial, 1969) *passim*.
6 This pattern holds to this day for non-Protestant religious denominations as well. American Catholics have created self-help associations such as the Knights of Columbus. Perhaps even more prolific are Jewish special interest groups such as B'nai B'rith, the American Jewish Congress, the American Jewish Committee, and the United Jewish Appeal. The new immigrants such as Muslims (not to mention indigenous Black Muslims who have created the Nation of Islam) and Hindus show a similar pattern.
7 Schlozman, Kay Lehman, and John T. Tierney, *Organized Interests and American Democracy* (New York: Harper and Row, 1986) p. 59.
8 Wilson, James Q., *Political Organizations* (New York: Basic Books, 1973) p. 79.
9 See Robert A. Dahl and Graham Wilson in Schlozman and Tierney, *Organized Interests and American Democracy*, p. 59.
10 Lipset, Seymour Martin, *American Exceptionalism: A Double-Edged Sword* (New York: W. W. Norton and Company, 1996) pp. 71–6.
11 The United States has the largest non-profit sector of Western democracies in both absolute and relative terms. Over 7 million people are employed in the sector, and it was a $341 billion industry as of 1994. According to Salamon and Anheier, NGOs tend to pick up on those social responsibilities (e.g. welfare, education and disaster relief) that the state ignores. Salamon, Lester M. and Helmut K. Anheier, *The Emerging Sector: The Nonprofit Sector in Comparative Perspective* (Baltimore MD: Johns Hopkins University Institute for Policy Studies, 1994) p. 10.
12 Salamon and Anheier, *The Emerging Sector*, p. 10. Although originally this theory was cast within the framework of welfare policy, one could find examples of it in other areas of public policy as well, such as to counter-terrorism and the response to right-wing extremism. Although from a comparative legal perspective the US government is more constrained by constitutional measures in combating political extremism, NGOs have filled this void and take a very proactive position in this area. This is parallel in other public responsibilities such as the welfare system.
13 Presthus, Robert, *Elites in the Policy Process* (New York: Cambridge University Press, 1974) p. 15.
14 For more on ethnic lobbying in the realm of US foreign policy see Deconde, Alexander, *Ethnicity, Race, and American Foreign Policy* (Boston MA: Northwestern University Press, 1992).
15 Anti-Defamation League, *Not the Work of a Day: The Story of the Anti-Defamation League of B'nai B'rith* (New York: Anti-Defamation League, 1965) p. 5.
16 Anti-Defamation League, *Not the Work of a Day*, p. 8.
17 The Leo Frank affair began in 1913 and involved a Jewish factory owner in Atlanta, Georgia, Leo Frank, who was convicted for the rape and murder of a fourteen year old girl, Mary Phagan, whom he employed at his factory. In this highly charged case, Frank eventually had his death penalty sentence commuted to life imprisonment by Georgia Governor John H. Slayton in 1915. When word of Governor Slayton's leniency reached the public, an angry vigilante crowd stormed the jail in which Frank was incarcerated, and hanged him. The public in Georgia by and large greeted news of this story with jubilation. The fear that this struck in the local Jewish population cannot be overstated, as the memory of the affair remained for quite some time. It is generally accepted by contemporary historians that Mr Frank was wrongly accused and convicted of this crime. For more on the Leo Frank affair see Myers, Gustavus, *History of Bigotry in the United States* (New York: Random House, 1943).

18 Hrebenar, *Interest Group Politics in America*, p. 17. It is worth mentioning that there was an overseas antecedent to the ADL. The ADL is in some ways reminiscent of a German Jewish defense organization that was active from 1870 to 1914, the *Zentralverein deutscher Staatsbüger jüdischen Glauben* (Central Association of German Citizens of Jewish Faith). This organization employed similar tactics to the ADL, such as lobbying the government and using libel and slander laws to undercut the effectiveness of anti-Jewish organizations. In short, it sought to make anti-Semitism a "disreputable, unsavory enterprise." See MacDonald, Kevin, *Separation and Its Discontents: Toward an Evolutionary Theory of Anti-Semitism* (Westport CT: Praeger, 1998) p. 190.
19 Goldberg, J. J., *Jewish Power: Inside the American Jewish Establishment* (New York: Addison-Wesley Publishing Company, 1996) p. 129.
20 Anti-Defamation League, *Not the Work of a Day*, p. 9.
21 Goldberg, *Jewish Power*, p. 129.
22 Anti-Defamation League, *Not the Work of a Day*, p. 8.
23 Anti-Defamation League, *Not the Work of a Day*, p. 14.
24 One can discern an alarmist tenor in many of the ADL's publications and pronouncements. And at times it has appeared to almost jealously control information about the far right. Take for example the case of sociologist James Aho, whose book, *The Politics of Righteousness* was cause for some consternation to the ADL. Essentially, Aho's research found that most of the far-rightists he studied in Idaho did not fit the alarmist stereotype, i.e. poorly educated, marginalized, unstable family background, etc. Much to Aho's dismay, the ADL, a private group, summoned him to explain his findings and activities! See Aho, James, *The Politics of Righteousness: Idaho Christian Patriotism* (Seattle WA: University of Washington Press, 1990) p. 29; and Kaplan, *Radical Religion in America*, p. 148.
25 Anti-Defamation League, *Not the Work of a Day*, p. 15.
26 This information is posted on the Guidestar web site, which tracks charities in the United States. See http://www.guidestar.org.
27 Wilcox, Laird, "Who Watches the Watchman?" in Kaplan, Jeffrey and Heléne Lööw, *The Cultic Milieu: Oppositional Subcultures in an Age of Globalization* (New York: Alta Mira Press, 2002) p. 294.
28 See Lipset, Seymour Martin and Earl Raab, *Jews and the New American Scene* (Cambridge MA: Harvard University Press, 1995) p. 69. Although current survey data point to a continuing diminution of anti-Semitic attitudes among the American public, many Jews have drawn lessons from Jewish history and realize that it can be activated very quickly given a specific constellation of circumstances. Lipset and Raab use a set of three interrelated variables to explain this phenomenon. The first variable is a target factor, i.e. a reservoir of anti-Jewish attitudes that exist at any given time. Second is a trigger factor, such as a condition or precipitating event that can transform passive attitudes into action. Finally, there is the constraining factor, or social and political conditions which repress the manifestation of anti-Jewish activities. See Lipset and Raab, *Jews and the New American Scene*, p. 76.
29 Lipset and Raab, *Jews and the New American Scene*, p. 107.
30 See for example, *Danger on the Right: The Attitudes, Personnel and Influence of the Radical Right and Extreme Conservatives*, and *The Radical Right: Report on the John Birch Society and Its Allies*, both of which are published by Random House.
31 George and Wilcox, *Nazis, Communists, Klansmen and Others on the Fringe*, p. 220.
32 Svonkin notes that the "Studies in Prejudice" research underwritten by the American Jewish Committee in the 1940s found that those people who evinced authoritarian tendencies, such as right-wing anti-communists, were susceptible to anti-Semitic appeals. Svonkin, *Jews Against Prejudice*, p. 115.

33 George and Wilcox, *Nazis, Communists, Klansmen and Others on the Fringe*, p. 260. According to Mike Piper of the Liberty Lobby, *The Spotlight* currently has a circulation of roughly 50,000 (interview with Mike Piper, July 10, 2000). This diminution in readership can be explained in large part by the fact that it is mostly a geriatric audience to which *The Spotlight* appeals. Thus over the years there has been a process of attrition as younger readers have not replaced those dying to maintain previous levels of circulation.
34 Anti-Defamation League, *Explosion of Hate: The Growing Danger of the National Alliance* (New York: Anti-Defamation League, 1998) p. 1.
35 Interview with Dr Mark Pitcavage, September 6, 2000.
36 To give an example of this perception, the fugitive financier, Marc Rich, enlisted the assistance of Abraham Foxman to intervene on his behalf to help secure a presidential pardon. Mr Foxman complied and sent an official ADL letter for such a request to President Clinton. Chafets, Zev, "Jewish Leaders' Unpardonable Role," *New York Daily News*, February 15, 2001.
37 One major setback for the ADL was the so-called San Francisco spy case, which will be covered in greater detail in Chapter 6. Another and more recent setback was a major defeat in a civil case in which a jury rendered a $10.5 million judgment against the organization. In a bizarre set of circumstances, this suit stemmed from a squabble between two neighbors over their pet dogs, which ultimately snowballed into a larger controversy in which the ADL recklessly involved itself. For more on this episode see Jordan, Michael J., "ADL Says Big Courtroom Defeat Won't Keep Group from Doing Its Job," *Jewish Telegraphic Agency*, http://virtualjerusalem.com/index.exe?0005153.
38 Schachner, Nathan, *The Price of Liberty: A History of the American Jewish Committee* (New York: The American Jewish Committee, 1948) pp. 1–28.
39 Schachner, *The Price of Liberty*, pp. 46–7.
40 Schachner, *The Price of Liberty*, p. 122.
41 Schachner, *The Price of Liberty*, pp. 123, 159–62.
42 Schachner, *The Price of Liberty*, p. 163.
43 See for example Danzig, David, *Rightists, Racists and Separatists: A White Bloc in the Making?* (New York: AJC, 1964).
44 Gerald L. K. Smith had a long and illustrious career in the far right. He once even served as an aide to Senator Huey Long, after which he went on to found the Christian Nationalist Party. He published a periodical called *Cross and Flag*, which remained in circulation from the late 1930s to the mid-1970s. By far-right standards, Smith built a very viable and financially successful enterprise. His activities occasioned fierce opposition from the Jewish watchdog groups. Finally, Smith was a very important bridge between the native fascists of the 1930s and 1940s and the contemporary far right. For more on Smith see Jeansome, Glen, *Gerald L. K. Smith: Minister of Hate* (New Haven CT: Yale University Press, 1988) and Smith, Geoffrey, S., *To Save a Nation: American 'Extremism,' the New Deal, and the Coming of World War II* (Chicago: Elephant Paperbacks, 1992).
45 For his part Rockwell claimed that he adopted the explicit trappings and symbols of Nazism such as the swastika, in order to create a shock effect for the very purpose of breaking what he referred to as the "silent treatment" by the media. For more on his decision, see his autobiographical *This Time the World*, 6th edn (Reedy WV: Liberty Bell Publications, 1993) pp. 136–42.
46 Simonelli, Frederick J., *American Fuehrer: George Lincoln Rockwell and the American Nazi Party* (Chicago: University of Illinois Press, 1999) p. 52. Fineberg expounded on the "quarantine treatment" in Fineberg, S. Andhil, "The Quarantine Treatment," in Newman, Edwin S. (ed.) *The Hate Reader* (New York: Oceana Publications, 1964) pp. 111–16.
47 Anti-Defamation League, *Not the Work of a Day*, p. 35.

48 Stern, Kenneth S., *A Force upon the Plain: The American Militia Movement and the Politics of Hate* (New York: Simon and Schuster, 1996). Stern also wrote a book on Holocaust revisionism, *Holocaust Denial* (New York: American Jewish Committee, 1993). Finally, he wrote a lengthy report under AJC auspices called "Hate and the Internet," 2000, and a report on the violence from "lone wolves" such as Benjamin Smith and Buford Furrow during the summer of 1999. See his "Understanding the Summer of Hate," 2000. The latter two reports are available on the AJC web site at http://www.ajc.org.
49 Cowell, Alan, "US Jewish Group Sets Up Office in Berlin to Watch for Demons," *New York Times*, February 10, 1998.
50 See http://www.guidestar.org.
51 Yaron Svoray wrote a book about his experiences in the German far-right underground. See Svoray, Yaron, and Nick Taylor, *In Hitler's Shadow: An Israeli's Amazing Journey inside Germany's Neo-Nazi Movement* (New York: Doubleday, 1994). Eventually, an HBO movie based on his story, "The Infiltrator," was made.
52 The meetings with the US House Foreign Affairs Subcommittee on Organizations and Human Rights, and on a separate occasion with German authorities, are recounted in Svoray and Taylor, *In Hitler's Shadow*, pp. 256–7. For more on the Center's meeting with FBI director Louis Freeh, see the "History of the Simon Wiesenthal" segment on the Center's website at http://www.wiesenthal.com/.
53 Furrow confessed this to FBI authorities after his surrender. He had carried a map with both the Simon Wiesenthal Center and its Museum of Tolerance circled as if to indicate they were targets. For more on this episode see "FBI: Wiesenthal Center Was Terrorist's Main Target," *Response*, 20 (2), pp. 2–3 (1999).
54 See http://www.guidestar.org.
55 The SWC has received two separate $5 million grants from the state of California; the first in 1985, the second in 1995. See Morain, D., "Lean Times Don't Imperil Wiesenthal Grant," *Los Angeles Times*, July 19, 1995.
56 For financial data on the SPLC see http://www.guidestar.org. The assertion that the SPLC is the wealthiest civil rights organization appeared in an article in *Harper's Magazine*. See Silverstein, Ken, "The Church of Morris Dees: How The Southern Poverty Law Center Profits from Intolerance," *Harper's Magazine*, November 2000, p. 56.
57 Robert Salisbury, in Hrebenar, Ronald J., *Interest Group Politics in America*, 3rd edn (New York: M. E. Sharpe, 1997) p. 20. Salisbury's contends that the key element in interest group formation is the organizer or entrepreneur of the group. As we shall later see, the success of both watchdog and far-right groups is often determined by charismatic leaders who have developed a "cult of personality" around themselves.
58 Stanton, Bill, *Klanwatch: Bringing the Ku Klux Klan to Justice* (New York: Mentor, 1991) p. 14.
59 Wilcox, *The Watchdogs*, p. 56.
60 Stanton, *Klanwatch*, p. 15.
61 Stanton, *Klanwatch*, p. 16.
62 Dees is the darling of many prominent liberals and has been lauded by such figures as former President Jimmy Carter, esteemed attorney Gerry Spence, novelist Kurt Vonnegut Jr, and ADL national director Abraham Foxman.
63 Stanton, *Klanwatch*, p. 15.
64 The most egregious example usually cited is the use of one Gary Thomas Rowe Jr as a Klan informant in Mississippi in the early 1960s. Some observers believe that he may have participated in the homicide of a civil rights worker Viola Liuzzo, in 1964.
65 Stanton, *Klanwatch*, p. 79.
66 Stanton, *Klanwatch*, p. 80.

67 A *Time* magazine article once referred to him as "the second most hated man in Alabama." Only a Montgomery judge who made several controversial pro-civil rights decisions, was more disliked. Stanton, *Klanwatch*, p. 16.
68 Interview with Mark Potock, August 18, 2000.
69 Dees, Morris and James Corcoran, *Gathering Storm: America's Militia Threat* (New York: HarperCollins, 1996); Dees, Morris and Steve Fiffer, *Hate on Trial: The Case against America's Most Dangerous Neo-Nazi* (New York: Villard Books, 1993); and Dees, Morris and Steve Fiffer, *Season for Justice: The Life and Times of Civil Rights Lawyer Morris Dees* (New York: Charles Schribner's Sons, 1991).
70 Interview with Mark Potok, August 18, 2000.
71 Stanton, *Klanwatch*, pp. 239–40.
72 The SPLC generated approximately $9 million in a fundraising appeal, which followed the United Klans of America suit. Although the jury awarded the plaintiff Mrs Beulah Donald a $7 million judgment in this case, she ultimately received only $51,875, because that was the extent of the UKA's assets. Silverstein, "The Church of Morris Dees," p. 54. It is believed that the SPLC did not share any of the funds with the plaintiff. In separate interviews, Tom Metzger and Dr William Pierce told me that the SPLC generated $7 million and $10 million respectively in appeals following the civil judgments against them. They both said that they did not believe that any of the money was shared with the plaintiffs.
73 Wilcox, *The Watchdogs*, pp. 56–8.
74 Wilcox, *The Watchdogs*, p. 57.
75 "Charity of Riches!" *Montgomery Advertiser*, February 13, 1994.
76 Silverstein, Ken, "The Church of Morris Dees: How The Southern Poverty Law Center Profits from Intolerance," *Harper's Magazine*, November 2000, pp. 54–7.
77 On the program, Daniel Burochoff, from the American Institute of Philanthropy, criticized the Center for not spending much of the money that it raises. In his view this presents an opportunity cost insofar as the money raised by the Center could have been donated to other civil rights organizations that would have put the money to use. *O'Reily Factor*, February, 2001.
78 See for example the comments of Stephen Bright, the director of the Southern Center for Human Rights in *Harper's Magazine*, November 2000, p. 57.
79 In 1983 members of a far-right underground group known as the Order once drew up a list of prominent figures marked for assassination. At the very top of the list was Morris Dees. See Flynn, Kevin and Gary Gerhardt, *The Silent Brotherhood* (New York: Signet, 1990) p. 233. Fortunately for Dees, authorities apprehended all members of the Order before they could carry out their plan.
80 Stanton, *Klanwatch*, pp. 159–70.
81 Members of the now defunct White Patriots Party were implicated in this plot. These repeated threats prompted the SPLC to construct a high-security system for its facility. See "Upgraded Security System Protects Center Employees," *SPLC Report*, March 1997.
82 For more on the Greensboro massacre see Wheaton, *Codename Greenkil*.
83 For a recounting of the creation of the Anti-Klan network see Center for Democratic Renewal, *When Hate Groups Come to Town: A Handbook of Effective Community Responses*, 2nd edn (Atlanta GA: Center for Democratic Renewal, 1992) pp. 7–8.
84 Interview with Chris Freeman, August 28, 2000.
85 Several of the CDR's founders, such as Leonard Zeskind and Lyn Wells, sojourned in Marxist-Leninist groups. For example, The Rev. C. T. Vivian, the chairman of the National Anti-Klan Network, was identified by the FBI as being an active Communist Party member during the 1940s. Executive Committee member Ann Braden was a founding sponsor of the US Peace Council. National Coordinator Lyn Wells is a former member of the Central Committee of the October League, a Marxist-

214 *Notes*

Leninist group, which evolved into the Communist Party, Marxist-Leninist. Finally, Leonard Zeskind, at one time a prominent researcher for the Center, was an organizer for a Marxist-Leninist-style group known as Sojourner Truth Organization. Researcher Laird Wilcox suggests that in essence the CDR has dropped its rhetoric of class warfare and has switched to anti-racism, because it is a much easier sell in contemporary American society. For more on the left-wing backgrounds of various staff members of the CDR, see Wilcox, *The Watchdogs*, pp. 68–85.

86 Interview with Chris Freeman, August 28, 2000.
87 Interview with Chris Freeman, August 28, 2000.
88 "Kansas Citian wins 'genius grant' for work studying hate groups," *Hannibal Courier-Post*, June 3,1998, http://www.fast-floweres.com/~hannibal/stories/060398/genius grant .html.
89 At one time Leonard Zeskind wrote regularly for *Searchlight* and served as its American correspondent. *Searchlight* is published in Britain and is the premier magazine which tracks the activities of right-wing extremists in Europe. *Searchlight* began publishing in 1975 and like the CDR, many of its staffers have sojourned in radical left-wing groups such as the Anti-Nazi League, which was launched by the Socialist Workers Party in 1977. Its most prominent staffer, Gerry Gable, was a member of the Young Communist League and once stood as a Communist Party candidate in a local election in London. For more on *Searchlight* and its ties to the CDR see Wilcox, *The Watchdogs*, pp. 77–81.
90 Interview with Chris Freeman, August 28, 2000.
91 See http://www.guidestar.org.
92 Interview with Chip Berlet, August 31, 2000.
93 PRA's most high profile research analyst, Chip Berlet, was affiliated with the left-leaning National Lawyers Guild as well as the Chicago Area Friends of Albania. For his part, Berlet explained to me in an interview that his affiliation with the latter stemmed more from his interest in the various ethnic communities in the Chicago area than with left-wing politics. Mr Berlet at one time wrote for the Marxist-Leninist-style *Guardian* newspaper. For more on Berlet's political background see Wilcox, *The Watchdogs*, pp. 86–101.
94 Interview with Chip Berlet, August 31, 2000. Berlet is alluding to the ADL San Francisco spy scandal, which will be covered in greater detail in Chapter 6.
95 See for example his essay he co-authored with Mathew N. Lyons, "Repression and the Patriot and Armed Militia Movements." This can be found at http://www.publiceye.org.pra/Repression-and-ideology.htm.
96 Berlet and Lyons are critical of the centrist/extremist model for a number of reasons, including what they see as its tendency to "obscure the rational choices and legitimate grievances that help fuel right-wing populist movements, [and that] it hides the fact that right-wing bigotry and scapegoating are firmly rooted in the mainstream social and political order." Further, they add that it "fosters a dangerous complacency about mainstream politics and institutions." Berlet and Lyons, *Right-Wing Populism in America*, p. 14.
97 I believe Berlet was alluding to Lipset *et al.*'s major study of right-wing extremism, *The Radical Right*. Some critics see this study as an effort to pathologize politically extremist views. See Bell, Daniel (ed.) *The Radical Right* (Garden City NY: Anchor Books, 1964).
98 Berlet was alluding to his book, *Right-Wing Populism in America: Too Close for Comfort*, which at the time of this interview was in preparation for publication.
99 Interview with Chip Berlet, August 31, 2000.
100 According to a PRA publication, in the three-week period following the April 19, 1995 bombing of the Murrah federal building in Oklahoma City, PRA received 218 media requests for information on the political right from various segments of the

media. Hardisty, Jean and Peter Snoad, *Unmasking the Political Right: A Fifteen Year Report 1981–1996* (Somerville MA, Political Research Associates, 1996).
101 Interview with Chip Berlet, August 31, 2000.
102 Interview with Chip Berlet, August 31, 2000.
103 See http://www.guidestar.org.
104 Holly Sklar is best known as a critic of US foreign policy and the Trilateral Commission. Her books include *Trilateralism* and *Washington's War on Nicaragua*. Sara Diamond, although progressive in background, wrote a well balanced and insightful book on the American right, *Roads to Dominion: Right Wing Movements and Political Power in the US*. Russ Bellant wrote two exposés which sought to connect the mainstream right with some of the more unsavory elements of the far right. See his *The Coors Connection: How Coors Family Philanthropy Undermines Democratic Pluralism*, and *Old Nazis, the New Right, and the Republican Party*.
105 In the vernacular of the racialist right this is often referred to as the "Northwest Imperative."
106 Interview with Bill Wassmuth, September 13, 2000.
107 "History and Organization of the NWC," from the Northwest Coalition Against Malicious Harassment website at: http://members.aol.com/ncamh?INTRO.HTM.
108 Interview with Bill Wassmuth, September 13, 2000.
109 This was the stated objective of one of NWC's founders, Dina Tanners. See Alibrandi, Tom and Bill Wassmuth, *Hate is My Neighbor* (Ellensburg WA: Stand Together Publishers, 1999) p. 79.
110 Interview with Bill Wassmuth, September 13, 2000.
111 Interview with Bill Wassmuth, September 13, 2000.
112 See http://www.guidestar.org.
113 Alibrandi and Wassmuth, *Hate is My Neighbor*, pp. 202–49.
114 Center for New Community, *"Creating" a Killer: A Background Report On Benjamin "August" Smith and The World Church of the Creator* (Oak Park IL: Center for New Community, 1999).
115 According to the Center's website, over half of its directors are reverends. The directors are Reverend Nancy Tannerthies, Chair, D. Bunyan Bryant; Reverend Barbara Essex, Reverend Ben Helmer, Reverend Dr Joe Hendrixson, Reverend Steven Johns-Boehme, Reverend Allison Phillips, and Delena Wilkerson. See http://www.newcomm.org/about%20us/index.htm.
116 Several groups in the racialist right, including the Liberty Lobby, Council of Conservatives, League of the South, and American Nationalist Union, endorsed the Buchanan candidacy and more than a few of their members actually worked in this campaign. At the center of this infiltration effort was one Mark Coterill, the leader of a Falls Church, Virginia-based organization known as the American Friends of the British National Party, which raised money for its parent organization in the United Kingdom. This resulted in a civil war of sorts in the Buchanan campaign organization, with stealth representatives of the far right in one camp and Pat's sister and campaign manager Bay Buchanan in the other. Eventually Bay Buchanan prevailed as she effectively cleaned house at campaign headquarters. The Center for New Community was one of the first to report on this story. See Center for New Community, *Party Crashers: White Nationalists and Election 2000* (Chicago: Center for New Community, July 2000). Also see Edsall, Thomas B., "Buchanan's Bid Transforms the Reform Party," *Washington Post*, July 23, 2000, A0, p. 4.
117 See http://www.guidestar.org.
118 For more on the Center for New Community see its website at http://www.newcomm.org/about%20us/index.htm.
119 Nizkor is Hebrew for "we will remember."

216 *Notes*

120 Hilliard, Robert L. and Michael C. Keith, *Waves of Rancor: Tuning in the Radical Right* (New York: M. E. Sharpe, 1999) p. 250.
121 Interview with Ken McVay, September 4, 2000.
122 Interview with Ken McVay, September 4, 2000.
123 Interview with Ken McVay, September 4, 2000.
124 Interview with Ken McVay, September 4, 2000.
125 Interview with Ken McVay, September 4, 2000.
126 Interview with Dr Mark Pitcavage, September 6, 2000.
127 Eddlem, Thomas, "Does SLATT Need a Watchdog?" *The New American*, 16 (19), (September 11, 2000), http://thenewamerican.come/tna2000/09-11-2000/vol6 no19_ slatt.htm.
128 Eddlem, "Does SLATT Need a Watchdog?" Guidestar reports that the Institute for Intergovernmental Research had assets of $709,998 as of 1998. Its annual income for that same year was reported at $5,886,503. See http://www.guidestar.org. No financial data were available for Militia Watchdog on Guidestar.
129 Interview with Dr Mark Pitcavage, September 6, 2000.
130 For more on Goldman's departing comments on the Hatewatch project, see http://www.hatewatch.org.
131 Memorandum from the Durham Board of Education, Whitby Ontario, subject: Hate and Violence Groups, December 6, 1996.
132 Padilla, "Race Violence Leads to Rise in Anti-Racism Groups."
133 Interview with Todd Ferguson, February 2, 2001.
134 Ferguson, Todd, "Youth Against Hate: Anti-Racist Action as a New Citizens' Movement," unpublished paper, December 2000, p. 1.
135 Ferguson, "Youth Against Hate," p. 1.
136 Ferguson, "Youth Against Hate," p. 2.
137 Interview with Todd Ferguson, February 2, 2001.
138 Ferguson, Todd, "A Case Study of Racist Extremism and Disintegrative Social Sanctioning," unpublished paper, December 2000, p. 2.
139 ARA member Scott Ferguson explains that ARA's "outing" measures are reminiscent of the French tradition of *charivaris*, which sought to shame wayward members of the community. It is meant to induce guilt and also shame and a fear of rejection by others in the community. For more on ARA's "outing" and "shaming" measures, see Ferguson, "A Case Study of Racist Extremism and Disintegrative Social Sanctioning."
140 Interview with Todd Ferguson, February 2, 2001.
141 Ferguson, "Youth Against Hate," p. 4.
142 Robert Clarkson, the leader of the Carolina Patriots – a Constitutional study group – is currently suing the Air Force for disseminating SPLC materials to DoD facilities. Clarkson claims that these materials encourage American soldiers to treat law-abiding citizens as terrorists. "US Air Force Sued Under Freedom of Information Act," *Citizens Informer*, May-June, 2000, p. 23.
143 For example the SPLC's publication, *False Patriots: The Threat of Antigovernment Extremists*, implies that the militias and other self-styled patriot groups are fronts for the racialist right. The leaders of the racialist right are depicted as the hidden hands behind the militias without any compelling evidence to support this supposition. Although there are some links between the two, often they are very tenuous, consisting of things such as a militia member attending a meeting of a racist organization at one time or another.

3 Overview of the contemporary American far right

1 For example, see Lipset, Seymour Martin and Earl Raab, *The Politics of Unreason: Right Wing Extremism in America, 1790–1970* (New York: Harper and Row, 1970); Goodman, Paul, *Towards a Christian Republic: Antimasonry and the Great Transition in New England, 1826–1836* (New York: Oxford University Press, 1988); Bennett, David H., *Party of Fear: From Nativist Movements to the New Right in American History* (New York: Vintage Books, 1988); and Myers, Gustavus, *History of Bigotry in the United States* (New York: Random House, 1943).
2 Lipset and Raab, *The Politics of Unreason*, p. 3.
3 Goodman made this observation in his *Towards a Christian Republic*, p. 237.
4 This observation is made in Hofstadter, Richard, *The Paranoid Style in American Politics and Other Essays* (New York: Vintage Books, 1967) p. 16.
5 See Goodman, *Towards a Christian Republic*, p. 8.
6 Bennett, David H., *Party of Fear: From Nativist Movements to the New Right in American History* (New York: Vintage Books, 1988).
7 See Beals, Carleton, *Brass-Knuckle Crusade: The Great Know-Nothing Conspiracy: 1820–1860* (New York: Hastings House, 1960) pp. 193–207.
8 For more on the Know-Nothing movement see Beals, Carleton, *Brass-Knuckle Crusade*; Lipset and Raab, *The Politics of Unreason*; Bennett, *Party of Fear*.
9 The literature on the Ku Klux Klan is vast. For more on the Reconstruction era Klan, see Trelease, Allen W., *White Terror: The Ku Klux Klan Conspiracy and Southern Reconstruction* (Baton Rouge LA: Louisiana State University Press, 1971); and Tougée, Albion Winegar, *The Invisible Empire* (Baton Rouge LA: Louisiana State University Press, 1989).
10 Dixon, Thomas, Jr, *The Clansman* (New York, 1905).
11 Bennett, *Party of Fear*, p. 173.
12 For more on the APA see Bennett, *Party of Fear*; Lipset and Raab, *The Politics of Unreason*; Myers, *History of Bigotry in the United States*.
13 Chalmers, David M., *Hooded Americanism: The History of the Ku Klux Klan*, 3rd edn (Durham NC: Duke University Press, 1981).
14 Chalmers, *Hooded Americanism*.
15 For more on the second-era Klan see MacLean, Nancy, *Behind the Mask of Chivalry: The Making of the Second Ku Klux Klan* (New York: Oxford University Press, 1994); Chalmers, *Hooded Americanism*; Jackson, Kenneth T., *The Ku Klux Klan in the City, 1915–1930* (New York: Oxford University Press, 1967); and Blee, Kathleen M., *Women of the Klan: Racism and Gender in the 1920s* (Berkeley CA: University of California Press, 1991).
16 Smith, Geoffrey S., *To Save a Nation: American "Extremism," the New Deal, and the Coming of World War II* (Chicago: Elephant Paperbacks, 1992).
17 For more on American far-rightists of the 1930s–1940s see Jeansome, Glen, *Gerald L. K. Smith: Minister of Hate* (New Haven CT: Yale University Press, 1988); Jeansome, Glen, *Women of the Far Right: The Mothers' Movement and World War II* (Chicago: University of Chicago Press, 1996); Jenkins, Philip, *Hoods and Shirts: The Extreme Right in Pennsylvania, 1925–1950* (Chapel Hill NC: University of North Carolina Press, 1997); Warren, Donald, *Radio Priest: Charles Coughlin, the Father of Hate Radio* (New York: The Free Press, 1996); Cannedy, Susan, *America's Nazis: A Democratic Dilemma* (Menlo Park CA: Markgraf Publications Group, 1990); Smith, *To Save a Nation*; Bennett, *Party of Fear*; Lipset and Raab, *the Politics of Unreason*; and Schonbach, Morris, "Native Fascism during the 1930s and 1940s: A Study of its Roots, its Growth, and its Decline," Ph.D. dissertation, University of California, Los Angeles, 1958. During the period of the "Brown Scare" there were several alarmist exposés which sought to link American far-rightists with continental European fascists. Subsequent research has

found little evidence to support this assertion. For instance, the German Foreign Office in America worried that the antics of Bund would alarm Americans and undercut the German government's efforts to keep America out of the war. Examples of this genre of literature include Piller, E. A., *Time Bomb: America's Sinister new Fascism – Will it Explode on Schedule?* (New York: Arco, 1945); Carlson, John Roy, *Under Cover* (New York: E. P. Dutton, 1943); Carlson, John Roy, *The Plotters* (New York: E. P. Dutton, 1946); and Sayers, Michael and Albert E. Kahn, *Sabotage! The Secret War against America* (New York: Harper and Brothers, 1942).

18 Broyles, J. Allen, *The John Birch Society: Anatomy of Protest* (Boston MA: Beacon Press, 1964).
19 Bell, Daniel (ed.) *The Radical Right* (Garden City NY: Anchor Books, 1964).
20 Adorno, T. W. *et al.*, *The Authoritarian Personality* (New York: Harper and Brothers, 1950), *passim*. A more recent study with a similar theme, i.e. fears of marginalization lead to scapegoating, is Ezekiel, Raphael S., *The Racist Mind: Portraits of American Neo-Nazis and Klansmen* (New York: Viking, 1995). For a critique of the Frankfurt School and its efforts to pathologize right-wing extremism see MacDonald, Kevin, *The Culture of Critique: An Evolutionary Analysis of Jewish Involvement in Twentieth-Century Intellectual and Political Movements* (Westport CT: Praeger, 1998) pp. 155–211. MacDonald puts the issue in an evolutionary framework, and argues that the fears of displacement to which far-rightists are responding are often not illusory but genuine. Thus right-wing movements are seen in some measure as an effort to prevent displacement and marginalization in an arena of "resource competition".
21 Hofstadter, *The Paranoid Style in American Politics*, p. 4.
22 *Ibid*., p. 5.
23 *Ibid*., pp. 29–30.
24 See for example Rowe, Gary Thomas, *My Undercover Years with the Ku Klux Klan* (New York: Bantam Books, 1976).
25 For more on George Wallace see Carter, Dan T., *The Politics of Rage: George Wallace, The Origins of the New Conservatism, and the Transformation of American Politics* (New York: Simon and Schuster, 1995).
26 See Goodman, *Towards a Christian Republic*, p. 5.
27 See Chalmers, David M., *Hooded Americanism*.
28 Lipset and Raab cite several factors, including the unique nature of the American political party system, the fluidity of social mobility, an educational system that instills democratic values, and the heterogeneity of the American nation as militating against extremist political parties. See Lipset and Raab, *The Politics of Unreason*, pp. 484–515.
29 There are some exceptions to this, such as the Populist Party, which fielded some candidates, including David Duke, for political office through the mid-1980s to the early 1990s. By and large such efforts have failed miserably. This is in contrast to the European parliamentary democracies, in which far-right political parties, although still minority parties, are able on occasion to win important political offices. Jörg Haider's Austrian Freedom Party recently demonstrated this by joining in a coalition to run the national government.
30 George, John and Laird Wilcox, *Nazis, Communists, Klansmen, and Others on the Fringe* (Buffalo NY: Prometheus Books, 1992) p. 214.
31 Birch was doing both missionary and intelligence work in China during the war. At the war's end he stumbled upon a communist force with which he became embroiled in a heated argument. Eventually the communist troops executed him. Welch considered Birch to be the first casualty in the Western world's war with communism and thus named his organization after him. For more on the life of John Birch see Welch's hagiographic *The Life of John Birch* (Chicago: Henry Regnery Company 1954).

32 In addition to this figure, George and Wilcox estimate that perhaps as many as 250,000 Americans had once been JBS members, most for only a few years. George and Wilcox, *Nazis, Communists, Klansmen and Others on the Fringe*, p. 220.
33 The Illuminati was founded by one Adam Weishaupt in 1776. Its worldview was similar to that of Freemasonry. Although Bavarian authorities dissolved the organization in 1785, many conspiracy theorists allege that it still exists, albeit in different guises. See for example Pat Robertson's *The New World Order* (Dallas TX: Word Publishing, 1991).
34 See for example Epstein, Benjamin R. and Arnold Forster, *Danger on the Right: The Attitudes, Personnel and Influence of the Radical Right and Extreme Conservatives* (New York: Random House, 1964); and Epstein, Benjamin R. and Arnold Forster *The Radical Right: Report on the John Birch Society and Its Allies* (New York: Random House, 1967).
35 Svokin notes that the "Studies in Prejudice" research underwritten by the American Jewish Committee in the 1940s found that those people who evinced authoritarian tendencies, such as right-wing anti-communists, were susceptible to anti-Semitic appeals. Svonkin, Stuart, *Jews Against Prejudice: American Jews and the Fight for Civil Liberties* (New York: Columbia University Press, 1997) p. 115.
36 Some leading anti-Semites at one time or another were JBS members, including Revilo P. Oliver, George Lincoln Rockwell, Willis Carto, Ben Klassen, Tom Metzger and Robert Jay Matthews. Virtually to a man, these disgruntled former members have renounced the JBS as a Zionist-led operation that confuses well meaning patriots and leads them down a blind alley. See for example George Lincoln Rockwell's criticism of the JBS in his book *White Power* (Reedy WV: Liberty Bell Publications, 1983) pp. 358–407. For its part, the Birch Society has excoriated the "collectivist tendencies" of their racism. Moreover, Birch Society founder Robert Welch went so far as to release a tape-recorded speech, "the Neutralizers," to his followers, in which he claimed that communists had planted anti-Semites into his organization to discredit it.
37 George and Wilcox, *Nazis, Communists, Klansmen, and Others on the Fringe*, p. 278.
38 *Ibid.*, p. 275.
39 Jones, J. Harry Jr, *The Minutemen* (Garden City NY: Doubleday, 1968) pp. 397–99.
40 Jones, *The Minutemen*, p. 321.
41 The ADL sponsored the following 1968 report: Albares, Richard P., *Nativist Paramilitarism in the United States: The Minutemen* (Chicago: Center for Social Studies, 1968).
42 Several top Minutemen were closely tied to Wesley Swift's Christian Identity Church, including Dennis Mower, Walter Peyson and Keith Gilbert. See Aho, James, *The Politics of Righteousness: Idaho Christian Patriotism* (Seattle WA: University of Washington Press, 1990) p. 57. The late Wesley Swift is thought to be the primary architect and promoter of the Christian Identity religion in the far-right movement.
43 Corcoran, James, *Bitter Harvest: Gordon Kahl and the Posse Comitatus: Murder in the Heartland* (New York: Penguin Books, 1990) p. 29.
44 See for example an FBI Internal Memorandum, File Number 100–487031–11, May 21, 1980.
45 According to an article by Leonard Zeskind and James Ridgeway, "[d]uring the 1980s federal law enforcement sources said that as many as one third of all Kansas state sheriffs were either involved in, or sympathetic to the Posse." Ridgeway, James and Leonard Zeskind, "Revolution USA," *Village Voice*, May 2, 1995. However, researchers Laird Wilcox and John George checked with the Kansas Attorney General's office and officers of the Kansas Sheriff's Association, and were informed that they did not know of a single sheriff who had been involved or sympathetic to the Posse. George, John and Laird Wilcox, *American Extremists* (Buffalo NY: Prometheus Books, 1996) p. 247. For more on the Posse Comitatus see Corcoran,

Bitter Harvest; and Coates, James, *Armed and Dangerous: The Rise of the Survivalist Right* (New York: Noonday Press, 1987).
46 Snow, Robert L., *The Militia Threat: Terrorists Among Us* (New York: Plenum Trade, 1999) pp. 14–15.
47 Interview with John Trochman, October 6, 2000.
48 Interview with Norm Olson, September 8, 2000.
49 Interview with John Trochman, October 6, 2000.
50 Interview with Norm Olson, September 8, 2000.
51 Interview with Norm Olson, September 8, 2000.
52 Interview with Norm Olson, September 8, 2000.
53 Interview with John Trochman, October 6, 2000.
54 Ironically this observation is made by a critic of the Militia movement. He seems to imply that it is a disingenuous public relations ploy to mask its "white supremacy roots." See Snow, *The Militia Threat: Terrorists Among Us*, p. 65. However, I would argue that there are segments of the far right that eschews racism of which the Militia movement is by and large part.
55 Two African-Americans, James M. Johnson, a member of the Ohio Unorganized Militia, and his associate, Imam A. Lewis, were arrested in connection with the Mountaineer Militia. FBI, *Terrorism in the United States 1996* (Washington DC: FBI, 1997) p. 7.
56 Interview with Norm Olson, September 8, 2000.
57 Interview with Norm Olson, September 8, 2000.
58 According to sources on virtually all sides of the issue, the Militia/Patriot movement is in decline. For example, according to the spring 2000 issue of the Southern Poverty Law Center's *Intelligence Report*, the number of militia organizations declined to 217 in 1999, substantially down from its high of 858 groups in 1996. Likewise, Laird Wilcox, who maintains the most comprehensive directory of right-wing groups in America (*Guide to the American Right*), also believes that the movement is quickly losing both members and organizations. Email from Laird Wilcox, March 30, 1999. Finally, Buck Revell, a former deputy director of the FBI, told me in a recent interview that he also saw a diminution of the Patriot movement. Interview with Buck Revell, February 16, 2001. It is important to note that while the Militia/Patriot movement is in decline, there is evidence to suggest that other segments in the racialist right are growing. The spring 2001 issue of the Southern Poverty Law Center's *Intelligence Report* identified 602 hate groups operating in the United States in 2000, up from 457 the year before.
59 The ADL has taken the lead in sponsoring anti-paramilitary training statutes. The Southern Poverty Law Center also took up the issue. This will be covered in greater detail in Chapter 6.
60 The Southern Poverty Law Center's publication *False Patriots: The Threat of Antigovernment Extremists* was widely disseminated to law enforcement authorities. Shortly after the Oklahoma City bombing in 1995, the SPLC released files containing thousands of names of alleged militia members to the FBI. See Wilcox, Laird, *The Watchdogs: A close look at Anti-Racist "Watchdog" Groups* (Olathe KS: Laird Wilcox Editorial Research Center, 1999) p. 8. For its part, the ADL has issued a number of reports, most notably *Armed and Dangerous: Militias Take Aim at America*.
61 During her two terms as a House Representative, Chenowith has sponsored and cosponsored several bills and resolutions that resonate with the Militia movement. These initiatives included a hearing she organized entitled "In the Matter of Excessive Use of Government Force;" the cosponsoring of a resolution that would abolish the Internal Revenue Service; and a resolution that would permit the display of the Ten Commandments in government offices and courthouses. See Snow, *The Militia Threat*, p. 172.

62 Bruce Hoffman explains Leonard Zeskind's "conveyor belt" metaphor in Hoffman, Bruce, *Inside Terrorism* (New York: Columbia University Press, 1998) p. 106.
63 This is the figure reported in the Southern Poverty Law Center's winter 1999 issue of its *Intelligence Report*. Gordon Baum, the leader of the organization, also gave me the same figure. Interview with Gordon Baum, August 3, 2000.
64 SPLC, *Intelligence Report*, winter, 1999. The Citizens Councils of America organization was more commonly known as the White Citizens Councils that were organized in the wake of the Supreme Court's landmark 1954 *Brown v. Topeka Board of Education* decision. It was primarily an effort to resist school desegregation in the South.
65 Interview with Gordon Baum, August 3, 2000.
66 Senator Trent Lott and Representative Barr both repudiated the Council when revelations of their meetings with the group were published in the national press. Both also sent separate letters to ADL national director Abe Foxman assuring him that they rejected affiliation with the Council. See the ADL press releases "Majority Leader Trent Lott Tells ADL He Rejects Association with Organizations that Support Any Form of Racial Supremacy," March 18, 1999; and "Rep. Bob Barr to ADL: Council of Conservative Citizens' White Supremacy Views are Repugnant." According to Gordon Baum, Governor Kirk Fordice made no apologies for meeting with the Council. Interview with Gordon Baum, August 3, 2000.
67 Interview with Gordon Baum, August 3, 2000.
68 Interview with Gordon Baum, August 3, 2000.
69 Quoted in Pitcavage, Mark, "The Council of Conservative Citizens 'in the News': A Chronology of Events," http://www.militia-watchdog.org/ccc.htm.
70 See for example the article "Sharks in the Mainstream" in the winter 1999 issue of the Southern Poverty Law Center's *Intelligence Report*; and Mark Pitcavage's article "The Council of Conservative Citizens 'in the News': A Chronology of Events," posted on his website at http://www.militia-watchdog.org/ccc.htm. The ADL also issued a critical report entitled "Council of Conservative Citizens: Promoting a Racist Agenda," which can be found at http://www.adl.org/special_reports/ccc/ccc_intro.html.
71 Interview with Mark Potok, August 18, 2000.
72 On February 2, 1999 Congressmen Robert Wexler and James Clyburn released the text of a resolution that denounced the Council, entitled "Condemning the racism and bigotry espoused by the Council of Conservative Citizens." The resolution accused the Council of promoting "intolerance," "divisiveness," promulgating a "dogma that supports white supremacy and anti-Semitism," and denigrating Abraham Lincoln and Martin Luther King. A copy of the resolution can be found at Pitcavage, Mark, "The Council of Conservative Citizens 'in the News': A Chronology of Events," http://www.militia-watchdog.org/ccc.htm.
73 As an aside, Sam Francis was fired from his position at the *Washington Times* for some of his public comments on race. Since then he has moved in a more radical direction as he writes for not only the Council, but also on occasion, for the *Spotlight*.
74 Interview with Jared Taylor, June 25, 2000.
75 Interview with Jared Taylor, June 25, 2000.
76 Interview with Jared Taylor, June 25, 2000.
77 Interview with Jared Taylor, June 25, 2000.
78 New Century Foundation, *The Color of Crime: Race, Crime, and Violence in America* (Oakton VA: New Century Foundation, 1999).
79 The article's author Mark Potok claimed that *The Color of Crime* report was faulty insofar as it did not use multivariate analysis and ignored variables such as income and education. Southern Poverty Law Center, "Coloring Crime," *Intelligence Report*, summer 2000.
80 Interview with Jared Taylor, June 25, 2000.

222 Notes

81 Professor Michael Levin has written controversial books and articles on race. Professor Robert Weissberg is perhaps best known for his research on Black-Jewish ethnic relations. Rabbi Mayer Schiller has emerged as the chief spokesman of the embattled New Square in New York, which is an Hasidic community that was linked to a pardon scandal involving Senator Hillary Clinton. Schiller occasionally expresses sympathy with some of the racialist right's positions, and actually addresses some of these groups such as the American Friends of the British National Party, in full Hasidic attire.
82 Interview with Jared Taylor, June 25, 2000.
83 This is implied in Piper, Michael Collins, *Final Judgement: The Missing Link in the JFK Assassination Conspiracy, Fifth Edition* (Washington DC: Center for Historical Review, 2000) pp. 322–3. Such allegations are not uncommon in the far-right milieu and should be met with skepticism.
84 For example, Glen Miller's now defunct White Patriots Party at times patterned itself as a southern secessionist organization. For more on Miller see his autobiography, Miller, Glenn, *A White Man Speaks Out* (self-published, 1999).
85 Southern nationalists could draw upon previous scholarship in this effort to downplay the moral failure of slavery. For example, the Nobel laureate economists Robert Fogel and S. L. Engerman once published a book titled *Time on the Cross*, which in essence argued that slavery was not as bad as previously thought. Fogel later distanced himself from this line of argument and was more critical of slavery.
86 This figure was given in Southern Poverty Law Center's summer 2000 edition of its *Intelligence Report*. The League president, Dr Hill, confirmed this same figure to me in a phone conversation in September 2000.
87 See Thornton, R. Gordon, *The Southern Nation: The New Rise of the Old South* (Gretna LA: Pelican Publishing Company, 2000).
88 Dougherty, Jon, "South seeks payback for Civil War 'injustices,'" *WorldNetDaily*, April 8, 2001. http://www.worldnetdaily.com/news/ARTICLE_ID=22326.
89 The Southern Poverty Law Center's summer 2000 edition of its *Intelligence Report*, which was devoted in its entirety to this issue. It is available online at http://:www.splcenter.org/intelligenceproject/ip-4.html.
90 For example, in February 2001, the Virginia chapter president, Ron Doggett, testified before the Virginia State Senate Rules Committee concerning recent statements of regret by that committee on the state's previous support for eugenics and anti-miscegenation laws. "NOFEAR Virginia Chapter leader Testifies before Virginia State Senate Rules Committee," http://www.duke.org/events/press_release/02-19-01.html. Doggett often attempts to meet with local politicians on the subject of Black-on-White violent crime.
91 Interview with Ron Doggett, August 20, 2000.
92 Interview with Ron Doggett, August 20, 2000.
93 To those in the racialist right, a trend of miscegenation is considered tantamount to genocide. This is because according to their reasoning, the phenotypical characteristics of the offspring of such unions are thought to resemble more the non-White parent. Interestingly, this is consistent with leading Afro-centrist theorist Dr Francis Cress Welsing's notion of "white genetic annihilation," the fear of which she posits is at the core of white racism. For more on Welsing's theory see Welsing, Frances Cress, *The Isis Papers: The Keys to the Colors* (Chicago: Third World Press, 1995) *passim*.
94 Foxman, Abraham, "David Duke's *My Awakening*: A Minor League Mein Kampf," ADL press release, January 1999.
95 ADL, "David Duke Launches Appeal to Russian Nationalists," Special Report, 2001.

96 "Ex-KKK Leader Duke Pleads Guilty to Charges," Associated Press, December 18, 2002.
97 As David Chalmers, the pre-eminent historian of the Klan, opined, "throughout its history the Klan has been a conservative, not a revolutionary, organization – The Klan has basically been a *revitalization movement* [emphasis in original]." Chalmers, David M., *Hooded Americanism: The History of the Ku Klux Klan*, 3rd edn (Durham NC: Duke University Press, 1981) p. 425.
98 Louis Beam and Dennis Mahon exemplified the revolutionary faction. Thom Robb is the leading proponent for the non-violent approach. Beam and Mahon have since parted from their respective Klan organizations. For more on this debate see Kaplan, Jeffrey, *The Encyclopedia of White Power: A Sourcebook on the Radical Racist Right* (New York: Alta Mira Press, 2000) pp. 163–6.
99 One terrorist expert, David Rapoport, estimated that the life expectancy of 90 per cent of terrorist organizations is less than one year. Rapoport, David, "Terrorism," in Mary Hawkesworth and Maurice Kogan (eds) *Routledge Encyclopedia of Government and Politics*, vol. 2 (London: Routledge, 1992) p. 1067. I don't know if Rapoport included the violence-prone Klan organizations in his analysis, but I suspect that his findings would hold up for them as well. However, in earlier eras, violent Klan organizations did have some staying power.
100 Kathleen Blee estimates that approximately 500,000 women joined the auxiliary organization. Her book is the definitive one on the subject. See Blee, Kathleen M., *Women of the Klan: Racism and Gender in the 1920s* (Berkeley CA: University of California Press, 1991).
101 Murray, Frank J., "Court delays move on KKK road signs," *Washington Post*, October 31, 2000, A11, p. 11.
102 Interview with Thom Robb, August 15, 2000.
103 During the 1940s and 50s, the Atlanta office of the ADL helped craft anti-mask laws for anti-Klan Southerners. Forster, Arnold, *A Measure of Freedom* (New York: Doubleday & Company, 1950) p. 210.
104 Despite its long history, the Klan's ideology has never really been well articulated. In her study of the Second Era Ku Klux Klan, Nancy MacLean gleaned some elements that inhered in the vigilantism of "hooded order." The Klan of that era evinced a populist tendency in which it believed that it had the right to take the law into its own hands if the government did not fulfill the will of the people. The notion of male honor also loomed large; men were expected to protect their households and be the defenders of White womanhood. Finally, there was an element of Protestant moralism, as Klansmen frequently flogged those who lapsed from community standards. See MacLean, Nancy, *Behind the Mask of Chivalry: The Making of the Second Ku Klux Klan* (New York: Oxford University Press, 1994).
105 One exception to this is Louis Beam's widely disseminated essay "Leaderless Resistance." Chapter 4 will cover this in greater detail, as it has been an important part of the far right's strategic approach to terrorism.
106 This even includes countries in which very few Jews reside. One bizarre example of this is the Japanese National Socialist Movement, as is illustrated by an announcement on its website:
    Our fight is principally dedicated to our fatherland (Japan) and Japanese-Turanian race. We also fight for the Freedom of Eurasia as well as that of Japan. And, we fight for the FREEDOM OF THE WORLD against Zionism and Marxism. We must establish the New Geopolitical Axis – as the World Union of National Socialists against ZOG in haste. We should expand our international cooperation with those who are fighting against our common enemies.
    See the Japanese National Socialist Movement website at http:// www.geocities.co.jp/WallStreet/1889/english.html.

224 *Notes*

107 In 1922 the American industrialist and automobile magnate Henry Ford began a fiercely anti-Semitic campaign in his newspaper *The Dearborn Independent*, which featured a series of articles titled "International Jew: The World's Foremost Problem." Some historians suspect that Ford hired William Cameron, an obscure Canadian, to write the series. The series accused Jews of subverting the Christian underpinnings of American society and included reprinted sections from the notorious *Protocols of the Elders of Zion*. A compilation of the series was published as a four-volume set of books also titled *The International Jew*. The *Protocols of the Elders of Zion* is believed to be a revision of a tract originating in nineteenth-century France which parodied a Masonic plot to take over Europe. Many historians believed that agents of the *Okhrana*, the Czar's secret police, appropriated the document and switched Jews for Masons as the culprits, for the purpose of fomenting ire against Russian Jews because of the role some of their members played in revolutionary activities. The Baltic German and Nazi philosopher, Alfred Rosenberg, brought the *Protocols* from Russia to Germany. From there the document spread to America and the rest of the world. the *Protocols* obviously inspired the myth of the "International Jew." There was much cross-fertilization as *The International Jew* influenced rightists in Europe including the Nazis and Hitler, who in turn inspired American far-rightists. Adolf Hitler was an admirer of Ford, and in 1938 awarded him with a high honor from the German state, the Grand Order of the German Eagle. Moreover, Hitler was rumored to have a portrait of Ford on his desk at his Nazi headquarters, the Brown House, and Ford was the only American mentioned by name in his tome, *Mein Kampf*. See Pool, James and Suzanne Pool, *Who Financed Hitler?* (New York: Dial Press, 1978) pp. 85–130. For its part, the ADL has sought to counter publications such as *The Protocols* and *The International Jew* with special reports of its own. See for example ADL, "The International Jew: Anti-Semitism from the Roaring Twenties is Revived on the Web," 1999; and "The Protocols of The Learned Elders of Zion: A Hoax of Hate," 1999.

108 The late Herbert Armstrong's Church of Christ, which publishes the periodical *The Plain Truth*, is one prominent exception. Others include the Church of Israel, and the National Message Ministry. For more on the Christian Identity sect see Barkun, Michael, *Religion and The Racist Right: The Origins of the Christian Identity Movement* (Chapel Hill NC: University of North Carolina Press, 1994); and Kaplan, Jeffrey, *Radical Religion in America: Millenarian Movements from the Far Right to the Children of Noah* (Syracuse NY: Syracuse University Press, 1997).

109 According to this theory, in the 8th Century, a Eurasian tribe known as the Khazars converted to Judaism and their descendants comprise the vast majority of contemporary Jews. Anti-Semites and occasionally some anti-Zionists invoke this theory to reject contemporary Jewish ancestral claims to Palestine. Ironically, the esteemed Hungarian-Jewish author Arthur Koestler unwittingly did much to popularize this theory in his book *The Thirteenth Tribe* (Koestler, Arthur, *The Thirteenth Tribe* [New York: Random House, 1976]). Far-rightists have in a sense arrogated this book as it has become a staple of their literature. Many far-right book distributors sell the title.

110 At first thought this might sound a little paradoxical, but according to this theory those terrorists who believe God is on their side are more self-assured in their mission and hence have less compunction about using violence. In recent years several terrorism scholars have propounded similar theories: see Bruce Hoffman's *Inside Terrorism* and his report, *Holy Terror: The Implications of Terrorism Motivated by a Religious Imperative* (Santa Monica CA: Rand Corporation, 1993); Flanagan, Thomas, "The Politics of the Millennium," *Terrorism and Political Violence*, 7 (3), pp. 164–75 (1995); and Barkun, Michael, "Religion, Militias and Oklahoma City: The Mind of Conspiratorialists," *Terrorism and Political Violence*, 8 (1), pp. 50–64 (1996).

111 For example, Brent Smith found that of the seventy-five persons indicted for right-wing terrorism during the 1980s, all were closely allied with the Christian Identity

movement. Smith, Brent L., *Terrorism in America: Pipe Bombs and Pipe Dreams* (Albany NY: State University of New York Press, 1994) p. 8.

112 George, John, "Emergence of a Euro-American Radical Right Book Review," *Menasha*, 93, (3), pp. 714–15 (September 1999).

113 This observation is made in Gallagher, Eugene V., "God and Country: Revolution as A Religious Imperative on the Radical Right," *Terrorism and Political Violence*, 9 (3), pp. 63–4 (1997).

114 Much like the Christian Identity movement, in the Third Reich the "German Christian Movement" espoused a "positive Christianity" which sought to expurgate all Jewish references from the Bible and claimed that Jesus was an Aryan Gentile. See Bergen, Doris L., *Twisted Cross: The German Christian Movement in the Third Reich* (Chapel Hill NC: University of North Carolina Press, 1996). Sounding much like an inverted version of Christian Identity, members of the Black Hebrew Israelite sect claim to be the true Jews of the Bible and identify Whites as devils and contemporary Jews as impostors.

115 For example, many members of the Montana Freemen were reported to be followers of Christian Identity. For more on the Freemen see Jakes, Dale and Connie Jakes with Clint Richmond, *False Prophets: The Firsthand Account of a Husband-Wife Team Working for the FBI and Living in Deepest Cover with the Montana Freemen* (Los Angeles CA: Dove Books, 1998).

116 There seems to be a generational shift in religious preferences taking place among the more radical elements of the far right. Younger activists are increasingly adopting Odinism, a form of neo-paganism, as their religion of choice. See the article "The New Romantics" in the spring 2001 issue of the Southern Poverty Law Center's *Intelligence Report* for more on this development.

117 Kaplan, *The Encyclopedia of White Power*, p. 130.

118 For the most comprehensive study of Yockey see Coogan, Kevin, *Dreamer of the Day: Francis Parker Yockey and the Postwar Fascist International* (New York: Autonomedia, 1999). Another good source is Lee, Martin A., *The Beast Reawakens* (New York: Little, Brown, 1997).

119 The World Union of National Socialists (WUNS) was one of the first major postwar efforts to create a united "Neo-Fascist International." Representatives included Colin Jordan and John Tyndall from Great Britain, Savitri Devi from France, Bruno Ludtke from Germany, Franz Pfeiffer from Chile, Horst Eichmann (son of Adolf Eichmann) from Argentina, and Rockwell from the United States among others. For more on WUNS see Simonelli, Frederick J., *American Fuehrer: George Lincoln Rockwell and the American Nazi Party* (Chicago: University of Illinois Press, 1999) pp. 81–95.

120 In 1959, a Washington, DC representative of the ADL forwarded information that Rockwell had been sending wires and registered letters to President Gamal Abdel Nasser of the United Arab Republic. Upon receipt of the information, the FBI opened an investigation. FBI Internal Memorandum, File Number 97–3835–33, July 13, 1959.

121 See the FBI Internal Memorandum, File Number 100–487473–50, January 23, 1987 and FBI Internal Memorandum, File Number: 100–487473–67, September 10, 1987. Robert Burnham, the FBI's section chief for domestic terrorism, remarked on the connection of the book to acts and potential acts of terrorism. According to Burnham, FBI field offices have received numerous calls from local police departments reporting that they found terrorist materials such as guns and bomb making materials in addition to copies of *The Turner Diaries*. "Domestic terrorism: the FBI view," MSBC, May 30, 2000, http:www.msnbc.com/news /272286.asp.

122 Interview with Dr William Pierce, July 12, 2000.

123 National Alliance, *National Alliance Handbook* (Hillsboro WV: National Vanguard Books, 1993) pp. 12–15.

226 *Notes*

124 The "Who Rules America?" pamphlet identifies prominent Jews in the various news and entertainment media, including Disney's Michael Eisner, Time Warner's Gerald Levin, and Viacom's Sumner Redstone among others. National Alliance, "Who Rules America?" 2000. For its part the ADL published a special report titled "Alleged Jewish 'Control' of the American Motion Picture Industry." Although the report acknowledged that Jews were disproportionately represented in the motion picture industry it pointed out that "those Jews who involve themselves in the motion picture industry do so as individuals, not as representatives of their religious group or with an aim to act in some coordinated conspiratorial manner."

125 See for example, Chomsky, Noam and Edward S. Herman, *Manufacturing Consent: The Political Economy of the Mass Media* (New York: Pantheon Books, 1988); and Parenti, Michael, *Inventing Reality: The Politics of the Mass Media* (New York: St Martin's Press, 1986).

126 Interview with Dr William Pierce, July 12, 2000.

127 According to a statement Pierce made in 1999, his website receives on average 8,500 hits per day. Barrett, Greg, "National Alliance grows quickly," *Detroit News*, July 16, 1999. http://detnews.com/1999/nation/9907/16/07160113htm.

128 An ADL report estimates that currently Resistance Records has the potential to draw in one million dollars in sales annually. ADL, "Deafening Hate: The Revival of Resistance Records."

129 Interview with Dr William Pierce, July 12, 2000.

130 Anti-Defamation League, "Eric Gliebe: 'The Aryan Barbarian,'" http://www.adl.org/learn/extus/gliebe.asp, August 5, 2002.

131 For more on the National Alliance demonstrations at the Israeli embassy see Brief, H. J., "White supremacist rally draws protestors," *Washington Times*, May 12, 2000; Lengel, "Neo-Nazis, Foes, Clash At Israeli Embassy," *Washington Post*, May 12, 2002, A19; and ADL, "Neo-Nazis Rally in Nation's Capital," August 26, 2002. *http://www.adl.org/Learn/news/Neo_Nazis_Rally.asp*. At the first demonstration in November, 2001, the National Alliance released a list of eighteen demands to the Israeli government, which sounded like anti-imperialist pronouncements of traditional left-wing groups. The demands included, *inter alia*, "Stop using American military aid to commit unlawful acts of terrorism, murder, and genocide against Palestinians … "; "Obey UN Resolution 242"; "Obey UN Resolution 194"; "Allow true freedom of speech and assembly for all people in Israel"; and "Turn Ariel Sharon, the 'Butcher of Beirut', over to the World Court – " For a complete list of the demands see *http://natall.com/demands/index.html*. For more on the leafleting campaign see Anti-Defamation League, "Hate Literature Blitz Planned By Neo-Nazi Groups To Coincide With Jewish Holidays and 9/11." *http://www.adl.org/PresRele?AUS_12/4148_12.asp*, August 27, 2002.

132 For more on "ethnic cleansing" see ADL, "Growing Proliferation of Racist Video Games Target Youth on The Internet," February 19, 2002.

133 Anti-Defamation League, *Explosion of Hate: The Growing Danger of the National Alliance* (New York: Anti-Defamation League, 1998).

134 In 1996 the Southern Poverty Law Center won an $85,000 judgment against Pierce. According to the suit, Pierce had been involved in a scheme to hide the assets of the Church of the Creator against which the Center had won an uncontested $1 million judgment in another civil suit. Just prior to the suit against the Church of the Creator, its leader, Ben Klassen, had sold Pierce real estate property at what the Southern Poverty Law Center argued was far below market value and thus constituted an effort to hide assets. For more on these suits see "Center Wins Judgment Against Neo-Nazi Leader," *SPLC Report*, 26 (2), p. 1 (June 1996).

135 Interview with Dr William Pierce, July 12, 2000.

136 Recently declassified FBI memoranda indicate that the FBI has kept close tabs on the organization virtually since the parent organization, the Youth Alliance for Wallace, was created in 1969. On numerous occasions the FBI justified its investigations on the assessment that the National Alliance was engaged in activities that could involve "rebellion or insurrection," "seditious conspiracy," "advocating the overthrow of the government," "civil disorders," and "conspiracy against rights of citizens," *inter alia*. This is according to a 1976 FBI report on the organization. See FBI File Number 157–12589.
137 Blythe, Will, "The Guru of White Hate," *Rolling Stone*, June 8, 2000, p. 100.
138 Eric Gliebe fired one Billy Roper, who served as the Alliance's deputy membership coordinator. Roper sought to unite various factions with the far-right movement into a broad coalition. According to a speech at the April 2002 National Alliance Leadership Conference, both Pierce and Gliebe expressed the desire to keep dysfunctional personalities out of the organization. Reportedly, Gliebe decided to remove Roper because of his efforts to recruit skinheads and marginal types, coupled with his brash street activism that risked potential conflict with authorities and anti-racist organizations. For more see an article posted on *http://www.tightrope.cc/update32.htm*, September 17, 2002.
139 Interview with Tom Metzger, July 7, 2000.
140 The Strasser brothers, Gregor and Otto, represented the left wing of the Nazi Party that was very critical of capitalism. Eventually, the two brothers had a falling out with Hitler. Gregor was killed in the "Night of the Long Knives" purge in 1934. Otto escaped to Canada. Some elements of the contemporary far right look to the Strasser brothers over Hitler for inspiration. This segment is sometimes referred to as "Third Positionist" and is especially popular among the British far right.
141 Interview with Tom Metzger, July 7, 2000.
142 McVeigh of course was convicted of bombing the Murrah federal building in Oklahoma City. Scott Baumhammers went on a shooting spree targeting Jews and minorities in Pittsburgh in the spring of 2000. Joseph Paul Franklin targeted interracial couples. John King was convicted in the grisly dragging homicide of James Byrd.
143 Ironically, Metzger claims that much of the government's attention given to him was because of his outspokenness on the issue of US intervention in Latin America. This was supposed to have involved him in an FBI probe. Carter, Jack, *In the Eye of the Storm: The True Story of Tom Metzger* (self-published, 1992) p. 166.
144 Interview with Tom Metzger, July 7, 2000.
145 Metzger, Tom, "Editorial by Tom Metzger," *WAR*, October 1997.
146 In a 1990 report, the ADL estimated that there were approximately 3,000 skinheads in the United States. ADL, "Neo-Nazi Skinheads: A 1990 Status Report," 1990, p. 3. A 1995 publication reported that the figure had risen to about 3,500 and has held steady at that figure. ADL, *The Skinhead International: A Worldwide Survey of Neo-Nazi Skinheads* (New York: ADL, 1995) p. 1.
147 Hewitt, Christopher, "Patterns of American Terrorism 1955–1998: An Historical Perspective on Terrorism-Related Fatalities 1955–98," *Terrorism and Political Violence*, 12 (1), pp. 1–14 (2000), p. 6.
148 Some of the special reports include "Shaved for Battle: Skinheads Target America's Youth," 1987; "Young and Violent: The Growing Menace of America's Neo-Nazi Skinheads," 1988; "Skinheads Target the Schools," 1989; and "Neo Nazi Skinheads: A 1990 Status Report."
149 In 1989, ADL representatives met with then Attorney General Dick Thornburgh to address the problem of skinhead violence. Soon thereafter a skinhead division was formed within the Civil Rights Division of the Justice Department. ADL, "Neo Nazi Skinheads: A 1990 Status Report," p. 1.

150 Contemporary Odinists face somewhat of a challenge because their religion was not handed down in the form of sacred books such as the Old and New Testaments and the Koran. However, they have culled much of the pagan ethos from the sagas in Snorri Sturluson's (1179–1241) *Prose Edda*.
151 The definitive book on this topic is Goodrick-Clarke's *The Occult Roots of Nazism*, which was also his Ph.D. dissertation. Goodrick-Clarke, *The Occult Roots of Nazism: Secret Aryan Cults and Their Influence on Nazi Ideology* (New York: New York University Press, 1992). Walter Laqueur pointed out that a similar effort was undertaken by nationalists in Russia to unearth evidence of a pagan golden age prior to its Christianization. See Laqueur, Walter, *Black Hundred: The Rise of the Extreme Right in Russia* (New York: HarperCollins, 1993) pp. 112–16.
152 Odinism is the mail order ministry *par excellence*. There are several Odinist journals such as *The Runestone*, *Vor Tru* and *Focus Fourteen*, but that is the extent of Odinism's institutional basis. Some Odinists have established "kindreds," that is, small circles of followers that occasionally get together to discuss things like the *Prose Edda* and other related issues.
153 Research indicates that Christian Identity draws very few from the Catholic Church or Mormon Church of Latter Day Saints, or the more established Protestant denominations. Identity believers tend to come from fundamentalist backgrounds. See Aho, *The Politics of Righteousness*.
154 Moynihan, Michael, and Didrik, Soderlind, *Lords of Chaos: The Bloody Rise of the Satanic Metal Underground* (Venice CA: Feral House, 1998) p. 102.
155 See Moynihan and Soderlind, *Lords of Chaos*, *passim*. It would be facile to dismiss the perpetrators as mere miscreants and psychopaths. As the interviews with the perpetrators conducted by Moynihan and Soderlind indicate, they were able to put forward detailed justifications for their actions and expressed no remorse. Generally, they hoped that their actions would draw attention to their religion and awaken the old gods in the hearts and minds of their kinsmen. The main figure behind the arsons is thought to be Varg Vikernes, who is currently serving a jail sentence for murder. While in prison he went through legal procedures to add "Quisling" to his name. Ominously, there has been a recent state-sponsored form of iconoclasm in Afghanistan, whereby the Taliban ordered the destruction of ancient Buddhist shrines in 2001.
156 *Project Megiddo* was a publication that was disseminated to police chiefs around the country to alert them to the potential violence that various groups holding millenarian beliefs might perpetrate around the turn of the century.
157 SPLC, "Pagans in the Prison," *Intelligence Report*, spring 2000.
158 SPLC, "The New Romantics," *Intelligence Report*, spring 2001.
159 Interview with Matt Hale, July 30, 2000.
160 Interview with Matt Hale, July 30, 2000.
161 According to Hale, not long before his death, Klassen had designated a small group of followers known as the "Guardians of the Faith" to carry on the religion. Reportedly, this body appointed Hales as Pontifex Maximus in 1996. Interview with Matt Hale, July 30, 2000.
162 Although the ADL condemned Hale's beliefs, the organization expressed concern over the decision and argued that it should be based upon an applicant's "individual conduct" and not "moral views." ADL, "ADL Reacts to Illinois Bar Panel's Rejection of Extremist Matt Hale: Well-Intentioned Yet 'Sets a Dangerous Precedent,'" February 4, 1999.
163 Interview with Matt Hale, July 30, 2000.
164 Richard Hirschault, the midwestern director of the ADL, gave the figure of 300 in the article Hughes, Jay, "Racist group growing a year after member's killing spree,"

USA Today, July 3–4, 2000, A-2. In 2002 the organization moved its headquarters to Riverton, Wyoming.
165 RAHOWA is an acronym for RAcial HOly WAr. It is meant to be a call to arms equivalent to the Arabic word *Jihad* that is used by Islamic militants.
166 The most notable example is Benjamin Smith, who went on a shooting spree on the July 4th weekend of 1999. Others include George Loeb, who shot and killed a Black veteran of the Gulf War in a parking lot altercation. In July of 1993, members near Los Angeles were arrested for conspiring to foment a race war, which was supposed to be sparked by assassinating Rodney King and Louis Farrakhan. Stewart, Sally Ann, "FBI: LA race war plot 'despicable,'" *USA Today*, July 16–18, 1993, A-1.
167 Rosenlum, Rebecca, "Justice Dept. Investigating World Church of the Creator," *Jewish Bulletin News*, August 20, 1999.
168 McDonald, Karen and Andy Kravetz, "Some Feel the World Church Will Falter, and Hale is Capable of Crime," *Peoria Journal Star Online*, January 9, 2003, http://www.pjstar.com/news/topnews/hold/g135498a.html.
169 ADL press release, "ADL Lauds Law Enforcement for Preventing Extremist Violence with Arrest of Matt Hale," January 8, 2003.
170 Interview with Mike Piper, July 10, 2000.
171 See Coogan, *Dreamer of the Day*. Yockey had several motivations for working with the Soviet Union. First, unlike most far-rightists at the time, he did not implicate the Soviet Union as part of a "Zionist conspiracy." In fact, he argued that the eastern bloc was becoming anti-Semitic and would thus be more amenable to neo-fascist overtures. Second, he envisaged a Western "Imperium" of which Russia would be an integral part. Finally, Yockey evinced an intense anti-Americanism. In that sense, it is somewhat ironic that Carto, who enthusiastically espouses Americanism, would choose to champion a figure like Yockey. However, in my meeting with Carto I found him to be very intellectually eclectic, and thus able to overlook certain aspects that might not necessarily fit into his overall worldview.
172 Yockey, Francis Parker, *Imperium*, 3rd edn (Costa Mesa CA: Noontide Press, 1991) p. ix.
173 Interview with Willis Carto, December 15, 2000.
174 Interview with Willis Carto, December 15, 2000.
175 The wide range of figures included in the book gives some insight in the diversity of figures from whom Carto draws inspiration: Thomas Jefferson, Andrew Jackson, Thomas Edison, Senator Robert LaFollette, Senator Thomas Watson, William Randolph Hearst, Henry Ford, Hiram Johnson, William H. Murray, Robert R. McCormick, H. L. Menken, Senator Burton K. Wheeler, Ezra Pound, Representative Hamilton Fish, Senator Robert A. Taft, Senator George W. Malone, Father Charles A. Coughlin, Senator Huey Long, Lawrence Dennis, Colonel Charles A. Lindbergh, and Mayor Frank Rizzo. One of the final chapters in the book ponders the question "Was Jesus Christ a Populist?" See Carto, Willis A. (ed.) *Populism vs. Plutocracy: The Universal Struggle* (Washington DC: Liberty Lobby, 2000). This book is an expanded version of a work that was originally published in 1982 as *Profiles in Populism*.
176 Interview with Willis Carto, December 15, 2000.
177 The Youth for Wallace was later reorganized as the National Youth Alliance after the defeat of Wallace in 1968. It sought to model itself as a right-wing counterpart to the various left-wing activist groups on college campuses at that time. A key leader in the group was Dr William Pierce. Pierce eventually had a falling out with Carto, and together with some members of the National Youth Alliance, went on to create the National Alliance, which exists to this day.
178 For more on this campaign see Liberty Lobby, *Conspiracy Against Freedom* (Washington DC: Liberty Lobby, 1986) *passim*.

230 *Notes*

179 See for example the ADL special report, "Liberty Lobby: Network of Hate," 1990. For its part, the Liberty Lobby occasionally issues critical reports on the ADL such as its "White Paper on the ADL," 1990.
180 Interview with Willis Carto, December 15, 2000.
181 For example, in 1984 the Bureau of Alcohol, Tobacco, and Firearms conducted an "Extremism and Terrorism School" in Missouri, at which it released a manual. The appendix included a list entitled "Paramilitary Groups Nationwide," which included the Liberty Lobby. Such a designation was a bit absurd for the Liberty Lobby, owing to its geriatric following. See George and Wilcox, *Nazis, Communists, Klansmen, and Others on the Fringe*, p. 373.
182 For more on Lipstadt's argument see Lipstadt, Deborah, *Denying the Holocaust: The Growing Assault on Truth and Memory* (New York: The Free Press, 1993).
183 Robert Griffin makes this observation with regard to Dr William Pierce, but I believe that it applies to many others in the far right as well. See Griffin, Robert S., *The Fame of a Dead Man's Deeds: An Up-Close Portrait of White Nationalist William Pierce* (self-published e-book, 2000) p. 259.
184 Although there is anecdotal evidence to suggest that David Irving sympathizes with elements of the far right's views, he has the reputation of being very contemptuous of individuals in the far right. He has lamented on several occasions that only they will provide him with an audience. Shermer, Michael and Alex Grobman, *Denying History: Who Says the Holocaust never Happened and why Do They Say It?* (Berkeley CA: University of California Press, 2000) p. 53.
185 In their content analysis, Schermer, Grobman and Sulloway referred to this category as "revisionism," which accounted for roughly 31 per cent of the articles, essays, book reviews, commentaries and editorials. This was followed by the "Holocaust" category, which accounted for roughly 21 per cent. Other categories in the order in which they followed include "Equivalency," a theme which seeks to relativize the Holocaust to other historical atrocities, "Nazis," "General," "Jews," "World War II," "Fascism" and "Other." See Shermer and Grobman, *Denying History*, pp. 77–80.
186 For example, the IHR building was burned down in 1984. The case was never officially solved but it was highly suspected that the Jewish Defense League (JDL) was responsible. The JDL had organized many demonstrations around the building and its leader, Irv Rubin, praised the arson attack at a press conference. The home of Canadian revisionist, Ernst Zündel, came under arson attack on two occasions. On another occasion members of a local Anti-Racist Action chapter broke into and ransacked his home.
187 For more on the Zündel trial see Barrett, Stanley R., *Is God a Racist?: The Right Wing in Canada* (Toronto: University of Toronto Press, 1987); Hoffman, Michael A. II, *The Great Holocaust Trial* (Torrance CA: The Institute for Historical Review, 1985); Kinsella, Warren, *Web of Hate* (Toronto: Harper Perennial, 1995); Prutschi, Manuel, "The Zündel Affair," in Alan Davies, *Anti-Semitism in Canada: History and Interpretation* (Waterloo, Ontario: Wilfrid University Press, 1992) pp. 249–77; and Weimann, Gabriel and Conrad Winn, *Hate on Trial: The Zündel Affair, the Media, Public Opinion in Canada* (New York: Mosaic Press, 1986).
188 Interview with Dr Ingrid Rimland, October 4, 2000.
189 For more on the Liberty Lobby's legal battles with the IHR see the *Spotlight*'s December 31, 2000 Emergency Edition; and Shermer and Grobman, *Denying History*, pp. 43–6.
190 Billups, Andrea, "Liberty Lobby Goes under, Ends Spotlight Publication," *Washington Times*, July 10, 2000.
191 For its part, the Liberty Lobby has claimed on numerous occasions that ADL operatives had orchestrated the dissension within the ranks of the IHR and purposefully

designed the Liberty Lobby's demise. Although the ADL has fiercely opposed the Liberty Lobby over the years, I know of no compelling evidence to support this claim. See Shermer, and Grobman, *Denying History*, pp. 43–6.
192 This is according to one Eric Owens, a former IHR staffer and assistant editor of the *Journal of Historical Review*. Owens widely disseminated an email message which alleged that IHR director Mark Weber and IHR member Greg Raven discussed selling the Liberty Lobby's mailing list to either the ADL or the Church of Scientology, another nemesis of the Liberty Lobby. Email from Eric Owens, June 19, 2001.
193 ADL, "Holocaust Deniers to Convene in Lebanon," ADL press release, February 11, 2001.
194 A Southern Poverty Law Center report commented on a trend of "Nazification" in the Ku Klux Klan and other segments of the far right. See Southern Poverty Law Center, *The Ku Klux Klan: A History of Racism and Violence* (Montgomery AL: Southern Poverty Law Center, 1991) pp. 40–6.
195 Lipset, Seymour Martin, "Failures of Extremism," *Society*, January/February, 1998.
196 Gallagher, "God and Country: Revolution as a Religious Imperative on the Radical Right," p. 70.
197 Laqueur, Walter, *Fascism: Past, Present, and Future* (New York: Oxford University Press, 1996) p. 224.
198 FBI, *Project Megiddo* (Washington DC: FBI, 1999) p. 22.
199 Far-right organizations are by and large shoestring operations. However, the movement may have found a financial angel in Vincent Bertollini, a multi-millionaire who made his fortune in the computer industry in Silicon Valley. In recent years he has given money to organizations such as the Aryan Nations. After a Southern Poverty Law Center civil suit bankrupted the organization, Bertollini took in its leader Richard Butler and built a home on his estate for him. For more on Bertollini see ADL, "Computer Millionaire$ Fund Hate: Carl Story, Vincent Bertollini and the 11th Hour Remnant Messenger," December 2000.
200 Kaplan, *The Encyclopedia of White Power*, p. 174. In another study, Kaplan and Weinberg observed that for all its apparent isolation, the far right is relatively well informed on world events and current affairs. Thus

> [I]n many ways the radical right serves as kind of a caged canary – the bird that miners take into the coal mines to warn of the hidden dangers long before they reach the level of consciousness. The study of this esoteric subculture can foretell national controversies yet to take place.

(Kaplan and Weinberg, *The Emergence of a Euro-American Radical Right*, pp. 109–10)

Likewise Wilcox and George opined that extremist groups sometimes fulfill a "watchdog" function in society insofar as they are especially sensitive to issues concerning their particular interests. George and Wilcox, *Nazis, Communists, Klansmen, and Others on the Fringe*, p. 61.

201 Examples include contemporary studies that warn of a burgeoning underclass, such as Charles Murray's *Losing Ground* and Murray and Herrnstien's *Bell Curve*. Also important are studies on the subject of civilizational decline such as Elmer Pendell's *Why Civilizations Self-Destruct*.

202 Leonard Zeskind makes this observation in the essay "Redefining America" in the Southern Poverty Law Center's spring 1999 *Intelligence Report*. Somewhat related to this issue, in their survey of individuals in the White separatist movement, Dobratz and Shanks-Miele found that the respondents asserted that their movement grows in hard economic times. Dobratz, Betty A. and Stephanie L. Shanks-Meile, *White Power, White Pride! The White Separatist Movement in the United States* (New York: Twayne Publishers, 1997) p. 23.

4 The far right and terrorism

1 See Beals, Carleton, *Brass-Knuckle Crusade: The Great Know-Nothing Conspiracy: 1820–1860* (New York: Hastings House Publishers, 1960) pp. 193–207.
2 Forster, Arnold and Benjamin R. Epstein, *Report on the Ku Klux Klan* (New York: Anti-Defamation League, 1965) p. 14.
3 Forster and Epstein, *Report on the Ku Klux Klan*, p. 14.
4 Hewitt, Chris, "Responding to Terrorism," unpublished manuscript, 2000, p. 5. According to Hewitt shootings accounted for 32 per cent of the incidents, followed by bombings (28 per cent), assaults (22 per cent) and other (18 per cent).
5 For a critical examination of the FBI's data collection on domestic terrorism see Hamm, Mark S., *Terrorism, Hate Crime, and Anti-Government Violence: A Preliminary Review of the Research* (Indiana: Indiana State University, 1996).
6 In 1976 the National Advisory Committee on Criminal Justice Standards and Goals issued a *Report on the Task Force on Disorders and Terrorism*, which listed violent incidents of a political or quasi-political nature in the period from January 1965 to March 1976. As the report demonstrates, violent incidents were practically daily occurrences throughout much of that period. Most of the incidents appear to emanate from the political left. See National Advisory Committee on Criminal Justice Standards and Goals, *Report on the Task Force on Disorders and Terrorism* (Washington DC: National Advisory Committee on Criminal Justice Standards and Goals, 1976).
7 Hewitt, Christopher, "Patterns of American Terrorism 1955–1998: An Historical Perspective on Terrorism-Related Fatalities 1955–98," *Terrorism and Political Violence*, 12 (1), p. 6 (2000).
8 Sprinzak, Ehud, "The Process of Delegitimation: Towards a Linkage Theory of Political Terrorism," *Terrorism and Political Violence*, 3 (1), pp. 50–68 (1991).
9 A case in point is the murder of three civil rights workers (Michael Schwerner, Andrew Goodman and James Chaney) in Philadelphia, Mississippi. Local law enforcement officers arrested the three on trumped-up traffic charges and then delivered them to the Klan to be executed.
10 Examples include the 1995 bombing of the Murrah federal building in Oklahoma City; the Oklahoma Constitutional Militia's alleged plans to bomb federal facilities in 1995; the Virginia-based Mountaineer Militia's alleged plan to blow up the FBI's fingerprint facility in Clarksburg, West Virginia in 1996; The Arizona-based Viper Militia's alleged plot to blow up federal buildings in Phoenix; the arrest of militia members for planning an attack on Fort Hood, Texas in 1997; the Colorado First Light alleged plot to disrupt the federal government in 1997; and the Republic of Texas, which allegedly planned to infect selected government officials with deadly toxins.
11 Hewitt, "Patterns of American Terrorism 1955–1998," p. 6.
12 See for example Wheaton, Elizabeth, *Code Name Greenkil: The 1979 Greensboro Killings* (Athens GA: University of Georgia Press, 1987).
13 See for example, Covington, Harold *The March up Country* (Reedy WV: Liberty Bell Publications, 1987).
14 Interview with Harold Covington, July 24, 2000.

15 In a civil trial however, a jury awarded approximately $400,000 for the death of one of the five slain and the injuries of two of the wounded. They found five Klansmen and Nazis, a police informant, and two police officers liable. Wheaton, *Code Name Greenkil*.
16 Coulson, Danny O. and Elaine Shannon, *No Heroes: Inside the FBI's Secret Counter-Terror Force* (New York: Pocket Books, 1999) pp. 192–3.
17 The organization used several names including "the Silent Brotherhood" and a German version of that same title, The *Brüder Schweigen*.
18 Aho, James, *The Politics of Righteousness: Idaho Christian Patriotism* (Seattle: University of Washington Press, 1990) p. 7.
19 Segal, David, "The Pied Piper of Racism," *Washington Post*, January 12, 2000, C1, p. 8.
20 In addition to the Order, *The Turner Diaries* has been linked to other episodes of right-wing terrorism as a possible source of inspiration, including the Aryan Republican Army, which committed approximately twenty-two bank robberies between 1992 and 1996; Dennis McGiffin, who was arrested by the FBI for conspiracy for planning to bomb state capitols and poison water supplies; David Copeland, who conducted a one-man campaign of terror in London in 1999; and Timothy McVeigh, who was convicted of the 1995 bombing of the Murrah federal building in Oklahoma City.
21 Macdonald, Andrew (pseudonym of William Pierce) *The Turner Diaries* (Hillsboro WV: National Vanguard Books, 1978) p. 210.
22 Interview with Dr William Pierce, July 12, 2000.
23 See the FBI Internal Memorandum, File Number 100–487473–50, January 23, 1987; and FBI Internal Memorandum, File Number: 100–487473–67, dated September 10, 1987.
24 Interview with Dr William Pierce, July 12, 2000.
25 Coulson and Elaine Shannon, *No Heroes*, p. 194.
26 This is according to the statements of Danny O. Coulson, the founder of the FBI's Hostage Rescue Team, who was involved in the Order investigation. Coulson and Shannon, *No Heroes*, p. 195. According to one estimate, the investigation is said to have involved one quarter of the total manpower resources of the FBI. Aho, *The Politics of Righteousness*, p. 61.
27 Interview with Dr William Pierce, July 12, 2000.
28 The prison addresses of the "POWs" are occasionally listed in the far-right literature, and readers are encouraged to write and provide material and moral support to them and their families.
29 Hawthorne, George Eric, "The Brüders Schweigen: Men against Time," in Lane, David, *Deceived, Damned, and Defiant: The Revolutionary Writings of David Lane* (St Maries ID: 14 Word Press, 1999) p. 157.
30 Hawthorne, George Eric, "History in the Making," in Lane, *Deceived, Damned, and Defiant*, p. 229.
31 For more on the Order II see Barker, William E., *Aryan America: Race Revolution and the Hitler Legacy* (St Maries ID: Falcon Ridge Publishing, 1993).
32 FBI, *Terrorism in the United States 1998*, p. 5.
33 This observation is made in Dobratz, Betty A. and Stephanie L. Shanks-Meile, *White Power, White Pride! The White Separatist Movement in the United States* (New York: Twayne Publishers, 1997) p. 193.
34 For more on the Order's donations to the White Patriots Party and WAR see Miller, Glen, *A White Man Speaks Out* (self-published, 1999) pp. 149–56. The White Patriots Party dissolved as a result of pressure from federal prosecutors and Morris Dees of the Southern Poverty Law Center. WAR continues operations to this day; however, it has lost strength due to a civil suit initiated by Dees.

234 *Notes*

35 According to an account of Matthews' former lover, Zillah Craig, Matthews stuffed a large amount of money in a paper bag. Later she saw Matthews hand the paper bag to Pierce. Flynn, Kevin and Gary Gerhardt, *The Silent Brotherhood* (New York: Signet, 1990) pp. 321–2. Soon after the meeting Pierce paid $95,000 in cash for a 346-acre plot in Hillsboro, West Virginia on which the National Alliance encampment is headquartered. Marks, Kathy, *Faces of Right Wing Extremism* (Boston MA: Branden Publishing Company, 1996) p. 59. The encampment has accorded the organization a good deal of privacy to go about its business unmolested and away from the watchful eyes of its opponents. A 1987 FBI memorandum on the activities of the National Alliance lamented that due to the remoteness of the West Virginia National Alliance encampment, "physical surveillance [was] nearly impossible." FBI Internal Memorandum, File Number: 100–487473–53X.
36 Coulson and Shannon, *No Heroes*, p. 212.
37 Coulson and Shannon, *No Heroes*, p. 222.
38 These members included Randy Evans, Tom Bentley, Jefferson D. Butler and James Wallington.
39 Coulson and Shannon, *No Heroes*, p. 222.
40 Some of the alleged plots included an attempt to blow up a natural gas pipeline in Fulton, Arkansas; however, the explosive failed. Some CSA members allegedly planned to assassinate several public offices, including those of federal judges H. Franklin Waters and Jack Knox, and also US Attorney Asa Hutchinson. Ellison and Noble planned to bomb a gay church in Kansas City, Missouri, but Noble lost his nerve and failed to carry out the attack. Finally, according to Ellison and Noble, the CSA planned to use a 30 gallon drum of cyanide that it had stockpiled to poison the water supplies of New York City and Washington DC. It was hoped that this would foment urban unrest and precipitate their anticipated revolution.
41 Hoffman, *Inside Terrorism*, pp. 178–9. Martha Crenshaw sees terrorism as the final outcome of a sequence of choices that extremist groups make. According to her theory, terrorism is part of a learning process in which terrorists weigh their available resources and resort to violence when other means of opposition seem unfeasible. Crenshaw, Martha, "The Logic of Terrorism," in Walter Reich (ed.) *The Origins of Terrorism* (Washington DC: Woodrow Wilson Center Press, 1998) pp. 7–24.
42 It took the far right quite a while to learn this lesson of how vulnerable they would be if isolated in a rural setting. As Smith and Damphousse observed, the far left had widely publicized in their publications the failure of Che Guevara's similar strategy in Bolivia. Smith, Brent L. and Kelly R. Damphousse, "Two Decades of Terror," in Kushner, Harvey W. (ed.) *The Future of Terrorism: Violence in the New Millennium* (Thousand Oaks CA: Sage, 1998) p. 142.
43 As described in Kaplan, Jeffrey, "Leaderless Resistance," *Terrorism and Political Violence*, 9 (3), p. 80 (1997).
44 As an example, a website operated by an anti-abortion activist in Oregon listed the names and addresses of doctors who performed abortions. The site contained unsubtle suggestions that there should be some kind of retribution against them. See "Anti-abortion Web Site Goes on Trial," *USA Today*, January 7, 1999. http://usatoday.com/news/ndswed05.htm. This is just one example of how this notion of leaderless resistance can work. Activists with no formal organizational ties and who don't even know one another can post information on the web, and others acting independently can take these cues and commit acts of terrorism as they see fit.
45 Hewitt, "Patterns of American Terrorism 1955–1998," p. 11.
46 Hewitt, "Responding to Terrorism," p. 5.
47 Aho, *The Politics of Righteousness*, pp. 8–9.
48 Aho, *The Politics of Righteousness*, p. 72.
49 According to an IRS manual intended for internal use only, Huberty was a subscriber to Mid-America Aryan Nations and was on Robert Miles' mailing list. The late Miles

was a prominent Christian Identity preacher from Michigan. For more on Huberty's connection to the far right via literature see Aho, *The Politics of Righteousness*, p. 10. Huberty had a history of mental problems, and it is very speculative to attribute his actions to any right-wing ideology. However, it is worth mentioning that some in the far right lauded his attack. For example, James Mason, a leading advocate of the leaderless resistance approach, described Huberty as a "hero of the first magnitude and beyond any reproach whatsoever." Mason, James, *Siege* (Denver CO: Storm Books, 1992) p. 219.

50 For more on Moody's campaign see Winne, Mark, *Priority Mail: The Investigation and Trial of a Mail Bomber Obsessed with Destroying Our Justice System* (New York: Scribner's, 1995).

51 Coates, James, *Armed and Dangerous: The Rise of the Survivalist Right* (New York: Noonday Press, 1987) pp. 157–61.

52 Hewitt, "Patterns of American Terrorism 1955–1998," p. 12. For more on Rudolph's connection to Christian Identity see Haught, James A., "Deadly Alliance," *Free Inquiry*, spring 1999.

53 Walsh, Edward. "'Appalled' Reno Pledges Review of Midwest Shootings," *Washington Post*, July 9, 1999, A12, p. 12.

54 Gibney, Frank Jr, "The Kids got in the Way," *Newsweek*, August 23, 1999, pp. 24–9.

55 Duke, Lynne, "Pittsburgh Reels From Another Apparent Hate Crime," *Washington Post*, April 30, 2000, A4, p. 4.

56 According to James Aho, roughly one half of all right-wing homicides from the period from 1980 through 1990 can be attributed to individuals acting alone. Aho, *The Politics of Righteousness*, p. 62.

57 Stickney, Brandon M., *All-American Monster: The Unauthorized Biography of Timothy McVeigh* (Amherst, NY: Prometheus Books, 1996) pp. 97–100, 158–9. One Michigan Militia member who was present at the meeting told me that McVeigh and Nichols were not well received because of their "extreme racial feelings" and were asked to leave. Interview with Norm Olson, September 8, 2000.

58 Michel, Lou and Dan Herbeck, *American Terrorist: Timothy McVeigh and the Oklahoma City Bombing* (New York: Regan Books, 2001) pp. 167–8.

59 McVeigh claims to have joined the Klan because he thought that it was "fighting for the restoration of individual rights, especially gun rights." After more research he discovered that the Klan was "almost entirely devoted to the cause of racism." Michel and Herbeck, *American Terrorist*, pp. 88–9. His naivete of the true nature of the Klan seems a bit disingenuous insofar as he was of above average intelligence and intellectually curious. However, it is also worth mentioning that he appears to have been a "seeker" in the truest sense of the word and was thus willing to look practically anywhere for knowledge.

60 Stern, Kenneth S., *A Force upon the Plain: The American Militia Movement and the Politics of Hate* (New York: Simon and Schuster, 1996) pp. 51, 192.

61 Griffin, Robert S., *The Fame of a Dead Man's Deeds: An Up-Close Portrait of White Nationalist William Pierce* (self-published e-book, 2000) p. 7.

62 McVeigh left several messages on the answering machine of Richard Coffman, an Arizona representative of the National Alliance. According to McVeigh he called the National Alliance before the bombing to make a "serious request for a safe haven." Michel and Herbeck, *American Terrorist*, p. 205.

63 Interview with Dr William Pierce, July 12, 2000.

64 Recent statements by McVeigh seem to indicate that *The Turner Diaries* may have been determinative in his choice of target and his decision to carry out the attack. While in prison, McVeigh read a novel called *Unintended Consequences*, which was published by John Ross in 1996. It tells the story of one Henry Bowman, a hunter and gun owner who is alarmed at government efforts to ban firearms. Bowman assembles a team of

assassins that kill government officials and agents one by one. Commenting on the book, McVeigh said, "If people say *The Turner Diaries* was my Bible, *Unintended Consequences* would be my New Testament. I [thought it] was a better book. It might have changed my whole plan of operations if I'd read that one first." Michel and Herbeck, *American Terrorist*, p. 304.
65 Griffin, *The Fame of a Dead Man's Deed*, p. 165.
66 Kaplan, Jeffrey, *The Encyclopedia of White Power: A Sourcebook on the Radical Racist Right* (New York: AltaMira Press, 2000) p. 182.
67 Kaplan, *The Encyclopedia of White Power*, p. 185.
68 Interview with Dr Mark Pitcavage, September 6, 2000.
69 Quoted in Coulson, *No Heroes*, p. 532.
70 Coulson, *No Heroes*, p. 533.
71 Coulson, *No Heroes*, p. 534.
72 McVeigh was calling for Andreas Strassmeir, a German national whom he had met at a gun show. Strassmeir's grandfather was supposedly an early Nazi Party member during Hitler's quest for power in Germany. Rumors circulated in the far-right milieu that Strassmeir was a German intelligence agent who was working with American authorities as part of a conspiracy to bomb the Murrah federal building and blame innocent people in the far-right movement.
73 See for example, Jones, Stephen with Peter Israel, *Others Unknown: The Oklahoma City Bombing Case and Conspiracy* (New York: Public Affairs, 1998); and Hoffman, David, *The Oklahoma City Bombing and the Politics of Terror* (Venice CA: Feral House, 1998). This theory is based on the premise that the accomplice Terry Nichols visited the Philippines on a couple of occasions, and it was suspected that possibly he and his wife consorted with Islamic extremists who may have been linked to the mastermind of the World Trade Center bombing, Ramzi Yousef.
74 Michel and Herbeck, *American Terrorist*, pp. 286–7.
75 Olson was pressured to resign from the Michigan Militia soon after making these comments. He later retracted his theory about Japanese culpability in the Oklahoma City bombing. However, he still believes that the US government was responsible for the Tokyo subway attack. Interview with Norm Olson, September 8, 2000.
76 This view was expressed to me in an interview with John Trochman, a leader of the Militia of Montana. Interview with John Trochman, October 6, 2000.
77 Partin's report is reprinted in Hoffman, *The Oklahoma City Bombing and the Politics of Terror*, pp. 461–9.
78 Partin lost some credibility when in his first report to Congress he attributed the attack to a communist conspiracy (The Third Socialist International). Hoffman, *The Oklahoma City Bombing and the Politics of Terror*, p. 23. Many theorists of the bombing still give credence to his report, although they disagree with his allegation that communists were responsible for the attack.
79 Interview with Dr William Pierce, July 12, 2000.
80 Metzger, Tom, "Editorial by Tom Metzger," *WAR*, July 1997, p. 1.
81 Interview with Tom Metzger, July 7, 2000.
82 The criminologist Mark Hamm posits the theory that the Aryan Republican Army was part of a larger conspiracy and revolutionary division of labor, in which the bandits would use their money to fund right-wing revolutionaries. He strongly suspects that members of the Aryan Republican Army were instrumental in the Oklahoma City bombing. For more on his theory see Hamm, Mark S., *In Bad Company: America's Terrorist Underground* (Boston MA: Northeastern University Press, 2001).
83 See for example Laqueur, Walter, *Guerrilla Warfare: A Historical Critical Study* (New Brunswick NJ: Transaction Publishers, 1998); and Laqueur, Walter, *The Age of Terrorism* (Boston MA: Little, Brown, 1987).

84 I borrow much of the analysis in this section from Kaplan's article "Leaderless Resistance," *Terrorism and Political Violence*, 9 (3), pp. 80–95 (1997).
85 Kaplan "Leaderless Resistance," pp. 81–2.
86 *The John Franklin Letters* (New York: The Bookmailer, 1959). Robert Griffin, the biographer of Dr William Pierce, believes that Revilo P. Oliver was the book's author. See Griffin, *The Fame of a Dead Man's Deeds*, p. 143.
87 DePugh, Robert B., *Blueprint for Victory*, 4th edn (Norborne MO: Salon Publishing Company, 1978).
88 Quoted in Kaplan "Leaderless Resistance," p. 83.
89 By "chiliastic" Kaplan refers to several themes, including a period of tribulation in which right-wing terrorists believe that they must engage in a violent struggle before they reach victory, which will result in a period of millennial bliss. Also, there is a Manichean theme to this struggle as the right wing sees themselves as a righteous remnant while their enemies are seen as the embodiment of evil. Kaplan argues that as the far right was banished from beyond the pale of respectability it abandoned any "reformist" ambitions that it once had:

> The state ZOG was increasingly seen as not worth claiming, and with this conclusion, the movement's dreams became increasingly chiliastic. With this too, the pattern of violence emanating from the fringes of the movement began to shift from vigilantism to anti-state terrorism.
>
> (Kaplan 1995, pp. 85–7)

90 Kaplan "Leaderless Resistance," p. 85.
91 Beam, Louis, "Leaderless Resistance," *The Seditionist*, issue 12, February 1992.
92 See Beam, Louis, "Understanding the Struggle or Why We have to Kill the Bastards," in *Essays of a Klansman* (Hayden Lake ID: AKIA Publications, 1983) pp. 45–51; and "Understanding the Struggle Part II," in Beam, *Essays of a Klansman*, pp. 52–72.
93 For example, the ADL issued a Special Edition report on Beam titled "Louis Beam: Dedicated to Hate," which alerted people of the dissemination of his assassination "point system" that he disseminated on the Aryan Nation's Liberty Net computer network.
94 According to Bruce Hoffman, the name Phineas is taken from a character in the Old Testament (Numbers 25), who became an avenger priest by murdering a Midianite woman whom he discovered having sex with her Israelite lover. Hoffman, *Inside Terrorism*, p. 119.
95 FBI, *Terrorism in the United States 1997*, p. 8.
96 Some members of the Aryan Republican Army, which went on a bank-robbing spree in the Midwest in 1994–5, invoked the term Phineas Priests. Paul Hill, the anti-abortionist activist who murdered Dr John Bayard Britton and his escort, had written an essay advocating "Phineas actions." Finally, Hoskins printed a letter from Byron de la Beckwith, the convicted killer of civil rights activist Medgar Evers, in which he concluded with the statement, "Phineas for president." See ADL, "The Order and Phineas Priesthood," August 11, 1999. As an aside, law enforcement authorities found a copy of another book by Hoskins, *War Cycles – Peace Cycles*, in the van of Buford Furrow. Some observers argued that this book motivated Furrow to commit his attack, but the book really has nothing do with terrorism; instead it focuses on international banking.
97 Interview with Dr William Pierce, July 12, 2000.

238 *Notes*

98 Several scholars have cited Pierce's *Hunter* as playing a part in the development of leaderless resistance concept in the far-right underground. See for example Hoffman, *Inside Terrorism*, p. 118, and Kaplan "Leaderless Resistance," p. 85.
99 Seymour, Cheri, *Committee of the States: Inside the Radical Right* (Mariposa CA: Camden Place Communications, 1991) p. 353.
100 The fourteen words are: "We must secure the existence of our people and a future for White children."
101 Wotan is another name for the god Odin of the Norse pantheon. His is considered to be a complex figure, both intellectually contemplative but also a fierce warrior.
102 Quoted in Kaplan "Leaderless Resistance," p. 89.
103 Quoted in Kaplan "Leaderless Resistance," p. 89.
104 This is according to an ADL report, "Alex Curtis: Lone Wolf of Hate Prowls the Internet," 2000, http://www.adl.org./curtis/default.htm.
105 Copeland single-handedly conducted a campaign of terror in 1999 during which he bombed Bangladeshi, Black and gay locations in London, England. Like several other right-wing terrorists, Copeland claimed to have been inspired by *The Turner Diaries*. For more on Copeland see McLagan, Graeme and Nick Lowles, *Mr Evil* (London: John Blake Publishing, 2000).
106 See Curtis, Alex, "Biology for Aryans," *The Nationalist Observer*, issue 21, June 2000, p. 1.
107 Quoted in the ADL report, "Alex Curtis: Lone Wolf of Hate Prowls the Internet."
108 The alleged offenses include placing racist stickers at some of the victims' offices; placing a snake skin in the mail slot of Congressman Filner's office; spray painting anti-Semitic words and symbols on a synagogue; and perhaps the most serious act, placing an inactive hand grenade at Mayor Madrid's residence. For more on this investigation see the FBI's report, "Operation Lone Wolf," 2000, http://www.fbi.gov/majcses/lonewolf1/htm.
109 See Liberty Lobby, *Survival and Leaderless Resistance* (Washington DC: Liberty Lobby, 1999). While not specifically calling for terrorism, the publication reprints an early version of Beam's "Leaderless Resistance" essay and offers tips on survival, physical fitness, creating resistance units, etc.
110 Hollyoak, Eric, "The Fallacy of Leaderless Resistance," *Resistance*, issue 10, winter 2000, pp. 14–18.
111 Barry is the founder of the Special Forces Underground, a covert right-wing organization composed of active duty and retired Special Forces soldiers. Barry and his organization will be covered in greater detail in Chapter 5. Barry is sometimes referred to as the "military advisor" to the National Alliance.
112 Crenshaw discusses some of the preparatory work that must go into an effective terrorist campaign in "The Logic of Terrorism," p. 17.
113 Interview with Steven Barry, October 3, 2000.
114 Interview with Dr William Pierce, July 12, 2000.
115 Laqueur, *The New Terrorism*.
116 As mentioned earlier, FBI data indicate that from 1993 to 1996 right-wing terrorists were responsible for the majority of domestic terrorist incidents in the United States. See Counter-terrorism Threat Assessment and Warning Unit National Security Division, *Terrorism in the United States 1996*.
117 Hewitt, "Patterns of American Terrorism 1955–1998."
118 Katz, Jesse, "Gang Killings in LA County Top a Record of 700," *Los Angeles Times*, December 8, 1991, A1, pp. 24, 26.
119 This observation is made in Gurr, Ted Robert, "Terrorism in Democracies," in Walter Reich, *The Origins of Terrorism*, p. 91. This is in marked contrast to other forms of terrorism such as Nationalist-Separatism, in which terrorists can often rely

on a sympathetic population of co-ethnics. It is generally believed that public support is essential for maintaining a viable resistance or terrorist movement.
120 Hewitt, "Patterns of American Terrorism 1955–1998," p. 8.
121 To recapitulate, Hewitt found that for his first wave of right-wing violence (1958–77) 50.0 per cent of those targeted fell into the "hate crime/random" category. Also for this period, 44.6 per cent of those targeted were "enemy activists," many of whom I suppose were racial minorities. In the second wave (1978–98) the hate crime and enemy activists categories were 70.8 per cent and 8.3 per cent respectively. By contrast another study, Hewitt found that in the Greek nationalist EOKA movement in Cyprus, "civilian victims selected on the basis of ethnic identity, or accidental victims" accounted for 13 per cent of the fatalities for which that group was responsible for the period from 1955–8. For the IRA of Northern Ireland, the figure was 35 per cent for that category for the period 1970–81. Finally, for the Basque nationalist ETA in Spain the figure was 20 per cent for the period 1975–81. Thus these figures are substantially lower than for American right-wing terrorists. Hewitt, Christopher, *The Effectiveness of Anti-Terrorist Policies* (Lanham MD: University Press of America, 1984) p. 29.
122 Ferguson, Todd, "Unjustifiable Force: Violence and Racist Extremism," unpublished paper, December 3, 1999.
123 Truman, David B., *The Governmental Process: Political Interests and Public Opinion*, 2nd edn (Berkeley CA: Institute of Governmental Studies, 1993).
124 As mentioned in the previous chapter, Brent Smith found that of the seventy-five persons indicted for right-wing terrorism during the 1980s, all were closely allied with the Christian Identity movement. Smith, Brent L., *Terrorism in America: Pipe Bombs and Pipe Dreams* (Albany NY: State University of New York Press, 1994) p. 8. Hewitt counted twenty-five homicides attributable to right-wing skinheads. Hewitt, "Patterns of American Terrorism 1955–1998," p. 6.
125 See Hoffman, Bruce, *Inside Terrorism* (New York: Columbia University Press, 1998); Barkun, *Religion and The Racist Right*; and Flanagan, Thomas, "The Politics of the Millennium," *Terrorism and Political Violence*, 7 (3), pp. 164–75 (1995).
126 Bruce Hoffman cites numerous examples, including the 1995 *Aum Shinrikyo* cult's attack on the Tokyo subway; the 1995 assassination of Yitzhak Rabin; the 1993 bombing of the World Trade Center in New York by Islamic extremists; the 1996 campaign of Hamas' suicide bombers, etc. See Hoffman, *Inside Terrorism*, pp. 92–3.
127 Adams, James, *The Financing of Terrorism* (New York: Simon and Schuster, 1986) in White, Jonathan R., *Terrorism: an introduction* (Stamford CT: Wadsworth, 2002) pp. 40–2.
128 Interview with Buck Revell, February 16, 2001.
129 FBI, *Terrorism in the United States 1997*, p. 8.
130 FBI, *Terrorism in the United States 1997*, p. 4.
131 FBI, *Terrorism in the United States 1996* (Washington DC: FBI, 1996) pp. 5–6.
132 Associated Press, "FBI: Militia leader directs attack plans," December 11, 1999.
133 Associated Press, "Two Men Arrested with Anthrax," February 19, 1998.
134 FBI, *Terrorism in the United States 1996*, p. 9.
135 Quoted in Hoffman, *Inside Terrorism*, p. 198.
136 Hoffman, *Inside Terrorism*, pp. 199–205.
137 Merari, Ariel, "Terrorism as a Strategy of Struggle: Past and Future," in Taylor, Max and John Horgan, *The Future of Terrorism* (London: Frank Cass, 1999) pp. 52–65.
138 Crelinsten, Ronald D., "Terrorism and Counter-Terrorism in a Multi-Centric World: Challenges and Opportunities," in Taylor and Horgan, *The Future of Terrorism*, p. 183.

240 *Notes*

139 Freeh, Louis, "The Threat to the United States Posed by Terrorists," testimony before the US Senate Committee on Appropriations, February 4, 1999.
140 This observation is made in Redden, *Snitch Culture*, pp. 145–59.
141 Southern Poverty Law Center, "Neither Left nor Right," *Intelligence Report*, winter, 2000.
142 Redden, *Snitch Culture*, p. 154.

5 The US government's response to right-wing extremism

1 Laqueur, Walter, *Guerrilla Warfare: A Historical Critical Study* (New Brunswick NJ: Transaction Publishers, 1998) p. 407.
2 Wilkinson, Paul, "Politics, Diplomacy and Peace Processes: Pathways out of Terrorism?" in Taylor, Max and John Horgan, *The Future of Terrorism* (London: Frank Cass, 1999) p. 66.
3 Trelease, Allen W., *White Terror: The Ku Klux Klan Conspiracy and Southern Reconstruction* (Baton Rouge LA: Louisiana State University, 1971) p. 383.
4 Trelease, *White Terror*, p. 384.
5 The Fifteenth Amendment to the US Constitution mandated that voting rights could not be denied on the basis of "race, color, or previous condition of servitude."
6 Trelease, *White Terror*, p. 385.
7 Trelease, *White Terror*, p. 387.
8 Trelease, *White Terror*, p. 389.
9 Trelease, *White Terror*, p. 391.
10 Trelease, *White Terror*, p. 417.
11 D'Sousa, Dinesh, *The End of Racism* (New York: The Free Press, 1995) p. 175.
12 Congress passed the Mann Act in 1910, which prohibited the transportation of women across state lines for immoral purposes.
13 FBI, "History of the Federal Bureau of Investigation,"http://www.fbi.gov.yourfbi /history/hist.htm.
14 Anti-Defamation League, *Not the Work of a Day: The Story of the Anti-Defamation League of B'nai B'rith* (New York: Anti-Defamation League, 1965) pp. 27–8.
15 Walker, Samuel, *Hate Speech: The History of an American Controversy* (Lincoln NE: University of Nebraska, 1994) pp. 25–6. Thirty years later, however, the Supreme Court overturned the *Bryan v. Zimmermann* decision in the 1958 *NAACP v. Alabama* case. In that decision the court ruled that the NAACP did not have to publicly disclose its members.
16 D'Sousa, *The End of Racism*, p. 191.
17 Chalmers, David M., *Hooded Americanism: The History of the Ku Klux Klan*, 3rd edn (Durham NC: Duke University Press, 1981) p. 323.
18 ADL, *Not the Work of a Day*, p. 32.
19 ADL, *Not the Work of a Day*, p. 32.
20 Schonbach, Morris, "Native Fascism during the 1930s and 1940s: A Study of Its Roots, Its Growth, and Its Decline," Ph.D. dissertation, University of California, Los Angeles, 1958, p. 367.
21 Schonbach, "Native Fascism during the 1930s and 1940s," p. 367.
22 Schonbach, "Native Fascism during the 1930s and 1940s," p. 369.
23 Cannedy, Susan, *America's Nazis: A Democratic Dilemma* (Menlo Park CA: Markgraf Publications Group, 1990) pp. 198–9.
24 Not long after the Dickstein-McCormack Committee investigation into the activities of the Friends of the New Germany in 1934, the German government decided to sever all ties with the organization and ordered all German national members to resign. Cannedy, *America's Nazis*, pp. 62–5. Likewise, in 1938, the German Foreign

Office ordered the breaking of any liaison between itself and the German American Bund. Cannedy, *America's Nazis*, pp. 156–68.
25 Cannedy, *America's Nazis*, p. 142.
26 In 1945 the CPUSA reached its highest membership count ever – between 75,000 and 85,000 members. Shannon, David A., *The Decline of American Communism* (Chatham NJ: Chatham Bookseller, 1959) p. 3.
27 Davis, James Kirkpatrick, *Spying on America: The FBI's Domestic Counterintelligence Program* (Westport CT: Praeger, 1992) p. 26.
28 Davis, *Spying on America*, p. 26.
29 In 1938 the FBI had a budget of $6.2 million, which amounted to 20 per cent of the Justice Department's total budget. By 1945, the FBI's budget was $45 million and accounted for approximated 43 per cent of the entire Justice Department's budget. Davis, *Spying on America*, pp. 28–9.
30 According to one interpretation, these unregulated investigative techniques developed during this period ultimately opened the door for the COINTELPRO initiative, which commenced in 1956. Davis, *Spying on America*, pp. 28–9.
31 Schonbach, "Native Fascism during the 1930s and 1940s," p. 389.
32 Redden, Jim, *Snitch Culture* (Venice CA: Feral House, 2000) p. 64.
33 For more on the efforts of the Anti-Nazi League and the World Anti-Nazi Council see Gottlieb, Moshe R., *American Anti-Nazi Resistance, 1933–1941: An Historical Analysis* (New York: KTAV Publishing House, 1982).
34 Schachner, Nathan, *The Price of Liberty: A History of the American Jewish Committee* (New York: The American Jewish Committee, 1948) pp. 123, 159–62; ADL, *Not the Work of a Day*, p. 32; Schonbach, "Native Fascism during the 1930s and 1940s," pp. 436–7.
35 Forster, Arnold. *Square One: The Memoirs of a True Freedom Fighter's Life-long Struggle Against Anti-Semitism, Domestic and Foreign* (New York: Donald I. Fine, 1988) p. 55.
36 Forster, *Square One*, p. 56.
37 Schachner, *The Price of Liberty*, p. 163.
38 Schonbach, "Native Fascism during the 1930s and 1940s," pp. 433–4.
39 Forster noted that his relationship with Winchell eventually soured after the latter became an ardent supporter of Senator Joseph McCarthy. Forster, *Square One*, p. 58.
40 Forster, *Square One*, p. 59.
41 Powers, Richard Gid, *Not Without Honor: The History of American Anticommunism* (New York: The Free Press, 1995) p. 185.
42 The historian Richard Gid Powers believes that *Undercover* was probably written, or at least edited, by ADL ghosts. Powers, *Not Without Honor*, pp. 184, 293.
43 Powers, *Not Without Honor*, p. 184.
44 Powers, *Not Without Honor*, p. 183.
45 Powers, *Not Without Honor*, pp. 183–4.
46 Powers, *Not Without Honor*, pp. 186–7.
47 Dennis, Lawrence and Maximilian St George, *A Trial on Trial: The Great Sedition Trial of 1944* (Torrance CA: The Institute for Historical Review, 1984) pp. 350–71.
48 Reilly, Lawrence, *The Sedition Case* (Metairie LA: Sons of Liberty, 1985) pp. 112–13. Other defense counsels, including Henry Klein and Albert Dilling, also asserted that the ADL was behind the prosecution. Jeansome, *Women of the Far Right*, pp. 161–2.
49 President Roosevelt ordered the investigation and Attorney General Biddle complied with some reluctance, as he thought that the trial amounted to political prosecution. Jeansome, *Women of the Far Right*, p. 152.
50 See for example Jeansome, *Women of the Far Right*; and Cannedy, *America's Nazis*.
51 There were allegations that some of the defendants had received money from Axis governments for their propaganda activities and the ACLU used this as pretext to withhold support. Dennis and St George, *A Trial on Trial*, p. 221.

52 Many of these cases remain unsolved, so they cannot all be imputed to the Klan with certainty. See Chalmers, *Hooded Americanism*, pp. 356–65.
53 Chalmers, *Hooded Americanism*, p. 398.
54 Davis, *Spying on America*, p. 76.
55 Chalmers, *Hooded Americanism*, p. 376. Chalmers also cites a study by Edgar Z. Friedenberg, which found that most accept violence if it is perpetrated by legitimate authority such as during wartime. Applying this logic to Klan violence in the Civil Rights era, the vigilantism of the Klan was often cloaked in such a way as to be seen as protecting the existing order against external disrupters. Thus a portion of the Southern population viewed it as legitimate and granted it a degree of immunity. Chalmers, *Hooded Americanism*, p. 387.
56 Katz, William Loren, *The Invisible Empire: The Ku Klux Klan's Impact on History* (Seattle WA: Open Hand Publishing 1986) p. 128.
57 Many violent acts of terrorism preceded the attacks on Jewish targets. Together they seemed to have a cumulative effect so that by the time the Klan's campaign ensued against the Jewish community, the FBI was prepared to meet the challenge. See Nelson, Jack, *Terror in the Night: The Klan's Campaign against the Jews* (New York: Simon and Schuster, 1993) p. 55.
58 Whitehead, Don, *Attack on Terror: The FBI Against the Ku Klux Klan in Mississippi* (New York: Funk & Wagnalls, 1970) p. 291.
59 According to one account, the police failed to administer the *coup de grace* to Tarrants because neighbors came out of their homes during the incident and would have thus been witnesses to such an execution. Nelson, *Terror in the Night*, p. 182.
60 Nelson, *Terror in the Night*, p. 224. The ADL's Botnick acknowledged to Jack Nelson that he had helped plan the ambush. However, he recounted that prior to his agreement, the FBI had played a provocative tape recording of a Klan threat to blow up a synagogue full of people, including women and children. Nelson, *Terror in the Night*, p. 219.
61 Nelson, *Terror in the Night*, p. 242.
62 Glick, Brian, *War at Home: Covert Action against US Activists and What We Can Do about It* (Boston MA: South End Press, 1989) p. 10.
63 This is according to the FBI testimony before the Senate Intelligence Committee. See Glick, *War at Home*, p. 10.
64 FBI Internal Memorandum, File Number 438611424445, September 8, 1964.
65 The Ku Klux Klan organizations targeted were: Association of Arkansas Klans of the Knights of the Ku Klux Klan; Association of Georgia Klans; Association of South Carolina Klans, Knights of the Ku Klux Klan; Christian Knights of the Ku Klux Klan; Dixie Klans, Knights of the Ku Klux Klan, Inc.; Improved Order of the US Klans, Knights of the Ku Klux Klan; Independent Klavern, Fountain Inn; Independent Klan Unit, St Augustine, Florida; Knights of the Ku Klux Klan, AR; Mississippi Knights of the Ku Klux Klan; National Knights of the Ku Klux Klan; National Knights of the Ku Klux Klan; Original Knights of the Ku Klux Klan; Pioneer Club, Orlando, Florida; United Florida Ku Klux Klan; United Klans of America, Knights of the Ku Klux Klan; US Klans, Knights of the Ku Klux Klan, Inc.; and White Knights of the Ku Klux Klan of Mississippi. The "hate organizations" consisted of the following: Alabama States Right Party; American Nazi Party; Council for Statehood; Fighting American Nationalists; National States' Rights Party; National Renaissance Party; United Freemen; Viking Youth of America; and White Youth Corps. FBI Internal Memorandum, File Number 438611424445, September 8, 1964.
66 Office of Attorney General Memorandum File Number 157–9–16, September 8, 1965.
67 Davis, *Spying on America*, p. 76.

68 Finch, Phillip, *God, Guts, and Guns* (New York: Seaview/Putnam, 1983) p. 158.
69 This figure of 2,000 informants is remarkable when one considers that it exceeds the number of informants (1,500) that were used against the Communist Party, USA, the *bête noire* of J. Edgar Hoover. See Davis, *Spying on America*, pp. 49, 88.
70 For example, the bureau xeroxed copies of an article that appeared in a rival organization's publication that accused Dr Ed Fields, the leader of the National States Rights Party, of bigamy. FBI Internal Memorandum, File Number 157–9–4–18, March 24, 1965. In another instance, the bureau sent postcards that contained a cartoon depicting James Robertson Jones, a Klan leader in North Carolina, of misusing Klan funds, and having extramarital relations. FBI Internal Memorandum, File Number 157–9–8–36, May 17, 1965.
71 FBI Internal Memorandum, File Number 157–9–23, March 18, 1966.
72 FBI Internal Memorandum, File Number 157–9–27, April 20, 1966.
73 Davis, *Spying on America*, p. 88.
74 An FBI memorandum recommended that insofar as the various Nazi organizations leveled attacks against the Jewish community, that the latter's organizations could be used to accumulate information. FBI Internal Memorandum, File Number 157–9–9–1, October 15, 1964. Another memorandum recommended sending an apocryphal inflammatory letter to the Jewish War Veterans organization in Chicago so that it would seek to counter the American Nazi Party in that city. FBI Internal Memorandum, File Number 157–9–9–5, February 26, 1965.
75 See for example FBI Internal Memorandum, File Number 157–9–2–4, September 25, 1964.
76 Chalmers, *Hooded Americanism*, p. 400.
77 Rowe maintained that he did not fire on Mrs Liuzzo. He became the government's star witness against the three Klan assailants who were convicted for this attack. Davis, *Spying on America*, p. 92.
78 Davis, *Spying on America*, p. 93.
79 One provision of the Levi Guidelines was that there must be clear evidence of criminal wrongdoing before the government could undertake surveillance or an investigation. Although this would seem to undercut the government's efforts to monitor extremist groups, watchdog groups have filled the void with their own informants, who often relay information to government sources.
80 The evidentiary criterion for a criminal predicate is slightly below the threshold of "probable cause," which is the less than absolute certainty but greater than mere suspicion or "hunch."
81 Methvin, Eugene H, "Anti-terrorism: How Far?" in Frank McGuckin (ed.) *Terrorism in the United States* (New York: H. W. Wilson, 1997) p. 104.
82 Smith, Brent L., *Terrorism in America: Pipe Bombs and Pipe Dreams* (Albany NY: State University of New York Press, 1994) p. 8.
83 Smith, *Terrorism in America*, p. 8.
84 Davis, *Spying on America*, p. 176.
85 Bridges, Tyler, *The Rise of David Duke* (Jackson MS: University of Mississippi Press, 1994) pp. 88–9.
86 Thompson, Jerry, *My Life in the Klan* (Nashville TN: Rutledge Hill Press, 1988).
87 Smith, *Terrorism in America*, p. 8.
88 In 1981 various members of the long dormant Weather Underground, Black Liberation Army and the Black Panther party coalesced to form the May 19th Communist Organization (M19CO). The new group began a terrorist campaign that included a robbery of a Brinks armored car. Moreover, the M19CO established links with and provided assistance to the Armed Forces of National Liberation (FALN), a Puerto Rican separatist terrorist group. Smith, *Terrorism in America*, p. 9.

244 *Notes*

89 General Accounting Office, *Combating Terrorism: FBI's Use of Federal Funds for Counterterrorism-Related Activities (FYs 1995–98)* (Washington DC: GAO, 1998) p. 26.
90 Quoted in The Center for National Security Studies, "The FBI Counter-terrorism Program," April 26, 1995.
91 Federal Bureau of Investigation, *99 Frequently Asked Questions About the FBI*, http://www.fbi.gov/faq.htm.
92 Smith, *Terrorism in America*, pp. 9–10.
93 Revell, Oliver "Buck," *A G-Man's Journal* (New York: Pocket Star Books, 1998) pp. 254–5. Dr James O'Connor, a former deputy assistant director of the FBI and currently a professor of criminology, communicated to me that the idea for the Hostage Rescue Team was conceived by the Training Division of the FBI. Phone conversation with Dr James O'Connor, June, 2002.
94 Coulson, Danny O. and Elaine Shannon, *No Heroes: Inside the FBI's Secret Counter-Terror Force* (New York: Pocket Books, 1999) pp. 209–313.
95 Seymour, Cheri, *Committee of the States: Inside the Radical Right* (Mariposa CA: Camden Place Communications, 1991) p. 5.
96 Coulson, and Shannon, *No Heroes*, p. 533.
97 Smith, *Terrorism in America*, p. 11.
98 This is the figure given by Miller and should be met with some skepticism in that he could be using puffery for self-serving purposes. Miller, Glen, *A White Man Speaks Out* (self-published, 1999) p. 103.
99 Stanton, Bill, *Klanwatch: Bringing the Ku Klux Klan to Justice* (New York: Mentor, 1991) p. 265.
100 According to independent researcher Laird Wilcox, the ADL played a major part in the Fort Smith trial and consulted with prosecutors. Irwin Suall, the ADL's chief investigator at that time, "flew to Arkansas when it looked bad for the prosecution." Letter from Laird Wilcox, April 29, 1999. This was corroborated by defense attorney Kirk Lyons, who pointed out that Suall had a personal interview with Judge Morris Arnold. Interview with Kirk Lyons, August 17, 2000.
101 Interview with Kirk Lyons, August 17, 2000.
102 Interview with Buck Revell, February 16, 2001.
103 The informant was a private investigator working on a contingency basis for the BATF. He would receive a $3,500 bonus for a conviction. This contingency practice was reportedly widespread in law enforcement and also very controversial insofar as it gives incentives for informants to inflate crimes. In 1995, BATF Director John Magaw promised to immediately end this practice in his agency. Kopel, David B. and Paul H. Blackman, *No More Wacos: What's Wrong with Federal Law Enforcement and How to Fix It* (Amherst NY: Prometheus Books, 1997) p. 32.
104 Coulson and Shannon, *No Heroes*, p. 395.
105 Kopel and Blackman, *No More Wacos*, p. 34.
106 Kopel and Blackman, *No More Wacos*, p. 35.
107 Louis Freeh stated that the FBI had exaggerated the threat posed by Randy in his testimony to Congress during its investigation of the incident. Freeh, Louis, "Opening Statement of Louis J. Freeh, Director Federal Bureau of Investigation Before the Subcommittee on Terrorism, Technology, and Government Information on the Judiciary United States Senate," Washington DC, October 19, 1995.
108 Coulson and Shannon, *No Heroes*, p. 402.
109 Kopel and Blackman, *No More Wacos*, p. 38.
110 According to Kopel and Blackman, not only did the Branch Davidians know that a raid was forthcoming, they also believed that the BATF had planned for a shootout. Kopel and Blackman, *No More Wacos*, p. 96–9.

111 According to Coulson, two Davidians were killed from BATF gunshots, one was a probable suicide, and two were murdered by other Davidians. Coulson and Shannon, *No Heroes*, p. 453.

112 Although the Posse Comitatus Act of 1878 forbids the use of federal troops for civilian law enforcement purposes, exceptions to the law have been created. Allegations of methamphetamine manufacturing were made against Koresh, which provided justification for the Army's involvement. The allegations proved unfounded. The House of Representatives Committee on Government Reform and Oversight, *Investigation in to the Activities of Federal Law Enforcement Agencies toward the Branch Davidians* (Washington DC, 1996). The US Marshals Service made an allegation of a drug connection in the Randy Weaver case in order to obtain military reconnaissance flights over his cabin. Kopel and Blackman, *No More Wacos*, pp. 87–9.

113 The House of Representatives Committee on Government Reform and Oversight, *Investigation in to the Activities of Federal Law Enforcement Agencies toward the Branch Davidians*, August, 1996.

114 Wright, Stuart A., "Anatomy of a Government Massacre: Abuses of Hostage-Barricade Protocols during the Waco Standoff," *Terrorism and Political Violence*, 11 (2), p. 47 (1999).

115 Barkun, Michael, "Millenarian Groups and Law Enforcement Agencies: The Lessons of Waco," *Terrorism and Political Violence*, 6 (1), p. 83 (1994).

116 Wright, "Anatomy of a Government Massacre," p. 55.

117 It was undetermined whether Koresh's fatal wound was self-inflicted or if another Davidian fired the shot. Coulson and Shannon, *No Heroes*, p. 453.

118 Kopel and Blackman, *No More Wacos*, p. 16.

119 Kopel and Blackman, *No More Wacos*, p. 49.

120 Coulson and Shannon, *No Heroes*, p. 432. Although these figures may sound alarming, according to Kopel and Blackman's research, the rate of gun ownership on a per capita basis for the Davidians was unremarkable by Texas standards. Kopel and Blackman, *No More Wacos*, p. 52.

121 Kopel and Blackman, *No More Wacos*, p. 61.

122 According to one researcher, CAN opened intelligence files on nearly 1,500 organizations that it classified as cults, including the Church of Scientology, the Nation of Islam and Reverend Sun Myung Moon's Unification Church, as well as far-right groups such as the Aryan Nations and the National Alliance. Redden, *Snitch Culture*, p. 85.

123 According to a sworn testimony, Ross deprogrammed David Block, a former Branch Davidian, from whom he received information on the allegations of child abuse and firearms violations. Wright, Stuart A., "Construction and Escalation of a Cult Threat," in Stuart A. Wright, *Armageddon in Waco: Critical Perspectives on the Branch Davidian Conflict* (Chicago: University of Chicago Press, 1995) pp. 88–9.

124 Redden, *Snitch Culture*, p. 87. Redden cites a letter Ross had written to Attorney General Janet Reno, which outlines his extensive contacts with both the BATF and the FBI.

125 Quoted in Ammerman, Nancy T., "Waco, Law Enforcement, and Scholars of Religion," in Stuart A. Wright, *Armageddon in Waco: Critical Perspectives on the Branch Davidian Conflict* (Chicago: University of Chicago Press, 1995) p. 289. The organization dissolved in 1995 after a Seattle jury ordered Ross to pay $2.5 million in punitive damages and CAN to pay $1 million in punitive damages for their conspiracy to kidnap a young man and attempt to deprogram him. Kopel and Blackman, *No More Wacos*, p. 143.

126 This story was originally reported in the *Heritage Southwest Jewish Press*, on April 16, just a few days prior to the final rail on April 19, 1993. The story praised the efforts of the ADL in this regard. Brin, Herb, "ADL travails bring glee to enemies of Jews,"

246   *Notes*

Heritage, April 16, 1993, p. 1. The far right *Spotlight* newspaper picked up on the article and based on that alone, claimed that the ADL had instigated the tragic raid. This appears, however, to be pure conjecture with virtually no evidence to support that claim. See Piper, Michael, "Waco Instigator Identified," *The Spotlight*, July 31, 1995, p. 10. At first it may seem odd that the ADL would take an interest in the Branch Davidians insofar as it was multi-racial and generally philo-Semitic. However, on occasion some Jewish parents have requested help in tracking down children who have joined cults. In fact Jewish parents were instruments in the creation of several of the "anti-cult" groups founded in the 1970s. For more on this issue see Melton, J. Gordon, "The Modern Anti-Cult Movement in Historical Perspective" in Kaplan, Jeffrey and Helène Lööw, *The Cultic Milieu: Oppostional Subcultures in an Age of Globalization* (New York: AltaMira Press, 2002) pp. 264–89.

127 The FBI maintained that the pyrotechnic tear gas that was used still did not cause the fire that engulfed the compound. FBI, press release, August 25, 1999.
128 Kaplan, Jeffrey, *The Encyclopedia of White Power: A Sourcebook on the Radical Racist Right* (New York: AltaMira Press, 2000) p. 323.
129 Kaplan, *The Encyclopedia of White Power*, p. 324.
130 This observation is made in Kaplan, *The Encyclopedia of White Power*, p. 334.
131 Michael Fortier and his wife Lori were accused of having foreknowledge of the planned bombing and not alerting authorities. Lori Fortier received "use immunity." Jones, Stephen with Peter Israel, *Others Unknown: The Oklahoma City Bombing Case and Conspiracy* (New York: Public Affairs, 1998) p. 96.
132 Heyman, Philip B., *Terrorism and America: A Commonsense Strategy for a Democratic Society* (Cambridge MA: MIT Press, 1998). p. 140.
133 Redden, *Snitch Culture*, p. 71.
134 Klaidman, Daniel and Michael Isikkoff, "The Feds' Quiet War: Inside the Secret Strategy to Combat the Militia Threat," *Newsweek*, 128, April 22, 1996, p. 47.
135 Kaplan, David E. and Mike Tharp, "Terrorism Threats at Home," *US News and World Report*, 123 (25), pp. 22–27 (December 29, 1997–January 5, 1998).
136 FBI, press release, October 20, 1999. The FBI released a guide for law enforcement personnel on how to make contact with militia organizations and cultivate relationships with them. See Duffy, James E. and Alan C. Brantley, "Militias: Initiating Contact," *Law Enforcement Bulletin*, July 1997,http://www.fbi.gov/library/leb/1997/july975.htm.
137 Interview with Buck Revell, February 16, 2001.
138 Interview with John Trochman, October 6, 2000.
139 Interview with Norm Olson, September 8, 2000.
140 GAO, *Combating Terrorism*, pp. 27–8.
141 For more on the exploits of the informants see Jakes, Dale and Connie Jakes with Clint Richmond, *False Prophets: The Firsthand Account of a Husband-Wife Team Working for the FBI and Living in Deepest Cover with the Montana Freemen*, (Los Angeles CA: Dove Books, 1998).
142 Interview with Kirk Lyons, August 17, 2000.
143 Interview with John Trochman, October 6, 2000.
144 Lackey, Tom, "Montana Freemen Leaders get Long Prison Terms, but Wives Walk," Associated Press, March 17, 1999.
145 Blitzer, Robert M., "FBI's Role in the Federal Response to the Use of Weapons of Mass Destruction: Statement of Robert M. Blitzer, Chief Domestic Terrorism/Counter-terrorism Planning Section FBI before the US House of Representatives Committee on National Security," November 4, 1997. This directive was later augmented by PDD 62, which creates a more systematic and integrated approach to fighting terrorism by establishing the National Coordinator for Security Infrastructure Protection and Counter-Terrorism, which oversees a

broad variety of relevant policies and program. The White House, Office of the Press Secretary, "Fact Sheet: Combating Terrorism: Presidential Decision Directive 62," May 22, 1998.
146 Redden, *Snitch Culture*, p. 71.
147 Freeh, "The Threat to United States Posed by Terrorists," pp. 12–13.
148 From the National Infrastructure Protection Center website at http://www.nipc.gov/history.htm.
149 Martinez, Barbara Y., "Congressional Statement on Preparedness for Terrorism Response," June 8, 1999.
150 FBI, press release, December 16, 1999.
151 Roos, John G, "It's All About Preparedness," *Armed Forces Journal*, November, 2000, pp. 42–3.
152 FBI, *CONPLAN: United States Government Interagency Domestic Terrorism Concept of Operations Plan* (Washington DC: FBI, 2001).
153 Federal Bureau of Investigation, *Project Megiddo* (Washington DC: US Department of Justice, 1999) p. 8.
154 O'Meara, Kelly Patricia, "FBI Targets Right Wing," *Insight on the News*, December 27, 1999, pp. 16–18.
155 Greg Rampton, the Assistant Special Agent in Charge of the Denver FBI field office, made this denial in an interview with Don Wiederman on the *Freedom Forum* radio call-in show. See *American NewsNet*, November 23, 1999, http://www.amerifree.com/front/front05.htm.
156 The report submitted in 1872 contained 632 pages; the accompanying testimony filled another twelve volumes. US Congress, *Report of the Joint Select Committee to Inquire into the Condition of Affairs in the Late Insurrectionary States* (Washington DC: US Congress, 1872).
157 The committee held hearings in several American cities including Washington DC, Los Angeles, New York and Chicago. Its interviews of hundreds of witnesses filled 4,300 pages of testimony. National Archives and Records Administration, "Special Committee on Un-American Activities Authorized to Investigate Nazi Propaganda and Certain Other Propaganda Activities," downloaded July 7, 2000, http:www.nara.gov/nara/legislative/house_guide/hgch22dh.html.
158 Powers, *Not Without Honor*, pp. 124–5.
159 Since the collapse of the Soviet Union, examinations of the Soviet archives have revealed that the Communist Party of America (CPUSA) was involved in espionage and received substantial funding from the Soviet government. See Klehr, Harvey, John Earl Jones and Friorikh Igorevich Firssov, *The Secret World of American Communism* (New Haven CT: Yale University Press, 1995).
160 Committee on Un-American Activities, *Preliminary Report on Neo-Fascist and Hate Groups* (Washington DC: Committee on Un-American Activities, 1954). The National Renaissance Party was founded by Madole in 1948 and lasted until his death in 1978. *Common Sense* ceased publication in 1972.
161 Sims, Patsy, *The Klan* (New York: Stein and Day Publishers, 1978) pp. 42–3.
162 House Committee on Un-American Activities, *The Present-Day Ku Klux Klan Movement* (Washington DC: US Government Printing Office, 1967) p. 136.
163 Sims, *The Klan*, p. 43.
164 House Committee on Un-American Activities, *The Present-Day Ku Klux Klan Movement*, p. 137.
165 House Committee on Un-American Activities, *The Present-Day Ku Klux Klan Movement*, p. 136.
166 Freeh, "Opening Statement of Louis J. Freeh, Director Federal Bureau of Investigation Before the Subcommittee on Terrorism, Technology, and Government Information on the Judiciary United States Senate."

185 "Klanwatch Director Urges Military to Discharge Troops with Extremist Ties," *SPLC Report*, 26 (3), September, 1996, p. 3.
186 The most notable example, Timothy McVeigh, received his training in explosives in the Army. Other prominent figures and leaders include Steven Barry, Louis Beam, William Potter Gale, James "Bo" Gritz, Tom Metzger, Norm Olson, George Lincoln Rockwell, Rodney Skurdal and Randy Weaver.
187 For example, Morris Dees discovered that during the mid-1980s some soldiers stationed at Fort Bragg had helped Glen Miller's White Patriots Party conduct paramilitary training. Dees filed a lawsuit, which persuaded a federal judge to prohibit Miller from conducting paramilitary training. Smith, *Terrorism in America*, pp. 85–6.
188 Laqueur estimated that in the period 1961–76 roughly 120 military coups have taken place, while only five guerilla movements have come to power. Laqueur, *Guerrilla Warfare*, p. 408.
189 Pate, James L, "Witch-Hunt for the Resister," *Soldier of Fortune*, February, 1996, p. 96.
190 Interview with Steven Barry, October 3, 2000.
191 Walker, Gregory A, "A Defector in Place," *Intelligence Report*, summer, 1999.
192 Walker, "A Defector in Place."
193 Peiper, Joachim, "Planning a Skinhead Infantry," *Resistance*, issue 9, fall 1999, p. 9.
194 Walker, *Hate Speech*, pp. 57–8.
195 Walker, *Hate Speech*, p. 105.
196 *Terminiello v. Chicago*, 337 US 1 (1949), quoted in Walker, *Hate Speech*, p. 106.
197 *Ibid*.
198 For more on *Brandenburg v. Ohio* see Epstein, Lee, and Thomas G. Walker, *Constitutional Law for a Changing America* (Washington DC: Congressional Quarterly Press, 1992) pp. 143–5.
199 Frank Collin was an odd choice to lead the NSPA. A homosexual pedophile, it was strongly suspected that his Jewish father was a survivor of the Dachau concentration camp of World War II. See George, John and Laird Wilcox, *Nazis, Communists, Klansmen, and Others on the Fringe* (Buffalo NY: Prometheus Books, 1992) pp. 360–1.
200 Neier, Aryeh, *Defending My Enemy* (New York: E. P. Dutton, 1979) pp. 31–2, p. 50.
201 Since Skokie, it is not uncommon to see public appearances in which a dozen or so right-wing activists are met by several thousand counter-demonstrators. This has rendered ineffective the demonstration tactic for the far right. Instead of a means by which to gain support, demonstrations have become pathetic displays of weakness. See George and Wilcox, *Nazis, Communists, Klansmen, and Others on the Fringe*, p. 361.
202 Interview with Harold Covington, January 10, 2001.
203 Samuel Walker noted that the ACLU was plunged into a financial crisis in the immediate aftermath of the Skokie decision. However, it quickly recovered and received a surge of new members to replace the losses attributable to Skokie. Walker, *Hate Speech*, p. 126.
204 Cleary, Edward J., *Beyond the Burning Cross* (New York: Vintage, 1994) p. 9.
205 For more on *R.A.V. v. St. Paul*, see Cleary, *Beyond the Burning Cross*.
206 See for example, Blain, "Group Defamation and the Holocaust," pp. 45–68. Analogously, Laurence Hauptman argues that the group defamation of Native Americans created an environment that led to their dehumanization and oppression. Hauptman, "Group Defamation and the Genocide of American Indians," pp. 9–22. More recently the genocidal violence in Rwanda has been ascribed to provocative "hate radio" that urged violence against the Tutsi tribe. ABC News, *Nightline*, November 21, 1996.
207 Walker, *Hate Speech*, p. 15.
208 Walker, *Hate Speech*, pp. 99–105.
209 Walker, *Hate Speech*, pp. 15–16.

167 The House of Representatives Committee on Government Reform and Oversight, *Investigation in to the Activities of Federal Law Enforcement Agencies toward the Branch Davidians*.
168 "History of the Simon Wiesenthal Center," http://www.wiesenthal.com/.
169 Risen, James, "Militia Leaders Bring Their Fiery Talk to Capitol Hill," *Washington Times*, June 16, 1995, A1, p. 26.
170 Minta, John, "Militias Meet the Senate With Conspiracies to Share," *Washington Post*, June 16, 1995, A1, p. 10.
171 ADL, *Not the Work of a Day*, p. 34.
172 See for example Tenney, Jack B., *Zionist Network* (Arabi LA: Sons of Liberty, n.d.).
173 Presley, Lieutenant Commander Steven Mack, USN, *The Rise of Domestic Terrorism and Its Relation to the United States Armed Forces* (Quantico VA: Marine Corps Command and Staff College, April 19, 1996) p. 26.
174 This observation is made in Curtin, Lawrence M. Jr, *White Extremism and the US Military* (Monterey CA: Naval Postgraduate School, 1997) pp. 96–8. To give an example, in 1976, fourteen Black Marines broke into what they thought was a Klan meeting at Camp Pendleton and stabbed six White soldiers. A subsequent study by Naval Investigative Service found that race relations had been severely strained at that and other Marine Corps and Naval facilities. Sims, *The Klan*, pp. 216–17.
175 Presley, *The Rise of Domestic Terrorism and Its Relation to the United States Armed Forces*, p. 8.
176 These regulations include DoD Directive 5200.2, Department of Defense Personnel Security Program, DoD Directive 1325.6, Guidelines for Handling Dissident and Protest Activities Among Members of the Armed Forces, Army Regulation 604–10, Military Personnel Security Program, and Army Regulation 380–67, Department of the Army Personnel Security Program. For more on the development of this policy see The Secretary of the Army's Task Force on Extremist Activities, *Defending American Values*, March 21, 1996, pp. 17–18.
177 "Deterring and Eliminating Hate Group Activities," *American Forces Information Service Defense Viewpoint*, 11 (57). http://www.defenselink.mil/speeches/1996/di1157.html.
178 Grigg, William Norman, "Racism in the Ranks," *The New American*, January 22, 1996, 12 (02).
179 The Secretary of the Army's Task Force on Extremist Activities, *Defending American Values*, p. 17.
180 The Secretary of the Army's Task Force on Extremist Activities, *Defending American Values*, p. 33.
181 Curtin, *White Extremism and the US Military*, p. 94. The NAACP released a separate report but it looked only at the state of North Carolina and consisted of a series of off-base community forums and on-base interviews. Among its policy recommendations were that the military should develop a uniform interpretation of polices concerning active versus passive participation in extremist groups; racist and offensive symbols (e.g. the Confederate battle flag) should be forbidden from display on military installations; and base commanders should appoint a senior officer to liaise with local NAACP branches to foster better community relations. NAACP, *Task Force Report on Community and Military Response to White Supremacist Activities In and Around Military Bases* (March, 1996) pp. 17–18.
182 The Secretary of the Army's Task Force on Extremist Activities, *Defending American Values*, p. 34.
183 The Secretary of the Army's Task Force on Extremist Activities, *Defending American Values*, p. ii.
184 Caldera, Louis, Memorandum on Army Policy on Extremist Activities, March 14, 2000.

210 Walker, *Hate Speech*, p. 160.
211 In his speech Freeh identified three chief threats: (a) the possibility that nuclear weapons or nuclear materials could be stolen by criminals and supplied to terrorists and/or rogue nations; (b) growth and spread of organized crime in Russia; and (c) hate crimes. Freeh, Louis, "Speech at the Berlin City Hall, Berlin Germany," June 28, 1994. http://www.fbi.gov.pressrm/dirspch/94–96archives/berlin.htm.
212 NSDAP-AO was the original name for the Nazi party's overseas organization, which coordinated party policy outside of the Reich.
213 George and Wilcox, *Nazis, Communists, Klansmen, and Others on the Fringe*, pp. 366–7.
214 Grigg, William Norman, "Crime Fighters Converge," *The New American*, 10 (17), August 22, 1994.
215 "Hamburg Court Convicts American Neo-Nazi Gary Lauck," *This Week in Germany*, September 6, 1996.
216 Schmidt, Hans, *Jailed in "Democratic" Germany: The Ordeal of an American Writer* (Milton FL: Guderian Books, 1997) p. 26. Schmidt reprints a German Interior Ministry memorandum, in the appendix of his book, which purports that the US embassy in Germany forwarded information from the ADL to German authorities to assist in his prosecution.
217 Vise, David A., "Fugitive Neo-Nazi From Germany is Captured in W. Va.," *Washington Post*, August 29, 2000, p. A02.
218 Southern Poverty Law Center, "Darker Than Black," *Intelligence Report*, fall 2000.
219 George, John and Laird Wilcox, *American Extremists* (Buffalo NY: Prometheus Books, 1996) p. 261.

6 The watchdogs' response to the far right

1 ADL press release, "ADL Commends President for Domestic Anti-Terrorism Initiative Calls on 26 States to Enact Anti-Paramilitary Training Statutes," April 24, 1998.
2 ADL, *The ADL Anti-paramilitary Training Statute: A Response to Domestic Terrorism* (New York: ADL, 1995) p. 3.
3 According to an SPLC report only one state, Texas, has ever challenged a group for violating these laws. SPLC, "Center attorneys craft model anti-militia law," http://www.splcenter.org/intelligenceproject/ip-6.html.
4 For more on this case see Stanton, Bill, *Klanwatch: Bringing the Ku Klux Klan to Justice* (New York: Mentor, 1991).
5 Weinberg, Leonard, Elizabeth Francis and Randall D. Lloyd, "Courts Under Threat," *Terrorism and Political Violence*, 11 (2), p. 95 (1999).
6 The researchers in this study sent mailed questionnaires to a randomly drawn sample of 3,000 sitting district and municipal judges throughout the United States, of which 426 responded. Weinberg *et al.*, "Courts Under Threat," pp. 93–109.
7 ADL, *Vigilante Justice: Militias and "Common Law Courts" Wage War Against the Government* (New York: ADL, 1997) p. 2.
8 FBI, *Terrorism in the United States 1997* (Washington DC: FBI, 1998) pp. 11–12.
9 It is difficult to estimate with great precision the number of common law courts. The aforementioned FBI report released in 1998 noted that some private and state sources estimated the number to be over 1,000. The study by Weinberg *et al.* reported that there were 131 common law courts operating in thirty-five states by 1996. A recent SPLC report stated that known common law courts have fallen from thirty-one in 1998 to just four in 1999. SPLC, "Red Hot Patriot Movement Cools Down," *Intelligence Report*, spring, 2000.
10 According to two researchers, hate crime perpetrators rely upon far-right organizations for "slogans, mottoes, and guidance," which can persuade them to commit hate

crimes. Levin, Jack and Jack McDevitt, *Hate Crimes: The Rising Tide of Bigotry and Bloodshed* (New York: Plenum Press, 1993) p. 104.

11 In 1995 the Southern Poverty Law Center reported that 15 per cent of those offenders arrested for hate crimes belonged to organized far-right groups. Dees, Morris and Ellen Bowden, "Taking Hate Groups to Court," http://www.splcenter.org/legalaction/la-3.html. This statistic must be taken with some caution in that these links are often very tenuous and consist of little more than subscribing to and reading extremist newsletters and literature, etc. The amorphous nature of the American far right makes such claims of affiliation very difficult.

12 From the Hate Crimes Statistics Act of 1990, in Jacobs, James B. and Kimberly Potter, *Hate Crimes: Criminal Law and Identity Politics* (New York: Oxford University Press, 1998) p. 39.

13 It is important to note that only 51 per cent of the American population was covered by hate crime reporting statistics in 1992. This figure increased to 85 per cent by 1999. Thus the modest increase between the 1992 and 1999 figures can be ascribed in part to two factors. First, more people are now covered by these statistics; and second, the general population has increased. Source: FBI Hate Crime Statistics.

14 Using data from the FBI's 1999 Uniform Crime Report, I calculated that approximately one out of every 191 persons was a victim of violent crime in 1999. Figures for other crimes for that year were property crime (one in 27); murder and non-negligent manslaughter (one in 17,544); forcible rape (one in 3,058); robbery (one in 666); aggravated assault (one in 298); burglary (one in 130); larceny theft (one in 39); and motor vehicle theft (one in 238). See FBI, *Uniform Crime Report, 1999*, http://www.fbi.gov.ucr/99cius.htm.

15 Jacobs and Potter, *Hate Crimes: Criminal Law and Identity Politics*, p. 33.

16 Levin and McDevitt cite a study that examined hate crimes committed in the city of Boston, which found that fully half of them were assaults. Moreover, almost three quarters of these assaults resulted in at least some physical injury to the victim. Levin, and McDevitt, *Hate Crimes*, p.11.

17 Jacobs and Potter, *Hate Crimes*, p. 131.

18 Wilcox, *Crying Wolf*, p. 20.

19 The FBI's 1999 hate crime statistics indicate that African-Americans are one-and-a-half times more likely to be arrested for committing hate crimes than whites. FBI, *Hate Crime Statistics 1999* (Washington DC: FBI, 2001) p. 12. Some minority activists believe that these laws have "boomeranged" against their communities and now call for their recision. Dougherty, Jon, "Blacks arrested more for hate crimes," WorldNetDail.com, March 6, 2001.

20 As of 1998 those states were Arkansas, Georgia, Indiana, Kansas, Kentucky, New Mexico, New York, South Carolina and Wyoming. ADL, *1999 Hate Crime Laws* (New York: Anti-Defamation League, 1998).

21 For example, the San Diego Police Department works very closely with the ADL in the area of hate crimes. Police officers are instructed to immediately contact an ADL crisis interventionist when a hate crime occurs. The crisis interventionist works directly with the victims at the scene of the crime to determine any support that they might need. Wessler, Stephen, "Promising Practices Against Hate Crimes: Five State and Local Demonstration Projects," May, 2000, p. 7. More recently, the ADL distributed clipboard cards imprinted with guidance on responding to hate crimes to over 2,000 members of the Boston Police Department. Meek, James Gordon, "Cops Get Guides to Hate Crimes," *APB News*, December 14, 2000.

22 "Gore in ADL Speech, Urges Federal Hate-crimes Law," *Jewish Bulletin News*, http://www.jewishsf.com /bk000512/usgore.shtml, downloaded March 1, 2001.

23 "FBI, Justice make hate top priority," *Jewish News of Greater Phoenix*, 39 (51) (June 25, 1999).

252 *Notes*

24 "Coalition Announces Plan for Hate Crime Prevention," US Newswire, April 2, 2001.
25 Kollman, Ken, *Outside Lobbying: Public Opinion and Interest Group Strategies* (Princeton, NJ: Princeton University Press, 1998) p. 156.
26 UKA members were involved in, among other things, the 1963 bombing of the 16th Street Baptist Church in Birmingham; the 1964 slaying of the Black Lieutenant Colonel Lemuel Penn; and the 1965 slaying of civil rights worker Viola Liuzzo. Stanton, Bill, *Klanwatch: Bringing the Ku Klux Klan to Justice* (New York: Mentor, 1991) p. 210.
27 For more on the civil suit against WAR see Dees, Morris, *Hate on Trial: The Case Against America's Most Dangerous Neo-Nazi* (New York: Villard Books, 1993).
28 Murphy, Kim, "Jury Verdict Could Bankrupt Aryans," *Los Angeles Times*, September 8, 2000.
29 Housing and Urban Development press release, "Cuomo Says Million Dollar Award Sends Clear Message against Racial Discrimination on the Internet," July 20, 2000.
30 Frederick Smith, quoted in Wilcox, Laird, "Who Watches the Watchman," in Kaplan, Jeffrey and Hélène Lööw, *The Cultic Milieu: Oppositional Subcultures in an Age of Globalization* (New York: Alta Mira Press, 2002) p. 309.
31 Quoted in Wilcox, Laird, *Crying Wolf: Hate Crime Hoaxes in America* (Olathe KS: Laird Wilcox Editorial Research Center, 1998) p. 15.
32 Wilcox, *Crying Wolf*, pp. 14–15.
33 Dees, Morris and Ellen Bowden, "Taking Hate Groups to Court."
34 Interview with Mark Potok, August 18, 2000.
35 Duke, David, *My Awakening* (Covington LA: Free Speech Press, 1998) p. 653.
36 Duke, *My Awakening*, pp. 655–6.
37 Duke, *My Awakening*, p. 670.
38 Black served over two years in prison for his role in a bizarre 1981 plot to invade the island of Dominica and overthrow its government. While in prison, he studied computers and became quite proficient in using them.
39 Kenneth Stern from the American Jewish Committee cites two studies on this issue. The *Ottawa Citizen* estimated approximately 600, while Gina Smith estimated 800. See Stern, Kenneth, *Hate on the Internet* (New York: American Jewish Committee, 1999) http://www.ajc.org/pre/interneti.htm.
40 Arent, Lindsey, "Net Group Stalks L.A. Gunman," *Wired News*, August 11, 1999, http://www.wired.com/news/news/politics/story/21163.html.
41 See for example, *Computerized Networks of Hate* (1985); *Web of Hate* (1996); *High-Tech Hate* (1997); and *Poisoning the Web* (1999).
42 "Statement of the Anti-Defamation League on Hate on the Internet Before the Senate Committee on the Judiciary," September 14, 1999.
43 Isaccs, Matt, "Spy vs. Spite," *Sfweekly.com*, February 2–8, 2000.
44 Isaccs, "Spy vs. Spite."
45 For example the ISP Prodigy removed offensive messages from one of the bulletin boards it hosted after receiving a complaint from the ADL. ADL press release, "Anti-Semitism Detoured on the Information Highway," February 24, 1999. The ADL persuaded Amazon.com and Barnes & Noble to place statements warning about the extremist content of certain books offered for sale such as *The Protocols of Zion*. ADL press release, "Amazon.com and Barnes&Noble.com Respond to ADL's Concerns on *Protocols* Book," March 28, 2000. Finally, the ADL recently persuaded the internet auction site, eBay, to refrain from listing items bearing extremist symbols. ADL press release, "ADL Applauds eBay for Expanding Guidelines to Prohibit the Sale of Items that Glorify Hate," May 4, 2001.
46 Isaccs, "Spy vs. Spite."

47 ADL memorandum to FBI Director William H. Webster, FBI File Number 100–530–526, December 10, 1980.
48 The USCCR ultimately declined to publish it because Paul Alexander, the acting counsel of the USCCR, believed that it was "too rhetorical" and "bordered on jingoism." George, John and Laird Wilcox, *Nazis, Communists, Klansmen, and Others on the Fringe* (Buffalo NY: Prometheus Books, 1992) pp. 238–9.
49 This program focuses on the role of law enforcement in the 1930s and 1940s in abetting the Holocaust. Recruits are required to tour the US Holocaust Museum in Washington DC, after which they write an essay on the relevance of this experience as "a human being and as a law enforcement officer." FBI press release, June 30, 2000.
50 ADL press release, "ADL Definitive Guide to Extremism in America now on CD-ROM. Resource will be Widely Distributed to Law Enforcement Agencies Nationwide," April 15, 2002.
51 ADL press release, "Law Enforcement From Across The US Participates in Joint ADL-FBI Conference on Terrorism," June 6, 2002.
52 Wessler, Stephen, "Promising Practices Against Hate Crimes: Five State and Local Demonstration Projects," p. 5.
53 For example, its September 8, 2000 "Changing Face of Hate and Terrorism" symposium brought together representatives of federal, state, and local law enforcement agencies as well as academics, and other government officials. Simon Wiesenthal Center, "Changing Face of Hate and Extremism," http://www.broadcast.com/events/swc/symposium0909/.
54 According to one report, SLATT received $2 million in government grants for fiscal year 1999 alone. Grigg, William Norman, "A Watchdog in Fedgov's Kennel," *The New American*, 16 (19), September 11, 2000.
55 From the Institute for Intergovernmental Research website at http:www.iir.com/slatt/.
56 Interview with Dr Mark Pitcavage, September 6, 2000.
57 See for example, Eddlem, Thomas, "Does SLATT Need a Watchdog," *The New American*, 16 (19) (September 11, 2000).
58 Dees, *Hate on Trial*, p. 19.
59 Shapiro, Joseph P., "Hitting before hate strikes," *US News and World Report*, September 6, 1999, pp. 56–7.
60 Arent, "Net Group Stalks L.A. Gunman."
61 Independent researcher Laird Wilcox has thoroughly examined various FBI and ADL memoranda, which indicate a close working relationship between the two entities. See Wilcox, Laird, *The Watchdogs: A close look at Anti-Racist "Watchdog" Groups* (Olathe KS: Laird Wilcox Editorial Research Center, 1999) pp. 45–6. My examination of Wilcox's archives on this subject confirms his assertion.
62 Wilcox, *The Watchdogs*, p. 46.
63 FBI Internal Memorandum, File Number 44-0-1204, February 4, 1985.
64 Interview with Buck Revell, February 16, 2001.
65 The Joint Terrorist Task Force is a joint program created in 1980 to pool the resources of both the FBI and the New York City Police Department to combat terrorism in New York. Herman was involved in several high-profile terrorist cases and led the investigation into the 1993 World Trade Center bombing. For more on the Joint Terrorist Task Force and Herman, see Reeve, Simon, *The New Jackals: Ramzi Yousef, Osama bin Laden, and the Future of Terrorism* (Boston MA: Northeastern University Press, 1999).
66 Rosenlum, Rebecca, "FBI surveillance of hate groups critical, Jewish leaders assert," *Jewish Bulletin of Northern California*, September 3, 1999.
67 Interview with Dr Mark Pitcavage, September 6, 2000.

68 George and Wilcox, *Nazis, Communists, Klansmen, and Others on the Fringe*, p. 394.
69 Redden, *Snitch Culture*, p. 78.
70 Oddly, Oakely later repudiated the book, expressed support for the groups on which he spied, and claimed that the ADL pressured him to continue his investigation. George and Wilcox, *Nazis, Communists, Klansmen, and Others on the Fringe*, pp. 361–2.
71 During the affair, it transpired that the ADL paid Bullock $170,000 for his services for the years 1985–93 through a conduit, ADL attorney Bruce Hochman. Friedman, Robert I., "The Enemy Within," *The Village Voice*, 38 (19) (May 11, 1993). The ADL's chief fact-finder at the time, Irwin Suall, once referred to Bullock as the ADL's "number one investigator." Blankfort, Jeffrey, "Unions Among 100s of Groups Spied on by ADL Informant," *Middle East Labor Bulletin*, 4 (3) (fall 1993).
72 Some of the groups on which the ADL had files included the ACLU, ACT-UP, African National Congress, National Lawyers Guild, NAACP, La Raza, CISPES, and Jews for Jesus.
73 Wilcox, Laird, "Who Watches the Watchman," in Kaplan, Jeffrey and Hélène Lööw, *The Cultic Milieu: Oppositional Subcultures in an Age of Globalization* (New York: Alta Mira Press, 2002) pp. 297–8.
74 Gerard is rumored to have worked closely with El Salvadoran death squads. When the police searched his locker they found a black executioner's hood, CIA manuals, a secret document on interrogation techniques referring to El Salvador, numerous passports and IDs, and photos of men bound and blindfolded. Friedman, "The Enemy Within."
75 "Former S.F. cop Target of Probe," *San Francisco Chronicle*, January 15, 1993.
76 "Police Said to Aid Spying on Political Groups," *San Francisco Chronicle*, March 9, 1993.
77 Court of Appeal of the State of California, *Anti-Defamation League of B'nai B'rith et al. v. Audrey Shabbas et al.*, November 16, 1998.
78 Wilcox, Laird, "Who Watches the Watchman," p. 301.
79 Friedman, Robert J, "The Anti-Defamation League Is Spying On You," *Village Voice*, May 11, 1993, in Wilcox, "Who Watches the Watchman," p. 301.
80 Zamora, Jim Herron and Ray Delgado, "The City Settles Suit for Police Spying," *San Francisco Examiner*, February 18, 1999.
81 See Friedman, "The Enemy Within."
82 Friedman, "The Enemy Within."
83 Friedman, "The Enemy Within."
84 "Hands Across the Water," *Intelligence Report*, fall 2001.
85 For more on this story see "US Support for UK Extremists," CNN.com, August 31, 2001.
86 To my knowledge a thorough study has yet to be conducted on this issue. However, a report prepared for Congress on the role of telecommunications in the commission of hate crimes, cites some examples in which the ADL and the Simon Wiesenthal Center made formal complaints to the FCC to remove offensive programming. In these cited cases the FCC decided that no action was warranted as long as the programming did not constitute an "imminent danger." See National Telecommunications and Information Administration, *The Role of Telecommunications in Hate Crimes* (Springfield VA: US Department of Commerce, 1993).
87 Liberty Lobby, *Conspiracy Against Freedom* (Washington DC: Liberty Lobby, 1986) p. 162.
88 Internal ADL documents made available as part of the discovery process of a Liberty Lobby lawsuit against the ADL, reveal that the latter exerted substantial pressure on radio station managers. Memos sent to the managers often implied that commercial pressure would be brought to bear against them if they did not stop airing the Liberty

Lobby radio program. The Liberty Lobby later reprinted these various documents in a book. See Liberty Lobby, *Conspiracy Against Freedom*, passim.
89 George and Wilcox, *Nazis, Communists, Klansmen, and Others on the Fringe*, pp. 259–60.
90 Although Stuart is Jewish and left wing in political orientation, he has consorted with right-wing extremists in the past. He has also been a fierce critic of the ADL. For more on Stuart see Coogan, Kevin, *Dreamer of the Day: Francis Parker Yockey and the Postwar Fascist International* (New York: Autonomedia, 1999).
91 "Dees Asks Booksellers To Consider Impact of Selling *The Turner Diaries*," *SPLC Report*, 26 (3), p. 3 (June, 1996).
92 The publisher, Barricade Books, was forced into bankruptcy not long after it published *The Turner Diaries* due to a libel suit brought by one Steve Wynn, who claimed that he was defamed in one of its publications. Wynn was awarded a $3 million judgment and Barricade closed down shortly after. See Griffin, Robert S., *The Fame of a Dead Man's Deeds: An Up-Close Portrait of White Nationalist William Pierce* (self-published e-book, 2000) p. 142.
93 This University of Florida study is cited in Padilla, Maria T., "Race Violence Leads to Rise in Anti-Racism Groups," *Salt Lake Tribune*, August 22, 1999, http://www.sltrib.com/1999/aug/08221999/nation_w/17231.htm.

7 Conclusion

1 Jacobs and Potter made this argument with regard to hate crime legislation, and I believe that it is applicable to the other legislative initiatives watchdog groups have sponsored as well. Jacobs, James B. and Kimberly Potter, *Hate Crimes: Criminal Law and Identity Politics* (New York: Oxford University Press, 1998) pp. 77–8.
2 Kaplan, Jeffrey, "Right Wing Violence in North America," in Tore Bjorgo (ed.), *Terror from the Extreme Right*. (London: Frank Cass, 1995), p. 75.
3 Malecki, Edward S. and H. R. Mahood, *Group Politics: A New Emphasis* (New York: Charles Scribner's Sons, 1972) p. 152.
4 Using the most recent financial data available on guidestar.org (fiscal year 2000), these four watchdog groups have as a mean, assets of $496,295 and an annual income of $650,478. Financial data on far-right organizations are extremely difficult to come by. In fact I could only find one such organization available on Guidestar – the New Century Foundation (an arm of American Renaissance), which had assets $325,555 and an annual income of $170,897 for fiscal year 2001. As mentioned in Chapter 3, the ADL estimates that Resistance Records – a subsidiary of the National Alliance – has the potential to draw in one million dollars in sales per year. That would make it one of the wealthiest organizations in the far-right movement, but still on nowhere near the financial footing of the top watchdogs. In sum, the watchdog organizations are at the present time almost infinitely better financed than their ideological opponents.
5 Rosenthal, Alan, *The Third House: Lobbyists and Lobbying in the States* (Washington DC: Congressional Quarterly Press, 1993) p. 214.
6 Wilson, Graham K., *Interest Groups* (Cambridge MA: Blackwell, 1990) p. 40.
7 Malecki and Mahood, *Group Politics*, p. 303.
8 An increasing awareness on an issue helps the interest group shape public opinion on that particular issue as well. See Kollman, Ken, *Outside Lobbying: Public Opinion and Interest Group Strategies* (Princeton NJ: Princeton University Press, 1998) p. 156.
9 This incident speaks volumes for Theodore Lowi's normative finding that interest group involvement can at times distort governmental authority, as explained in Ornstein and Elder, *Interest Groups, Lobbying and Policymaking*, p. 16.

10 Hewitt, Christopher, "Patterns of American Terrorism 1955–1998: An Historical Perspective on Terrorism-Related Fatalities 1955–98," *Terrorism and Political Violence*, 12 (1), pp. 1–14, 12 (2000).

11 The high-profile defense attorney and civil libertarian, Alan Dershowitz, along with US Appeals Court Judge Stephen Trott, acknowledged that informants are essential in criminal investigations. Trott commented, "Informers are very important. They give you leads and tips. They tell you where the guns are buried." See Curriden, Mark, "No Honor Among Thieves," *ABA Journal*, June 1989. In a study on US spy culture, Jim Redden agreed, but also called for a balance which, takes into account privacy and civil liberty concerns. Redden, Jim, *Snitch Culture* (Venice CA: Feral House, 2000) p. 64.

12 The FBI's Buck Revell commented that after the House of Representative's Judiciary Committee held hearings on the FBI's handling of its investigation into the Committee in Solidarity with the People of El Salvador (CISPES) in 1988, that the bureau's counter-terrorism section was "effectively neutralized." The various censures and removals resulting from the House investigation devastated morale, and according to Revell, the FBI had to practically "order people to work on counter-terrorism." Revell, Oliver "Buck," *A G-Man's Journal* (New York: Pocket Star Books, 1998) p. 349.

13 For example, as mentioned in Chapter 5, the FBI spent two years investigating one Alex Curtis under its "Operation Lone Wolf." Curtis' alleged offenses were amateurish and should probably have been handled by local authorities; they did not really warrant such involvement from the FBI. For more on this investigation see the FBI's report "Operation Lone Wolf," 2000, http://www.fbi.gov/majcses/lonewolf1/htm.

14 This is according to Ivan C. Smith, former head of the Analysis, Budget and Training section of the FBI's National Security Division. See Sperry, Paul, "Why FBI Missed Islamic Threat," *WorldNetDaily*, July 25, 2002, http://www.worldnetdaily.com/news/printer-friendly.asp?ARTICLE_ID=28400.

15 The report was released in 1999. David Holmes, at that time the head of security, is now a security official in the Department of Transportation's Transportation Security Agency. See Sperry, Paul, "TSA Honcho Nixed Islamic Groups in Terror Report," *WorldNetDaily*, July 23, 2002, http://www.worldnetdaily.com/news/printer-friendly.asp?ARTICLE_ID=28374.

16 Coulson and Shannon, *No Heroes*, p. 415.

17 Interview with Buck Revell, February 16, 2001.

18 Interview with Ed Meese, August 31, 2000.

19 According to some accounts a BATF agent, Bernard Butkovich, infiltrated the neo-Nazi Party involved in the Greensboro Massacre and encouraged the members to bring weapons to the anti-Klan rally at which five members of the Communist Workers Party were slain. Redden, *Snitch Culture*, p. 87.

20 According to a July 2000 phone conversation I had with Steve Berry, a Supervisory Special Agent with the FBI's National Press Office, this outreach program does not extend to other groups in the far right beyond the Patriot/Militia movement.

21 For more on the FBI's Militia Outreach Program see Duffy, James E. and Alan C. Brantley, "Militias: Initiating Contact," *Law Enforcement Bulletin*, July 1997, http://www.fbi.gov/library/leb/1997/july975.htm.

22 Crelinsten, Ronald D., "Terrorism and Counter-Terrorism in a Multi-Centric World: Challenges and Opportunities," in Taylor, Max and John Horgan, *The Future of Terrorism* (London: Frank Cass, 1999) pp. 192–3.

23 A similar recommendation is made in King, Dennis and Chip Berlet, "ADLgate," *Tikkun*, 8 (4), pp. 101–2 (1993).

24 Combining Hewitt's figure of 501 domestic terrorist fatalities for the period 1958–98 with the fatalities resulting from the Oklahoma City bombing sums to a figure of 669. The number of gang-related deaths in L.A. for 1991 exceeded 700. Katz, Jesse, "Gang Killings in LA County Top a Record of 700," *Los Angeles Times*, December 8, 1991, A1, pp. 24, 26.
25 Center for Democratic Renewal, *The Changing Face of White Supremacy* (Atlanta GA: CDR, 1996).
26 Lipset, Seymour Martin and Earl Raab, *The Politics of Unreason: Right Wing Extremism in America, 1790–1970* (New York: Harper and Row, 1970) pp. 499–503.
27 Lipset and Raab, *The Politics of Unreason: Right Wing Extremism in America*, p. 506.
28 This theory is further developed in Kaplan, Jeffrey, and Leonard Weinberg, *The Emergence of a Euro-American Radical Right* (New Brunswick NJ: Rutgers University Press, 1998). In essence, the "Euro-American radical right," as they call it, seeks to develop a new identity based on race and civilization that transcends national borders.
29 Mudde, Cas, *The Ideology of the Extreme Right* (Manchester: Manchester University Press, 2000) p. 171.
30 The American legal position on hate speech is *sui generis* compared to other Western counties, and the latter are much more restrictive on issues of free speech. For example, a French court ordered National Front leader Jean-Marie LePen to pay a fine for his trivializing remark that the Jewish Holocaust of World War II was only "a detail of history." There is no codified free speech protection in England, and its 1965 Race Relations Act has been used to mute the discourse of British far-right groups. Because of First Amendment protections, America has become the propaganda mill of sorts for the international far right, as American right-wing groups supply their comrades in other countries with printed literature often in the language of the recipient countries. A case in point is the American neo-Nazi Gerhard Lauck, whose NSDAP-AO supplies literature to the "neo-fascist International" in about ten different European languages.
31 As mentioned in Chapter 3, George Lincoln Rockwell made overtures to President Gamel Abdul Nasser of the United Arab Republic, and even considered becoming a registered foreign agent of Arabic governments. During the late 1970s and early 1980s, members of a small German neo-Nazi group, *Hoffmann-Wehrsportgruppe*, reportedly received paramilitary training under the auspices of the Fatah faction in camps in Jordan. See Hoffman, Bruce, *Right-Wing Terrorism in Europe since 1980* (Santa Monica CA: Rand Corporation, 1984) pp. 6–7. In 1989 Libyan leader Mu'ammar Qadhafi hosted various far-right individuals from North America and Europe in an effort to create an anti-Zionist united front. Kinsella, Warren, *Web of Hate: Inside Canada's Far Right Network* (Toronto: Harper Perennial, 1995) pp. 258–9, 276, 295–6.
32 John Miller, "Osama Bin Laden: The ABC Interview," May 18, 1998.
33 Interview with Buck Revell, February 16, 2001.
34 Interview with Pövl Riis-Knudsen, August 15, 2000.
35 Fukuyama, Francis, *The End of History and the Last Man* (New York: The Free Press, 1992).
36 Moynihan, Patrick Daniel, *Pandemonium: Ethnicity in International Politics* (New York: Oxford University Press, 1993).
37 Huntington, Samuel P., *The Clash of Civilizations: Remaking of World Order* (New York: Touchstone, 1996).
38 Weinberg and Eubank argue that the wave of street-corner assaults by youth gangs in European cities in the 1990s constitute a form of inter-civilization conflict. Weinberg, Leonard and William Eubank, "Terrorism and the Shape of Things to Come," in Taylor, Max and John Horgan, *The Future of Terrorism* (London: Frank Cass, 1999) p. 104.

258 *Notes*

39 As Tocqueville saw it, the three major races which inhabited North America in the early part of the nineteenth century (Native Americans, European Americans and African Americans), were on a collision course to racial violence. He was not sanguine that the three races could coexist peacefully on the continent; he believed that ultimately one race would rule over the others or widespread racial expulsions would result in racially homogeneous regions in the hemisphere. Tocqueville, Alexis de, *Democracy in America* (New York: Harper Perennial, 1969) pp. 316–407.

40 Chittum, Thomas W., *Civil War Two: The Coming Breakup of America* (Show Low AZ: American Eagle Publications, 1996).

41 Interview with Chris Freeman, August 28, 2000.

42 For example, in the Senate by a vote of 98–0, and in the House of Representatives by a vote of 420–1, Congress passed a joint resolution authorizing President Bush to use "all necessary and appropriate force" for those responsible for the September 11 terrorist attack.

43 Herman, Susan, "The USA Patriot Act and the US Department of Justice: Losing our Balances?" *Jurist*, http://law.pitt.edu/forum/formnew40htm.

44 ADL, "ADL Applauds President Bush for Signing into Law Landmark Anti-Terrorism Bill," October 26, 2001.

45 ADL, "ADL Calls Bush Administration Military Commission Guidelines 'A Significant Step Forward,'" March 25, 2002.

46 US Department of Justice Civil Rights Division, "Civil Rights Division National Origin Working Group Initiative to Combat the Post-9/11 Discriminatory Backlash," January 16, 2002. http://www.usdoj.gov/crt/legalinfo/nordwg_mission.html.

47 Community Relations Service, "CRS Sponsors Briefing on the USA Patriot Act for Arab Americans and Muslim Leaders," December 19,2001.http://www.usdoj.gov/crs/pr12192001.htm.

48 See for example, "ADL Responds to Violence and Harassment against Arab Americans and Muslim Americans."

49 Shortly after the September 11 attack, rumors circulated on the internet that Israeli intelligence operatives in America had shadowed the Al-Qaeda terrorist hijackers, yet deliberately failed to warn American authorities. According to the rumor, Israeli nationals working in the World Trade Center were warned approximately two hours before the first plane struck the tower, and accordingly evacuated the building. David Duke asserted in his newsletter that the Jerusalem Post had reported that 4,000 Israelis were missing from the WTC and furthermore, only one Israeli was killed in the attack, which suggested Israeli foreknowledge of the terrorist plot. The rationale for failing to warn the Americans was supposed to be that the attack would so enrage the American public that it would support a broad war against those countries that sponsor terrorism in the Middle East, many of which are hostile to Israel (e.g. Iraq and Iran). For more on the ADL's analysis of these rumors see ADL, "Conspiracy Theories and Criticism of Israel in the Aftermath of Sept. 11 Attacks," November 1, 2001; and "4,000 Jews Absent During World Trade Center Attack," downloaded November 15, 2001. Both are available on the ADL's website at http://www.adl.org. For more on David Duke's allegations see "How Israeli Terrorism and American Treason Caused the September 11 Attack," *The David Duke Report*, issue 52, November, 2001.

50 See for example, Brackman, Harold, *9/11 Digital Lies: A Survey of Online Apologists for Global Terrorism* (Los Angeles: Simon Wiesenthal Center, 2001).

51 Stahl, Julie, "Greater Danger In Islamic Anti-Semitism, Expert Says," *CNS News*, October 25, 2002,http://www.cnsnews.com/ViewForeignBureaus.asp?Page=\Foreign Bureaus\archive\200210FOR.

52 Mahler, Horst, "The Fall of the Judeo-American Empire," http://vanguardnewsnetwork.com/h_mahler4htm, downloaded November 5, 2001.

53 Duke, David, "The Big Lie: The True Reason Behind the Attack of September 11," October 8, 2001, htttp://www.duke.org.
54 Taylor, Jared, "Will America Learn its Lessons? Paying the Price for Foolish Policies," *American Renaissance*, 12 (11), pp. 1–8 (November 2001).
55 Taylor, Jared, "Teaching More Millions to Hate Us," *Battleflag*, October, 2001, p. 4.
56 ADL, "New ADL Poll Shows No Anti-Semitic and Blame Israel Fallout from Sept. 11 Attack," November 2, 2001.
57 American Jewish Committee, "Talking Points: The Agenda of Islamic Extremism, the War on Terrorism and the US-Israel Alliance," October 8, 2001.
58 Simon Wiesenthal Center, "Trans-National Hate: Technology Unites Anti-Semites and Haters around the Globe," February 27, 2001.
59 Solomon, John, "US extremists' links with terror groups watched," *Salon.com*, February 28, 2002.
60 "Report: Anthrax Could be from Domestic Extremists," *CNN*, October 26, 2001.
61 Foxman, Abraham, "New Excuses, Old Hatred: Worldwide Anti-Semitism in Wake of 9/11," February 8, 2002.
62 British National Party, "Islam, Bush and the BNP," http://www.bnp.org, downloaded April 6, 2002.
63 BNP, "'Islam – a threat to us all!' BNP Launches Joint Anti-Islam Campaign with Sikhs and Hindus," http://www.bnp.org.uk, downloaded April 6, 2002.

Bibliography

Primary sources

Interviews:

Interview with Steven Barry, October 3, 2000.
Interview with Gordon Baum, August 3, 2000.
Interview with Willis Carto, December 15, 2000.
Interview with Harold Covington, July 24, 2000.
Interview with Todd Ferguson, February 2, 2001.
Interview with Chris Freeman, August 28, 2000.
Interview with Matt Hale, July 30, 2000.
Interview with Kirk Lyons, August 17, 2000.
Interview with Ken McVay, September 4, 2000.
Interview with Ed Meese, August 31, 2000.
Interview with Tom Metzger, July 7, 2000.
Interview with Norm Olson, September 8, 2000.
Interview with Dr William Pierce, July 12, 2000.
Interview with Dr Mark Pitcavage, September 6, 2000.
Interview with Mark Potok, August 18, 2000.
Interview with Buck Revell, February 16, 2001.
Interview with Pövl Riis-Knudsen, August 15, 2000.
Interview with Jared Taylor, June 25, 2000.
Interview with John Trochman, October 6, 2000.
Interview with Bill Wassmuth, September 13, 2000.

Government sources

ADL Memorandum to FBI Director William H. Webster, FBI File number 100–530–526, December 10, 1980.
Blitzer, Robert M., "FBI's Role in the Federal Response to the Use of Weapons of Mass Destruction: Statement of Robert M. Blitzer, Chief Domestic Terrorism/Counter-terrorism

Planning Section FBI before the US House of Representatives Committee on National Security," November 4, 1997.
Bureau of Justice Assistance, *A Policymaker's Guide to Hate Crimes* (Washington DC: Bureau of Justice Assistance, 1997).
Caldera, Louis, Memorandum on Army Policy on Extremist Activities, March 14, 2000.
Court of Appeal of the State of California, *Anti-Defamation League of B'nai B'rith* et al.*v. Audrey Shabbas* et al., November 16, 1998.
"Deterring and Eliminating Hate Group Activities," *American Forces Information Service Defense Viewpoint*, 11 (57), http://www.defenselink.mil/speeches/1996/di1157.html.
Duffy, James E. and Alan C. Brantley, "Militias: Initiating Contact," *Law Enforcement Bulletin*, July 1997, http://www.fbi.gov/library/leb/1997/ july975.htm.
Federal Bureau of Investigation, *99 Frequently Asked Questions About the FBI*, http://www.fbi.gov/faq.htm.
——File Number 157–12589, 1976.
——"History of the Federal Bureau of Investigation,"http://www.fbi.gov.yourfbi/history/hist.htm.
——Internal Memorandum, File Number 97–3835–33, July 13, 1959.
——Internal Memorandum, File Number 157–9–2–4, September 25, 1964.
——Internal Memorandum, File number 157–9–9–1, October 15, 1964.
——Internal Memorandum, File Number 157–9–9–5, February 26, 1965.
——Internal Memorandum, File Number 157–9–8–36, May 17, 1965.
——Internal Memorandum, File Number 157–9–23, March 18, 1966.
——Internal Memorandum, File Number 157–9–27, April 20, 1966.
——Internal Memorandum, File number 44-0–1204, February 4, 1985.
——Internal Memorandum, File Number 100–487473- 50, January 23, 1987.
——Internal Memorandum, File Number: 100- 487473–67, September 10, 1987.
——Internal Memorandum, File Number: 100–487473–53X, 1987.
——"Operation Lone Wolf," 2000, http://www.fbi.gov/ majcses/lonewolf1/htm, 2001.
——"Press Release," October 20, 1999.
——"Press Release," June 30, 2000.
——"Press Release," August 25, 1999.
——*Project Megiddo* (Washington DC: US Department of Justice, 1999).
——*Terrorism in the United States: 1990* (Washington DC: FBI, 1991).
——*Terrorism in the United States 1995* (Washington DC: FBI, 1995).
——*Terrorism in the United States 1996* (Washington DC: FBI, 1996).
——*Terrorism in the United States 1996* (Washington DC: FBI, 1997).
——*Terrorism in the United States 1997* (Washington DC: FBI, 1998).
——*Terrorism in the United States 1998* (Washington DC: FBI, 1999).
Freeh, Louis, "Opening Statement of Louis J. Freeh, Director Federal Bureau of Investigation Before the Subcommittee on Terrorism, Technology, and Government Information on the Judiciary United States Senate," Washington DC, October 19, 1995.
——"Speech at the Berlin City Hall, Berlin, Germany," June 28, 1994. http://www.fbi.gov.pressrm/dirspch/94–96archives/berlin.htm.
——"The Threat to the United States Posed by Terrorists," Testimony before the US Senate Committee on Appropriations, February 4, 1999.
General Accounting Office, *Combating Terrorism: FBI's Use of Federal Funds for Counterterrorism-Related Activities (FYs 1995–98)* (Washington DC: GAO, 1998).

House Committee on Un-American Activities. *Preliminary Report on Neo-Fascist and Hate Groups* (Washington DC: Committee on Un-American Activities, 1954).

House Committee on Un-American Activities, *The Present-Day Ku Klux Klan Movement* (Washington DC: US Government Printing Office, 1967).

House of Representatives Committee on Government Reform and Oversight, *Investigation in to the Activities of Federal Law Enforcement Agencies toward the Branch Davidians*, August, 1996.

Housing and Urban Development Press Release, "Cuomo Says Million Dollar Award Sends Clear Message against Racial Discrimination on the Internet," July 20, 2000.

National Advisory Committee on Criminal Justice Standards and Goals, *Report on the Task Force on Disorders and Terrorism* (Washington DC: National Advisory Committee on Criminal Justice Standards and Goals, 1976).

National Archives and Records Administration, "Special Committee on Un-American Activities Authorized to Investigate Nazi Propaganda and Certain Other Propaganda Activities," Downloaded July 7, 2000, http:www.nara.gov/nara/legislative/house_guide/hgch22dh.html.

National Telecommunications and Information Administration, *The Role of Telecommunications in Hate Crimes* (Springfield VA: US Department of Commerce, 1993).

Office of the Attorney General Memorandum File Number 157–9–16, September 8, 1965.

Secretary of the Army's Task Force on Extremist Activities, *Defending American Values* (March 21, 1996).

"Statement of the Anti-Defamation League on Hate on the Internet Before the Senate Committee on the Judiciary," September 14, 1999.

US Congress, *Report of the Joint Select Committee to Inquire into the Condition of Affairs in the Late Insurrectionary States* (Washington DC: US Congress, 1872).

Watchdog sources

ADL Press Release, "ADL Applauds eBay for Expanding Guidelines to Prohibit the Sale of Items that Glorify Hate," May 4, 2001.

—— "ADL Commends President for Domestic Anti-Terrorism Initiative Calls on 26 States to Enact Anti-Paramilitary Training Statutes," April 24, 1998.

—— "ADL Lauds Law Enforcement for Preventing Extremist Violence with Arrest of Matt Hale," January 8, 2003.

—— "ADL Reacts to Illinois Bar Panel's Rejection of Extremist Matt Hale: Well-Intentioned Yet 'Sets a Dangerous Precedent,'" February 4, 1999.

—— "Amazon.com and Barnes&Noble.com Respond to ADL's Concerns on *Protocols* Book," March 28, 2000.

—— "Anti-Semitism Detoured on the Information Highway," February 24, 1999.

—— "Holocaust Deniers to Convene in Lebanon," February 11 2001.

Anti-Defamation League, *1999 Hate Crime Laws* (New York: Anti-Defamation League, 1998).

—— *The ADL Anti-Paramilitary Training Statute: A Response to Domestic Terrorism* (New York: Anti-Defamation League, 1995).

—— "Alex Curtis: Lone Wolf of Hate Prowls the Internet," 2000, http://www.adl.org./curtis/default.htm.

—— *The Church of the Creator: Creed of Hate* (New York: Anti-Defamation League, 1993).

——"Col. Gordon 'Jack Mohr': An Officer and a Hatemonger," *ADL Special Edition*, November, 1992.
——"Computer Millionaire$ Fund Hate: Carl Story, Vincent Bertollini and the 11th Hour Remnant Messenger," December 2000.
——*Danger: Extremism: The Major Vehicles and Voices on America's Far-Right Fringe* (New York: Anti-Defamation League, 1996).
——"David Duke Launches Appeal to Russian Nationalists," Special Report, 2001.
——"Deafening Hate: The Revival of Resistance Records," 2000.
——*Explosion of Hate: The Growing Danger of the National Alliance* (New York: Anti-Defamation League, 1998).
——*Extremism on the Right: A Handbook* (New York: Anti-Defamation League, 1988).
——"Hate and the Law: Kirk Lyons, Esq," *ADL Special Edition*, June, 1991.
——*Hate Groups in America: A Record of Bigotry and Violence* (New York: Anti-Defamation League, 1988).
——*High-tech Hate: Extremist Use of the Internet* (New York: Anti-Defamation League, 1996).
——*Hitler's Apologists: The Anti-Semitic Propaganda of Holocaust "Revisionism"* (New York: Anti-Defamation League, 1993).
——"Liberty Lobby: Network of Hate," *ADL Special Report*, 1990.
——"Louis Bean: Dedicated to Hate," *ADL Special Edition*, February, 1990.
——"Neo-Nazi Skinheads: A 1990 Status Report," 1990.
——*Not the Work of a Day: The Story of the Anti-Defamation League of B'nai B'rith* (New York: Anti-Defamation League, 1965).
——"Shaved for Battle: Skinheads Target America's Youth," 1987.
——"Shawn Slater: The Hate Movement's New Face," *ADL Special Edition*, October, 1990.
——*The Skinhead International: A Worldwide Survey of Neo-Nazi Skinheads* (New York: Anti-Defamation League, 1995).
——"Skinheads Target the Schools," 1989.
——"Tom Metzger's Long March of Hate," *ADL Special Edition*, June, 1993.
——*Vigilante Justice: Militias and "Common Law Courts" Wage War Against the Government* (New York: ADL, 1997).
——"Young and Violent: The Growing Menace of America's Neo-Nazi Skinheads," 1988.
Berlet, Chip and Mathew N. Lyons, "Repression and the Patriot and Armed Militia Movements," http://www.publiceye.org.pra/Repression-and-ideology.htm.
Center for Democratic Renewal, *The Changing Face of White Supremacy* (Atlanta GA: CDR, 1996).
——*When Hate Groups Come to Town: A Handbook of Effective Community Responses*, 2nd edn (Atlanta GA: CDR, 1992).
Center for New Community, *"Creating" a Killer: A Background Report On Benjamin "August" Smith and The World Church of the Creator* (Oak Park IL: Center for New Community, 1999).
——*Party Crashers: White Nationalists and Election 2000* (Chicago: Center for New Community, July 2000).
"Center Wins Judgement Against Neo-Nazi Leader," *SPLC Report*, 26 (2), June 1996, p. 1.
Danzig, David, *Rightists, Racists and Separatists: A White Bloc in the Making?* (New York: AJC, 1964).
"Darker Than Black," *Intelligence Report*, fall 2000.

"Dees Asks Booksellers To Consider Impact of Selling *The Turner Diaries*," *SPLC Report*, 26 (3), June 1996, p. 3.

Dees, Morris, and Steve Fiffer, *Season for Justice: The Life and Times of Civil Rights Lawyer Morris Dees* (New York: Charles Scribner's Sons, 1991).

Dees, Morris and Ellen Bowden, "Taking Hate Groups to Court," splc.org.

Epstein, Benjamin R. and Arnold Forster, *Danger on the Right: The Attitudes, Personnel and Influence of the Radical Right and Extreme Conservatives* (New York: Random House, 1964).

—— *The Radical Right: Report on the John Birch Society and Its Allies* (New York: Random House, 1967).

"FBI: Wiesenthal Center Was Terrorist's Main Target," *Response*, 20 (2), pp. 2–3 (1999).

Ferguson, Todd, "A Case Study of Racist Extremism and Disintegrative Social Sanctioning," unpublished paper, December 2000.

—— "Youth Against Hate: Anti-Racist Action as a New Citizens' Movement," unpublished paper, December 2000.

Fineberg, S. Andhil, "The Quarantine Treatment," in Newman, Edwin S. (ed.) *The Hate Reader* (New York: Oceana Publications, 1964) pp. 111–116.

Foxman, Abraham, "David Duke's *My Awakening*: A Minor League Mein Kampf," ADL Press Release, January 1999.

Hardisty, Jean and Peter Snoad, *Unmasking the Political Right: A Fifteen Year Report 1981–1996* (Sommerville MA: Political Research Associates, 1996).

"Klanwatch Director Urges Military to Discharge Troops with Extremist Ties," *SPLC Report*, 26 (3), p. 3 (September 1996).

"Neither Left nor Right," *Intelligence Report*, winter 2000.

Pitcavage, Mark, "The Council of Conservative Citizens 'in the News': A Chronology of Events," http://www.militia-watchdog.org/ccc.htm.

"Red Hot Patriot Movement Cools Down," *Intelligence Report*, spring 2000.

Schachner, Nathan, *The Price of Liberty: A History of the American Jewish Committee* (New York: The American Jewish Committee, 1948).

Southern Poverty Law Center, "Center Attorneys Craft Model Anti-militia Law," http://www.splcenter.org/ intelligenceproject/ip-6.html.

—— *The Ku Klux Klan: A History of Racism and Violence* (Montgomery AL: Southern Poverty Law Center, 1991).

Stern, Kenneth S., *Hate on the Internet* (New York: American Jewish Committee, 1999) http://www.ajc.org/pre/interneti.htm.

—— *Holocaust Denial* (New York: American Jewish Committee, 1993).

Walker, Gregory A, "A Defector in Place," *Intelligence Report*, summer 1999.

Far-right literature

Beam, Louis, "Leaderless Resistance," *The Seditionist*, issue 12, February 1992.

Carter, Jack, *In the Eye of the Storm: The True Story of Tom Metzger* (self-published, 1992).

Chittum, Thomas W., *Civil War Two: The Coming Breakup of America* (Show Low AZ: American Eagle Publications, 1996).

Covington, Harold, *The March up Country* (Reedy WV: Liberty Bell Publications, 1987).

Curtis, Alex, "Biology for Aryans," *The Nationalist Observer*, issue 21, June 2000, p. 1.

DePugh, Robert B., *Blueprint for Victory*, 4th edn (Norborne MO: Salon Publishing Company, 1978).

Duke, David, *My Awakening* (Covington LA: Free Speech Press, 1998).

Ford, Henry Sr, *The International Jew: The World's Foremost Problem*, date and publisher unknown.
Hollyoak, Eric, "The Fallacy of Leaderless Resistance," *Resistance*, issue 10, winter 2000, pp. 14–18.
Hoskins, Richard Kelly, *War Cycles, Peace Cycles, Fifth Edition* (Lynchburg VA: Virginia Publishing Company, 1994).
——*Vigilantes of Christendom: The History of the Phineas Priesthood* (Lynchburg VA: Virginia Publishing Company, 1997).
Klassen, Ben, *Nature's Eternal Religion* (Church of the Creator, 1973).
——*The White Man's Bible* (Church of the Creator, 1981).
Koestler, Arthur, *The Thirteenth Tribe* (New York: Random House, 1976).
Lane, David, *Deceived, Damned and Defiant: The Revolutionary Writings of David Lane* (St Maries ID: 14 Word Press, 1999).
Liberty Lobby, *Conspiracy Against Freedom* (Washington DC: Liberty Lobby, 1986).
——*Survival and Leaderless Resistance* (Washington DC: Liberty Lobby, 1999).
Macdonald, Andrew (pseudonym of William Pierce) *Hunter* (Hillsboro WV: National Vanguard Books, 1978).
——*The Turner Diaries* (Hillsboro WV: National Vanguard Books, 1978).
Mason, James, *Siege* (Denver CO: Storm Books, 1992).
Metzger, Thomas, *WAR Editorials 1984–1996* (self-published, 1996).
Miller, Glenn, *A White Man Speaks Out* (self-published, 1999).
National Alliance, *National Alliance Handbook* (Hillsboro WV: National Vanguard Books, 1993).
——"Who Rules America?" (Hillsboro WV: National Alliance, 2000).
New Century Foundation, *The Color of Crime: Race, Crime, and Violence in America* (Oakton VA: New Century Foundation, 1999).
Nilus, Sergius A., *The Protocols of Zion*, trans. Victor Marsden, 1934.
Peiper, Joachim, "Planning a Skinhead Infantry," *Resistance*, issue 9, fall 1999, p. 9.
Pendell, Elmer, *Why Civilizations Self-Destruct* (Cape Canaveral FL: Howard Allen, 1977).
Piper, Michael Collins, "Waco Instigator Identified," *The Spotlight*, July 31, 1995, p. 10.
——*Final Judgement: The Missing Link in the JFK Assassination Conspiracy*, 5th edn (Washington DC: Center for Historical Review, 2000).
Robertson, Wilmont, *The Dispossessed Majority, Third Edition* (Cape Canaveral FL: Howard Allen, 1981).
Rockwell, George Lincoln, *White Power* (Reedy WV: Liberty Bell Publications, 1983).
——*This Time the World*, 6th edn (Reedy WV: Liberty Bell Publications, 1993).
Schmidt, Hans, *Jailed in Democratic Germany: The Ordeal of an American Writer* (Milton FL: Guderian Books, 1997).
Taylor, Jared, *Paved with Good Intentions: The Failure of Race Relations in Contemporary America* (New York: Carroll and Graf Publishers, 1992).
Tenney, Jack B., *Zionist Network* (Arabi LA: Sons of Liberty, n.d.).
Thornton, R. Gordon, *The Southern Nation: The New Rise of the Old South* (Gretna LA: Pelican Publishing Company, 2000).
Welch, Robert H. W. Jr, *The Life of John Birch* (Chicago: Henry Regnery Company 1954).
Yockey, Francis Parker, *Imperium*, 3rd edn (Costa Mesa CA: The Noontide Press, 1991).

Secondary literature

Books

Abanes, Richard, *American Militias: Rebellion, Racism, and Religion* (Downers Grove IL: Inter Varsity Press, 1996).

Adorno, T. W., Frenkel-Brunswick, E., Levinson, D. J. and Sanford, R. N., *The Authoritarian Personality* (New York: Harper & Brothers, 1950).

Aho, James, *The Politics of Righteousness: Idaho Christian Patriotism* (Seattle WA: University of Washington Press, 1990).

Albares, Richard P, *Nativist Paramilitarism in the United States: The Minutemen* (Chicago: Center for Social Studies, 1968).

Alibrandi, Tom and Bill Wassmuth, *Hate is My Neighbor* (Ellensburg WA: Stand Together Publishers, 1999).

Barker, William E., *Aryan America: Race, Revolution and the Hitler Legacy* (St Maries ID: Falcon Ridge Publishing, 1993).

Barkun, Michael, *Religion and The Racist Right: The Origins of the Christian Identity Movement* (Chapel Hill NC: University of North Carolina Press, 1994).

Beals, Carleton, *Brass-Knuckle Crusade: The Great Know-Nothing Conspiracy: 1820–1860* (New York: Hastings House Publishers, 1960).

Bell, Daniel (ed.) *The Radical Right* (Garden City NY: Anchor Books, 1964).

Bennett, David H., *Party of Fear: From Nativist Movements to the New Right in American History* (New York: Vintage Books, 1988).

Bergen, Doris L., *Twisted Cross: The German Christian Movement in the Third Reich* (Chapel Hill NC: University of North Carolina Press, 1996).

Bjorgo, Tore (ed.) *Terror from the Extreme Right* (London: Frank Cass, 1995).

Blee, Kathleen M., *Women of the Klan: Racism and Gender in the 1920s* (Berkeley CA: University of California Press, 1991).

Bridges, Tyler, *The Rise of David Duke* (Jackson MS: University of Mississippi Press, 1994).

Broyles, J. Allen, *The John Birch Society: Anatomy of Protest* (Boston MA: Beacon Press, 1964).

Cannedy, Susan, *America's Nazis: A Democratic Dilemma* (Menlo Park CA: Markgraf Publications Group, 1990).

Carlson, John Roy, *Under Cover* (New York: E. P. Dutton, 1943).

——*The Plotters* (New York: E. P. Dutton, 1946).

Carter, Dan T., *The Politics of Rage: George Wallace, The Origins of the New Conservatism, and the Transformation of American Politics* (New York: Simon and Schuster, 1995).

Chalmers, David M., *Hooded Americanism: The History of the Ku Klux Klan*, 3rd edn (Durham NC: Duke University Press, 1981).

Cheles, Luciano, Ronnie Ferguson and Michalina Vaughan, *Neo-Fascism in Europe* (New York: Longman, 1991).

Chomsky, Noam and Edward S. Herman, *Manufacturing Consent: The Political Economy of the Mass Media* (New York: Pantheon Book, 1988).

Christensen, Loren, *Skinhead Street Gangs* (Boulder CO: Paladin Press, 1994).

Churchill, Ward, and Jim Vander Wall, *Agents of Repression: The FBI's Secret Wars Against the Black Panther Party and the American Indian Movement* (Boston MA: South End Press, 1990[a]).

——*The COINTELPRO Papers* (Boston MA: South End Press, 1990[b]).

Cleary, Edward J., *Beyond the Burning Cross* (New York: Vintage, 1994).

Coates, James, *Armed and Dangerous: The Rise of the Survivalist Right* (New York: Noonday Press, 1987).

Cohn, Norman, *Warrant for Genocide: The Myth of the Jewish World Conspiracy and the Protocols of the Elders of Zion* (London: Serif, 1996).
Coogan, Kevin, *Dreamer of the Day: Francis Parker Yockey and the Postwar Fascist International* (New York: Autonomedia, 1999).
Coppola, Vincent, *Dragons of God: A Journey through Far-Right America* (Atlanta GA: Longstreet Press, 1996).
Corcoran, James, *Bitter Harvest: Gordon Kahl and the Posse Comitatus: Murder in the Heartland* (New York: Penguin Books, 1990).
Coulson, Danny O. and Elaine Shannon, *No Heroes: Inside the FBI's Secret Counter-Terror Force* (New York: Pocket Books, 1999).
Curtin, Lawrence M. Jr, *White Extremism and the US Military* (Monterey CA: Naval Postgraduate School, 1997).
Davies, J. C. (ed.) *When Men Revolt and Why?* (New York: Free Press, 1971).
Davis, Daryl, *Klan-Destine Relationships: A Black Man's odyssey in the Ku Klux Klan* (Far Hills NJ: New Horizon Press, 1998).
Davis, James Kirkpatrick, *Spying on America: The FBI's Domestic Counterintelligence Program* (Westport CT: Praeger, 1992).
Deconde, Alexander, *Ethnicity, Race, and American Foreign Policy* (Boston MA: Northwestern University Press, 1992).
Dees, Morris, *Hate on Trial* (New York: Villard Books, 1993).
Dees, Morris and James Corcoran, *Gathering Storm: America's Militia Threat* (New York: HarperCollins, 1996).
Dennis, Lawrence and Maximilian St George, *A Trial on Trial: The Great Sedition Trial of 1944* (Torrance CA: The Institute for Historical Review, reprinted 1984).
Dixon, Thomas, Jr, *The Clansman* (New York, 1905).
Dobratz, Betty A. and Stephanie L. Shanks-Meile, *White Power, White Pride! The White Separatist Movement in the United States* (New York: Twayne Publishers, 1997).
D'Sousa, Dinesh, *The End of Racism* (New York: The Free Press, 1995).
Dyer, Joel, *Harvest of Rage: Why Oklahoma City is only the Beginning* (Boulder CO: Westview Press, 1997).
Eatwell, Roger and Noel O'Sullivan, *The Nature of the Right* (Boston MA: Twayne Publishers, 1989).
Epstein, Lee, and Thomas G. Walker, *Constitutional Law for a Changing America* (Washington DC: Congressional Quarterly Press, 1992).
Ezekiel, Raphael S., *The Racist Mind: Portraits of American Neo-Nazis and Klansmen* (New York: Viking, 1995).
Fears, Karla P., *FBI and Domestic Counterterrorism: A Comparative Analysis* (Monterey CA: The Naval Postgraduate School, 1995).
Finch, Phillip, *God, Guts, and Guns* (New York: Seaview/Putnam, 1983).
Flynn, Kevin and Gary Gerhardt, *The Silent Brotherhood* (New York: Signet, 1990).
Ford, Glyn, *Fascist Europe: The Rise of Racism and Xenophobia* (Boulder CO: Pluto Press, 1992).
Forster, Arnold, *A Measure of Freedom* (New York: Doubleday & Company, 1950).
——*Square One: The Memoirs of a True Freedom Fighter's Life-long Struggle Against Anti-Semitism, Domestic and Foreign* (New York: Donald I. Fine, 1988).
George, John and Laird Wilcox, *Nazis, Communists, Klansmen, and Others on the Fringe* (Buffalo NY: Prometheus Books, 1992).
——*American Extremists* (Buffalo NY: Prometheus Books, 1996).

Glazer, Nathan, *We are all Multiculturalists Now* (Cambridge MA: Harvard University Press, 1997).
Glick, Brian, *War at Home: Covert Action Against US Activists and What We Can Do about It* (Boston MA: South End Press, 1989).
Goldberg, J. J., *Jewish Power: Inside the American Jewish Establishment* (New York: Addison-Wesley, 1996).
Goodman, Paul, *Towards a Christian Republic: Antimasonry and the Great Transition in New England, 1826–1836* (New York: Oxford University Press, 1988).
Goodrick-Clarke, Nicholas, *The Occult Roots of Nazism: Secret Aryan Cults and Their Influence on Nazi Ideology* (New York: New York University Press, 1992).
——*Hitler's Priestess: Savitri Devi, the Hindu-Aryan Myth, and Neo-Nazism* (New York: New York University Press, 1998).
Gottlieb, Moshe R., *American Anti-Nazi Resistance, 1933–1941: An Historical Analysis* (New York: KTAV Publishing House, 1982).
Greene, Melissa Fay, *The Temple Bombing* (New York: Addison-Wesley, 1996).
Griffin, Robert S., *The Fame of a Dead Man's Deeds: An Up-Close Portrait of White Nationalist William Pierce* (self-published e-book, 2000).
Griffin, Roger, *The Nature of Fascism* (New York: Routledge, 1993).
——*Fascism*, Oxford Readers (Oxford: Oxford University Press, 1995).
Gurr, Ted, *Why Men Rebel* (Princeton NJ: Princeton University Press, 1970).
Hamm, Mark S., *American Skinheads: The Criminology and Control of Hate Crime* (Westport CT: Praeger, 1993)
——*Terrorism, Hate Crime, and Anti-Government Violence: A Preliminary Review of the Research* (Indiana: Indiana State University, 1996).
——*In Bad Company: America's Terrorist Underground* (Boston MA: Northeastern University Press, 2001).
Hasselbach, Ingo with Tom Reiss, *Führer-Ex: Memoirs of a former Neo-Nazi* (New York: Random House, 1996).
Heyman, Philip B., *Terrorism and America: A Commonsense Strategy for a Democratic Society* (Cambridge MA: MIT Press, 1998).
Hill, Ray with Andrew Bell, *The Other Face of Terror: Inside Europe's Neo-Nazi Network* (London: Grafton Books, 1988).
Hilliard, Robert L. and Michael C. Keith, *Waves of Rancor: Tuning in the Radical Right* (New York: M. E. Sharpe, 1999).
Hoffman, David, *The Oklahoma City Bombing and the Politics of Terror* (Venice CA: Feral House, 1998).
Hofstadter, Richard, *The Paranoid Style in American Politics and Other Essays* (New York: Vintage Books, 1967).
Hoffman, Bruce, *Right-Wing Terrorism in Europe since 1980* (Santa Monica CA: The Rand Corporation, 1984).
——*Holy Terror: The Implications of Terrorism Motivated by a Religious Imperative* (Santa Monica CA: The Rand Corporation, 1993).
——*Inside Terrorism* (New York: Columbia University Press, 1998).
Hrebenar, Ronald J., *Interest Group Politics in America*, 3rd edn (New York: M. E. Sharpe, 1997).
Jackson, Kenneth T., *The Ku Klux Klan in the City, 1915–1930* (New York: Oxford University Press, 1967)

Jacobs, James B. and Kimberly Potter, *Hate Crimes: Criminal Law and Identity Politics* (New York: Oxford University Press, 1998).
Jakes, Dale and Connie Jakes with Clint Richmond, *False Prophets: The Firsthand Account of a Husband-Wife Team Working for the FBI and Living in Deepest Cover with the Montana Freemen* (Los Angeles CA: Dove Books, 1998).
Jeansome, Glen, *Gerald L. K. Smith: Minister of Hate* (New Haven CT: Yale University Press, 1988).
—— *Women of the Far Right: The Mothers' Movement and World War II* (Chicago: University of Chicago Press, 1996).
Jenkins, Philip, *Hoods and Shirts: The Extreme Right in Pennsylvania, 1925–1950* (Chapel Hill NC: University of North Carolina Press, 1997).
Jones, J. Harry Jr, *The Minutemen* (Garden City NY: Doubleday & Company, 1968).
Jones, Stephen with Peter Israel, *Others Unknown: The Oklahoma City Bombing Case and Conspiracy* (New York: Public Affairs, 1998).
Kaplan, Jeffrey, *Radical Religion in America: Millenarian Movements from the Far Right to the Children of Noah* (Syracuse NY: Syracuse University Press, 1997).
—— *The Encyclopedia of White Power: A Sourcebook on the Radical Racist Right* (New York: AltaMira Press, 2000).
Kaplan, Jeffrey, and Leonard Weinberg, *The Emergence of a Euro-American Radical Right* (New Brunswick NJ: Rutgers University Press, 1998).
Katz, William Loren, *The Invisible Empire: The Ku Klux Klan Impact on History* (Seattle WA: Open Hand Publishing, 1986).
Kennedy, James Ronald and Walter Donald Kennedy, *The South was Right!* (Gretna LA: Pelican Publishing Company, 1996).
Kennedy, Stetson, *The Klan Unmasked* (Boca Raton FL: Florida Atlantic University Press, 1991).
Kinsella, Warren, *Web of Hate: Inside Canada's Far Right Network* (Toronto: Harper Perennial, 1995).
Klehr, Harvey, John Earl Jones, and Friorikh Igorevich Firssov, *The Secret World of American Communism* (New Haven CT: Yale University Press, 1995).
Kollman, Ken, *Outside Lobbying: Public Opinion and Interest Group Strategies* (Princeton NJ: Princeton University Press, 1998).
Kopel, David B. and Paul H. Blackman, *No More Wacos: What's Wrong with Federal Law Enforcement and How to Fix It* (Amherst NY: Prometheus Books, 1997).
Laqueur, Walter, *The Age of Terrorism* (Boston: Little, Brown, 1987).
—— *Black Hundred: The Rise of the Extreme Right in Russia* (New York: HarperCollins, 1993).
—— *Fascism: Past, Present, and Future* (New York: Oxford University Press, 1996).
—— *Guerrilla Warfare: A Historical Critical Study* (New Brunswick NJ: Transaction Publishers, 1998).
—— *The New Terrorism: Fanaticism and the Arms of Mass Destruction* (New York: Oxford University Press, 1999).
Lee, Martin A., *The Beast Reawakens* (New York: Little, Brown, 1997).
Levin, Jack and Jack McDevitt, *Hate Crimes: The Rising Tide of Bigotry and Bloodshed* (New York: Plenum Press, 1993).
Lifton, Robert Jay, *Destroying the World to Save it: Aum Shinrikyo, Apocalyptic Violence, and the New Global Terrorism* (New York: Metropolitan Books, 1999).
Lipset, Seymour Martin, *American Exceptionalism: A Double-Edged Sword* (New York: W. W. Norton, 1996).

Lipset, Seymour Martin and Earl Raab, *The Politics of Unreason: Right Wing Extremism in America, 1790–1970* (New York: Harper and Row, 1970).
——*Jews and the New American Scene* (Cambridge MA: Harvard University Press, 1995).
Lipstadt, Deborah, *Denying the Holocaust: The Growing Assault on Truth and Memory* (New York: The Free Press, 1993).
MacDonald, Kevin, *The Culture of Critique: An Evolutionary Analysis of Jewish Involvement in Twentieth-Century Intellectual and Political Movements* (Westport CT: Praeger, 1998[a]).
——*Separation and Its Discontents: Toward an Evolutionary Theory of Anti-Semitism* (Westport CT: Praeger, 1998[b]).
MacKenzie, Angus, *Secrets: The CIA's War at Home* (Berkeley CA: University of California Press, 1997).
MacLean, Nancy, *Behind the Mask of Chivalry: The Making of the Second Ku Klux Klan* (New York: Oxford University Press, 1994).
Malecki, Edward S. and H. R. Mahood, *Group Politics: A New Emphasis* (New York: Charles Scribner's Sons, 1972).
Marks, Kathy, *Faces of Right Wing Extremism* (Boston MA: Branden Publishing Company, 1996).
Martinez, Thomas with John Guinther, *Brotherhood of Murder* (New York: McGraw-Hill, 1988).
McGuckin, Frank (ed.) *Terrorism in the United States* (New York: H.W. Wilson, 1997).
McLagan, Graeme and Nick Lowles, *Mr. Evil* (London: John Blake Publishing, 2000).
Michel, Lou and Dan Herbeck, *American Terrorist: Timothy McVeigh and the Oklahoma City Bombing* (New York: Regan Books, 2001).
Moynihan, Michael and Didrik Soderlind, *Lords of Chaos: The Bloody Rise of the Satanic Metal Underground* (Venice CA: Feral House, 1998).
Mudde, Cas, *The Ideology of the Extreme Right* (Manchester: Manchester University Press, 2000).
Myers, Gustavus, *History of Bigotry in the United States* (New York: Random House, 1943).
National Association for the Advancement of Colored People, *Task Force Report on Community and Military Response to White Supremacist Activities In and Around Military Bases* (March 1996).
Neier, Aryeh, *Defending My Enemy* (New York: E. P. Dutton, 1979).
Nelson, Jack, *Terror in the Night: The Klan's Campaign against the Jews* (New York: Simon and Schuster, 1993).
Noble, Kerry, *Tabernacle of Hate: Why they bombed Oklahoma City* (Presscott, Ontario: Voyageur Publishing, 1998).
Oakely, Andy, *"88" An Undercover News Reporter's Exposé of American Nazis and the Ku Klux Klan* (Skokie IL: P. O. Publishing Company, 1987).
Ornstein, Norman J. and Shirley Elder, *Interest Groups, Lobbying and Policymaking* (Washington DC: Congressional Quarterly Press, 1978).
Parenti, Michael, *Inventing Reality: The Politics of the Mass Media* (New York: St Martin's Press, 1986).
Piller, E. A., *Time Bomb: America's Sinister new Fascism – Will it Explode on Schedule?* (New York: Arco Publishing Company, 1945)
Pool, James and Suzanne Pool, *Who Financed Hitler?* (New York: Dial Press, 1978).
Powers, Richard Gid, *Not Without Honor: The History of American Anticommunism* (New York: The Free Press, 1995).

Presley, Lieutenant Commander Steven Mack, USN, *The Rise of Domestic Terrorism and Its Relation to the United States Armed Forces* (Quantico VA: Marine Corps Command and Staff College, April 19, 1996).

Presthus, Robert, *Elites in the Policy Process* (New York: Cambridge University Press, 1974).

Redden, Jim, *Snitch Culture* (Venice CA: Feral House, 2000).

Reeve, Simon, *The New Jackals: Ramzi Yousef, Osama bin Laden, and the Future of Terrorism* (Boston MA: Northeastern University Press, 1999).

Reilly, Lawrence, *The Sedition Case* (Metairie LA: Sons of Liberty, 1985).

Revell, Oliver "Buck," *A G-Man's Journal* (New York: Pocket Star Books, 1998).

Richter, Michaela W., *The Verfassungsschutz* (Washington DC: American Institute for Contemporary German Studies, 1998).

Rosenthal, Alan, *The Third House: Lobbyists and Lobbying in the States* (Washington DC: Congressional Quarterly Press, 1993).

Rowe, Gary Thomas, *My Undercover Years with the Ku Klux Klan* (New York: Bantam Books, 1976).

Salamon, Lester M. and Helmut K. Anheier, *The Emerging Sector: The Nonprofit Sector in Comparative Perspective* (Baltimore MD: Johns Hopkins University Institute for Policy Studies, 1994).

Sayers, Michael and Albert E. Kahn, *Sabotage! The Secret War against America* (New York: Harper and Brothers, 1942).

Shermer, Michael and Alex Grobman, *Denying History: Who Says the Holocaust Never Happened and why Do They Say It?* (Berkeley CA: University of California Press, 2000).

Schlozman, Kay Lehman and John T. Tierney, *Organized Interests and American Democracy* (New York: Harper & Row, 1986).

Schmaltz, William H., *Hate: George Lincoln Rockwell and the American Nazi Party* (Washington DC: Brassey's, 1999).

Schmidt, Michael, *The New Reich: Violent Extremism in Unified Germany* (New York: Pantheon Books, 1993).

Schonbach, Morris, "Native Fascism during the 1930s and 1940s: A Study of its Roots, its Growth, and its Decline," (Ph.D. dissertation, University of California Los Angeles, 1958).

Schweitzer, Glenn E., *Super-Terrorism: Assassins, Mobsters, and Weapons of Mass Destruction* (New York: Plenum Trade, 1998).

Seymour, Cheri, *Committee of the States: Inside the Radical Right* (Mariposa CA: Camden Place Communications, 1991).

Shannon, David A, *The Decline of American Communism* (Chatham NJ: Chatham Bookseller, 1959).

Simonelli, Frederick J., *American Fuehrer: George Lincoln Rockwell and the American Nazi Party* (Chicago: University of Illinois Press, 1999).

Sims, Patsy, *The Klan* (New York: Stein and Day, 1978).

Smith, Brent L., *Terrorism in America: Pipe Bombs and Pipe Dreams* (Albany NY: State University of New York Press, 1994).

Smith, Geoffrey, S., *To Save a Nation: American "Extremism," the New Deal, and the Coming of World War II* (Chicago: Elephant Paperbacks, 1992).

Snow, Robert L., *The Militia Threat: Terrorists Among Us* (New York: Plenum Trade, 1999) 14–15.

Stanton, Bill, *Klanwatch: Bringing the Ku Klux Klan to Justice* (New York: Mentor, 1991).

Sterling, Claire, *The Terror Network* (New York: Berkley Books, 1986).

Stern, Kenneth S., *A Force upon the Plain: The American Militia Movement and the Politics of Hate* (New York: Simon and Schuster, 1996).

Stickney, Brandon M., *All-American Monster: The Unauthorized Biography of Timothy McVeigh* (Amherst NY: Prometheus Books, 1996).

Svonkin, Stuart, *Jews Against Prejudice: American Jews and the Fight for Civil Liberties* (New York: Columbia University Press, 1997).

Svoray, Yaron and Nick Taylor, *In Hitler's Shadow: An Israeli's Amazing Journey inside Germany's Neo-Nazi Movement* (New York: Doubleday, 1994).

Swearingen, M. Wesley, *FBI Secrets: An Agents Exposé* (Boston MA: 1995).

Thompson, Jerry, *My Life in the Klan* (Nashville TN: Rutledge Hill Press, 1988).

Tocqueville, Alexis de, *Democracy in America* (New York: Harper Perennial, 1969).

Tomajczyk, S. F., *US Elite Counter-Terrorist Forces* (Osceola WI: MBI Publishing Company, 1997).

Tougée, Albion Winegar, *The Invisible Empire* (Baton Rouge LA: Louisiana State University Press, 1989).

Trelease, Allen W., *White Terror: The Ku Klux Klan Conspiracy and Southern Reconstruction* (Baton Rouge LA: Louisiana State University Press, 1971)

Truman, David B., *The Governmental Process: Political Interests and Public Opinion*, 2nd edn (Berkeley CA: Institute of Governmental Studies, 1993).

Walker, Samuel, *Hate Speech: The History of an American Controversy* (Lincoln NE: University of Nebraska Press, 1994).

Walter, Jess, *Every Knee Shall Bow: The Truth and Tragedy of Ruby Ridge and the Randy Weaver Family* (New York: Regan Books, 1995).

Warren, Donald, *Radio Priest: Charles Coughlin, the Father of Hate Radio* (New York: The Free Press, 1996).

Welsing, Frances Cress, *The Isis Papers: The Keys to the Colors* (Chicago IL: Third World Press, 1995).

Wheaton, Elizabeth, *Code Name Greenkil: The 1979 Greensboro Killings* (Athens GA: University of Georgia Press, 1987).

Whitehead, Don, *Attack on Terror: The FBI Against the Ku Klux Klan in Mississippi* (New York: Funk & Wagnalls, 1970).

Wilcox, Laird, *Guide to the American Right: Directory and Bibliography* (Olathe KS: Laird Wilcox Editorial Research Center, 1994).

——*Crying Wolf: Hate Crime Hoaxes in America* (Olathe KS: Laird Wilcox Editorial Research Center, 1998).

——*The Watchdogs: A close look at Anti-Racist "Watchdog" Groups* (Olathe KS: Laird Wilcox Editorial Research Center, 1999).

Wilson, Graham K., *Interest Groups* (Cambridge MA: Blackwell, 1990).

Wilson, James Q., *Political Organizations* (New York: Basic Books, 1973).

Winne, Mark, *Priority Mail: The Investigation and Trial of a Mail Bomber Obsessed with Destroying Our Justice System* (New York: Scribner, 1995).

Witte, Rob (ed.) *Racist Violence and the State* (New York: Longman, 1996).

Articles

Ammerman, Nancy T., "Waco, Law Enforcement, and Scholars of Religion," in Stuart A. Wright (ed.) *Armageddon in Waco: Critical Perspectives on the Branch Davidian Conflict* (Chicago: University of Chicago Press, 1995) p. 289.

"Anti-abortion Web Site Goes on Trial," *USA Today*, January 7, 1999, http://usatoday.com/news/ndswed05.htm.

Arent, Lindsey, "Net Group Stalks L.A. Gunman," *Wired News*, August 11, 1999, http//www.wired. com/news/news/politics/story/21163.html.

Armond, Paul de, "Rock, Paper, Scissors: Counter-Terrorism, Anti-Terrorism and Terrorism," *Public Good Occasional Paper no. 6* (1997) http://www.nwcitizen.com/publicgood/reports/rockpaper/scissors/.

Barkun, Michael, "Millenarian Groups and Law Enforcement Agencies: The Lessons of Waco," *Terrorism and Political Violence*, 6 (1), pp. 75–95 (1994).

—— "Religion, Militias and Oklahoma City: The Mind of Conspiratorialists," *Terrorism and Political Violence*, 8 (1), pp. 50–64 (1996).

Barrett, Greg, "National Alliance grows quickly," *Detroit News*, July 16, 1999. http://detnews.com /1999/ nation/9907/16/07160113htm.

Billig, Michael, "The Extreme Right: Continuities in Anti-Semitic Conspiracy Theory in Post-War Europe," in Eatwell, Roger and Noel O'Sullivan (eds) *The Nature of the Right* (Boston MA: Twayne Publishers, 1989) pp. 146–66.

Billups, Andrea, "Liberty Lobby Goes under, Ends Spotlight Publication," *Washington Times*, July 10, 2000.

Blankfort, Jeffrey, "Unions Among 100s of Groups Spied on by ADL Informant," *Middle East Labor Bulletin*, V (4), p. 3, fall 1993.

Blythe, Will, "The Guru of White Hate," *Rolling Stone*, June 8, 2000, p. 100.

Brin, Herb, "ADL Travails Bring Glee to Enemies of Jews," *Heritage*, April 16, 1993, p. 1.

Center for National Security Studies, "The FBI Counter-terrorism Program," April 26, 1995.

Chafets, Zev, "Jewish Leaders' Unpardonable Role," *New York Daily News*, February 15, 2001.

"Charity of Riches!" *Montgomery Advertiser*, February 13, 1994.

"Coalition Announces Plan for Hate Crime Prevention," *US Newswire*, April 2, 2001.

Cohen-Almagor, Raphael, "Combating Right-Wing Political Extremism in Israel: Critical Appraisal," *Terrorism and Political Violence*, 9 (4), pp. 16–23 (1997).

Cole, David, "Spying on Hate," *Cal Law*, September 1, 1999, http://www.calllaw. com /weekly/last906.html.

Cowell, Alan, "US Jewish Group Sets Up Office in Berlin to Watch for Demons," *New York Times*, February 10, 1998.

Crenshaw, Martha, "The Logic of Terrorism," in Walter Reich (ed.) *The Origins of Terrorism* (Washington DC: Woodrow Wilson Center Press, 1998) pp. 7–24.

Curriden, Mark, "No Honor Among Thieves," *ABA Journal*, June 1989.

Docherty, Jayne Semnare, "There is no Cookbook for Crisis Negotiation: A Response to Stuart Wright," *Terrorism and Political Violence*, 11 (2), pp. 74–82 (1999).

"Domestic Terrorism: The FBI View," MSBC, May 30, 2000, http:www.msnbc.com/news /272286.asp.

Dougherty, Jon, "South Seeks Payback for Civil War 'Injustices,'" *WorldNetDaily*, April 8, 2001, http://www.worldnetdaily.com/news/ARTICLE_ID=22326.

Duke, Lynne, "Pittsburgh Reels from another Apparent Hate Crime," *Washington Post*, April 30, 2000, A4, p. 4.

Eddlem, Thomas, "Does SLATT Need a Watchdog?" *The New American*, 16 (19) (September 11, 2000), http://thenewamerican.come/tna2000/09–11–2000/vol6 no19_slatt.htm.

"Ex-KKK Leader Duke Pleads Guilty to Charges," Associated Press, December 18, 2002.
"FBI, Justice Make Hate Top Priority," *Jewish News of Greater Phoenix*, V (51), p. 39 (June 25, 1999).
Flanagan, Thomas, "The Politics of the Millennium," *Terrorism and Political Violence*, 7 (3), pp. 164–75 (1995).
"Former S.F. Cop Target of Probe," *San Francisco Chronicle*, January 15, 1993.
Friedman, Robert I., "The Enemy Within," *The Village Voice*, V 38 (19) (May 11, 1993).
Gallagher, Eugene V. "God and Country: Revolution as A Religious Imperative on the Radical Right," *Terrorism and Political Violence*, 9 (3), pp. 63–4 (1997).
——"Going by the Book: A Response to Stuart Wright," *Terrorism and Political Violence*, 11 (2), pp. 69–73 (1999).
George, John, "Emergence of a Euro-American Radical Right Book Review," *Menasha*, 93 (3), pp. 714–15 (September 1999).
Gibney, Frank Jr, "The Kids got in the Way," *Newsweek*, August 23, 1999, pp. 24–9.
"Gore in ADL Speech, Urges Federal Hate-crimes Law," *Jewish Bulletin News*, http://www.jewishsf.com /bk000512/usgore.shtml, downloaded March 1, 2001.
Grigg, William Norman, "Crime Fighters Converge," *The New American*, 10 (17) (August 22, 1994).
——"Racism in the Ranks," *The New American*, 12 (02) (January 22, 1996).
——"A Watchdog in Fedgov's Kennel," *The New American*, V 16 (19) (September 11, 2000).
Groenwold, Kurt, "The German Federal Republic's Response and Civil Liberties," *Terrorism and Political Violence*, 9 (4), winter 1997, pp. 136–50.
Gurr, Ted Robert, "Terrorism in Democracies," in Walter Reich (ed.) *The Origins of Terrorism* (Washington DC: Woodrow Wilson Center Press, 1998).
"Hamburg Court Convicts American Neo-Nazi Gary Lauck," *This Week in Germany*, September 6, 1996.
Hewitt, Christopher, "Patterns of American Terrorism 1955–1998: An Historical Perspective on Terrorism-Related Fatalities 1955–98," *Terrorism and Political Violence*, 12 (1), pp. 1–14 (2000[a]).
——"Responding to Terrorism," unpublished manuscript, 2000(b).
Hughes, Jay, "Racist Group Growing a Year after Member's Killing Spree," *USA Today*, A-2, July 3–4, 2000.
Isaccs, Matt, "Spy vs. Spite," *Sfweekly.com*, February 2–8, 2000.
Jordan, Michael J., "ADL Says Big Courtroom Defeat Won't Keep Group from Doing Its Job," *Jewish Telegraphic Agency*, http://www.jta.virtualjerusalem. com/index. exe?0005153.
Kaplan, David E. "Hitting before Hate Strikes: Private Groups Pick up the Slack, Is it Time for the Feds to Step up?" *US News and World Report*, September 6, 1999.
Kaplan, David E. and Mike Tharp, "Terrorism Threats at Home," *US News and World Report*, 123 (25), pp. 22–7 (December 29, 1997–January 5, 1998).
Kaplan, Jeffrey, "Right Wing Violence in North America," in Tore Bjorgo (ed.) *Terror from the Extreme Right* (London: Frank Cass, 1995).
——"Leaderless Resistance," *Terrorism and Political Violence*, 9 (3), pp. 80–95 (1997).
"Kansas Citian Wins 'Genius Grant' for Work Studying Hate Groups," *Hannibal Courier-Post*, June 3, 1998, http://www.fast-floweres.com/~hannibal/stories/060398/ genius-grant.html.

Katz, Jesse, "Gang Killings in L.A. County Top a Record of 700," *Los Angeles Times*, December 8, 1991, A1, pp. 24, 26.

King, Dennis and Chip Berlet, "ADLgate," *Tikkun*, 8 (4), pp. 101–2 (1993).

Klaidman, Daniel and Michael Isikkoff, "The Feds' Quiet War: Inside the Secret Strategy to Combat the Militia Threat," *Newsweek*, 128, April 22, 1996, p. 47.

Lackey, Tom, "Montana Freemen Leaders Get Long Prison Terms, but Wives Walk," Associated Press, March 17, 1999.

Lipset, Seymour Martin, "Failures of Extremism," *Society*, January/February, 1998.

Lodhi and C. Tilly, "Urbanization, Crime, and Collective Violence in 19th Century France," *Journal of Sociology*, 2 (1972).

McDonald, Karen and Andy Kravetz, "Some Feel the World Church Will Falter, and Hale is Capable of Crime," *Peoria Journal Star Online*, January 9, 2003, http://www.pjstar.com/news/topnews/hold/ g135498a.html.

Meek, James Gordon, "Cops Get Guides to Hate Crimes," APB News, December 14, 2000.

Methvin, Eugene H., "Anti-terrorism: How Far?" in Frank McGuckin (ed.) *Terrorism in the United States* (New York: H. W. Wilson Company, 1997).

Minta, John, "Militias Meet the Senate With Conspiracies to Share," *Washington Post*, June 16, 1995, A1, p. 10.

Morain, D., "Lean Times Don't Imperil Wiesenthal Grant," *Los Angeles Times*, July 19, 1995.

Murphy, Kim, "Jury Verdict Could Bankrupt Aryans," *Los Angeles Times*, September 8, 2000.

Murray, Frank J., "Court Delays Move on KKK Road Signs," *Washington Post*, October 31, 2000, A11, p. 11.

Noble, Kerry, "In Response to Stuart Wright," *Terrorism and Political Violence*, 11 (2), pp. 83–6 (1999).

Padilla, Maria T., "Race Violence Leads to Rise in Anti-Racism Groups," *Salt Lake Tribune*, August 22, 1999, http://www.sltrib. com/1999/ aug /08221999/ nation_w/17231.htm.

Pate, James L., "Witch-Hunt for the Resister," *Soldier of Fortune*, February, 1996, p. 96.

"Pentagon Plans Domestic Terrorism Team," *Washington Post*, February 1, 1999, A2, p. 2.

"Police Said to Aid Spying on Political Groups," *San Francisco Chronicle*, March 9, 1993.

Rapoport, David C., "Fear and Trembling: Terrorism in Three Religious Traditions," *American Political Science Review*, 78, pp. 658–77 (September, 1984).

Risen, James, "Militia Leaders Bring Their Fiery Talk to Capitol Hill," *Washington Times*, June 16, 1995, A1, p. 26.

Rosenlum, Rebecca, "Justice Dept. Investigating World Church of the Creator," *Jewish Bulletin News*, August 20, 1999(a).

——"FBI Surveillance of Hate Groups Critical, Jewish Leaders Assert," *Jewish Bulletin of Northern California*, September 3, 1999(b).

Segal, David. "The Pied Piper of Racism," *Washington Post*, January 12, 2000, C1, p. 8.

Shapiro, Joseph P., "Hitting before Hate Strikes," *US News and World Report*, September 6, 1999, pp. 56–7.

Silverstein, Ken, "The Church of Morris Dees: How The Southern Poverty Law Center Profits from Intolerance," *Harper's Magazine*, November, 2000, pp. 54–7.

Smith, Brent L. and Kelly R. Damphousse, "Two Decades of Terror," in Kushner, Harvey W. (ed.) *The Future of Terrorism: Violence in the New Millennium* (Thousand Oaks CA: Sage, 1998).

Sprinzak, Ehud, "The Process of Delegitimation: Towards a Linkage Theory of Political Terrorism," *Terrorism and Political Violence*, 3 (1), spring 1991, pp. 50–68.

Stahl, Julie, "Greater Danger In Islamic Anti-Semitism, Expert Says," *CNS News*, October 25, 2002, http://www.cnsnews.com/ViewForeignBureaus.asp?Page=\ForeignBureaus\archive\200210FOR.

Stewart, Sally Ann, "FBI: LA Race War Plot 'Despicable,'" *USA Today*, July 16–18, 1993, p. a-1.

"US Air Force Sued Under Freedom of Information Act," *Citizens Informer*, May-June, 2000, p. 23.

Vise, David A. "Fugitive Neo-Nazi From Germany is Captured in W. Va," *Washington Post*, August 29, 2000, A02.

Walsh, Edward, "'Appalled' Reno Pledges Review of Midwest Shootings," *Washington Post*, July 9, 1999, A12, p. 12.

Weinberg, Leonard, book review of Laqueur, Walter, *The New Terrorism: Fanaticism and the Arms of Mass Destruction* (New York: Oxford, 1999), *Terrorism and Political Violence*, 12 (1), pp. 125–8 (2000).

Weinberg, Leonard, Elizabeth Francis and Randall D. Lloyd, "Courts Under Threat," *Terrorism and Political Violence*, 11 (2), p. 95 (1999).

Wessler, Stephen, *Promising Practices Against Hate Crimes: Five State and Local Demonstration Projects* (Washington DC: Bureau of Justice Asssistance, May 2000) p. 7.

Wright, Stuart A., "Construction and Escalation of a Cult Threat," in Stuart A. Wright, *Armageddon in Waco: Critical Perspectives on the Branch Davidian Conflict* (Chicago: University of Chicago Press, 1995) pp. 88–9.

——"Anatomy of a Government Massacre: Abuses of Hostage-Barricade Protocols during the Waco Standoff," *Terrorism and Political Violence*, 11 (2), pp. 39–68 (1999[a]).

——"Cookbook or Cooking the Books?: A Rejoinder to Gallagher, Docherty and Noble," *Terrorism and Political Violence*, 11 (2), pp. 87–92 (1999[b]).

Zamora, Jim Herron and Ray Delgado, "The City Settles Suit for Police Spying," *San Francisco Examiner*, February 18, 1999.

Index

affirmative action 10
Afghan *Mujihadeen* 7
Al-Qaeda 194
American interest group structure 11, 13–15; non-governmental organizations (NGOs) 14; Protestantism 13; volunteerism 13
American Jewish Committee (AJC) 8, 12, 18–19; dynamic silence 18–19; finances 19, 191; government authorities 18
American Nazi Party 16, 19, 43, 67–8, 113
American Protective Association (APA) 42
American Renaissance 55–8, 60, 204; civil liberties implications 192–3; race 55–8
anti-abortion groups 1
Anti-Defamation League (ADL) 8, 10–11, 15–18, 60, 89; American Nazi Party 16; anti-Semitism 10; Christian National Party 16; finances 16, 191; HateFilter 180; intelligence sharing 181–6; John Birch Society 16–17, 45; Liberty Lobby 17; National Alliance 17; San Francisco Spy Scandal 183–6; Second Era Ku Klux Klan 132; September 11 2001 204; training/educational programs 180–1; US Dept Justice 15; *Y2K Paranoia* 155
anti-democracy 5
anti-globalists 127
Anti-Masonic Party 40–1, 44
anti-paramilitary training statutes 171–2
Anti-Racist Action (ARA) 8, 11–12, 35–8; finances 37
anti-Semitism 6, 10, 198
anti-statism 6
anti-Zionism 198–202
Aryan Nations 50, 66, 98, 104; civil suit 177–8; internet 179; September 11 2001 205
Aryan Republican Army 112

Atwater, Lee 71

bacteriological warfare 126–7
Barr, Bob 53
Barry, Steven 161–2; leaderless resistance 120–1
Baum, Gordon Lee 53, 55
Baumhammers, Richard Scott 75, 106, 119
Beach, Henry L. 46
Beam, Louis 115–16, 144–5, 171–2; phantom cell model 115–16
Belgium: Vlams Blok 5
Bellant, Russ 30
Bennett, David 41
Berlet, Chip 3–4, 27–30
Black, Don: Stormfront 179
Blodgett, Todd 71
Bo Gritz: September 11 2001 205
Bond, Julian 22
Brady Bill 44, 47
Branch Davidians 107, 147–9, 192
Brandenburg v. Ohio 163–4
British National Party: September 11 2001 206
Brookings, Clifford 50–1
Brown Scare 129, 133–7; German American Bund 133–4; Great Sedition Trial 1944 135–7
Brown v. Topeka Board of Education 137
Brüder Schweigen Strike Force II 32, 103
Bryant v. Zimmermann 132
Buchanan, Pat 33
Butler, Richard 30, 66
Caldera, Louis: Policy on Extremist Activities 160
Cameron, William 64
Carlson, John Roy: *Under Cover* 135–6, 186
Carto, Willis 17, 67–8, 81–5; Center for

Historical Review 87; Institute for Historical Review 86–90
Center for Democratic Renewal (CDR) 8, 10, 12, 25–7, 201; finances 27, 191; Greensboro Massacre 25, 96–7; National Anti-Klan Network (NAKN) 25; right-wing extremists 197
Center for New Community 8, 12, 32–3; finances 33, 191; *Midwest Action Report* 32
Chenowith, Helen 52
Chomsky, Noam 70
Christian Identity 2, 52, 65–6, 73; leaderless resistance 114–17; and terrorism 124
Christian National Party 16
Christian Patriot movement 4, 12, 44–52, 66, 107; John Birch Society 44–5; militia movement 46–52; Minutemen 45–6; Posse Comitatus 46
Christopher, Joseph 105
Church of Jesus Christ Christian 66
civil liberties implications 192–3
civil litigation watchdog: Southern Poverty Law Center (SPLC) 12, 21–5
civil suit use to silence far right 176–9
COINTELPRO *see* Federal Bureau of Investigation (FBI)
Columbians 67
common law courts 172–3; paper terrorism 172–3
Confederate Society of America 59
Congress 129, 155–8; House Un-American Activities Committee (HUAC) 155–6; recent investigations 156–8
conservative right wing 3
conspiracy view of history 6
Cooper, Rabbi Abraham 81
Coughlin, Father: Christian Front 42
Council of Conservative Citizens (CofCC) 52–5, 59; civil liberties implications 192–3
counter-terrorism 7–8, 194–7
Covenant, Sword, and Arm of the Lord (CSA) 103–4; Hostage Rescue Team 143; McVeigh, Timothy 110
Covington, Harold 96–7
Cult Awareness Network (CAN) 192; Waco 148
Curtis, Alex: leaderless resistance 118–20, 206; *Nationalist Observer* 118–19

de Tocqueville, Alexis 13, 201
Dees, Morris S. 11, 21–5, 49, 144, 186; United Klans of America (UKA) 176–7
Defending American Values 159–609
democracy: low regard 6
Dept of Defense (DOD) 130, 158–62; Caldera's Policy on Extremist Activities 160; *Defending American Values* 159–60; Special Forces Underground 161–2; Weinberger's restrictions in armed forces 158–9
DePugh, Robert Bolivar 45–6; cellular model 114
Dershowitz, Alan 80
Detroit Constitutional Militia 51
Diamond, Sara 30
Digital Hate 2000 180
Doggett, Ron 60–1
Duke, David 53, 60–2; internet 179; Knights of the Ku Klux Klan 62

eco-terrorists 1
economic rights 10
Ellison, Jim 103–4, 110, 144
environmentalism 10
ethnic chauvinism 6
European-American Unity and Rights Organization (EURO) 60–2

far right: anti-statism 6; confrontation 186–8; conspiracy view of history 6; definition 3–6; development of theoretical approach 113–23; and domestic terrorism 8; low regard for democracy 6; particularism 5–6; racial/ethnic component 6; significance 197–202, *see also* far right contemporary overview
far right contemporary overview 39–92; Christian Patriot movement 44–52; historical background 40–4; Holocaust 85–90; Liberty Lobby 81–5; non-revolutionary racialist right 52–64; revolutionary racialist right 64–81
far right and terrorism, development of theoretical approach 113–23; Know-Nothing movement 93; Reconstruction Era Ku Klux Klan 93; right-wing terrorism patterns 94–6; right-wing terrorism significant episodes 96–112; Second Era Ku Klux Klan 93, *see also* far right; far right contemporary overview

Farmer, Milliard 24
fascism 4
Federal Bureau of Investigation (FBI) 1, 129, 141–55; Brown Scare 134–5; COINTELPRO 68, 139–41, 194–5; CONPLAN 154; Counter-terrorism Center 153; Counter-terrorism Division 154; Critical Incident Response Group (CIRG) 151; Hoover, J. Edgar 134–5, 139–41; Hostage Rescue Team 143; intelligence sharing 181–6; Levy Guidelines 141–3; Montana Freemen 151–2; National Directive Preparedness Office 153; National Infrastructure Protection Center (NIPC) 153; new initiatives 152–5; Oklahoma City bombing 149–51; Oklahoma City National Memorial Institute 154; Operation Clean Sweep 143–5; Presidential Decision Directive (PDD) 153; *Project Megiddo* 154–5; Ruby Ridge 145–7; terrorism 7, 125–6; Waco 147–9
Ferguson, Todd 35–8
Fineberg, Solomon Andhil 18
Fleming, Thomas 59
Fordice, Kirk 53
Fortier, Michael 106
Foxman, Abraham 18, 55, 61–2, 204; internet 205–6
Francis, Sam 55
Frank, Leo 15
Frankfurt School 43
Franklin, Joseph Paul 75, 105
Freeman, Chris 25–6, 201
Freemasons 49–50
Friends of the New Germany 66, 155
Fuller, Milliard 21
Furrow, Buford O'Neal 20, 106, 121

Gale, William Potter 46
Gayman, Dan 66
George, John 65
German American Bund 66, 133–4, 136, 155; Kuhn, Fritz 134
Germany, Deutsche Volksunion 5; Office of the Protection of the Constitution 2; Republikaner Party 5
Gilbert, Keith 45
Gliebe, Eric 71–3
Goldman, David 35; Paragraph175.org 35
Great Sedition Trial 1944 135–7, 186
Greensboro Massacre 25, 96–7
Griffin, Nick 62, 206

Griffin, Roger 4
Gutstadt, Richard 15

Habitat for Humanity 21
Haider, Jörg 202
Hale, Matt 32, 79–80
Hardisty, Jean 27, 30
Harris, David A. 19
hate crime legislation 173–6
HateFilter 180
Hatewatch 8, 12, 35, 179
Hewitt, Chris 94–5, 123–4, 193
Hier, Rabbi Marvin 20
Hill, Michael 59
historical background 40–4, 130–41; American Nazi Party 43; American Protective Association (APA) 42; Anti-Masonic Party 40–1, 44; Brown Scare 133–7; COINTELPRO 139–41; John Birch Society 43; Know-Nothing movement 41; Ku Klux Klan 41–2; McCarthyism 43; National Renaissance Party 43; National States' Rights Party 43; Reconstruction Era Ku Klux Klan 130–2; Second Era Ku Klux Klan 42, 132–3; Third Era Ku Klux Klan 43, 137–9; World War II 42
Holocaust revisionism 85–90; Zündelsite 87–9
Hoover, J. Edgar 134–5, 139–41
Hoskins, Richard Kelly 66; leaderless resistance 116–17
House Un-American Activities Committee (HUAC) 129, 155–6
Huberty, James Olive 105
Huffington, Arianna 55
Hunter 116–18
Huntington, Samuel: clash of civilizations 201

Independent Order of B'Nai B'rith 15
Institute for Historical Review (IHR) 86–90; September 11 2001 205–6
intelligence sharing 181–6, 193–7; ADL San Francisco spy scandal 183–6
international cooperation 167–9
internet 104; and far right 179–80
internet-based watchdog groups 12, 33–5; Hatewatch 35; Militia Watchdog 34; Nizkor Project 33–4
Irving, David 86
Israel: Kach movement 2

Italian American Fascist League of North America 42

Jewish defense organizations 11, 15–21; American Jewish Committee (AJC) 18–19; Anti-Defamation League (ADL) 15–18; Simon Wiesenthal Center (SWC) 19–21
John Birch Society (JBS) 16–17, 43–5, 73; Illuminati 45; Insiders 45; *New American* 45; resistance approach 114
Johnson, Eddie 62
Johnson, J. J. 50

Kahl, Gordon 46, 104, 116; Posse Comitatus 97–8
Kaplan, Jeffrey 4–5, 64, 66–7, 114, 198
Kennedy, Robert 45
King, John 75
Klassen, Ben 78, 80
Knights of the Ku Klux Klan 73; Duke, David 62
Know-Nothing movement 41, 93
Koehl, Matt 68
Koresh, David 147–9, 156–7
Ku Klux Klan 15, 23, 41–2, 62–4; Duke, David 63; Greensboro Massacre 96–7; McVeigh, Timothy 107; Women of the Ku Klux Klan 63
Kuhn, Fritz: German American Bund 42, 134

Lane, David: leaderless resistance 118
Laqueur, Walter 3
LaRaza 60
Le Pen, Jean-Marie 62, 202
leaderless resistance 104–6, 114–15; Baumhammers, Richard 106; Christopher, Joseph 105; Franklin, Joseph Paul 105; Furrow, Buford 106; Huberty, James Olive 105; internet 104; Moody, Walter Leroy 105; Rice, David Lewis 106; Rudolph, Eric 106; Smith, Benjamin 106; Spisak, Frank 105
League of the South 55, 59–60; civil liberties implications 192–3
Lefkow, Joan Humphrey 81
Levin, Joseph J. 21
Levin, Michael 58
Levy Guidelines 141–3
Liberty Lobby 17, 68, 81–5, 119, 206; *Spotlight* 81–2

Lipset, Seymour Martin 13; American creed 13
Lipstadt, Deborah 86
Livingston, Simon 15
Lott, Trent 53
Lyons, Kirk 59, 144–5, 151–2
Lyons, Matthew N. 4

McCarthy, Jamie 88
McCarthyism 43
McVay, Ken 33–4, 88
McVeigh, Timothy 75, 106–12, 192; *Turner Diaries* 107
McWhiney, Grady 59
Makashov, Albert 62
Matthews, Robert Jay 98–103, 116
Metzger, Tom 24, 73–6, 103, 111–12; law suit 177; leaderless resistance 120–1
Michigan Militia 48, 106, 111, 157; September 11 2001 206
militia measures 171–3; anti-paramilitary training statutes 171–2; common law courts 172–3
militia movement 46–52, 124; Aryan Nations 50; Christian Identity 52; Detroit Constitutional Militia 51; Freemasons 49–50; Michigan Militia 48; Montana Freemen 51; Mountaineer Militia 51; New World Order 48–9; Ohio Organized Militia 50; paper terrorism 124; Patriot movement 47, 52; Ruby Ridge 47; Waco 47
Militia Watchdog 8, 12, 34, 179; finances 34; State and Local Anti-Terrorist Training Program (SLATT) 34
Miller, Glen 103, 144, 171, 186
Minutemen 45–6; resistance approach 114
miscellaneous: Anti-Racist Action 35–8
Montana Freemen 51, 124, 151–2; paper terrorism 151–2
Moody, Walter Leroy 105
Mountaineer Militia 51
Mudde, Cas: right-wing extremism 5, 198

National Alliance 17, 68–73, 103, 107; National Vanguard Books 70–1; Order 98; Resistance Records 71; *Spotlight* 108; ZOG 70, 103
National Anti-Klan Network (NAKN) 25
National Association for the Advancement of Colored People (NAACP) 60
National Renaissance Party 43, 67
National Socialism 6, 66–8

National Socialist Liberation Front (LSLF) 113
National States' Rights Party 43
nationalism 5
Nationalist Observer: Curtis, Alex 118–19
Nationalist Socialist Party of America: Greensboro Massacre 96–7
neo-Confederates 58–60; American Renaissance 60; Confederate Society of America 59; Council of Conservative Citizens (CofCC) 59; Kennedy brothers 58–9; League of the South 59–60; Rockford Institute 60; Sons of Confederate Veterans 59; Southern Legal Resource Center (SLRC) 59; Southern Military Institute 59; Southern Party 59; United Daughters of the Confederacy 59
Neo-Nazis 2
Netherlands: Centrumdomocraten 5; Centrumparti '86 5
New Order 68
New World Order 48–9
Nichols, Terry 106
Nicholson, Jim 54–5
Nizkor Project 8, 12, 33–4, 179; Zündelsite 88
Noble, Kerry 110
non-governmental organizations (NGOs) 2–3, 8–9, 14; effectiveness 190–2; prosecutions 186
non-revolutionary racialist right 52–64; American Renaissance 55–8; Council of Conservative Citizens (CofCC) 52–5; European-American Unity and Rights Organization (EURO) 60–2; Ku Klux Klan 62–4; neo-Confederates 58–60
Northwest Coalition Against Malicious Harassment (NWC) 8, 12, 30–2; Aryan Nations 30–2; finances 32, 191; *Northwest Beacon* 31

Odinism 77–8
Ohio Organized Militia 50
Oklahoma City bombing 1, 29, 34, 106–12, 149–51, 157; Fortier, Michael 149; Nichols, Terry 149; technology 124–5
Olson, Norman 48–50, 111, 150–1, 157, 206
Operation Clean Sweep 143–5, 188; Fort Smith sedition trial 1988 144–5

Order 98–104, 124; cellular model 114
Order II 103
Osama Bin Laden 7, 121, 199

paper terrorism 172–3
Paragraph175.org: Goldman, David 35
Parenti, Michael 70
particularism 5–6
Patler, John 68
Patriot movement 47–52
Pelley, William Dudely: Silvershirts 42
Peters, Pete 47, 66, 114–15
Peyson, Wally 46
Phineas Priests 116–17
Pierce, William 17, 24, 68–73; foreign policy 199; *Hunter* 116–18; leaderless resistance 120–3; September 11 2001 205; *The Turner Diaries* 68, 98–103
Piper, Mike 81–2
Pitcavage, Mark 17, 34; State and Local Anti-Terrorism Training (SLATT) 181
Political Research Associates (PRA) 8, 10, 12, 27–30; finances 30, 191; Midwest Research 27; *The Public Eye* 29
Posse Comitatus 46, 97–8; September 11 2001 205
Potok, Mark 22, 55, 60, 81, 186
producerism 4
progressive-oriented watchdog groups 11, 25–30; Center for Democratic Renewal (CDR) 25–7; Political Research Associates (PRA) 27–30
Protestantism 13
public policy recommendations 193–7
Puerto Rican separatists 1, 127

racial/ethnic component 6
racism 5–6
Rassinier, Paul 86
R.A.V. v. St Paul 166–7
Reconstruction Era Ku Klux Klan 4, 93, 129–32; Grant, General Ulysses S. 130
regional watchdog groups 12, 30–3; Center for New Community 32–3; Northwest Coalition Against Malicious Harassment (NWC) 30–2
Revell, Buck 145, 149–50, 182, 195; foreign policy 200
revolutionary racialist right 64–81; Christian Identity 65–6; National Alliance 68–73; National Socialism 66–8; Odinism 77–8; skinheads 76–7; White Aryan Resistance 73–6; World

Church of the Creator 78–81; Zionist Occupation Government (ZOG) 64
Rice, David Lewis 106
right-wing extremism 2, 5, 7–8, 127; core ideology 5, *see also* US government response
right-wing terrorism episodes 96–112; Aryan Republican Army 112; Covenant, Sword, and Arm of the Lord 103–4; Greensboro Massacre 96–7; leaderless resistance 104–6; Oklahoma City bombing 106–12; Posse Comitatus 97–8; The Order 98–103
right-wing terrorism patterns 94–6; terrorist fatalities 94–5
Riis-Knudsen, Pövl H. 200
Robb, Thom 63, 66
Rockford Institute 60
Rockwell, George Lincoln 16, 19, 67–8; mass action theory 113
Roosevelt, Theodore 42; Brown Scare 134–6
Ruby Ridge 8, 44, 47, 107, 114, 145–7; civil liberties implications 192–3; Weaver, Randy 145–7
Rudolph, Eric 106

Schiff, Jacob 18
Schiller, Rabbi Mayer 58
Second Era Ku Klux Klan 42, 93, 132–3; *Bryant v. Zimmermann* 132
September 11 2001 9, 121, 194–7, 202–6
Simmons, William J. 42
Simon Wiesenthal Center (SWC) 8, 12, 19–21, 157; Digital Hate 2000 180; finances 20; National Task Force Against Hate 20; September 11 2001 203–5; training/eductional programs 180–1; Zündelsite 88–90
single-issue terrorists 1
skinheads 2, 76–7; Hammerskin Nation 76; Outlaw Hammerskins 76; Underground Skinhead Action 76
Sklar, Holly 30
Skokie v. Illinois 164–5
Smith, Benjamin 78, 81, 106, 119, 121
Smith, Geoffrey 42
Smith, Gerald L. K. 17–19
Snell, Richard Wayne 104, 110
Snyder, Steven 143–5
Sons of Confederate Veterans 59
Southern Legal Resource Center (SLRC) 59

Southern Military Institute 59
Southern Party 59
Southern Poverty Law Center (SPLC) 8, 11, 21–5; Dees, Morris S. 11, 21–5; finances 21, 24, 191; *Intelligence Report* 22–3; intelligence sharing 181–6; Klanwatch Project 22; Ku Klux Klan 23; Militia Task Force 22
Special Forces Underground (SFU) 161–2; *The Resister* 161–2
Spisak, Frank 105
State and Local Anti-Terrorism Training (SLATT) 181
State v. Klapprott 162–3
Stern, Kenneth 19
Stockman, Steve 52
Stormfront 179
Straus, Oscar 18
Strom, Kevin Alfred 71
strong state 5
Sulzberger, Cyrus L. 18
Supreme Court 162–7; *Brandenburg v. Ohio* 163–4; *R.A.V. v. St Paul* 166–7; *Skokie v. Illinois* 164–5; *State v. Klapprott* 162–3; *Terminiello v. Chicago* 163
Swift, Wesley 66

Tanner, Harold 19
Taylor, Jared 55–8, 204
Te-Ta-Ma Truth Foundation 81
Terminiello v. Chicago 163
terrorism: definition 6–7; far right theoretical approach 113–23; mass action theory 113, 1132
Third Era Ku Klux Klan 43, 137–9; *Brown v. Topeka Board of Education* 137; COINTELPRO 139; White Knights of the Ku Klux Klan 138
Thornton, R. Gordon 60
Tomassi, Joseph 113
training/educational programs 180–1; Anti-Democratic League (ADL) 180–1; State and Local Anti-Terrorism Training (SLATT) 181
Trochman, John 47–8, 50–1, 150, 152, 157
Turner Diaries 68, 98–103; McVeigh, Timothy 107

UK: British National Party 2; National Front 2; Race Relations Act 1965 2
United Daughters of the Confederacy 59
US government response to right-wing

extremism 129–70; Congress 155–8; Dept of Defense 158–62; FBI in contemporary era 141–55; historical background 130–41; international cooperation 167–9; Supreme Court 162–7
US v. McWilliams: *see* Great Sedition Trial
US v. Reese 132
USA: First Amendment 2; free speech 130; response to terrorism 8–9

volunteerism 13

Waco 8, 29, 44, 47, 114, 147–9; civil liberties implications 192–3; Koresh, David 147–9
Wallace, George 44, 84–5
Wassmuth, Bill 30–2
watchdogs 10–38; American interest group structure 13–15; civil litigation watchdog: Southern Poverty Law Center (SPLC) 21–5; internet-based watchdog groups 33–5; Jewish defense organizations 15–21; miscellaneous: Anti-Racist Action 35–8; progressive-oriented watchdog groups 25–30; regional watchdog groups 30–3; typology 11
watchdogs' response to far right 171–89; civil suit use to silence far right 176–9; far right confrontation 186–8; hate crime legislation 173–6; intelligence sharing 181–6; internet and far right 179–80; militia measures 171–3; non-governmental organizations prosecutions 186; training/educational programs 180–1
weapons of mass destruction (WMD) 127
Weaver, Randy 145–8

Weinberger, Caspar: restrictions in armed forces 158–9
Weisman, Charles A. 66
Weissberg, Robert 58
Welch, Robert H. W. Jr 44–5
White Aryan Resistance (WAR) 73–6, 103, 177
White Patriot Party 103, 144, 171
Wilson, Clyde 59
Winchell, Walter: Brown Scare 135, 138
Winrod, Gerald 42; Defenders of the Christian Faith 42
women's rights 10
World Church of the Creator 32–3, 78–81; RAHOWA 80; September 11 2001 205
World Trade Center *see* September 11 2001
World Union of National Socialists 67–8

xenophobia 5–6

Yockey, Francis Parker 67, 82

Zeskind, Leonard 27
Zhirnovsky, Vladimir 62
Zionist Occupation Government (ZOG) 64
Zündelsite 87–9